INHERITING THE EARTH

The Long family's 500 year reign in Wiltshire

CHERYL NICOL

First published in 2016 by
The Hobnob Press, 30c Deverill Road Trading Estate, Sutton Veny,
Warminster BA12 7BZ
www.hobnobpress.co.uk

British Library Cataloguing in Publication Data
A catalogue record for this book is available from the British Library

ISBN 978-1-906978-37-2

Typeset in Adobe Garamond Pro 11/14 pt. Typesetting and origination by
John Chandler
Printed by Lightning Source

*The cover illustration incorporates details from John Speed's map of Wiltshire,
1610*

'The life of Mann is a trewe Lottarie'
Epitaph to Robert Long of Broughton Gifford, 1620

Contents

X

XI

XII

XIII

XIV

XV

Preface

By the time my great-grandfather Ernest Walter Long emigrated to New Zealand in the late nineteenth century, his cousin Walter, 1st Viscount Long of Wraxall, was the last real land czar in the family. I first became aware of my English heritage in 1966 when a small box of family memorabilia belonging to my late grandfather arrived at our modest suburban home. A lengthy yellowed newspaper clipping of Lord Long's funeral in 1924 particularly intrigued me.

It would be nearly forty years before I got around to delving into the dusty nooks and crevices of my family history, and what I found was a surprising revelation at almost every turn. The accumulation of a large amount of material and the lack of any comprehensive written history of the family as a whole, that is, one which encapsulates all the branches and their collective role in England's social and political landscape over five centuries, meant the decision to write this book was not a difficult one. Putting it all together in a comprehensible way was another thing entirely.

I have endeavoured to check and cross-check historical details from a large number of sources to ensure the accuracy of the information presented here, and any errors are unintentional. Where pounds sterling are quoted I have added a comparison value in some instances, calculated using the National Archives online Currency Converter. It should be noted that converting historical monetary values to present day is notoriously difficult and these must be regarded as estimations only.

The extensive original pedigrees are available at: http://longfamilyofwiltshire.webs.com/

Cheryl Nicol

Acknowledgements

I am very grateful to those individuals who have contributed either photographs, information, or both, including Viscount Long, Mike Pease and Lord Gisborough, each descendants of the Longs of Rood Ashton; Julia Crane, who kindly provided scans of William Long of Wrington's diary and other material, also Ian Macalpine Leny and Brigitte Neal, each descendants of the family of Long of Preshaw; Janet Davis, descended from the Longs of Devon, for the many hours spent in the Wiltshire and Swindon Archives with her trusty camera; William J. Long, descended from the family who made their mark in Jamaica; Mrs Beverley Booty, a previous owner of Rood Ashton House, and the collaborative exchange of research with Tim Couzens on the Longs of Draycot.

Mention must be made also of the able assistance given by the archivists at the Wiltshire and Swindon Archives, as well as the British Museum, National Portrait Gallery, National Library of Wales and several other institutions. Thanks also to the inimitable Guy Pease for his support and encouragement to resist procrastinating and just get on with it. Last but not least, I owe a debt of gratitude to my publisher, John Chandler of Hobnob Press, who kindly came to my rescue.

List of Images

Coat of Arms, Long of Wraxall

Pieux Quoique Preux
Pious Although Chivalrous

Introduction

Promoting the first episode of *A Country House Revealed* in 2011 the BBC proclaimed the Long family 'one of the most powerful dynasties in England'. Architectural historian Dan Cruickshank took 1.6 million British viewers on a fascinating tour of South Wraxall Manor, the elegant fifteenth-century pile built by the Long family. Mr Cruickshank enthusiastically told us the early Longs were power hungry, ruthless capitalists, brutal, fiercely ambitious, double-crossing, cunning, conniving and guilty of dodgy dealing – willing to get their way by any means – fair or foul.

The pedigree of Long, 'the most flourishing and numerous family in the county of Wiltshire', so said seventeenth-century historian John Aubrey, is a vast and convoluted one, with frequent intermarriages between the various branches. Their habit of often marrying close cousins served to consolidate and expand their wealth, but may have partly contributed to the extinction of the Longs of Wraxall, Draycot and other offshoots in the male line, which culminated in unmarried daughters or childless marriages. The origin of the earliest known common ancestor is somewhat vague. Roger Le Long, thought to have descended from a Norman noble of Preux, is believed to have married the daughter and heir of St Maur (Seymour) by the daughter and heir of Zouche.[1]

The early public records of Wiltshire show Longs as landowners at Alton and Ablington near Figheldean in 1258, in Coulston near Lavington in 1267, and at Bratton and Westbury in 1279. In later centuries, besides Wraxall, Draycot and Rood Ashton, subsequent branches of the family also established themselves at Semington, Potterne, Little Cheverell, Trowbridge, Monkton Farleigh and elsewhere in Wiltshire, Somerset, Hampshire, Gloucestershire

---

1 Letter extract dated 16 October 1688 to Mr Panchrinch at Cossam; from the original, Penes Dom. from Sir Robert Long, 1st Baronet of Westminster

and Devon. While some old-established families declined through misfortune, excess, incompetence or failure of male heirs, the Longs consistently maintained their position as landowners and county administrators for many centuries, underlining the importance of the gentry as a major political influence. Land was far more than a secure investment and permanent asset, it was power.

They were staunch Royalists, with one or two exceptions, and a few enjoyed the trust of their reigning sovereign, luxuriating amid the splendours of the royal circle. Partly founded on the wool industry, which had its golden age in the reign of Henry VIII, their wealth was further increased by advantageous marriages, closely interlinking them with other ruling Wiltshire families. While opposition to royal policies proved fatal to many, the dissolution of the monasteries during Henry's reign provided enrichment to the Longs of Wraxall for their unswerving loyalty. Another branch of the family became one of the most distinguished groups of clothiers in the West of England, based around Trowbridge and Bradford on Avon.

The continual acquisition of land from one generation to the next consolidated their position in a social class which practically monopolised not only the administration of the county of Wiltshire, but also its parliamentary representation. In order to defend and extend their estates it was necessary to acquire knowledge of the rudiments of law, and many sons became members of the Inns, though few were practising lawyers. This also provided a useful grounding for their political ambitions, and from 1414 until the twentieth century an almost unbroken line of Longs served Parliament in the House of Commons.

In 1919, while preparing to write his autobiography (*Memories*, 1923), the 1st Viscount Long asked his Parliamentary Secretary Sir William Bull to compile a comprehensive list, with a few brief genealogical notes. Perhaps not surprisingly, Bull's research resulted in two rather bookish volumes which eventually found their way into the library of Wiltshire-based Norris McWhirter, co-founder of the Guinness Book of Records. The Longs belonged to quite an exclusive political club. *A History of the County of Wiltshire: Volume 5* (1957) tells us that Wiltshire was represented by members drawn from a very small circle of long-settled families, and during the period 1689–1832, for example, only seventeen different family names appear in the complete list of Members of Parliament.

The years 1722–1812 represent the heyday of the Deptford (Wylye) and Beckhampton (Avebury) Clubs – originally begun as a means of combatting 'an aristocratic ascendancy and a most unwarrantable interference of the Peerage'. These gatherings of the justices of the peace and principal gentry met for the purpose of choosing candidates whenever a vacancy occurred through death or retirement. A case in point is the choice behind closed doors of Richard Godolphin Long in 1806. He was accepted by the freeholders, though some resented the manner with which he was presented. One observer later described him as 'a man of no public worth or value, though a plain and respectable man in his private character'. At his retirement came the first real challenge to the dominance of the clubs and the ascendancy of the Long family.

The election literature of 1818 made pointed references to the dictation of these clubs, which had become what they once sought to eliminate: a monopoly by just a few families, and in particular the Longs. The influence of the clubs was well known in the county and William Long Wellesley, the candidate put forward by the Longs in 1818, was at pains to declare his independence from both the clubs and government. While some members of the Long family branched out and were elected in other counties, the Longs of Rood Ashton were the last successful candidates in Wiltshire, whose representation continued until 1931.

While their changing fortunes didn't propel them all the way back to rags, by the twentieth century the family's once great estates were gone. Many other landed families found themselves in the same position, partly because of the hostility of the government towards large landowners and the threat of confiscatory taxes. Between the end of the First World War and 1921 a quarter of English land had changed hands.[2] One historian remarked that such an enormous and sudden transfer of land had not been seen since the dissolution of

---

2   *Estates Gazette*, 31 Dec 1921

the monasteries, and perhaps not even equalled since the Norman Conquest. The Longs' estates that survived into the twentieth century were more often than not purchased by the sitting tenants, giving rise to a new class of owner. This was the beginning of the disintegration of a system of landholding which had characterised England for centuries, carefully orchestrated by a government intent on gradually reducing the power of a disproportionate few.

The researches of two nineteenth-century gentlemen have added much to our knowledge of the Longs: historian Canon Jackson, who delved into the history of the family and their estates, and antiquarian Charles Edward Long, nephew of Sir Charles Long, Baron Farnborough, who painstakingly constructed what others had deemed impossibly difficult – the family tree. The access allowed him to the College of Heralds by his uncle by marriage, Lord Henry Molyneux Howard, Deputy Earl Marshal, furthered his historical and genealogical studies.

An extensive archive of documents relating to the Longs held by the Wiltshire & Swindon Archives *(ref. 947)* has also been an invaluable source of information for this book. While not an exhaustive account of the family, which by necessity would fill several volumes, we look at the role they played throughout the turbulent reigns of the Tudor and Stuart monarchies and follow the descent of the manors of South Wraxall, Draycot, Rood Ashton and others, giving some idea of the complex relationships between the different branches, the circumstances leading to the breakup of all the estates, and ultimately, their loss of power and influence.

Prologue: A Death in Paris

On an almost unbearably hot midsummer day in 1863 Lady Victoria Long Wellesley sat comforting her dying brother, slowly and painfully succumbing to the effects of cancer of the tongue. She had no inkling of the betrayal her 'darling invalid' had already inflicted upon her. It was late July, and there was no longer the need for chloroform to help him sleep. The 5th Earl of Mornington, William Richard Arthur Pole Tylney Long Wellesley, was lying unconscious and close to death at the Hotel du Rhin in the historic Place Vendôme. He was not quite fifty when he died the next day, 25 July. With the exception of two elderly aunts, Lady Victoria, the heir presumptive, was now the last living representative of the Tylney Long family. She was certain her brother had left her what remained of the once extensive estates passed down from their mother, and in particular her beloved Draycot.

William had indeed left all his landed estates to his 'dear little sister' in a second will, but as Lady Victoria prepared to leave Paris to accompany her brother's body for burial at Draycot, the shock discovery of a third will written just three weeks before left her devastated. He had bequeathed all the property away from the family, to his father's first cousin, Earl Cowley, then Ambassador to Paris, and to her he left only an annuity of £1,000. Draycot had been owned by the Longs for four centuries, and despite maintaining an apparently cheerful resignation to its fate Lady Victoria felt the loss acutely for the rest of her long life.[3]

Thus ended the association between the Long family and Draycot, the most sudden and unexpected loss of all.

But to begin at the beginning . . .

---

3   Octavia Barry, *The Lady Victoria Tylney Long Wellesley*, 1899, p. 122

I
Long of Wraxall and Draycot

Robert Long of Wraxall (c.1391–1446)

In the last decades of the fifteenth century plague remained endemic in England, Henry VI died a prisoner in the Tower of London and a new law was passed banning certain games of skittles. But it was not all doom and gloom. In Wiltshire, one hundred miles to the west of the capital, the booming cloth industry had become of major economic importance, aiding the recovery of the depressed rural economy and increasing the demand for grain, wool and meat. This came as a welcome relief for the local populace who had suffered bitterly during the mid-century collapse of the export market, partly associated with a severe European bullion shortage.

By this time Robert Long of Wraxall had already made his fortune, laying the foundation for subsequent generations of his family. He had exploited opportunities that came his way, deriving profit as sheriff, coroner, escheator and justice of the peace. In the scheme of things he ranked as gentry, a diverse social group that embraced very different levels of wealth, from humble country gentlemen and members of learned professions to titled owners of several thousand acres.

Historians are divided on the question of whether the success of men of Robert's status was due to increased economic strength or enhanced political power, but certainly a substantial source of his wealth lay in the acquisition of land. The son of Roger Le Long, Robert was a lawyer, and the first of the family to own land in South Wraxall, where he had a house in 1429. Always on the lookout for small properties to round out his estate and extend his influence, he expanded his stake in 1433 by exchanging lands with the Abbess of Shaftesbury.[4] He also

4   Nat. Arch. SC 8/26/1290B

enjoyed, with all its associated benefits, a friendship with Sir Walter
Hungerford, Lord High Treasurer, a man of considerable power who
had also prospered in the service of the Crown.

On the subject of the origin of the name Long, historians John
Leland (1506–52) and William Camden (1551–1623) disagree on the
first name of Hungerford's friend: the latter calls him 'Long Thomas'
or 'Long H'. A traditional view is that the name of Long related to
physical height. Camden says:

> In respect of stature, I could recite to you other examples, but
> I will onely adde this which I have read, that a young Gentleman
> of the house of Preux, being of tall stature, attending on the Lord
> Hungerford, Lord Treasurer of England, was among his fellows called
> Long H., who afterwards preferred to a good marriage by his Lord,
> was called H. Long, that name continued to his posteritie, Knights
> and men of great worship.

It is thought Robert was in some way indebted to Hungerford
for his rising affluence. Certainly his name occurs regularly in Lord
Hungerford's deeds as one of the feoffees to purchases of land from at
least 1422, when he became trustee of Hungerford's Somerset estates.
There was considerable activity in the land market during this period,
and until about 1444 he also held in trust for the Hungerfords a number
of properties in Wiltshire, as well as estates in Devon and Cornwall,
and premises in London.[5] However, it is a contentious point that the
association with Hungerford was entirely the method of his rise, and it
is probable the Long family was already of some substance before this.

Hungerford's influence as sheriff may have helped Robert to
obtain a seat in the Leicester Parliament of 1414 for Old Sarum, along
with William Chesterton, another of his retainers. Old Sarum was a
so-called rotten borough with few resident voters. Three years later he
was returned for Calne, another rotten borough close to Wraxall. Over
the next ten years he rose in the administrative ranks. He was twice

5   J.S. Roskell, L. Clark, C. Rawcliffe, *The House of Commons, 1386–1421*, v.4
1993

returned as knight of the shire, becoming a Justice of the peace and
county coroner. His appointment as escheator jointly for Wiltshire
and Southampton in 1428,[6] where he held lands at Barton Sacy in
right of his wife, Margaret Popham, pushed him a little further up the
power ladder.

He was building an empire to which a viable heir would be
vital. In addition to Wraxall, Robert purchased the manor of Draycot[7]
as a future estate for his second son John by his first wife Margaret
Godfrey. The acquisition of these two manors would form the basis of
the family's identity and wealth, ensuring his hierarchical line was set
to benefit, over time, from a large accumulation of land – as long as
there were heirs. Continuity of family as well as wealth was a constant
concern; under the law if there was no living person of a designated
class to inherit, the king took the property by escheat. Fortunately
Robert had four sons; an heir and three spares.

He fulfilled his role as escheater with gusto, which occasionally
caused disputes and accusations he abused his power. In one Chancery
case during this period, Edmund Ford of Swainswick complained
Robert had encouraged one William Juet to dispossess his feoffees of
property in Melksham, and claimed he could get no redress at common
law 'by cause of grete power, consideration, mayntenance and aliance
of the sayd Robert Longe in the sayde shyre by menys of embrasyng
and other unlawful demenyng'.[8]

The patronage of Hungerford as treasurer saw Robert join the
Court of Exchequer for five years as foreign apposer, whose business it
was to oversee the Sheriff's accounts. This allowed him the right to farm
the subsidy of cloth in Somerset. In 1430, during the Hundred Years'
War, he was relieved of his duties as coroner while he 'abided' in France
on the king's service, 'for the safeguard of those parts'.[9] Those parts
were French territories won in battle by the English. The two countries
had been engaged in a sporadic series of conflicts since 1337, which

6   *Calendar of the Fine Rolls Vol. XV, 1422–30*
7   Tim Couzens, *Hand of Fate*. It was previously believed Draycot had come
into the Long family by inheritance through the de Cernes
8   *The House of Commons, ibid*
9   *Calendar of the Close Rolls, 1441–7*

for the most part, were fought on French soil. The profitable English export trade in wool and cloth to Flanders was a significant factor in hostilities, but the main struggle centred on the French possessions of the kings of England and their claim to be kings of France.

In 1422 Henry VI had ascended the English throne at the age of nine months on the death of his father Henry V. Less than a decade later ten-year-old Henry was crowned King of France in Paris, an attempt to reinforce England's position in the war. But it would be only a matter of time before territory wrested from the French slipped out of English control. In 1436 calls went out to fund a new army to prop up the English forces and Robert contributed £40 towards equipping it. To put this amount into context, at that time tradesmen such as roof thatchers earned about £1 a year, putting Robert's wealth in stark contrast to the miserable poverty of most of the common people. But for the boy king Henry, his minders and Robert especially, it was not money well-spent; the English lost Paris that year.

Robert easily maintained his position of authority, with reappointments to the Wiltshire Commission of the Peace continuing until his death. His career in parliament lasted almost as long. He was returned for the last time in 1442 as member for Salisbury, where for the previous fifteen years he had acted as bailiff of the episcopal liberty, firstly under Bishop Neville and later under Bishop Aiscough.[10] This association with the Bishops of Salisbury was a key factor in the rise of the Long family during this period, and Robert's son Henry became steward to Bishop Richard Beauchamp from 1455.

Robert's power as bailiff to the bishops is demonstrated when he had three of his sons in Parliament with him in 1442; that year Richard, the youngest at nineteen, sat for Old Sarum. After Robert's death in 1446 his younger son John inherited his estate at Draycot with Wraxall descending to his eldest son Henry.

Henry Long (1420–90)

Not surprisingly, Henry, also a lawyer, followed in his father's footsteps, beginning his political career at the extraordinarily

young age of fifteen,[11] firstly as MP for the rotten borough of Old
Sarum in 1435, then for Devizes in 1442, being returned for the
final time in 1454.[12] It was not uncommon for men of status to start
their sons early on a political career, and Henry has the distinction,
according to the *Guinness Book of Records*, of being one of Britain's
youngest ever MPs.

Henry served three terms as sheriff between 1456 and 1483,[13]
and was appointed to various commissions between 1450 and 1488.
Recent research on the role of medieval sheriffs and other local officials
suggests they were tightly regulated bureaucrats whose latent value was
as pawns, manipulated by the crown and the nobility to their own
advantage. This was demonstrated in June 1460 when a commission
empowered Henry to arrest and imprison all adherents of Richard,
3rd Duke of York, together with Richard Neville, Earl of Warwick
(the Kingmaker), and the latter's father, the Earl of Salisbury, three of
the main protagonists against Henry VI during the Wars of the Roses.
Some historians believe a contributory cause of the war was financial
loss by English landowners whose continental holdings were seized
by the triumphant French following the English defeat in the earlier
Hundred Years' War.

Henry's association with Bishop Richard Beauchamp endured
until at least 1470, when he joined him as feoffee for the goods of a
certain William Bewshin, Esquire. Henry was also closely associated
with other prominent men such as John Whittocksmead[14] and
Thomas Tropenell, for whom he acted as one of the feoffees for the
manor of Great Chalfield.[15]

In 1471, while Henry was busy with business in Wiltshire, the
embattled Henry VI was imprisoned in the Tower of London where
he died, probably murdered at the behest of Edward IV who seized
the throne in his place. Two years later with the last of the Lancastrian
revolt dealt with, revenue and tax evasion became the royal focus when

11   Anne Holt, *History of Parliament 1439–1509*, vol. 1, 1938
12   Holt, *ibid,* Old Sarum, Devizes, p. 550
13   C.F.R.1452–61 p. 175, C.F.R.1471–85 pp. 245, 257
14   A lawyer who sat in twelve Parliaments between 1427 and 1472,
15   Ed. Davies, *The Tropenell Cartulary*, Wilts Archaeological Society, pp. 285–6

Henry was appointed to a commission investigating the concealment in Wiltshire of wardships, marriages and other feudal dues, the escape of felons and illegal alienations in mortmain.[16] On another commission in 1475 he was asked to enquire into certain treasons, lollardries, heresies and errors in Dorset and Wiltshire.

Eight years later Edward IV was dead. His son, twelve-year-old Edward V, reigned for 86 days with his uncle Richard as Protector. After some political sleight of hand which resulted in the disappearance of young Edward V and his brother, his uncle took over the throne as Richard III. Accusations circulated that the boys had been murdered on Richard's orders, giving rise to the legend of the Princes in the Tower. Considering the questionable method of his accession, not surprisingly, Richard had enemies of his own lurking in the wings.

In his play *Richard III* Shakespeare refers to the Sheriff of Wiltshire leading Henry Stafford, 2nd Duke of Buckingham to his execution at Salisbury. This occurred in 1483, the first year of Richard's reign and Henry Long's last term as sheriff. Buckingham had hatched a plot to dethrone the king, and while Richard was marching with a large army towards Salisbury expecting to intercept him, Buckingham was betrayed to the Sheriff of Shrewsbury by one of his followers, hoping to claim the large reward offered for his capture. After interrogation, Buckingham was conveyed to Salisbury and given into the custody of Sheriff Henry Long who refused his request to see the king, temporarily resident in 'the King's house' in The Close. Buckingham, given no time to argue, was executed without trial.

Being sheriff was an expensive business. The fees payable at the beginning and end of the appointment were far heavier than the value of personal benefits, and there was the expense of entertaining assize judges and the provision of accoutrements for their ceremonial retinue. In 1485, shortly before Richard III died he pardoned Henry for all outstanding arrears relating to his time as sheriff.[17]

Henry outlived two of his three wives but had no children. When he died in 1490, he left among other bequests 20s for vestments to the

---

16   C.P.R. 1467–77, p. 408
17   ffarl. MSS 433, p. 35

parish church at Bradford. According to his *Inquisition Post Mortem* he held the manor of Combe in Gloucestershire, and in Wiltshire the manors of Wraxall, Bradley, Tidcombe and Etchilhampton, as well as lands in Box, Farley and Melksham. His nephew Sir Thomas Long – then aged 'forty or more' – inherited these estates.

South Wraxall Manor, courtyard view

Sir Thomas Long (c.1451–1509)

Thomas, son of Henry's brother John Long and his wife Margaret Wayte, succeeded to the estates at Draycot by the will of his father in September 1478, afterwards inheriting his Uncle Henry's estates in 1490. Thus began the descent of the manors of Draycot and Wraxall together. He was elected Member of Parliament for Westbury the following year, and served two terms as High Sheriff, once in 1500 and again in 1506.

While the treacherous plots and conspiracies continued to unsettle the country, now hatched by those intent on wresting the throne from the tenuous grip of Richard III's successor, Henry VII, Thomas was busy sprucing up his armour, preparing to defend his sovereign. He galloped off with the 'great compaignye of noble menne' who went with Edward, 3rd Duke of Buckingham in 1497 to meet

Henry VII at Taunton,[18] then in pursuit of the pretender to the throne, Perkin Warbeck, who had proclaimed himself 'Richard IV'.

Gathered from members of the nobility and gentry, this troop of patriotic volunteers included his good friend Richard Beauchamp, Lord St Amand. Armoured and battle-ready, their animated gathering at Taunton so intimidated some of Warbeck's men, they deserted, causing Warbeck to retreat to the New Forest and subsequently take refuge in Beaulieu Monastery, near Southampton. The pretender's days in the sun were numbered, and after surrendering to the king's mercy and making a full confession, he was committed to the Tower, from where he later escaped. He was eventually hanged at Tyburn in 1499.

The name of Thomas Long began to appear in the A-lists and, again in the royal orbit in November 1501, he was present at the reception of thirteen-year-old Princess Katherine of Aragon at Shaftesbury, a costly spectacle involving a series of pageants which preceded her marriage ten days later to Henry VII's eldest son Arthur, Prince of Wales, a boy of just fifteen. Having performed the required ritual bathing and vigils the night before, Thomas was made Knight of the Bath[19] during the marriage celebrations, elevating his rank above 'esquire' and the gentry, but one notch below a baronet.

Unhappily for the young Spanish princess, who had been formally betrothed to Prince Arthur since the age of five, she was widowed just five months after her marriage. This was not a complete disaster for Arthur's father Henry VII, still determined to secure a friendly alliance with Spain. Two months after his brother's death, young Prince Henry and Katherine were betrothed.

Sir Thomas Long rose in the ranks of Henry VII's courtiers to become perhaps one of the most important commoners in England.[20] He married Margery, sister of Katherine of Aragon's vice-chamberlain, Sir Edward Darrell, whose father George Darrell of Littlecote had been on friendly terms with the Longs. Sir Edward Darrell and Sir Thomas were appointed assessors of aid for Wiltshire in 1504. One of his last

18   John Burke, *Burke's Extinct & Dormant Baronetcies of England*, p. 321
19   Robert Beatson, *A Political Index to the Histories of Great Britain & Ireland*, 1806, p. 422
20   Hubert Hall, *Society in the Elizabethan Age*, 1886, p. 188

duties at court was his attendance at the coronation of seventeen-year-old Henry VIII in June 1509, and he died a few months later. He was succeeded by his eldest son Henry (d. 1556), who was later knighted.

According to John Aubrey writing of his burial in the church at Draycot, 'Sir Thomas Long, Knight, lies buried by the North Wall on the Chancel, under a rich gothique altar monument without inscription: his heaume and crest do yet hang up over it.' His jousting helmet ('heaume'), hinged at the back, with a working visor, has been authenticated by the Tower of London and dated to the late fifteenth century. With it hangs a pair of gauntlets and a sword. His tomb is embellished with family crests and heraldic devices, including the fetterlock, borrowed from the original owners of Draycot, the de Cernes.

Sir Richard Long (c.1474–1546)

Sir Thomas Long's third son Richard was in his thirties when Henry VIII came to the throne in 1509. Loyal and ambitious, he quickly rose in prominence at the Tudor court, a more than willing confidante and facilitator who carefully cultivated favour with the ruthless chief minister Thomas Cromwell. Some of the greatest changes ever made in England occurred during Henry's reign, and it was Cromwell who ably assisted the king to become, in modern terms, a totalitarian dictator with a thirst for plunder, financially independent of Parliament. To this end King Henry employed Richard and his brother Sir Henry Long as enforcers of his new regime, and in return they derived great wealth from grants of confiscated lands after the dissolution of the monasteries.

Richard joined the 'great retinue' of some thirty to forty thousand men who accompanied Sir Gilbert Talbot in 1513 to Calais to reinforce Henry's claim to the French throne. Captured by Edward III early in the Hundred Years War, Calais became an important strategic asset for the English, allowing them to safely keep troops in northern France. The war officially ended in 1453, but it was not until 1558 that the French eventually recovered the town. Although Richard was appointed a Spear of Calais in 1515, a position he retained for life, Cromwell arranged that he be a non-resident except in times of war.

His loyal service over the next twenty years was rewarded with a knighthood following the baptism celebrations for Prince Edward in 1537. [21] The name of Long appears frequently in the New Year's Gift Rolls. The king's wardrobe inventory taken at the Tower towards the latter end of his reign records 'one paire of upper stockes, (meaning the hose alone without the stocking parts annexed to them), of purple satten, embrauded all over with pirles of damask gold and damask silver, the gift of Sir Richard Longe'.[22] A few years later Richard made the king another gift of a similarly elaborate doublet, probably an extra-large one, since by then the royal girth had expanded considerably. The next year, in a more than fair exchange, Henry granted Richard the manor of Shingay in Cambridgeshire, at the time worth £176 4s 6d per annum (about £54,000 today).

His star continued to rise; 1538 saw his appointment as master of the buckhounds and master of the hawks, and chief master of the royal games. His performance in this role so impressed Henry VIII's daughter, the young Princess Elizabeth, that when she later became queen she instructed her new chief master Ralph Bowes that 'our game pastymes and sportes' should be in as large and ample manner and form as when Sir Richard Long had been master. The yearly payment Richard received during this appointment was £33 6s 8d (about £10,200), a sum which continued to be paid to subsequent masters of the royal pack until the accession of Charles II more than 100 years later.[23]

Richard had proved his loyalty beyond all doubt by the time he was appointed one of about six gentleman of the Privy Chamber, also in 1538, a position which gave him daily access to the king as confidante and companion. By this time the dissolution of the monasteries and confiscation of their property was well underway, and Richard took receipt of jewels, plate, ornaments of shrines and relics seized from Abingdon Abbey in Oxfordshire, including two mitres, three pontifical

21   Richard Turpyn, *The Chronicle of Calais: In the Reigns of Henry VII and Henry VIII to the Year 1540*, 1846, p. 21
22   Joseph Strutt, *A Complete View of the Dress and Habits of the People of England, Vol. 2*, 1799, p. 241
23   J.P. Hore, *The History of the Royal Buckhounds*, 1895, p. 50

gold rings set with stones and a silver gilt cross, which he deposited in the king's Treasury. He was one of two commissioners appointed by Cromwell to regulate the importation of wine into England, and he was made keeper of the king's hunting park at Greenwich.

In 1540 he and his brother Sir Henry attended the reception of Anne of Cleves, the king's fourth wife. Also on the guest-list was Robert Long Esquire, probably their younger brother Robert of Box, one rung lower in the social pecking order. A man with the rank of 'esquire' followed a knight to war and rendered him personal services. The next year, as keeper of the newly-acquired royal palace in Southwark, Richard was petitioned together with Robert Acton against numerous alleged abuses by the master and brethren of St Thomas's Hospital. It was possibly under pretext of this appointment he was elected MP for Southwark in 1539.

Described by the king as 'our trusty and right well-beloved Councillor', the relationship between Richard and the king was one of mutual respect, and it was in everyone's interest to keep Henry in good humour. Known for his gluttony, ostentation and gambling, Henry had a ready supply of courtiers willing to bet on anything that took his royal fancy and Richard was also happy to oblige. The Privy Purse expenses record money paid for a wager he won while hunting with the king.

A serial gamester himself, Richard had an old gambling debt catch up with him when his friend Robert Acton wrote reminding him of the time they both had 'lesse than we now have', mentioning a loan he obtained from the Treasurer of the Chamber, Brian Tuke, for Richard to play dice. On that occasion Acton loaned him a further 40 angels (about £6,000 today), because 'at my going home ye told me ye must ryde to the Courte, the King's Majestie being in his progress, and could not go w'out money'. [24]

Having survived the fall of his patron Cromwell in 1540, Richard continued to serve the government throughout the decade that followed. For his loyalty, in addition to Shingay, he was granted

---

24   John Gage, *The History and Antiquities of Suffolk: Thingoe Hundred*, 1838, p. 103

Felix Hall and Coggeshall, Essex, also Old Court, Greenwich, the
latter for his life only. Reading Place, in London, with certain farms
and rents there, was granted to him in 1541.

This was an eventful year for Richard, and his growing wealth
dictated the need for an heir. By the time he married thirty-two-
year-old Margaret Donnington, widow of Sir Thomas Kytson, he
was probably in his sixties. The new Lady Long's introduction into
the royal circle gave her the right to lodge at court, and in 1544 she
appeared on a list of Katherine Parr's ladies-in-waiting at Hampton
Court as one of 'The Queenes Highness Maides Ordinary', together
with Lady Lisle.

Richard received further grants, including lands in Surrey, Kent,
Buckinghamshire, Leicestershire, Essex and Gloucestershire. These
had belonged to St Thomas's Hospital and the abbeys of Reading
and Malmesbury. The same year the king granted Richard and his
wife the Suffolk manor of Great Saxham in tail male, parcel of the
possessions of the dissolved monastery of Bury St Edmunds. Richard
was appointed bailiff of the manor of Gravesend, keeper of the parks
in Kent at Panthurst, also Otford and Knole – both confiscated from
Archbishop Thomas Cranmer. The prizes were beginning to mount.

When Richard was sent to Calais in 1541 to inspect and
report on the fortifications there and elsewhere in France, the French
ambassador, Charles de Marillac, Bishop of Vienne, commended him
to the French king as 'a personage of a certain authority and experience
in military affairs'.[25] Another sometime gentleman of the Privy
Chamber, ambassador Sir John Wallop, was also in Calais sending
back reports of the army, for which Richard had furnished one body
of men himself. Wallop remarked that those sent from Mr. Long were
tall men and right warlike trimmed, 'yet lacking swords'.[26]

As one of Henry's most senior Privy Councillors, Richard
enjoyed an intimacy with the king that perhaps Wallop did not. In
fact Henry suspected Wallop of colluding against him with Cardinal

25   *Calendar of Letters, Despatches and State Papers Relating to the Negotiations*
Between England and Spain: pt.1. Henry VIII, 1538-1542, p. xviii
26   *Letters and Papers, Foreign and Domestic, Henry VIII, Volume 17, 1542*, ed.
James Gairdner and R H Brodie (London, 1900), p. 380

Reginald Pole. Making use of Richard's presence in Calais to carry out a clandestine operation, Henry wrote to him, beginning with his usual 'Trustie and welbeloved, we grete you well', giving instructions to intercept Wallop on his return. A master of flattery, patronage and sudden betrayal, Henry urged Richard to greet Wallop on the highway and 'with gentill and frendely countenaunce' welcome him home, all the while under pretence he was there on his own private business. But Wallop had already got wind of some sort of ambush on Henry's orders.

Richard's instructions were to arrest Wallop immediately, but they instead went to Richard's lodgings at Sittingbourne and had dinner, during which Wallop had wept, complaining to Richard how much it grieved him to be thought of so badly by the king – a potential death sentence by any other name. Afterwards Richard took him aside out of earshot of the servants, suggesting he would be better off surrendering himself willingly. The subsequent failure of this mission was blamed not on Richard but on his kinsman Sir Edward Seymour, who had sent him to intercept Wallop too early.[27] Wallop, in view of his long and loyal service was given the opportunity to explain himself to the council, and after intervention by Henry's new wife Catherine Howard he was pardoned.

But young Catherine would soon find a charge of treason hanging over her own head. Later in 1541 Richard worked on various commissions and juries investigating her behaviour. When Henry discovered several of Catherine's family covertly knew all about her infidelity and apparently condoned it, he instigated a train of events which would see the ransacking and sequestration of their houses and possessions, and their imprisonment in the Tower. The fact that these were Catholic families did nothing to improve Henry's mood. He sent Sir Richard Long and Sir Thomas Pope to houses in Kent and Southwark occupied by Catherine's aunt, the Countess of Bridgewater, to sequester her property. For their prior knowledge and concealment

27   On this matter Seymour wrote to Henry VIII on 2 March, referring to 'mi cosen Long'. *State Papers, Vol. 8, Part V, Foreign Correspondence, 1537–1542*, p. 538. Sir Richard Long's maternal aunt was the wife of Sir John Seymour of Wolf Hall, grandfather of the Protector.

of the young queen's conduct, the countess and several others were imprisoned, but later pardoned and their possessions reinstated.

Also in 1541, after an affray on the tennis court at Greenwich Palace, we find Richard again acting as royal messenger, following Henry VIII's condemnation of his long-time sergeant-porter Sir Edmund Knyvett for an assault on Thomas Clere, a cousin of Anne Boleyn. Henry's court was a model of decorum compared with most others in contemporary Europe, with harsh punishments for breaking the peace, so no one would have been surprised when Knyvett was sentenced to have his hand severed. Later, as the knife and mallet were readied and searing irons laid in the fire with the 'Kinges Mr Surgeon' on standby, the proceedings were stopped at the last minute while Henry considered it over his all-important dinner.

Notorious for his tactical intimidation, he often said the best way of managing people was through fear, and with his belly full and humour improved, Henry sent Richard to Knyvett after dinner with a pardon. Afterwards, to ensure no further expectations of clemency, a proclamation was made that 'whosoever gave any stroke heareafter in the court, or a certaine precinct therunto, should lose his hand without redemption'.[28]

Richard's military experience proved useful when he was made governor of Guernsey, Alderney, and Sark later that year. In the year that followed he was given a place on the king's council of the north, when he was appointed captain of Kingston upon Hull. Henry's long-standing ambition to conquer France and his constant need to prove himself was enough impetus to launch a fresh attack, and he wrote to Richard ordering his attendance on his person with a hundred able footmen and six horsemen, being 'determyned to invade the Realme of ffraunce this somer with a Roiall Armye in our owne personne'.[29]

There is no doubt Richard was genuinely trusted and 'welbeloved' by Henry, a boisterously affectionate man who did have a few notable virtues; he took an interest in people and had a desperate desire to please. He stood as godfather to Richard's only son in 1544.

28   Charles Wriothesey, *A Chronicle of England during the Reigns of the Tudors*, Vol. I, 1875, p. 125
29   Hengrave Hall Manuscripts preserved by the University of Cambridge

The previous year Richard had been present at Henry's marriage to Katherine Parr, a very intimate low-key affair. As one of only eleven men to witness the ceremony performed by the Bishop of Winchester, Richard attended the private oratory of the Queen's Closet at Hampton Court with other family and close friends, which included Sir Edward Seymour and Lady Lisle as one of the queen's supporters.

While Henry had a new wife, Richard at last had a family of his own. After the baptism of their son Henry – prudently named after the king – Lady Long noted in her household account book 'that Mr Harrie Long was born the xxxj day of March, in the reign of the King, between v and vj of the clock in the morning; godfather the King's Majesty, his deputy my Lord of Essex, otherwise my Lord Parr, and my Lord of Northfolke; godmother my Lady Russell. God make him a good old man and much cause of worship.'[30]

Bound to the Crown by past favours and personal association, Richard was again obliged to fight the king's war at the second siege of Boulogne in September 1544. By this time he was father to two more children, both daughters. By November he was back in England lying seriously ill. Sir William Paget wrote to Secretary Petre, doubting his ability to continue in his numerous administrations, 'as he is, through age and infirmity, unable to perform his office of Gernesey'.[31] His ongoing illness forced him to retire in 1545, by which time his wife had another daughter. He was granted an annuity of £100 – about £20,000 in today's money.

The large grants of abbey lands resulting from his long service to the Crown, together with his marriage settlements, meant he was a very rich man when he died in September the following year, just three days after making his will. His estates in Cambridgeshire alone were worth £510 a year, and he left two-thirds of his lands to his widow as her jointure, naming her sole executor of his estate.

In his will he wrote that he had expended large sums of money in the king's yearly wars and other services on behalf of His Majesty, being obliged to sell some of his estates not in jointure, so that there

---

30   John Gage, *History and Antiquities of Hengrave, in Suffolk*, p.120
31   *Letters and Papers, Foreign and Domestic, of the Reign of Henry VIII*, Vol XX, Pt. I, p. 127

was not a full third part of his lands, which in case of his death, and having no time to purchase others, would descend in possession to his heir. Richard humbly besought the king to accept the lands that remained. King Henry had only a short time to consider this before he too died, exactly four months later, leaving England virtually penniless after squandering much of the riches gained from the monasteries on his fruitless wars against France.

Soon after her husband's death Lady Margaret Long married a third time to John Bourchier, 2nd Earl of Bath, being styled thereafter as Countess of Bath. She had made a dramatic social ascent throughout her three marriages. As daughter and sole heir of John Donnington, 'an ordinary Middlesex gentleman', Margaret also benefitted from the death of her first husband Sir Thomas Kytson, who left her the Suffolk manors of Hengrave and Feltons, and all his other property.

Kytson had been a successful mercer and merchant adventurer who had exported cloth almost from the beginning of Henry VIII's reign, much of which he had sourced from the clothiers of West Wiltshire. He had a posthumous son with Margaret, (afterwards Sir Thomas Kytson), and four daughters. Her step-daughter, Catherine, married Sir John Spencer of Wormington, from whom the Earls Spencer and Dukes of Marlborough descend.

Unusually for the times, Margaret's marriage settlement with the Earl of Bath gave her complete control over the extensive personal property she brought into their marriage, including the right to devise it by will should she predecease him. Lord Bath lived with her at Hengrave, though she insisted his five daughters from his previous marriage went to live elsewhere. She kept her own family close; one of her daughters from the Kytson marriage and her three daughters, Jane, Mary and Catherine from her marriage to Sir Richard Long, resided with them.[32]

During her attendance on Katherine Parr as Lady Long, Margaret's name appeared on a list of courtiers, the queen's friends

32   Barbara J. Harris, *English Aristocratic Women, 1450–1550: Marriage and Family, Property and Careers*, 2002, p. 122

who had become ardent Protestants, but on the death of Edward VI in 1553 she, together with her husband Lord Bath – both rigid Catholics – sided with Queen Mary. Consequently Margaret rose to considerable power and influence during her reign. She outlived her third husband, dying in 1562.

Despite Margaret's negotiations to marry off one of her daughters by Sir Richard Long to Lord Mordaunt's grandson and heir, there was little success for the Long girls on the matrimonial front. The youngest, Catherine, was the only one to marry, after the death of her mother. Catherine's marriage to Edward, heir of Thomas Fisher (secretary to the Duke of Somerset), was not all she had hoped, although it had begun promisingly enough. Early in their marriage she and her husband provided Queen Elizabeth with dinner at their manor house at Itchington during her 1572 progress.

But Fisher, a man of dissipated habits, soon squandered his inheritance, and in 1582 was accused of fraud when he sold the Priory estate to Sir John Puckering, then lord keeper of the Great Seal of England. The estate was encumbered with debts, but when Fisher received payment he 'wasted it all upon a bankett [banquet] on[e] night where he had musick and hores'.[33] Consequently he was a prisoner in the Fleet in 1584–7, and prosecuted for fraud in the most notorious court in English history, the Star Chamber.[34] He died in poverty in 1601.

Henry Long of Shingay (1544–73)

With the deaths of his elderly father and munificent godfather the king, a grant was made by Edward VI to Sir Edward Montagu of the wardship of young Harry Long, Sir Richard Long's only son and heir, aged two years and nine months. Montagu was a friend of Harry's father and a former Privy Councillor to Henry VIII. At age eighteen Henry Long was admitted fellow-commoner to Gonville and Caius College, a year after Queen Elizabeth visited his manor house Felix Hall (or Filliol Hall) on her progress of 1561.

33   D.M. Dean, *Law-Making and Society in Late Elizabethan England: The Parliament of England, 1584–1601*, 2002, p. 226
34   Alan Dyer, 'Fisher, Thomas (1515/16–1577)', *Oxford Dictionary of National Biography*, Oxford University Press, 2004, online edn.

As a newly established gentleman, Henry, who had been brought up a Catholic, took up residence at Shingay, granted to his father in 1538. During his marriage to Dorothy, daughter of Nicholas Clarke, he served as sheriff for Cambridgeshire and Huntingdonshire in 1569–70, gaining entry to the Cambridgeshire commission of the peace in 1571. Despite an apparent lack of integration with the established ruling elite who monopolised the elections, he was elected to the junior Cambridgeshire parliamentary seat, also in 1571. He died in London aged twenty-nine, and was buried there in April 1573.

Lady Elizabeth Russell, née Long (1568–1611)

Barely five years old at the death of her father Henry, as heir to his estates the infant Elizabeth became a ward of the queen. The wardship of under-aged heirs was a system dating back to the Norman invasion, and Elizabeth's proved to be a profitable speculation for three men in particular. The Crown sought to bolster revenues by its sale, and within a year of Henry's death her wardship was granted to Thomas Cecil, son of Lord Burghley, for a fixed price of £250 and an annuity of £40. Before Cecil had paid a penny he sold it to John Manners for £1,350 – more than five times the price.[35] Elizabeth's mother Dorothy had remarried a year after Henry's death, to Sir Charles Morrison of Watford, Hertfordshire, who purchased the wardship from Manners for £2,450. In effect the queen had received only a tenth of the price it had realised on the open market.

Elizabeth spent her formative years in Watford at Cassiobury House, home of her stepfather. She was sixteen when she married Sir William Russell in February 1585, youngest son of the 2nd Earl of Bedford. Notable among their descendants is Charles, the present Prince of Wales.[36] Sir William Russell had earned his reputation as a soldier and administrator in Ireland. In 1581 he was knighted and later recognised for his exploits during a battle as new lord deputy

---

35   Joel Hurstfield, *The Queen's Wards: Wardship and Marriage Under Elizabeth I*, 1958, p. 275

36   Gerald Paget, *The Lineage and Ancestry of H.R.H. Prince Charles, Prince of Wales*, 1977, Vol. II, p. 88

against the O'Byrne clan in 1594, which had long been a threat to Tudor authority. He was created 1st Baron Russell of Thornhaugh in 1603.

Elizabeth accompanied her husband when he was in Ireland, where they frequently participated in the pleasures of the chase, amusing themselves at different times with hawking, fishing and even wolf-hunting – according to William's journal entry of May 1596. She died in 1611, and on her memorial in the parish church at Watford, erected by her mother (who survived her by seven years), is a long epitaph, describing her as 'having lived religiouslie, vertuouslie, and honorablie 43 years and of them 27 in holie and unspotted Wedlocke'. Before her death Elizabeth had quarrelled with her only son Francis, and had directed her feoffees to sell the manor of Duxford, Cambridgeshire, part of the estates inherited from her father, to pay certain legacies. However, Francis paid the legacies himself and retained Duxford until 1637.

The manor was sold a number of times over the course of the next 150 years or so, when it came into the possession of Charles Long, Baron Farnborough (descended from the Longs of Netheravon), through a legacy from his great uncle Richard Cropp. Originally granted to Sir Richard Long in 1540 by Henry VIII, the property remained in Baron Farnborough's branch of the Long family until 1906.

Francis became 2nd Baron Russell of Thornhaugh on the death of his father in March 1613, and later 4th Earl of Bedford in 1627, succeeding his cousin Edward, the 3rd Earl. Francis moved in the same circles as another of his cousins, Sir Robert Long, later auditor of the Exchequer, who was also involved in the Lincolnshire fen drainage projects. Francis wrote to him in 1637 thanking him for speaking to Lord Holland, to whom he owed £2,500. In the habit of writing a new will every year, he was at the height of his parliamentary career when he died of smallpox in 1641, aged forty-eight. He was succeeded by his son William as 5th Earl, later 1st Duke of Bedford. William's great-granddaughter Henrietta Greville many years later married Sir James Long, 5th Baronet of Draycot, her fifth cousin.

Sir Henry Long (c.1472–1556)

The heir to the Wraxall and Draycot estates, Elizabeth's great uncle Henry, eldest son of Sir Thomas Long and Margery Darrell, was also prominent at court in the early years of Henry VIII 's reign. He was among the courtiers who jousted at Greenwich in 1510, and took part in the king's expedition to France in 1513, being present at the siege of Therouenne in Picardy, an ultimately fruitless campaign. He was knighted in September 1513 for making a gallant charge in the sight of the king, for which he was granted a new crest. Preserved in the Herald's College is a drawing of Sir Henry's standard depicting this new crest – a white lion's head holding a bloodstained gauntlet in its mouth with the fringe and motto in gold: *Es-Evreux – Fortune Soi.*[37]

Sir Henry accompanied the king in 1520 to the Field of the Cloth of Gold, an ostentatious three-week-long display of wealth and prowess of the English and French monarchs, with banqueting, jousting and other competitions of skill and strength. Much of it was organised by Cardinal Wolsey, whose diplomatic foreign policy had pressed for an alliance with France.

Serving several terms as sheriff of Wiltshire, Dorset and Somerset in the thirty years between 1512 and 1542 Sir Henry's workload was such that in 1523 when he was summoned as one of the loan commissioners to be assessed for unpaid monies, the Bishop of Winchester complained to Cardinal Wolsey that 'Long is so busy about the temporal subsidy that he cannot come to the writer till Martinmas, when he will pay what is due'.[38] The eventful decade at court between 1533 and 1543 kept everyone on their toes. When the king lost confidence in Cardinal Wolsey for his failure to secure an annulment of his first twenty-four year marriage to Katherine of Aragon, Sir Henry was appointed one of the commissioners to make inquisition into Wolsey's possessions.

Wolsey was stripped of his government office and property, the king got his annulment and he immediately married Anne Boleyn.

37   Evreux is a region in Upper Normandy, captured in 1418 by Henry V: this may be a clue as to the origin of the family
38   *Letters and Papers Foreign and Domestic, of the Reign of Henry VIII Vol. 3. Part II: 1521–23*

Sir Henry was present at her coronation in 1533, his name appearing on the list of 'Knights and Gentlemen to be servitors'. He probably kept his distance when she was executed three years later for alleged adultery, incest and high treason. Indeed, on that fateful morning of 19 May 1536 King Henry was near Epping Forest attired for the chase with his hounds and attendants around him, including Henry Long's brother Sir Richard, master of the buckhounds.

Two days earlier Sir Richard' s predecessor, Anne's brother George Boleyn, Viscount Rochester, was executed for alleged incest with his sister despite a complete lack of evidence, an oft-used tactic of Thomas Cromwell, who took a central role in her trial and execution. The king was keen to try a new method of decapitation on his unfortunate wife, copying the French in their dispatch of criminals with a sword rather than an axe. No man in London could be found with the necessary experience, and Cromwell had to send to Calais for an expert.

A horrified Anne expressed her doubts about the efficiency of such a novelty to the lieutenant of the Tower, and he kindly assured her that her head would be off in no time – as indeed it was. As the sound of the death salute boomed along the Thames, King Henry is supposed to have shouted with ferocious joy, 'Ha, Ha! The deed is done. Uncouple the hounds and let us follow the sport!' According to tradition, after the hunt the king and his party proceeded to Wiltshire, spending the night at Wolfhall, the house of his soon-to-be brother-in-law Edward Seymour, Earl of Hertford, later 1st Duke of Somerset – 'The Protector'.

The death of his once 'entirely beloved' Anne paved the way for the king's betrothal the next day, and marriage ten days later to Seymour's sister Jane, mother of his only legitimate son, Prince Edward, whose baptism Sir Henry Long attended on 15 October 1537. Jane died from puerperal fever nine days later, following a difficult birth.

Over the course of his life Sir Henry, like his brother, had acquired much wealth, not only from royal favours. The manor of Charlton came to him by the will of Richard Beauchamp, Lord St

Amand in 1508.[39] As hereditary bailiff of Charlton Wood and ranger
of Braden Forest, he received a weekly pension in Malmesbury Abbey
of seven white loaves and seven flagons of beer, compounded for in
money with an estimated annual value of 60s per annum.[40] He later
bequeathed this to his daughter Elizabeth, wife of Michael Quinton.
In 1509 he succeeded to Draycot, South Wraxall and other properties
at his father's death. This gave him considerable dominance over his
tenants and neighbours who occasionally took issue with his high-
handedness. The belief by men such as Sir Henry in their inherent and
natural right to regulate the 'lower orders' sometimes led to overbearing
pride and misuse of the extensive powers they commanded.[41]

Walter Fynemore and his son Richard enjoyed a brief victory
in Chancery over a land dispute, but the timing was unfortunate; Sir
Henry happened to be sheriff at the time. He responded by paying
various poor men to harass them, ordering the arrest of Fynemore
the elder, which drew the accusation he behaved 'more like an
oppressor, cruel tyrant and extortioner, than an indifferent executor
and minister'. They sued Sir Henry's bailiff, John Mawditt, for arrest
and false imprisonment.

Perhaps Sir Henry, like Cromwell – notoriously one of the
most ruthless and potent operators ever to dominate the politics
of England – took to heart lessons from the writings of Florentine,
Niccolo Machiavelli, whose work *The Prince* was published in 1532.
Machiavelli describes with unflinching cynicism the grim truth about
how political power is actually seized and maintained. He observed
that: 'A man who strives after goodness in all his acts is sure to come to
ruin, since there are so many men who are not good.'

In 1531, Henry, again over-exercising his powers, together
with Sir Anthony Hungerford and Sir John Bridges, sought the
favour of Cromwell on behalf of the abbot, who was behind with his
'temporalities' to the king. The abbot's predecessor had left him little
ready money, and during the vacancy part of the plate and much of the

---

39   Nicholas Harris, *Testamenta Vetusta: Being Illustrations from Wills, of
Manners, Customs, &c, Vol II*, p. 491
40   *Valor Ecclesiasticus Temp Henry VIII*, Wilts. p. 122
41   G. E. Mingay, *The Gentry, The Rise and Fall of a Ruling Class*, 1976, p. 164

goods of the house had been embezzled. Sir Henry was not inclined to take the side of the abbot after the death of a keeper during an affray between the abbot's and Sir Henry's men, who objected to the abbot's men hunting in parts of the forest.

At the inquest Sir Henry blamed the abbot for the keeper's death and indicted him as an accessory to murder. Later at the trial he had the jury imprisoned when he discovered they were about to acquit, and after intervention by the king at Sir Henry's personal instigation, and his firm instruction to the jury to deliver a guilty verdict, the abbot and three other monks were duly convicted.[42]

While serving on the Commission of the Peace in 1535, Sir Henry found himself mediating in a dispute between the Prior of Bath, William Holloway, and William Crouch, a quarrelsome, grasping, ruthless man, who disrupted the economy of Bath yet later became its MP. Crouch claimed the prior had reneged on a promise to give him the reversion of St John's Hospital, and resorted to the law. When a servant of Crouch's attempted to serve Prior Holloway with a subpoena in Bath Cathedral, he was frogmarched out by two priory servants, Baten and Horner, with threats that if he came back they would cut off his ears.[43]

Crouch went to Sir Henry Long's house at Draycot, requesting his intervention. Shortly afterwards he was pursued by an armed band of priory supporters who put him in the stocks with a horselock on his leg, Crouch later claiming he was derided, threatened and 'shaken by the beard'. After three days of imprisonment he was made to sign a £200 bond for his good behaviour.

Humiliated and enraged, he waited three weeks to exact retribution, imprisoning Horner in his house at Englishcombe. A mass of priory servants and tenants besieged the house and attacked the doors with hatchets. Crouch retaliated with arrows, but eventually released Horner when the mob threatened to burn the house down. Vehemently denying he was a 'maintainer of thieves, vagabonds and ill-doers', Crouch was imprisoned by Sir Henry Long with the

---

42   June Badeni, *Wiltshire Forefathers*, 1959, p. 45
43   *Proceedings in the Court of the Star Chamber in the Reigns of Henry VII* Somerset Record Society 1911, p.24

assistance of the mayor. The case was heard in the Star Chamber before Sir Henry and Sir William Stourton. It wouldn't be the last the courts would see of Crouch however; he spent the rest of his life mired in lawsuits over property.

At the time of this suit Sir Henry and his brother Richard were in high favour with Cromwell, well on the way to becoming the king's chief minister after the death of Cardinal Wolsey in 1530. Indeed, Sir Henry was described as Cromwell's friend by Dr John London, Cromwell's agent in the dissolution of the monasteries. Sir Henry joined the House for various sessions around 1533 on Cromwell's nomination, but during the next few years his parliamentary career would be interrupted – perhaps distracted by a financial crisis. In 1537 he wrote to Cromwell requesting reimbursement of £55 for expenses relating to his term as sheriff, making the point that it was 100 marks short of what he had spent.

The following year he found himself under further financial strain after the ransacking of Abingdon Abbey. There was a huge revolt in the north, known as the Pilgrimage of Grace, perpetrated by a menacing ragtag army of some twenty to thirty thousand outraged peasants and gentry. Appeased by King Henry who agreed to their demands, they went home, but he did nothing except raise an army of his own.

This was more a peacekeeping operation than war, nevertheless Sir Henry and his cohorts were obliged to pay the wages of men raised against the rebels. Early in his reign Henry had enforced the Acts of his father Henry VII decreeing that all who had grants of land, held office or received an annuity must either accompany him on military expeditions or make a suitable payment in lieu. It was bad timing for Sir Henry. Having already exhausted his available money after mortgaging his manor at Calne, he earnestly requested Cromwell's financial assistance. The penalty for non-payment of soldiers was harsh: forfeiture of all personal goods and chattels and a free cart ride to prison, although his friendship with both the king and Cromwell guaranteed immunity on that score.

He also asked Cromwell to grant a convenient living for his daughter Jane from her estranged husband's lands, 'and I care not if she never see him again. I desired your favour for him at the time of his trouble, trusting he would amend, but since then he is rather worse than better.'[44] This errant husband was Robert Leversege of Frome, son of Sir Henry's second wife, Elinor Wrottesley – clearly not a favourite son-in-law. Sir Henry was appointed guardian of Robert Leversege, son and heir of Edmund Leversege, Esquire.[45] The younger Leversege was a volatile man who on at least one occasion was brought before the Court of Chancery for failure to pay for goods supplied to him, and assaulting the unfortunate merchant when he asked for his money.[46]

During Sir Henry's third term as sheriff a riot broke out in Somerset at Taunton early in 1536, sparked by the activities of a commission to take up corn. The townsfolk were desperately aggrieved; 'the poor people doth much complain of the scarceness and dearth of grain'. An armed mob of about sixty men and women took to the streets, shouting accusations against several magistrates, warning 'it shall cost a thousand lives'. In a panic, the authorities alerted Sir Henry that they were headed towards Frome. He made the 26 mile dash on horseback to meet them, but it was all over before he got there. His son-in-law Robert Leversege had already disarmed the mob, probably unleashing a few choice threats of his own. Whatever he said, it had the effect that 'they delivered their weapons to him and were contented to obey at the first word'.

Sir Henry informed Cromwell that his son-in-law had arrested twenty-eight rioters, receiving the reply in no uncertain terms that they should be severely dealt with.[47] The arrest a few years earlier of another son-in-law who fell foul of the law, Michael Quinton, led to Sir Henry being accused by Sheriff Thomas Yorke of rescuing him from lawful custody. Perhaps another instance of Sir Henry's high-handedness; either way, he considered it an outrageous slander and sued Yorke for £100 damages.

44   J. S. Brewer, R. H. Brodie, J. Gairdner, *Letters and Papers, Foreign and Domestic, of the Reign of Henry VIII*, PRO, 1932, p. 403
45   Henry Churchill Maxwell-Lyte, *The Registers of Thomas Wolsey, Bishop of Bath and Wells, 1518–23*, p. 43
46   *Court of Chancery: Six Clerks Office: Early Proceedings, Richard II to Philip and Mary* C1/1124/56
47   G.R. Elton, *Policy and Police: The Enforcement of the Reformation in the Age of Thomas Cromwell*, 1985, p. 109

In an attempt to alleviate his financial pressures, Sir Henry joined with Walter, Lord Hungerford, who wrote to Cromwell in June 1539 requesting a grant from the king of several manors, including lands in Somerset formerly belonging to the priory of Hinton Charterhouse, confiscated from the Carthusian monks. Hungerford mentioned his 'old friend Sir Henry Long desires to have part of it of me'.

It is evident from the state papers that Sir Henry and his brother Sir Richard were not averse to a little grovelling for the substantial crumbs after the Thynnes and Hungerfords had their slice of the cake. Sir Henry sent a very ingratiating letter to Cromwell requesting his appointment as steward of the Somerset estates as a reward for his work as commissioner, reporting on the smaller monasteries to the Court of Augmentation. 'In my hartieste maner I recommende me', he wrote, pleading Cromwell's approbation to the king 'to helpe me to be his grace's farmer to the house of Henton', otherwise fearing he would be ruined. 'Unlesse the kynges grace be gode & gracyous unto me I shalbe fayne to geve over my house, and to gette me yn to some corner'.[48] His obligation to the king's military ambitions continued to shrink his purse, and on at least five further occasions between 1542 and 1545 he sold some of his Wiltshire landholdings.

Cromwell, meanwhile, was about to come undone. He had made a serious misjudgement in trying to keep alive the marriage he had arranged between Anne of Cleves and the king, who insisted he had detested her from the moment of their first meeting. Henry got his annulment on 9 July 1540. Attainted for treason, Cromwell was beheaded at the Tower nineteen days later, his head stuck on a pike facing away from the city in disgrace. Henry's reign probably had more political executions than any other of comparable length in English history – 330 in the years 1532-40 alone.

With heads rolling all around him, Sir Henry Long carried on the work Cromwell had masterminded, and in December he sent Thomas Horton, vicar of Calne, before the Privy Council on suspicion of being a papist, after Thomas Becket's name was found in one of his

---

48   o. Crom. Corresp. xxiv. 5 *The Somerset Religious Houses and their Suppression*, p. 66

service books. The Privy Council having satisfied themselves that the vicar had 'left the same unput out of negligence rather than malice', ordered him to be bound over with a payment of £40 to appear at the next assizes, and make a public declaration in his church acknowledging his offence and folly in disobeying the king's injunction, promising to mend his wicked ways. He was then dismissed with a letter to Sir Henry to monitor his future compliance.[49]

When the king again went to war with France in 1544 it was probably under some financial pressure that Sir Henry, aged in his fifties, commanded a troop of 200 men at the siege of Boulogne. Amongst other Wiltshire magnates accompanying him on that expedition was Edward Bayntun, and the king's brothers-in-law Thomas and Edward Seymour, kinsmen by marriage on Sir Henry's mother's side. The steward's accounts held at Longleat tell us that in the autumn of 1537, Edward Seymour, travelling with a cavalcade of forty mounted servants and retainers, made a progress from his Wiltshire residence of Wolfhall, and 'on the 8th he lay at Sir Henry Long's, at Draycote'.

A century later historian John Aubrey gives some idea of what a typical dinner at Draycot must have been like. The lords of the manor dined in their great Gothic halls at the high table, and the halls of the justices of the peace were dreadful to behold: 'the skreens [were] garnished with corselets and helmets gaping with open mouth, with coats of mail, lances, pikes, halberts, brown bills, and batterdashes'.

After the death of Henry VIII in 1547, his widow Katherine Parr remarried Sir Thomas Seymour, who, like his brother Edward the Protector, was also later executed. Shortly before this marriage Katherine encountered problems that turned into a three-way bun-fight with the Protector over a lease he had made to Sir Henry Long as tenant of her dower property Fasterne (or Vasterne), about a mile from Wootton Bassett in Wiltshire.

The Protector coveted Fasterne and negotiated with Sir Henry Long to resign his lease without notable success, which may have soured the previous good relations between them. Katherine wrote to her husband-to-be from Chelsea expressing her outrage at his brother's conduct towards her, which 'made me a little warm'. She complained the Protector had given 'Master Long such courage that he refuseth to receive such cattle as are brought here for the provision of my house'.

Sir Thomas Seymour immediately advised her to ask the Protector 'not to meddle, for you will take wrong at his hands rather than claim your right against his pleasure. If you find him, stick fast to Mr Long's interest.' The Protector overrode the furious Katherine's wishes, and for a while he succeeded in getting Fasterne from Sir Henry Long, who somewhat unwillingly agreed to part with it for a sum of money and the lifetime office of ranger of Braden Forest.

Sir Henry wasn't going to leave it at that, however. He wrote to the Protector from Draycot in July 1547 asking that the lease be restored to him. Hoping to enlist the aid of a go-between, he had already written to the Earl of Warwick requesting he intercede,[50] and also to Sir John Thynne, who reminded him of his earlier agreement to surrender the lease, urging him to stick to the arrangement.

A later suit shows Sir Henry's younger son Richard Long of Bradenstoke sold the keepership of the park at Fasterne to his brother-in-law John Newborough,[51] suggesting an eventual victory over Seymour. Another dispute arose between them over property leased by Sir Henry at Littlecote in exchange for lands at Wraxall, involving the Protector's second son, Sir Edward Seymour junior.

Like his brother Richard, Sir Henry Long did extremely well from his close relationship with the king, despite the cash flow problems he encountered. At the Dissolution he was granted land that had belonged to St Mary's Priory, near Kington St Michael and also Lyneham and Littlecote in Hilmarton, formerly belonging to Bradenstoke Priory. He later received a grant of land confiscated from Malmesbury Abbey.

He married firstly Frideswyde Hungerford[52] and secondly Elinor Wrottesley, the young widow of Edmund Leversege, who between

50   *Calendar of the Manuscripts of the Marquis of Salisbury,* vol. 9, pt.1, Sir Henry Long to the Duke of Somerset, p. 48
51   Nat Arch. C 1/1250/26
52   Named as Jane in her father's will pr. 1524, extract *Collectanea Topographica et Genealogica,* 1841, ʃp. 71

them produced thirteen children. Eleanor's uncle Richard Dudley, chancellor of Salisbury, stood godfather to Richard and Thomasine, two of her children by Sir Henry Long.

At South Wraxall Manor there is a fireplace in one of the bedrooms on the south side of the house with the initials 'SHL' (Sir Henry Long) engraved into one of the spandrels, and into another tied by a lover's knot, the initials H and E, thought to stand for 'Henry and Elinor'. After Lady Elinor died in 1543, Sir Henry turned his attention to Parliament. He represented Wiltshire briefly, in 1552–3 and died in 1556. He was succeeded by his eldest son, Robert.

Sir Robert Long (c.1517–81)

At the age of twenty-three Robert was elected to the junior knighthood of the shire, probably with the assistance of his influential father. In 1545 he was MP for Calne, but other than these early forays into the world of politics, and unusually for this family, Robert had little involvement in local administrative matters, preferring instead a life at court. Two years later he was rewarded by Henry VIII, becoming a gentleman pensioner and Esquire of the King's Body. This afforded him intimate access; he was required to be attendant upon the royal person, to array and unray him, and to watch day and night, because 'no man else [is] to set hands on the king'. Robert was with his uncle Sir Richard Long at the reception of Anne of Cleves at Calais in 1539, and five years later fought in the siege of Boulogne with his father. When the siege ended in 1546 he returned to England and married Barbara Carne, eventually fathering five children.

After inheriting his father's estates in 1556 and purchasing more land in Wiltshire to add to his patrimony, Sir Robert began alterations to the manor house at South Wraxall and the enclosure of the Longs' chapel in the church. His initials with the date 1566 can be seen carved above the doorway. It was not until his later years he was pricked as sheriff and knighted in 1575. Before he died in 1581 he appointed as one of his overseers 'my trustie and welbeloved' friend Sir John Danvers, a magistrate whose actions, as we shall see, would later trigger a calamitous chain of events leading to the murder of one of Sir Robert's sons.

After leaving provision for his wife he left annuities to his younger sons, and to his eldest son Walter *(see Sir Walter Long the Elder, 1561–1610)* he left nine manors and other property. In 1588 his widow remarried, to Simon Bowyer, gentleman usher to Queen Elizabeth. She continued to be styled Lady Barbara Long after this marriage.

II
Long of Ashley

Another younger son of Sir Henry Long, Anthony of Ashley, also had property at Wraxall. Tithe suits enrolled in the Exchequer of Pleas beginning in 1577 show a six year wrangle over this property between Anthony Long and Hugh Sexey, which was continued after his death by Anthony's widow Alice and their son Thomas. Anthony died at the end of April 1578 and is buried at St Thomas A'Beckett church, about three miles from Wraxall at the village of Box.

His monument, depicting a bearded figure incumbent on the altar in armour, was removed from its original position some time during the early part of the nineteenth century and only rediscovered after renovations revealed it stored under the old three-decker pulpit of the church. The effigy was placed in a rebuilt tomb recess in 1896. Also buried at Box is one of Sir Henry Long's grandsons – son of Sir Robert, named Jewel, after his godfather John Jewel, bishop of Salisbury. Anthony's widow Alice (*née* Butler), continued to live at the manor house at Ashley possessed of considerable property in Wiltshire and Somerset, the source of a long-running family dispute.

It is not certain Anthony Long was a Catholic; his brother Robert apparently was not. Persecution of Catholics was at a peak during this time, and the Act Against Reconciliation to Rome was passed in 1581 establishing heavy fines for recusancy or attending Catholic mass. Laymen who sheltered priests were liable to the death penalty, and suspected papists were subjected to house searches. In 1582 the finger of suspicion was pointed at Anthony's widow Alice and their son Thomas.

On the order of the sheriff, William Brouncker, (brother-in-law of Edward Long of Monkton), a search was made of Alice's house at Ashley, and the undersheriff Michael Cuffe seized 'certen

Popishe trashe . . . divers popish books, beads, holy candles &c.',[53] possession of which constituted a felony. These items were taken to Sir Francis Walsingham to be kept as evidence. The instigator of the allegations was none other than Alice's eldest son William, a man of little conscience who coveted her property.

His brother Thomas, it was alleged, was 'an earnest and disorderly Papist, and harbourer of Papists'. His mother, an 'obstinate Recusant', said to be guided by the perverse direction of a schoolmaster called Wells,[54] 'a dangerous Papist', fled to Wells's house in nearby Monkton Farleigh, a haven for 'suspected persons'. The unannounced arrival at Monkton Farleigh of the undersheriff and three justices resulted in the arrest of Wells, together with Mrs Long and anyone else in the house thought worthy of suspicion.

In 1584 a Bill of complaint made in Alice's name was brought before the Star Chamber by Thomas against his brother William, Michael Cuffe and the others who had forcibly entered the house. It was maintained that Alice was 'a simple old woman not acquainted with the practices of her son Thomas and his adherents', but the evidence was stacked against her and the Bill declared 'most slanderous'. After Thomas's death the following year William took advantage of his mother's increased vulnerability. He determined to gain possession of her estate at Ashley and other lands in Wiltshire which she claimed in descent from her ancestor Thomas Mountford.

With no love lost between them, in March 1586 he callously cast his mother 'out of dores, making great waste and spoyle' of her house and goods therein. A distraught Alice petitioned the queen, who referred the matter to her Privy Council. The result was yet another Bill of complaint being heard in the Star Chamber, brought by Alice against William for redress of 'certain wrongs, injuries and oppressions'. She won an order from the court for her return to the house, pending further legal action on behalf of William to decide ownership of the title, but Alice's reinstatement was not as

---

53   *Calendar of State Papers, Domestic Series 1547–1625*, p. 158
54   St Swithun Wells, one of the forty martyrs of England and Wales canonised by Pope Paul VI, 25 October 1970. He was sent to the gallows for treason 10 December 1591

straightforward as it should have been.

William and his wife Lucy stayed put and by August were well and truly ensconced. On being ordered to leave, the pair refused, creating a 'royotous and disorderlie dysturbaunce'. William's wife was the most obstinate and outspoken, and the sheriff, Sir John Danvers, had orders to charge William with his wife's misdemeanour and a further order to return possession of the property to Alice. Their continued refusal culminated in both being arrested and imprisoned until the next sitting of the Star Chamber. The court ruled against them and Alice regained control of her estates, but William again attempted to dispossess his mother by procuring a writ against her. Fortunately for Alice this was unsuccessful, and for the time being William was thwarted.

This was not the end of the matter, however. William, obsessed with desire for what he believed was his rightful inheritance, continued to persecute his elderly mother, and in 1593, seven years after he had first thrown her out of the house, the Star Chamber was once again reverberating with evidence of his cruelty. This time he was found guilty of riotous entry into the house and imprisoning his mother, said to be 'a widow of 80 years of age', and keeping her locked up for eight weeks, destroying her goods and eating her provisions; 'a very barbarous and cruell matter'. He was fined 100s, his servants 20s each, and all were dispatched immediately to prison.[55]

For the three years that remained of her life Alice had the satisfaction justice had been done, and she died at her house in September 1596.

Nathaniel Long (1652–1714)

Nathaniel, grandson of Anthony and Alice's son Henry, was baptised at Bath Abbey, Somerset, in the autumn of 1652, later inheriting his father's modest property at Minchinhampton. Mr C.E Long 's printed pedigree of 1878 incorrectly records Nathaniel's parents as Anthony and Ann Long of Walcot, Somerset. The confusion

55   John Hawarde, *Les Reportes Del Cases in Camera Stellata, 1593 to 1609,* 1894, p. 323

no doubt arose due to close intermarriage between cousins, all with
the name Long and two wives called Ann. Nathaniel was in fact the
son of Anthony's *sister* Ann[56] and her husband the Rev. George Long
of Bath. Confusingly, George was the brother of Anthony's *wife* Ann,
both children of the Rev. Richard Long (correctly noted as of Avening,
Gloucestershire, in the pedigree).

Nathaniel, aged thirteen at his father's death, was perhaps too
young to have been unduly influenced by George's zealous Puritanism.
Styled colonel, he rose up the ranks of Sir Robert Vyner's Red
Regiment of the Honourable Artillery Company, one of six militia
units in London during the 1670s. In the early years of his marriage
to Sarah Lytcott, and with his father-in-law Giles Lytcott comptroller
of customs, he left the army and reinvented himself as a merchant,
an employment deemed perfectly acceptable for a man of his social
status, although on this point his contemporary John Locke would
have disagreed. Locke took the traditional view that trade was 'wholly
inconsistent with a gentleman's calling.' But for Nathaniel it was the
best means of improving his fortune.

From premises in London and with assistance from his younger
brother Josias – official printer to the Customs House – Nathaniel
published daily news-sheets giving particulars of entries and clearances
of ships in the port of London, which he sold to subscribers for 40s a
year. This had once been a profitable side-line of the Custom House
clerks until Nathaniel became patentee, possibly a perk influenced by
his father-in-law.

Managing risk and cost in London's complex commercial
environment was vital to Nathaniel's success; in one instance he had
an entire shipment of Spanish wine condemned, having already sent
woollen manufactures in part payment. Facing a loss, he petitioned the
customs commissioners to be released from his obligation to pay the
rest of the assessed value. Wary of pirates active on the trade routes, in
December 1693 he sought permission for the ship *Three Sarahs*, with a
crew of seven, to retrieve a parcel of Spanish wines already bought and
paid for the previous summer, awaiting shipping from Coruña.

56   Baptised 25 November 1618 at Box

While briefly a tenant of Aldersbrook House he was appointed commissioner to raise a £2m government fund by subscription to aid trade to the East Indies in 1698. Once part of the manor of Wanstead, Essex, Aldersbrook House was bought by Sir James Long nearly one hundred years later, when it was again merged with that manor. At about this time Nathaniel had warehouses built in Mark Lane, which not only provided rental income and storage space but also premises for his brother Josias's printing operation.

Temporarily escaping the stress of business and a pending court case after a mishap with a merchant ship in Portsmouth Harbour, he took a short holiday with fellow merchant and adventurer Thomas Bowrey. On the evening of 28 May 1698 with a crew of three, the friends set sail from Greenwich down the Thames in Bowrey's yacht *The Duck,* anticipating a relaxing six week tour to France, Holland and Flanders.

Only rediscovered in 1913, a diary Bowrey kept of the trip provides a meticulous record of their shared expenses and an insight into their adventure. Bowrey had stocked up on provisions and they dined like kings, purchasing more fresh food along the way. Overnight stays in the towns necessitated the hire of transport to and from the inns, and there were sundry expenses to get the boat through the canals. They paid locals to help lower and raise the mast, hinged to allow the yacht to pass under the low bridges. And to compensate for his absence, 'Madm Long' instructed Nathaniel bring her back three pieces of lace.

The lawsuit to which they returned involved the freighting of the galley *St George* for a voyage to India in the winter of 1696 by Bowrey, Nathaniel and others. Bowrey was to have sailed in her as master but the vessel proved unseaworthy. On her way into Portsmouth Harbour for overhauling she collided with a Swedish vessel, the damage so serious her voyage had to be abandoned. With the owners of the *St George* facing a loss, an action was brought against Bowrey. He and Nathaniel had been great friends during their trip abroad but before the litigation ended their friendship had considerably cooled.[57]

57   *The Papers of Thomas Bowrey, 1669–1713*

A little note written probably not long after the holiday was sent from London from Nathaniel's son Lytcott, then aged about twelve, to Bowrey in connection with *The Duck*:

> Captain Bowrey, my father shewed me your letter wherein you have ordered me the care of your yatt which I will be shure to do and make much of our leftenant[58] till I se you again; and the next time you goo to sea you have promiseed to take me with you and I rely on you that you will be as good as your word. I am Sir, your humbell sarvant to command – Lytcott Long. [59]

Nathaniel was one of the twelve jurors who convicted Captain William Kidd at the Old Bailey for murder and piracy in 1701. He died in August 1714, outliving four of his five sons, leaving four infant daughters and his surviving heir, five-year-old John. As sole executor his widow Sarah had the task of tying up loose ends, and in 1718 her petition to the House of Lords was granted allowing the sale of his estate to pay his debts and apply the residue as per his will. His freehold property was mostly in London at Allhallows and elsewhere; his only stake in the country was the modest house and land in Gloucestershire at Minchinhampton, inherited from his father.

Sarah spent her last years in London at Bloomsbury, dying in early January 1731. Written informally in her own hand, her will makes clear the distribution of her personal and household effects among her daughters, but also her despair over her last remaining son John. She had apprenticed him to Sherman Godfrey of the Distillers' Company, London, in retrospect an unfortunate choice of career. Just ten years later John was 'the grief of my heart, pray God turn him from his evill ways and if ever he proves a sober man I desire his sisters to give him the ruby ring that was his deare fathers, but not [until] they are well assured he will not part with it'.

58   Lieutenancy, delegated authority
59   Bowrey *ibid*

Long of Minchinhampton

The Rev. George Long of Bath (1621–65)

Baptised at Minchinhampton, Nathaniel's father George received his early education at nearby Tetbury under a certain Mr Webb, later graduating Bachelor of Arts from St John's College, Cambridge. Following in his Puritan vicar father's footsteps he was appointed pastor and incumbent of Bath Abbey, recommended by the Assembly of Divines as 'a learned orthodox and godly Divine'. Twenty-five-year-old George and his assistant Matthew Randall were each granted a maintenance allowance of £100 a year, while George was also allowed to 'receive and enjoy houses, Glebe Lands, tythes and profits of the churches and chapells within and belonging to the Cittie of Bath'. These were estimated to be worth a further £60 per annum.[60]

George was a zealous supporter of Oliver Cromwell's crusade to reform the nation's morals. He testified against several accused clerics in the West Country and denounced the vicar of Box, Walter Bushnell, to the Wiltshire commissioners in 1656. George was incensed Bushnell had preached at a funeral at St James's church without his permission, telling him he was not well thought of by the godly, i.e. Cromwell's henchmen. After further investigation Bushnell was charged with drunkenness, profanation of the Sabbath, gaming and disaffection of the government. During the proceedings Bushnell slighted George as an outsider – 'the intruder of Bath' – accusing him of slander and backbiting, and not being as godly as his reputation suggested.

Despite a vigorous defence Bushnell was found guilty and ejected. George continued as minister at Bath until the tables were turned on Puritanism at the Restoration in 1660, when Bushnell was restored once again to the living of Box. Moves were afoot to reintroduce the many conventions and rites of the church abolished by the Puritans, enforced by the Act of Uniformity passed by Parliament in 1662. In what became known as the 'Great Ejection', nearly 2,000

60 John Wroughton, *A Community at War: the Civil War in Bath and North Somerset, 1642–1650*, 1992, p. 183

clergymen chose to leave the Established Church, but by this time George's tenure at Bath was already history.

William Prynne, MP for Bath, sometime Puritan turned Presbyterian and supporter of the Act, wrote in September 1661 that a number of persons 'all liveing in or neare the city of Bath', including 'George Long, Clerke' and his faithful assistant Greene, had been secured as prisoners by two of the deputy lieutenants for the purpose of interrogation. In what must have seemed like sweet justice to Walter Bushnell, George now found himself one of those ejected. He, together with Greene, removed to a non-conformist church at Trim Street, just a few minutes' walk from Bath Abbey, to minister to the dissenting congregation there.

George died in January 1665, having written his will shortly before. To his wife Ann he left his property in Gloucestershire, including the house and garden at Minchinhampton, inherited from his father.

The Rev. Richard Long (1598–c.1645)

George's father also suffered for his beliefs. Oxford University educated, the Rev. Richard Long was born at Ashleworth, Gloucester[61], where a branch of the Long family had been yeomen since 1491. His forebears possibly descended from Wiltshire's wealthy gentry, but Richard's means were more modest. Without the advantages of old family money, his house in Minchinhampton was not a valuable freehold inheritance but a copyhold cottage for the three lives of himself, Anne his wife and their son George. He did briefly attempt to improve his position; in partnership with three other London gentlemen he dabbled in the land market in 1639 receiving several grants of 'various properties in divers counties' by virtue of the commission for defective titles. This appears to have been for short-term profit, in some cases reselling within weeks of the grants.

While Richard left the business of generating long-term wealth to others, he earned a reasonable living by holding jointly the vicarages of Chewton Mendip, Somerset, and Winterborne Monkton,

61   *Deposition Book, Sarum Consistory Court*, WSA ref D1/42/43

Wiltshire, between 1627 and 1645. During the 1620s and '30s he acted as surrogate judge of the Consistory Court of Bath and Wells, his initial appointment favoured by the bishop's registrar James Huishe, after he promised to be there on all court and market days. Clerical justices such as Richard were few in the seventeenth century, becoming more prevalent in the mid-eighteenth.

One morning session he held in Wells Cathedral in 1638 dealt with the fornication between William Lane and Agnes Kilbie of Chewton Magna. The accusation was that Lane, 'beeinge att Staunton Drewe att a bull bayting and beare bayteinge, mett with her, and Carryed her home to Chewe behinde him, and weare found in her howse alone togeather about midnight verie suspiciouslie of Incontinent lief togeathers.'

The standard punishment was public penance. The offenders were instructed to stand in church during morning prayers for three consecutive Sundays, bare legged and bare headed, attired in a white sheet and carrying a white rod. Denunciation by the vicar and confessions of guilt by the couple completed the humiliation. This usually had the effect of deterring attendance at church rather than reforming immoral behaviour, however.

While not an extremist, Richard nevertheless interpreted and enforced the rules with typical Puritan enthusiasm. One Sunday in the pulpit while reading the first lesson he was disturbed by John Edgill, who shouted: 'You that read prayers, see you goe not to the communion table, your bowinge and bendinge to superstition and idolitrie.' Richard viewed this as a refusal to conform to the newly emphasised ceremony of bowing at the name of Jesus, which resulted in his presentment of Edgill.

The circumstances of Richard's unhappy fate were not dissimilar to those that led to the downfall of his son George some twenty years later during the Civil War. Richard 'was vilely treated by the rebels, and died of poison. The four persons chiefly concerned in his prosecution, were Job Emlin, Robert Wilcox, James Hoskins, and Thomas Philips. The first died soon after, the second was taken speechless and never spoke more, the third was distracted in his head before, and after grew downright mad, and the last died in a barn. Two others, who were

going to London to swear against Mr Long, died on the road thither
of small-pox.'[62]

Another account says Richard died in Axbridge prison, his wife
and children taken into the care of Alexander Popham, MP of Bath.[63]

62   Henry Spelman, Charles Frere Stopford Warren, *The History and Fate of
Sacrilege*, 1853, p. 44
63   David Underdown, *Somerset in the Civil War and Interregnum*, 1973, p.144

III
Long of Lyneham

Richard Long (c.1526–58)

Here we leave the scattered fragments in Gloucestershire, Somerset and London, and return to Wiltshire and another son of the Longs of Wraxall and Draycot. Richard, third son of Sir Henry Long and Elinor Wrottesley, acquired the keepership of the park of Vastern which had earlier given his father such a headache, and he too became involved in a lawsuit over the property with his brother-in-law John Newborough, to whom he sold it.

In 1556, about a year after his marriage to Marian Browne Richard inherited his father's lands at Bradenstoke. They had an only child, Edmund, born in January 1556, but Richard died aged thirty-two, less than three years later, barely having had time to enjoy fatherhood. His widow purchased the wardship of their infant son giving her control of management and estate revenue, with an annuity of £4 a year for his maintenance. Outliving her second husband Robert Geale, Marian married a third time to Oliver Pleydell.

Edmund Long (1556–1635)

On his marriage to Emund's mother, Pleydell gave a bond to provide his stepson with the lease of a house at Lyneham purchased by his father, and one half of all his father's goods. By the time Edmund came of age ten or twelve years later, Pleydell had hatched a plan to defraud him. From his point of view it was opportune that his wife Marian was on her deathbed. Hoping to profit from her inability to prevent the wicked deed and perhaps also her son's ignorance of his own affairs, Pleydell moved out of the house, taking all the chests containing the wills of Edmund's father Richard Long and first stepfather Geale, as well as the bond. Marian's death shortly afterwards allowed Pleydell to remarry, and to this wife he left what rightfully belonged to Edmund.

Pleydell died nearly ten years later and it was left to Edmund to sue his widow Margaret through the court of Chancery.

Practically predestined by virtue of his family name, Edmund was appointed to the Commission of the Peace. The office of justice became increasingly popular as their sphere of influence and responsibility grew, but the strict enforcement of regulations made the justice himself rather less well-liked. On one occasion during the arduous and complex business of assessing property for the collection of subsidies, Edmund's unpopularity and self-aggrandising forced him to court. He was accustomed, it was alleged in a Star Chamber case in 1621, 'to win applause to himself and increase an estimation of greatness' at the expense of his fellow justices. He had spread such 'a false conceipt of his, the said Edmund Long's unlimited authority by virtue of the said commission, that he might induce ignorant people to believe that he had absolute power and authority in himself to raise or abate their several rates'.[64]

Edmund's sense of power over the people had begun long before. In a bastardy case in 1607 with his fellow justice John Hungerford they meted out a 'sentence and finall doome' to a young unmarried couple who produced a child. Economic provision for illegitimate children was of direct concern to parish officials and it was not unusual for local magistrates to deal with such flouting of the rules by ordering public whipping of the parents, but on this occasion they were made to do public penance at morning prayers in the church. This was followed by an hour standing in the stocks to be derided by the morally upright citizens of Lyneham. At evening prayers the guilty couple were displayed for the parishioners to 'behold, look upon and take warning by',[65] an ineffective deterrent as the registers of baptisms attest.

Some years later the beginnings of another power struggle emerged between Edmund and fellow JP, William Button, both men accusing each other of misuse of office. Edmund would have been all too aware of the risks involved in taking on a man like Button, who

64   R B Pugh, Elizabeth Crittall, *A History of the County of Wiltshire*, 1953, vol. 5, p. 120
65   WAM v. 22

– according to Edmund – was usually armed with a pistol and wore a 'privy doublet' – light body armour under his clothes. Edmund also accused Button of being boldly cruel to the people, who dared not seek redress because of his greatness and wealth. Edmund could hardly have forgotten the strikingly similar circumstances of the infamous feud in which he was also involved, that led to the murder in 1594 of his cousin Henry Long of Draycot. *(See Murder Most Foul)*

During Star Chamber proceedings Edmund charged Button with organising a violent intrusion into his park at midnight, killing deer and assaulting his servants who came out to investigate the 'braying and noise'. One servant lost the fingers of his right hand during the scuffle. It was alleged an encounter had been deliberately set up by Button's brother in pretence of friendship, inveigling Edmund's sons away to an alehouse beforehand, exposing the deer park as an easy target for plunder.[66]

The Long and Button families had a long association. Edmund's grandfather Sir Henry Long appointed his 'sonne in lawe Henry Buttayne' one of the overseers of his will. When his father died, as his underage heir Edmund automatically became a ward of the queen, and in the few months until his mother was granted wardship, a William Button – possibly the father of his adversary – was administrator of his estates. In 1627 Sir William Button was granted a pardon for acquiring, without having obtained licence from the king, the hay, corn, wool of West Tokenham, Preston and Lyneham from Edmund, his son Richard and daughter-in-law Mary. Button was a Royalist who during the Civil War had his estate at Tokenham raided on at least two occasions, suffering great losses at the hands of the Parliamentarians and was fined more than £2,000 for his delinquency.

Edmund lived at the moated manor house of Lyneham Court, demolished by the RAF in 1939. His marriage in 1576 to Rachel Coxwell and the subsequent birth of eight children ensured the continuation of the line, although his eldest son Henry predeceased him. Richard, the second son, would inherit his father's estates and become progenitor of at least another two generations.

66   Alison Wall, *Power & Protest in England, 1525–1640*

As a young man Richard engaged in an enterprise with his first cousin Henry Coxwell of Cirencester, who went with him to St Lucar, Spain, to buy merchandise in 1604. Shortly beforehand James I had given his opening speech to the first English Parliament outlining his desire to secure peace, by 'profession of the true religion'. Less than a month later a Bill was introduced in Parliament which threatened to outlaw all English followers of the Catholic Church, causing some alarmed Catholics to flee England.

During his stay in St Lucar Richard heard that a group of newly-arrived English Catholics in the town, one by the name of Percy, had implicated themselves in a papist plot to overthrow the king, the architect being a 'great nobleman' pulling the strings while imprisoned in the Tower of London. What Richard had stumbled on was the notorious Gunpowder Plot; Thomas Percy was one of the main conspirators. A year earlier the explosives expert they recruited, Guy Fawkes, had gone to Spain with a Catholic delegation to Philip III pleading for an invasion of England. While the Spanish king was sympathetic to the Catholic cause he declined, wishing to keep the peace.

Richard's first port of landing on his return home in November 1604 was Chepstow, Wales, and he immediately reported to the bishop of Llandaff with the story. On arrival in Wiltshire Richard ensured it reached the ears of magistrate Sir Thomas Snell of Kington St Michael (whose wife Anne was the daughter of Sir Robert Long of Draycot), and a report signed by Long and Snell was sent to the Privy Council in January 1605.[67]

Parliament was due to resume in February, but due to concerns about the plague it did not return until October, allowing the plotters time to bolster their ranks and perfect their plan. They were thwarted after William Parker, 4th Baron Monteagle, received an anonymous letter revealing existence of the plot, and Percy and his cohorts went into hiding with the Catholic Littleton family at Holbeche House. Their escape plan began to unravel after the gunpowder became wet during their flight and they foolishly tried to dry it in front of the fire.

67   *Calendar of the Cecil Papers in Hatfield House*, vol. 18, January 1606, 1-15

It exploded, injuring several of those present. The sheriff of Worcester and his men, now alerted to their whereabouts, attacked the house, and Thomas Percy was fatally struck by a musket ball, sparing him the gruesome execution which befell some of his co-conspirators.

Some thirty years later Richard was forced to defend the good name of Long during a session at the Wiltshire assizes in July 1637, after Philip Sticklow of Chippenham, bailiff and alehouse keeper, called him an 'impudent and audacious fellowe'. Richard complained that another man, Edward Hellier, had ridiculed him as a 'base gentleman', challenging him to fight, confident Richard 'would make a poore condiconed fellowe'. Evidence by witnesses supported the libel case, confirming Richard was 'descended of an ancient worshipful family' and his father was a JP, whereas Sticklow, a common bailiff, was a man of mean condition and estate. Brought before the assizes again in March 1638/9, Sticklow was ordered to acknowledge Richard's gentility and crave forgiveness for his 'rash and inconsiderate speeches'. Richard was awarded £12 expenses with £13 6s 8d damages[68] but had only a year to savour the victory before he died.

Neither Richard nor his seven siblings lived to any great age. When his younger brother Walter died in 1630 he had a two-year-old son, Walter junior of Lyneham, who at the age of thirty became caught up in one of many abortive Royalist risings in August 1659, seeking to restore the exiled monarchy of the future Charles II. Early that year Oliver Cromwell's Protectorate had disintegrated and the former republic restored by the resurrection of the Rump Parliament, whose first business was to reorganise the army. A general rising of Royalists was planned to occur on 1 August, but with only one notable demonstration in Cheshire the revolt was a flaccid affair and quickly suppressed.

In Wiltshire they were more enthusiastic, organising themselves into huddles in the countryside expecting word of a declaration on the restoration of King Charles from former parliamentarian Colonel Edward Massey and his Cavaliers. Massey was one of eleven impeached

---

68   Richard Cust, Andrew Hopper, *Cases in the High Court of Chivalry, 1634–1640*, vol. 18, 2006

members of parliament whom the army sought to remove in 1647, along with his Presbyterian crony Sir Walter Long (1st baronet of Whaddon). The parliamentary army were in pursuit with bloodhounds on his trail; he eluded them, heading for Lansdowne to muster supporters with the intention of riding *en masse* with a large body of horse and foot into Bristol to proclaim Charles Stuart rightful king. His plans were foiled by the army who quickly moved in, making several arrests.

The interrogations went on for several days, and among those arrested was Richard's nephew, Walter Long of Lyneham. He said he'd ridden from Wraxall to Lansdowne where he met 100 or more men waiting on the arrival of Colonel Massey and another 400 to swell their numbers. Walter stayed only a quarter of an hour at Landsdowne before sidling off and hiding in a wood. Asked why he retreated, he replied, 'in consequence of a message from Mr James'. He was admitting nothing.

Edmund Long junior (c.1642–81)

Edmund, great grandson of the preceding Edmund Long, and eldest son of Edmund Long and Barbara Ayliffe[69] inherited his father's estates but appears to have made little commitment to them. He sold Lyneham and Bradenstoke and went to live in London, taking up residence at St Olave's, Hart Street, a few miles from the home of his future wife Mary Otger at Battersea. Recently widowed, she was the daughter of Dutch Calvinists, Abraham and Mary Otger.

Her late husband Samuel de Visscher, a Dutch merchant, was barely cold when she married Edmund in early June 1676, and there were no children born during their five year marriage. Edmund died intestate in 1681 aged thirty-nine and Mary married a third time three years later to Samuel Pett, Royal Navy Commissioner. Edmund's brother Oliver took Mary to court in a dispute over her first husband's estate at about the same time.

Why did Edmund sell the estates that had been in the family so long? Ordinarily only outlying land would be sold if there was need for

---

69   Her sister Anne Ayliffe was briefly the wife of Edward Hyde, 1st Earl of Clarendon

money, never the main property that gave families status and a sense of permanence. From this property the heir's sisters would be provided with dowries, younger brothers a small inheritance to get them started in the world, and his mother a jointure. But Edmond's mother had predeceased his father and his sisters were already successfully married off. He knew Oliver was still living, and there was also younger brother George who had gone to sea, whereabouts unknown. Oliver was a career soldier in Ireland, unlikely to return, and for all anyone knew, George, not heard from for years, was already dead.

Perhaps through lack of interest or ability he failed to adequately exploit the resources of his inheritance, feeling disinclined to retain them due to interests in London. Whatever the case, the Longs of Lyneham were doomed to extinction.

Oliver Long (c.1643–1716)

Oliver – or Nol to his closest friends – Edmund 's flaxen-haired[70] brother, is described in the will of Lady Martha Ayliffe as the 'very welbeloved cozen' to whom she bequeathed £10 in 1667. She left the residue of her estate to Oliver's sister Martha. Lady Ayliffe (*née* Blount) was the second wife of Oliver's grandfather Sir George Ayliffe of Grittenham, and with no children of her own she took a motherly interest in her late husband's grandchildren.

Lady Ayliffe and her sisters were co-heiresses of the manor of Dedisham, Sussex, where Oliver's name appears as owner of freehold property. One of these sisters, Elizabeth Mohun, was appointed his guardian in 1658.[71] Oliver and his surviving siblings all left Wiltshire. In addition to Edmund in London and younger brother George somewhere at sea, his sister Martha married John Danvers of Slinfold, Sussex, and Elizabeth lived in Gloucestershire with her husband Christopher Guise.

Oliver's destiny was preordained. Younger sons, who could not expect to inherit the family estate, were instead urged into professions of state service. The Longs followed a pattern similar to many other

---

70   *Manuscripts of the Marquis of Ormonde, preserved at the Castle Kilkenny,* 1899. Description on the Muster Roll of the Kings Guard, p. 238
71   Wiltshire & Swindon Archives Add MS 49,844

gentry families which usually determined the eldest son would inherit the estate and enter politics, the second would join the army, the third went into law, and the fourth joined the clergy. As second son Oliver slotted neatly into the second designation, serving in the army in Ireland, appearing on the muster roll of the King's Guard of Horse in 1670 at the age of twenty-seven, the only man in his troop from Wiltshire. He went on to become captain of Colonel Francis Willoughby's company in 1677.

It was largely due to a chance meeting while in France in 1668 that Oliver's sometime uncle by marriage, Edward Hyde, Earl of Clarendon, survived an assassination attempt. The original letter giving an account of this event is held in the Bodleian Library at Oxford. Dated 26 April, it was written by Oliver from Evreux in Normandy to Secretary of State Sir William Cromwell:

As I was travelling from Rouen towards Orleans, it was my fortune, April 23, to overtake the earl of Clarendon, then in his unhappy and unmerited exile, who was going towards Bourbon, but took up his lodgings at a private hotel in a small walled town called Evreux, some leagues from Rouen. I, as most English gentlemen did to so valuable a patriot, went to pay him a visit near supper-time; when he was, as usual, very civil to me. Before supper was done, twenty or thirty English seamen and more came and demanded entrance at the great gate; which, being strongly barr'd, kept them out for some time. But in a short space they broke it, and presently drove all they found, by their advantage of numbers, into the earl's chamber; whence, by the assistance of only three swords and pistols, we kept them out for half an hour, in which dispute many of us were wounded by their swords and pistols, whereof they had many. To conclude, they broke the windows and the doors, and under the conduct of one Howard, an Irishman, who has three brothers, as I am told, in the King of England's service, and an ensign in the company of cannoneers, they quickly found the earl in his bed, not able to stand by the violence of the gout; whence, after they had given him many blows with their swords and staves, mixed with horrible curses and oaths, they dragged him on the ground in the middle of the yard, where they encompassed him around with their swords, and after they had told him in their own language, how he had sold the kingdom, and robbed them of their pay, Howard commanded them all, as one man, to run their swords through his body. But what difference arose among themselves before they could agree, God above, who alone sent this spirit of dissection, only knows. In this interval their lieutenant, one Swaine, came and disarmed them.

Sixteen of the ringleaders were put into prison; and many of those things they had rifled from him, found again, which were restored, and of great value. Mons. la Fonde, a great man belonging to the King of France's bed-chamber, sent to conduct the earl on his way thither, was so desperately wounded in the head, that there were little hopes of his life. Many of these assassins were grievously wounded; and this action is so much resented by all here, that many of these criminals will meet with a usage equal to their merit. Had we been sufficiently provided with fire-arms, we had infallibly done ourselves justice on them; however, we fear not but the law will supply our defect.

Clarendon, as a mark of his gratitude probably rewarded Oliver in some way for his bravery, and the relationship between the two was referred to in a letter written many years later by Clarendon's son Henry Hyde, the 2nd earl, when he was lord lieutenant of Ireland. It was when Oliver was with the Duke of Ormond's regiment in 1686 that Hyde wrote from Dublin Castle to his brother Lawrence, Lord Rochford, at that time lord treasurer. He lamented the actions of Sir Thomas Newcomen, who had 'filled the town with many rumours of changes', saying that all the officers of the regiment of Guards were to be displaced, except one, Captain Morice.

[This] makes poor Captain Long almost out of his wits. He is captain of the King's company, which he purchased; and by the rules of war (if those were observed) he ought naturally to rise to be major. He is a very honest man: his family were always loyal, and sufferers for being so. You know the dependence he had upon, and relation to my father; and therefore I hope you will do him what good you can.[72]

Hyde mentions Oliver again two years later in his diary on 12 December 1688,[73] one month after the Scottish Catholic King James VII invaded England during the Glorious Revolution. The conflict that followed between the Jacobites and Williamites (supporters of the Dutch Protestant Prince William of Orange) was to decide who would be King of England, Scotland and Ireland. The Irish Williamite War raged from 1688-91.

As part of a multi-national force being sent into Ireland, Hyde had collected Oliver and his friend Captain Thomas Flower at Oxford. They were *en route* to Wallingford to meet the Duke of Ormond, together with Hyde's brother-in-law Thomas Keightley, commissioner of Irish Revenue. It was an interesting little family circle; Keightley's wife's niece – the future queen Mary – was married to William of Orange, and his sister Mary Keightley had recently married Oliver's alcohol-fuelled cousin, James Long junior of Draycot.

Oliver was a great friend of Keightley's future son-in-law Lucius O'Brien (son of Sir Donat O'Brien of Dromoland) who married Keightley's daughter Catherine in 1701. Lucius was a profligate spendthrift, accumulating debts of £3,543.16s (about £277,000 today) in their first five years of marriage.[74] A few years later, Oliver, one of his creditors, wrote to him at Cratloe, near Limerick, with a cryptic request for repayment:

> Concerning the similitudes between lovers and borrowers; no sooner has parson or scrivener made use of these fatal words know all men by these presents but the borrower grows cool and the lover indifferent . . . which generally leaves men of my tribe as melancholy as you will me, if you doe not send some subsistance to your most humble servant, Oliver Long. [75]

Early in 1689 Oliver returned to England after he, his friend Thomas Flower and their fellow comrades-in-arms were 'declared and

---

73   *Ibid* v.2, p.113
74   *Dictionary of Irish Biography* (Butler, James (1665-1745)) Sir Donat O'Brien to Thomas Keightley 21 Feb 1706/7 (NLI, MS 45, 295/4)
75   Inchiquin MS 45,296/4

adjudged Traytors, convicted and attainted of High Treason' for their support of William of Orange. The battle went on in his absence, and he received a letter from Tipperary, dated January 1689, two months before James VII landed in Ireland. Beginning 'Dear Nol,' the writer bemoans the paucity of good wine in the nation and talks light-heartedly of the ongoing Irish conflict. 'We are continually alarmed by my Lord Deputy, sometimes he swears he will send 10,000 of his red locusts to devour us and when he hears we have 20,000 to oppose them he burns his periwig. So that his Lordship and the friars that are all running away make the barber's trade the best in Dublin.'

'Little Nol' had made a name for himself; he was 'often talked of by our great council. If we had you among us we would make you a Brigadier at least'. Oliver is urged to return to Ireland; 'If you love land come over, for debentures are suddenly to be given out.' He should bring with him a 'good horseman's sword' and also 'a good scarfe, belt, a good saddle, horse and furniture and you shall have either horse or money for them.'[76]

Oliver's attainder prevented his immediate return to Ireland, and in the March following this letter he was in London seeking another appointment. He and comrades Captain Thomas Flower and Captain Nicholas Sankey were named on a list of Protestant officers lately in the army in Ireland, 'and are now out of employment in and about London, and desire to be entertained in his Majesty's Service'. Oliver, Flower and Sankey had been through thick and thin together, fighting not only the Jacobites, but also each other. During a duel a year or so earlier, in which Oliver also concerned himself, Flower had grievously wounded Sankey, landing all three of them in prison. Their trial was postponed pending either Sankey's recovery or death.

A few days before this, Sankey had been reported to the lords' justice by the Earl of Sunderland, who had disposed of his command to Lord Galmoy, recommending he be cashiered. After the duel Sankey recovered from his wounds and Captains Flower and Long regained their liberty. Sankey kept his commission into the bargain, eventually rising to the rank of lieutenant general in 1710.

76 *Analecta Hibernica,* Issues 32-34, 1985 p. 51

The Irish Jacobites were finally defeated after the Battle of Aughrim in 1691. Promoted to lieutenant colonel, by 1702 Oliver was a member of Colonel Robert Ecklin's Inniskilling Dragoons, having been recommended to the post as 'an honest gentleman'. He retired from the army in 1705. Seeking a new post and a change of scenery he wrote from Dublin to Ormond on St George's Day in 1706, asking to be recommended for an appointment as governor of Barbados, replacing the recently deceased Sir Beville Granville. Although Oliver had made many visits to Barbados over the years, being 'well acquainted with that island', his request was denied in favour of Johnathan Swift's friend Mitford Crowe.

He also asked Ormond to recommend his newly rediscovered younger brother George Long to the admiral of the fleet, Sir Cloudesley Shovell, a request Oliver – and very briefly George – would live to regret. With the family believing George was long dead, Oliver was surprised to learn from Ormond's cousin, Captain Butler, that he was in fact alive and well on board the *Exeter* at Plymouth.

Oliver lived out his days in Dublin, unmarried, dying there in 1716. His property descended to Captain John Bateman, son of his army friend Colonel Charles Bateman. Pursuant to his will Bateman took the additional name of Long and laid out £10,000 for the erection and maintenance of a hospital near Dublin for the blind and lame. He died after being thrown from his horse in 1744.

Oliver made mention of his sister in his will, Mrs Elizabeth Guise, widow of Christopher Guise of Abbots Court, Gloucester. The Guises' daughter Eleanor married Robert Mann of Linton, whose son Sir Horace Mann, 1st baronet, sometime resident at the court of Tuscany and Venice, was a close friend of Horace Walpole, featuring regularly in his correspondence. Mann was also acquainted with Sir Robert Long, 6th baronet of Draycot, through the latter's brother-in-law Lord Tylney.

Oliver's other sister Martha, widow of John Danvers of Slinfold, Sussex, was included with Elizabeth in a small annuity each, 'as evidence that I never intend them any further part or profit of any [of] my estate, both real or personal whatsoever'.[77] Oliver never did receive repayment of the loan to his impecunious friend Lucius O'Brien. Three years later there appears a panicky letter to Catherine, Lucius's widow, from Captain Christopher O'Brien who had stood security for the loan. Oliver's executors were calling in the debt but finding himself without the funds, he hoped to borrow from the estate of Catherine's son Sir Edward O'Brien, then still in his minority.[78]

George Long (c.1656–1707)

Oliver's brother George was about eight years old when he and his siblings were orphaned, their parents Edmund and Barbara dying within two years of each other in 1662 and 1664 respectively. As a younger son George set his course in the navy, though he appears not to have attained any substantial rank. His occupation at death was merely 'mariner'.

When Queen Anne declared war on France in May 1702 to preserve 'the liberty and balance of Europe', George was involved in naval operations that allied England with the Dutch against the Spanish and French. In what became known as the War of the Spanish Succession (1702–13), England's first focus was on the acquisition of a Mediterranean base, culminating in an alliance with Portugal and the capture of Gibraltar (1704) and Port Mahon in Minorca (1708).

For whatever reason, George had neglected to keep in touch with his family, and they were quite unaware he was not only alive but in the port of Plymouth on the last day of January 1705, about to set sail on the *Exeter* under command of Captain Thomas Swanton. Sir George Byng, vice-admiral of the Blue, was also on board. He had been engaged to protect outward and homeward-bound merchantmen in their passage past the island of Ushant in the English Channel, close to the French naval base of Brest where the French squadron was active. Besides the *Exeter*, Byng's squadron also included the *Medway*, *Rochester* and *Deptford,* and their task was to convoy forty-one merchantmen safely through the gauntlet of privateers. On leaving

77   Will of Oliver Long, 1716 PROB 11/554
78   Inchiquin MS 45,348 /3, 1719–1722

port, George spent an uneventful night under sail. Next morning saw the capture by the *Medway* of a ten-gunned privateer, and they retook an English vessel laden with salt which was sent into Falmouth.

At dawn on 14 February – Valentine's Day – after a fairly uneventful fortnight, five ships were discovered ahead of them at a distance of about twelve nautical miles. The *Exeter* led the squadron, and with a strong easterly wind and rough seas the men prepared the ship for a chase under full sail. With the real possibility of sudden death just hours away, George readied himself for the battle ahead and took aside two of his shipmates, Walter Blackie and John Hague, asking that one of them should ensure all his worldly goods went to his niece Barbara, wife of John Satchwell of London, if he 'happened to die or [be] knocked on the head'.[79] Blackie and Hague would later testify that at the time their position was 'about sixty leagues west-south-west from Scilly'.[80]

As they drew nearer their quarry it became obvious the convoy was French, and it took until nearly noon to pass the first three ships. The *Exeter*'s target was a French man-of-war, the *Thetis*, and once they were within range the *Exeter* fired as many guns into her as the weather conditions would allow. During a desperate and noisy battle lasting six or seven hours, fourteen men on the *Exeter* were killed and thirty-one wounded, all the sails and rigging were cut and the foremast wrecked. Likewise the *Thetis* sustained thirty-three dead and wounded, a similar mess was made of her sails and rigging with all masts shot through. Once the smoke had cleared there was no doubt she had sustained considerably more damage, her flank sporting 'four holes between wind and water'.[81]

An account of the battle was afterwards sent to the Duke of Ormond by the chaplain on the *Exeter*, Marius D'Assigny, who acted as interpreter when the French prisoners were brought on board. The three other ships in the English squadron each took an enemy vessel in the convoy, laden with cargo; however the *Thetis* was the most valuable prize with 300 hogsheads of sugar, 44 guns, 244 men, 250

---

79   Nuncupative will of George Long, mariner, PROB 11/491
80   PROB 11/491, *ibid*
81   *Report on the Manuscripts of the Duke of Portland*, 1907, p. 172

hides, 25 hogsheads of indigo, a large amount of cacao and tobacco and more than £2,000 in coin and plate. The efforts of Admiral Byng and Captain Swanton to return triumphantly to port with the *Thetis* in tow were frustrated by the tempestuous weather and seawater entering the holes in the hull.

Attempts were made to lighten the load by removal of the sugar, indigo and cacao, but they encountered crosswinds that twice blew away the main mast. Realising the *Thetis* was just too leaky and would be impossible to bring into harbour it was set alight. Its captured master, Le Chevalier de Sourjon, could do nothing as his ship burned. Captain Swanton was later awarded a share of the £4,000 prize money allocated by an Act of Parliament.[82]

George lived to tell the tale, and thanks to his brother Oliver he secured a position with Sir Cloudesley Shovell, the fleet's commander in chief. When Shovell and his fleet were returning to England from an unsuccessful attempt on Toulon on 22 October 1707, his ship HMS *Association* struck the rocks near the Isles of Scilly along with several other vessels. His ship was seen by those on HMS *St George* to go down in three or four minutes, not a soul being saved of the 800 men on board.

This was later found to be a result of a disastrous navigational error attributed to Shovell, once described as 'a very lusty, comely man, and very fat'. His corpulent body was one of the first washed ashore the next day, and in total, 1,400 sailors were lost from his squadron, George Long among them. Probate was granted on his nuncupative will in December 1707 to his niece Barbara Satchwell.

82 *Calendar of Treasury Books*, vol. 24, 1710, Declared Accounts: Navy, British History Online

IV
The Split of Wraxall and Draycot

Sir Walter Long the Elder (1561–1610)

Leaving behind the extinct Longs of Lyneham we backtrack 150 years and four generations to Wraxall and Draycot once again, where Sir Walter, the eldest son of Sir Robert Long and his wife Barbara Carne, had only just come of age five days before his father's *Inquisition Post Mortem* on 15 April 1582. Walter is distinguishable from his kinsmen as being the last to own both manors of South Wraxall and Draycot together.

His first wife was Mary, youngest daughter of Sir Thomas Pakington of Aylesbury, Buckinghamshire. Pakington had married Dorothy Kytson, Sir Richard Long 's stepdaughter. Lady Mary Long was on friendly terms with Elizabeth I, exchanging New Year gifts,[83] and her brother Sir John Pakington became a favourite courtier of the queen, who nicknamed him Lusty Pakington. The flamboyant Lusty lived in great splendour but his expenditure exceeded his income and he inevitably depleted his fortune. The Longs also maintained the ostentatious lifestyle of the times: Aubrey says 'Old Sir Walter Long of Draycot kept a trumpeter', and when he went to Marlborough 'rode with 30 servants and retainers'.[84]

After Mary's premature death Sir Walter married Catherine, daughter of Sir John Thynne of Longleat. Thynne's gentleman of the horse, Carew Raleigh, later married his widow Dorothy Thynne. Sir Walter's close friendship with Carew and his younger brother Sir Walter Raleigh arose from their 'consimility of disposition' according to Aubrey. 'Old John Long, who then waited on Sir Walter Longe, being one time in the privy gardens with his master, saw

---

83   John Nichols, *The Progresses and Public Processions of Queen Elizabeth*, 1823
84   John Burke, *A Genealogical and Heraldic History of the Commoners of Great Britain*, vol. 3, 1836, p. 215

the Earl of Nottingham wipe the dust from Sir Walter R.'s shoes in compliment.'[85] Aubrey also says Sir Walter Long was the first to introduce the fashion of smoking tobacco into Wiltshire, his friend Sir Walter Raleigh being the first to bring it to England. 'They had first, silver pipes', and the legend has endured that the two Sir Walters enjoyed many a pipeful of tobacco at South Wraxall Manor. A sceptical visitor to the house remarked some 420 years later that he could not detect any lingering aroma of tobacco in the room named after Raleigh; all he got in his nostrils was Jeyes cleaning fluid, with perhaps a hint of mothballs.[86]

Towards the end of Elizabeth's reign Sir Walter Long embarked on a programme of enlarging and remodelling the manor house at South Wraxall in an ostentatious style, which was continued after his death by his son Walter junior. The exterior also received extra flamboyant touches, one nineteenth-century visitor noting 'the gargoyles are singularly large and hideous'. Between father and son the house benefited from the addition of a series of magnificent chimneypieces carved from stone, a panelled timber screen concealing a passageway and a decorative plaster ceiling in the hall, since removed. Another two east-facing wings were also added. The hall fireplace is dated 1598 and the ceiling in the withdrawing chamber is signed and dated 1611, the year after Sir Walter's death.

While other large landowners were exploiting the mineral potential of their estates, mining for lead, coal and iron, Sir Walter also had hopes his land would yield treasure. As Aubrey tells it,

[He] digged for silver, a deep pitt through blew clay and gott five pounds worth, for sixty pounds charges or more. It was on the west end of the stable but I doubt there was a cheat put upon him. Here are great indications of iron and it may be of coale; but what hopes he should have to discover silver does passe my understanding.[87]

85   Edward Walford, John Charles Cox, George Latimer Apperson, *The Antiquary* 1890, p. 163,
86   *Daily Telegraph* p. 8, 17 May 2003
87   John Aubrey, *Aubrey's Collections for Wilts., part I*, Chapter V, 1821

Murder Most Foul

A bitter quarrel arose between Sir Walter and his neighbours, the Danvers' of Dauntesey, which turned into one of the most long-lasting and divisive feuds between prominent gentry in Elizabethan England – resulting in the murder of Sir Walter's brother Henry in 1594. The quarrel had started almost twenty years before, with Sir James Marvin and Sir John Danvers leading one faction, together with Danvers' hot-headed twenty-something sons Sir Charles and Sir Henry. Leading the other was John Thynne, with the help of his friend and new brother-in-law Walter Long, and to a lesser degree Sir Henry Knyvett, who made attempts to mediate. There are several versions of events depending on which side was telling the story, and historians are unable to agree on the exact origins of the feud.

Draycot was only a few miles from the Danvers' seat at Dauntesey, and there can be no doubt both sides sought domination of its county government. The divisions were deep-rooted, and at the height of the feud Sir Walter had strengthened the Thynne alliance with his marriage to Catherine. One of the Danvers' sons, Sir Charles, served under the Earl of Essex in Ireland and developed a close friendship with him, later taking a prominent part in the revolt there. Sir Walter Long, on the other hand, sided with his friend Sir Walter Raleigh, who was deeply hostile to Essex.[88]

Already a dominating element in Wiltshire politics for some years, in 1589 the feud descended into public brawls at the Marlborough and Salisbury assizes. Injuries were sustained on both sides triggering lengthy Star Chamber suits, each side accusing the other of instigating the affrays. The list of witnesses included almost all the local gentry who were divided between the two factions. With news of the dispute spread beyond the boundaries of Wiltshire the main players were well known in London and at Court, prompting the Crown to intervene by raising a Privy Council commission. Notoriety was no barrier to Sir Walter's career, however. Although he had been dismissed in a purge of JPs in 1587 and again in 1592-3,[89] he was elected MP for Wiltshire

88   John Aubrey, *Letters written by Eminent Persons and Lives of Eminent Men*, 1813
89   Alison Wall, *'The Greatest Disgrace', The Making and Unmaking of JPs in*

in 1592, together with Sir William Brouncker.[90]

The catalyst seems to have been the committal at the assizes by Sir John Danvers of one of Sir Walter Long's servants for robbery. On rescuing his servant, Sir Walter argued that Danvers' malice and spleen had interfered with justice, and after he complained at the next assizes Sir John had him locked up in the Fleet prison. In no mood to tolerate a challenge to his authority Danvers then committed another of Sir Walter's servants on a charge of murder.[91] Danvers had a reputation, according to Aubrey, 'of a most beautifull and good and even tempered person'; indeed he was 'trustie and welbeloved' by Sir Walter's father.

But the Danvers' brothers hatred of the Longs increased, and with the exchange of further mutual insults and injuries the violence escalated, resulting in the death of one of the Danvers' servants during another affray. Henry Long goaded Sir Charles Danvers, threatening to untie his points, probably the ones holding together his breeches, since Henry also promised he would whip his bare backside with a rod. And he derided him as a liar, fool, puppy dog and a mere boy.[92]

The climax came on 4 October 1594. The Danvers' brothers led a band of followers 'to the number of seventeen or eighteen persons, in most riotous manner appointed for that most foul fact', and attacked the Longs in the company of several of their own followers, dining at 'one Chamberlayne's house' at Corsham. Sir Henry Danvers bludgeoned Henry Long but was trapped and injured while trying to escape. He then shot Henry dead with his pistol, 'a certain engine called a dagge, worth 6s 8d, charged with powder and bullet of lead'.[93] A serving boy named Barnard also died in the mêlée.

The circumstance of the Longs being attended by so many followers was not unusual during family hostilities, which were frequent at this time. Strype the historian mentions that in Queen Elizabeth's reign licences from the Crown were often granted to lords

Elizabethan and Jacobean England; Source: *The English Historical Review*, vol. 119, No. 481 (Apr. 2004) p. 321

90   HOC Papers, part I, Parliaments of England, 1213–1702
91   Anthony Burgess, *Shakespeare*, 1970, p. 133
92   Burgess, *ibid*
93   BL, Lansdowne MS 827, fols 25-9

and gentlemen to have twenty or more retainers for the purpose of maintaining quarrels, by which means many murders were committed and feuds maintained.[94]

After the dreadful deed the Danvers brothers fled, riding for several hours to Hampshire, where they initially took refuge at Whitley Lodge near Tichfield. Here they met with their young friend Henry Wriothesley, 3rd Earl of Southampton, who happened to be in the midst of his coming of age celebrations.[95] Southampton was a patron of William Shakespeare who dedicated to him two of his poems, *Venus and Adonis* (1593) and *The Rape of Lucrece* (1594). Some literary critics[96] have conjectured that the feud, ending as it did in death, inspired Shakespeare's *Romeo and Juliet*, and Romeo's exile may allude to Southampton's protection of Sir Charles and Sir Henry Danvers, whom he aided in their escape to France. They fled by boat from Cawshot Castle, a fort on the opposite side of Southampton Water.

The timing of the murder corresponds closely with the widely accepted belief that Shakespeare wrote his play in 1595, and the presence of the company of players in the area with whom Shakespeare was at that time associated coincides with the public feuding in Wiltshire. A clandestine marriage[97] and the many other parallels with the feud and the play are carefully explored by Alison Wall in her article '*The Feud and Shakespeare's Romeo and Juliet: a Reconsideration*' (Sydney Studies, 1979–80), which makes a compelling argument.

An inquest was held at Corsham on 5 October detailing the events, and two days later an order from the Lords of the Council at Nonsuch was issued to apprehend Sir Charles and Sir Henry Danvers, 'because Her Majestie is desirous to be informed of the Truth of so outrageous a fact'.[98] Together with another gentleman, Southampton was indicted as an accessory and imprisoned in the Fleet, and initial endeavours by the Earl of Essex to secure his release proved unsuccessful.

---

94   Strype Memor. III. II. 61
95   Anthony Holden, *William Shakespeare: The Man Behind the Genius*, 2000, pp.139-40
96   A.L. Rowse, Anthony Burgess, M.C. Bradbrook
97   John Thynne's son 16 year-old Thomas secretly married a teenaged Maria
98   Marquis of Bath's papers at Longleat

He was later allowed licence to return home for his health.

During the course of the enquiry Sir Walter Long, together with his uncle and brothers, were accused of corrupting 'very partial and undue witnesses'. His stepfather Simon Bowyer was one of the queen's favourites, which would explain his mother Lady Barbara Long being able to immediately inform the queen of the 'verie strange owtrage' committed by the Danvers brothers. Aubrey wrote that the events relating to the Danvers' escape and concealment hastened the death of their father Sir John, who died two months after the slaying of Henry Long.

Their mother soon remarried, to Sir Edmund Carey, a cousin of the queen, which Aubrey says was an attempt to influence the granting of a pardon for her sons. The new Lady Carey wrote to Sir Robert Cecil in 1596 complaining that the letters written by Henry Long were 'of such a form as the heart of a man indeed had rather die than endure'.[99] She hints at her willingness to make payment of some 'reasonable composition' if it might help bring to a practical issue her majesty's good inclination of mercy.

Sir Henry Danvers, outlawed for not surrendering, sued out a writ of error, assigning various exceptions presented at the inquest. Sir Edward Coke's report of the exceptions taken to the wording in 'bad Latin' led to the examination by four justices, including Lord Chief Justice Sir John Popham. After much splitting of hairs all exceptions were overruled except the last, which was held to be fatal. The coroner's conclusion was accordingly found invalid, the outlawry was reversed, and consequently no indictment was ever brought against the Danvers' by either the state or the Long family.

The exiled brothers were well received by the French king, and managed to evade justice for several years without being actively pursued by the English authorities, their crime considered more in the nature of a gentleman's disagreement. In October 1596 they were met by the Earl of Shrewsbury at Rouen, who wrote favourably of them to Sir Robert Cecil, applauding their soldierly bearing. Back in England their mother did everything she could to secure her sons'

99   A.L. Rowse 'Oxford's Relic of the English Romeo', The Times, 24 July 1971

pardon, and an agreement was finally reached involving a certain sum of money. Diplomat Dudley Carleton, later 1st Viscount Dorchester, wrote to John Chamberlain at the beginning of August 1598, saying 'the two knights, Danvers, are stayed at Paris by sickness. Their pardon is conditional on their contenting Sir Walter Long, by paying £1,500; £1,200 is paid; the rest they think too late in the reckoning.'[100]

The young Earl of Southampton, meanwhile, had got heavily into debt, which he blamed on 'following the Queen's Court', and he sought respite in France from his troublesome creditors. He had intended to journey to Italy with the younger of the Danvers brothers but just before departure they received word of their pardon, and in August 1598 they returned to England while Southampton waited in vain at Paris, complaining of this last-minute change of plan as 'an exceeding maim' to him.

Sir Henry Danvers was later created 1st Earl Danby, privy councillor and knight of the garter, and became a very rich man. His brother Sir Charles fared rather poorly in comparison: he was beheaded in 1601 on Tower Hill for joining in a plot with the Earl of Essex against Queen Elizabeth. A younger brother, the regicide Sir John Danvers, was MP for Malmesbury when he became an enthusiastic signatory to the death warrant of Charles I.

The earlier incident involving the death of the Danvers' servant was dealt with separately in the Star Chamber, after it was found the coroner and undersheriff, a certain Mr Mathew of Thavies Inn, solicitor and steward to Sir Walter Long, had acted corruptly in collaboration with Walter and his cousin Edmund Long of Lyneham in an attempt to sweep it under the carpet. Matthews had never viewed the body and arranged for the inquest to be held outside the area where the death occurred, contrary to the law.

The jury were said to be wrongly drawn from Hundreds 'where Walter Longe commands and is JP'.[101] Their verdict of not guilty by virtue of self-defence was considered 'most absurde', the fatal blow being behind the ear. Sir Walter and Edmund Long were dismissed

100   *Calendar of State Papers, Domestic Series, 1598–1601*, vol. CCLXV
101   WAM, vols 70–75, 1975, p. 124

but not acquitted, and Matthews for his 'subtle carriage' was sentenced to imprisonment, fined £500, removed from his posts as coroner and undersheriff, disbarred as a solicitor and expelled from Thavies Inn. In addition he was ordered to 'have a paper' and go through Westminster Hall to be 'impilloride' there, and to be again pilloried with the paper on his head at the assizes in Wiltshire.

Of course the feud didn't end with Henry Long's murder. Sir Walter supported the claims of the Danvers' tenants to rights of common, and consequently hedge-breaking on land enclosed by the Danvers'. In 1596 the Star Chamber decided Sir Walter was to blame; he was ordered to pay £100 and sentenced to imprisonment for inciting a great riot in a 'most contemptuous and outrageous manner'.

There is no evidence he went to prison however, although the Exchequer records of 1596 show he was fined £200. His cousin Edmund was also charged but acquitted because he testified against him. The two warring families continued to annoy each other in a tit-for-tat fashion, and there were instances of servants being poached from Lady Danvers' household by the Longs, also in 1596.

Some thirty years and a generation later, the names of two JPs – another Sir John Danvers and Henry Long's cousin Gifford Long of Rood Ashton – are linked in more conciliatory circumstances in the Assizes: mediating in someone else's dispute.

Legend of the White Hand

Sir Walter's second marriage to Catherine Thynne would see the split of South Wraxall and Draycot by the disinheritance of his eldest son, John. The events which inspired the story of a ghostly hand are related by Bernard Burke in *Anecdotes of the Aristocracy*, in which he says that after returning to his paternal halls at Draycot following the wedding, Walter and his new bride were met with joyous festivities by his tenants. Frequent episodes of gout had soured his disposition and he was not so beloved by them, rather they feared him.

The new Lady Long was determined to prejudice her husband against John, who stood in the way of whatever children there might be from the second marriage. Contriving with her brother Sir Egremont Thynne, they took advantage of John's weakness for gambling and drink. Sir Walter had already remonstrated with John about his undesirable pastimes, so he was not surprised to hear of further excesses, aided and magnified into heinous crimes by the unscrupulous stepmother and uncle.

Influenced by the pair Sir Walter agreed to make a will, disinheriting John and settling all his property on his second wife and her family. Sir Egremont Thynne, an eminent barrister, presented Sir Walter with a draft of the will which he approved and ordered to be copied. Aubrey's account of the legend recalls that the sudden apparition of a ghostly hand prevented the clerk finishing the revised will, thus temporarily thwarting the new wife's plans; however, the will was completed by another clerk and duly signed and sealed.

Sir Walter died not long afterwards, in October 1610, aged forty-nine. His estates and great fortunes were bequeathed to his younger son, Walter, and the execution of his will was to be overseen by his cousin Edmund Long of Lyneham and Sir Egremont Thynne. The clerk's tale of the ghostly apparition quickly became the subject of popular conversation. Trustees of the first Lady Long sympathetic to John's cause disrupted the burial of Sir Walter's corpse and commenced a suit against the intended heir, which ended in a compromise between the two parties; John took possession of South Wraxall and his half-brother Walter retained Draycot.

The legend would be perpetuated in the mind of a later descendant, Lady Victoria Long Wellesley, the heir apparent deprived of Draycot in the nineteenth century, who said she sometimes thought the white hand which sought to arrest Sir Walter Long's unjust deed was the foreshadowing of her own disinheritance.[102] In the twentieth century the 'Long curse' continued to make its presence felt. Richard, the 4th Viscount Long had been brought up with the terror of Wraxall deeply instilled into him, weaned from nursery days on doom-laden threats from the curse. 'If you hear the clock strike thirteen you will die.' In an ominous voice, Richard's father (the 3rd Viscount) would

102   Octavia Barry, *op. cit.* p. 11

point his finger at his daughter-in-law Margaret and say, 'When I am gone you will be married to the head of the Long family. But you will have nothing to do with South Wraxall Manor. You will not put a foot inside that house. Always beware of a curse on the Long Family.'[103]

In his *Brief Lives* Aubrey tells another tale: that Dame Catherine made her husband a solemn promise on his death bed that she would not remarry; not long afterwards 'a very beautiful gentleman did win her love'. This was Sir Edward Fox, whom Aubrey names only as Sir __ Fox, giving rise to an often repeated confusion with his son Somerset who married Sir Walter Long's daughter Anne. Catherine married Sir Edward at South Wraxall as his third wife, and Aubrey relates what happened when he led her by the hand from the church into the parlour:

> . . . the picture of Sir Walter that then hung over the parlour door (the string being eated off with the rust of the nail) fell down upon her ladyship and cracked in the fall (it was painted on wood as was the fashion in those days). This made her ladyship reflect upon her promise and drew some tears from her eyes.

In a less romantic theory, the falling picture could just as easily have been caused by the rush of wind as they slammed the door in their delirious dash to consummate their union. The notion that old Sir Walter was a disapproving and jealous ghost was probably a more appealing one to an imaginative storyteller such as Aubrey.

Somerset Fox, son of Sir Edward Fox and his second wife Elizabeth Somerset, married his step-sister Anne Long in about 1617. By this time Anne's mother was dead, and Sir Edward had already been married for a year to his fourth wife, Elizabeth Palgrave, wasting no time after the death of Catherine, the former Lady Long. Somerset and Anne Fox lived at Gwernygo, Montgomeryshire, and several of their nine children were baptised at Kerry. He took the side of Charles I in the Civil War and was with him at Oxford where he made his will

---

103   Margaret, Viscountess Long of Wraxall, *Treasures of Darkness*, unpublished memoir, *pers. com.*

in May 1643. It was proved there on 20 July in the same year by his widow, Anne.[104]

Sir Walter Long's grandson, Somerset Fox junior (described as a young city apprentice) naturally shared his father's allegiance to the monarchy. He was charged with high treason in 1654, together with his cousin John Gerard and a schoolmaster from Islington, Peter Vowell, for conspiring to murder Cromwell, the lord protector, and replace him with Charles II as rightful monarch. After being overheard hatching the plot in a tavern Somerset pleaded guilty, though the other two refused to confess. The sentence was death by hanging, but Gerard petitioned Cromwell for a more noble death by beheading or shooting. His wish was granted, and on his way to Tower Hill to have the connection severed betwixt head and shoulders an observer noted Gerard's manner was 'spritely, the substance of his discourse Cavalier-like'. Vowell was hanged, and for his confession Somerset Fox was reprieved.

Two of Sir Walter's sons-in-law are known to have gone to the New World colony of Virginia, one of Sir Walter Raleigh's projects. Maurice Berkeley, husband of Barbara Long, had accompanied his father John, sent to oversee the mining of iron ore in 1621. His father was slain in a massacre by Indians eight months later. Colonel Gerard Fowke, after his marriage to Sir Walter's other daughter Olivia, also went to the colony. It is uncertain if their wives accompanied them.

John Long of Haugh (1619–52)

Another of Sir Walter Long's grandsons, John, second son of the previously dispossessed John Long and his wife Anne Eyre, entered Pembroke College, Oxford, in October 1634 aged fifteen. His elder brother William had inherited several estates, including the manors of South Wraxall and Kellaways from his father, but died childless at the age of thirty-two in 1647. These properties then passed to John. Kellaways had been purchased in 1500 by their great-great-great-grandfather Sir Thomas Long, and for twenty years a portion

104   *Collections Historical & Archaeological Relating to Montgomeryshire*, 1893, vol. 27, p. 104

was in the occupation of Vincent Smith under John's Royalist uncles, Thomas and Robert (later Sir Robert Long, 1st baronet).

The political and religious arguments raised by the Civil War divided counties, towns and families, and John was one of the few in the family to support the cause of Parliament in both martial and civil offices. He had written in March 1647 to Colonel Edward Ludlow at Holborn, describing himself as his 'unfeigned friend', offering his services after hearing 'of a northern vapour, I mean a wind which seems to threaten a persecution. Brave Christian and Wiltshire's honoured servant fear not, they can but kill the body. Be pleased if there be occasion to give me timely notice'. Alluding to his breaking with the Longs' ancient attachment to monarchy, he continues: 'The antiquity and honour of my family I value much, but not comparably with the Christian honour which obliges me to suffer affliction with the people of God.'[105] In April 1650 he was granted a commission as captain of a troop of horse with the Wiltshire Militia under Colonel Ludlow, but it was a short-lived appointment. Six months later Ludlow was ordered to find another captain of horse and within fourteen days John's commission was withdrawn.

Perhaps there were suspicions his loyalties were divided. A few months later in December his manor of Kellaways was sequestered as one of the estates of his Royalist uncles, declared delinquents. The tenant Smith was ejected from the farm and mill and other lands he had occupied. John petitioned Parliament to have it restored to himself, so that 'I may enjoy my rents', reminding them of his faithful service through the wars.[106] In March 1651 Smith tendered his own petition, blaming John's uncles Thomas and Robert Long for his losses amounting to £1,000 for siding with Parliament, having given two men for service, complaining that the Longs were neither compounding nor likely to repay him. He feared further frustrations if John regained possession, and offered the same amount of rent, pleading his case. He gained the sympathy of the lord-general, and in July Smith was re-admitted as tenant at £70 a year.

105 *Calendar of State Papers, Domestic Series, 1625–[1649,]* vol. 22
106 M. A. E. Green, *Calendar of the Proceedings of the Committee for Advance of Money, 1642–56,* 1888, parts I, II & III, p. 550

It was not the outcome John had hoped for, nor would he live long enough to enjoy his rents and the relative peace after the end of the war. Surviving only another seven months, he died in February the following year aged thirty-three in London – like his brother William before him, in the prime of his life. Also prematurely relinquishing his grip was another brother, Edward, who had died two years before, aged twenty-three, but it would be Walter, the third brother, who outlived all five of his siblings, dying at the ripe old age of forty-six in 1669.

John's widow Catherine (*née* Paynter) leased part of the manor house and outbuildings at South Wraxall to Walter in 1654, and by 1660 she had married again, to Edward Aubrey, who entered into an agreement with Walter to occupy part of the house and a farm at St Audoen's, another house known as The Lodge and a property called Crooke's Living.

Catherine's three surviving children with John may have unwittingly contributed to the Wraxall Longs' extinction. Each married into another branch of the Long family, no doubt under the assumption that such close alliances would keep the estates in the family, one way or the other. John and Catherine optimistically named their only son Hope, and he inherited his father's estates, including South Wraxall. His gene-compromising hat-trick was to marry Mary, daughter of John Long of Monkton, and while she would have brought a handsome dowry, any expectation of a continuation of the line evaporated when his only child John died unmarried aged twenty-two. Hope had no children with his second wife Grace, and South Wraxall passed to his first cousin, Walter Long, who in 1731 also died childless.

Sir Robert Long (c.1598–1673), 1st Baronet of Westminster, Auditor of the Exchequer

Sir Walter Long had thirteen children with his second wife Catherine Thynne, but it was the youngest son Robert who eventually rose to prominence in the service of Charles II. Inheriting no property, his father had provided an annuity of £20 and provision for his education at Lincoln's Inn, where he was admitted in 1619. Eight years later he was called to the bar. By then he was acting as secretary to his brother's father-in-law, the elderly lord treasurer, Sir James Ley, 1st Earl of Marlborough, who affectionately addressed him as 'Good Robin'.[107] It was in his interest he was elected for Devizes to the Parliaments of 1626 and 1628–9, though he was inactive in the House, later becoming MP for Sussex in 1640 and Boroughbridge, Yorkshire, in 1661.

Robert entered the royal service after Marlborough's long-overdue resignation. He was writer of the tallies in the Exchequer

Sir Robert Long 1st Bt, © *National Portrait Gallery, London*

107 *Calendar of the Manuscripts of the Marquis of Bath, 1904, p. 73.* Letter to Robert Long from the Earl of Marlborough

during the Civil War when he joined the king at Oxford; he became surveyor-general of the queen's lands, and was appointed secretary of the council for Charles II, then Prince of Wales. Initially engaged in minor commissions and reversions, he was excused from military service against the Scots in 1639 when he was appointed to oversee the Lincolnshire drainage project of the Wildmore and East and West Fens, commissioned to increase agricultural production. During the reign of Charles I his yearly salary was £316 13s, and the house in the Cloisters (formerly belonging to Sir Walter Mildmay) for life.[108] The increase in his personal wealth enabled him to purchase three Yorkshire manors and the manor of Athelhampton in Dorset, which he bought in 1665 from Sir Ralph Bankes.

Charles I and his queen entrusted the education of the Prince of Wales to their friend William Cavendish, Marquess of Newcastle (grandson of Bess of Hardwick), who received the royals and their select entourage at his estates of Bolsover, Derbyshire, and Welbeck in Nottinghamshire, where he entertained on a lavish scale. A patron of drama and former courtier to James I, Cavendish, famous for his 'banquets of the senses', was a rampant womaniser hotly in pursuit of a third wife right up until his death at the age of eighty-three. He designed the interior of Bolsover Castle for sensual indulgence, decorating it with erotic Ovidian pictures.

In his article 'Pleasure Reconciled to Virtue' Timothy Raylor describes an essay by Cavendish, found among his surviving holograph manuscripts, on the relative efficacy of various aphrodisiacs. Entitled 'Whatt are aproved remedies to helpe Venus as the Lerned saye', the essay enumerates some seventy-eight items: viper wine is 'powerfull', canthrides (better known today as Spanish fly) 'mighteleye provokes, butt is dangerous', and he believed foods such as lambs' testicles, sparrows' brains, 'all younge meates', chestnuts and melons were effective provokers of lust. Apparently Robert Long shared this interest: in a letter of 10 August 1637 he promised to send Cavendish some melons.[109] Years later when he was auditor of the Exchequer

---

108   Florence R. Scott, *Sir Robert Howard as a Financier*, 1937, p. 1098
109   Timothy Raylor, *Pleasure Reconciled to Virtue: William Cavendish, Ben Jonson, and the Decorative Scheme of Bolsover Castle*, Renaissance Quarterly, vol.

writing to his servant, Burges, on official business in 1665 during the Great Plague, Robert followed with instructions for precautions to be taken, and the importance of certain foods:

> I pray use all possible care to preserve yourselves and my house. Send for things to burne, and make use of them dayly; lett noe body stirre out, nor any suitors come into the house or office. Lett every one take every morning a little london treacle, or the kernell of a walnutt with 5 leaves of rue and a grayne of salt beaten together and rosted in a figg and soe eaten, and never stirre out fasting. Lett not the porter come into the house; take all course you can agaynst the ratte, and take care of the catts; the little ones that will not stirre out may be kept, the great ones must be killed or sent away. [110]

He had fled England with the exiled court during the Civil War, during which time his estates in England were placed under a sequestration order by Parliament, who later rejected his petition to compound. With the intention of managing communications with Royalist conspirators, the queen sent him from Paris to Jersey to rejoin sixteen-year-old Prince Charles, who had fled there with the chancellor Sir Edward Hyde from the Isles of Scilly one stormy night in April 1646.

Although trusted implicitly by the queen and her son, Robert's ambition made him very unpopular in some quarters, and his reputed love of money was so notorious that suspicion easily attached to him. His arch-rival Hyde, in his *History of the Rebellion,* dismisses Robert as 'a creature of the Queen's', believing him so corrupt that he was always thought guilty of more than he was charged with.

One such example occurred in 1648 when part of the Parliamentary fleet placed itself at the prince's disposal. Robert went aboard to replenish the Royalist coffers from a blockade of the Thames, seizing a quantity of merchandise. He, together with John, 1st Baron Culpepper, was accused of lining his own pockets by improperly

52, No. 2, p. 434
110   British Library manuscripts

retaining money and disposing of cloth, sugar and other goods for his own benefit. The pair adamantly denied any wrongdoing.[111]

After the execution of Charles I in 1649, the Royalist councils, dominated by Queen Henrietta Maria and her favourite, Henry Jermyn, relied on Robert to keep the prince focused on the Presbyterian alliance. Their move to Scotland from The Hague in 1650 met with Jermyn's warm approval. But the Scots did not approve of Robert and he had to return to the Continent. In December 1651, after Jersey surrendered to Parliamentary forces, he left the court in disgrace after the discovery by the government of a trunkful of compromising letters. Sir Edward Hyde then took his place as secretary of state.

In his defence Robert wrote to the king: 'Your Majesty may be pleased to remember that upon your remove from Jersey you were to passe through all France and Flanders to Breda, and that there was but one cart in all allowed for your Majesty's robes and necessaries and particular trunks, in which I was permitted to carry one little trunke of papers and one box', adding that he had entrusted the trunk, filled with state papers, to the charge of Sir George Carteret. Robert may have been in Rouen when he wrote this, and he stayed away from the court for many months.

Sometime later an accusation of treachery surfaced relating to his time in Wiltshire with the prince, alleging he had provided Parliament with intelligence about divisions among the commanders, thereby precipitating the final Royalist collapse. Convinced of his guilt, Hyde wrote to Sir Richard Nicholas expressing his confidence that 'Mr Long's reign is drawing towards an end'. Faced with a charge of treason and fiercely maintaining his innocence, Robert petitioned the king (by now Charles II in exile) and sent Hyde a list of pertinent questions to be put to his accuser Colonel Edward Wogan, who alleged as evidence a letter supposed to have been written by him and signed 'Robert Long'.

Robert insisted it was a forgery; for twenty years he had signed his name 'Rob. Long'. Despite putting forward a very credible

111   Samuel Elliott Hoskins, *Charles the Second in the Channel Islands: A Contribution to His Biography and to the History of His Age*, vol. 2, p. 231

argument he was ordered to resign the seals of his office, but he absolutely refused. His office, he said, was held under the great seal, and his patent as secretary could only be terminated in a regular court of law, while a voluntary surrender would amount to a tacit confession of misdemeanour.

On learning of the denials, Wogan wrote to Robert challenging him to a duel, but wisely Robert showed the letter to the king, who would not, he said, suffer him to be 'so used'. Charles justified his confidence by having Wogan arrested and assured Robert of his protection, much to Hyde's frustration, who wrote again to Sir Richard Nicholas: 'Mr Long is a spy upon all; the King knows it and neglects to remedy it.' At the time Robert was in Paris, but he yielded to panic and fled, leaving no address.

He did eventually resurface, and while still on the Continent his battle to gain supremacy over Hyde raged on behind the scenes. In 1654 Robert contrived a plot to discredit him, but despite attempts to keep his own name out of it he was embroiled, together with Sir Richard Grenville, who had also long cherished a grudge, accusing Hyde of paying a secret visit to Cromwell and receiving a pension for intelligence. This story, they said, was told to them by a chambermaid. In an effort to disassociate himself, Robert wrote a lengthy letter to the king complaining of his 'well known implacable enemy' Sir Edward Hyde 's 'great power and malice' towards him, saying it was Grenville who accused Hyde, and that 'the accusation against me was managed by persons that were no friends to me'.

Nevertheless, he told the king whether Hyde was guilty or innocent he should 'be deprived of his place, dismissed with disgrace from Your Majesty's service and be left under the suspicion of the crimes he is now accused of, and thereby condemned in the opinion of the world'. He hoped 'that Sir Edward Hyde [would] descend into his own heart and confess his iniquity'. Indeed Hyde wished much the same fate for Robert. The accusation against Hyde was considered totally preposterous and dismissed without further investigation by the king, who said it discredited all who were concerned in it. 'A libell', declared His Majesty, 'derogatory against my own honour and justice, and full of malice against Mr Chancellor.'[112]

Robert backed down. In early 1660 he wrote to the king suing for a free pardon for past offences and begging compassion for his destitution. Swallowing his pride he went to Hyde 'making great acknowledgments and asking pardon', and confessed that the whole story had been maliciously concocted. He was again restored to favour, Hyde generously agreeing 'to make no more words of it',[113] and Robert resumed his former position with Queen Henrietta Maria in 1661.

After the Restoration, King Charles was generous towards his faithful supporters, rewarding them with lucrative offices, grants and beneficial leases of Crown lands. Robert was created a baronet (Long of Westminster), followed one week later by his appointment as chancellor of the Exchequer, and for eleven years from 1662 until his death he held the position of auditor of the receipt in the Exchequer. He also acquired an interest from the queen's jointure in the forest of Galtres, between York and Boroughbridge,[114] and Higham Ferrars Park in Northamptonshire.

These perks did not sit well with some of his rivals, one accusing him of making at least £50,000 from the management of her affairs. Accurate or not, Robert was further enriched by gifts of land from the king, including a long lease of Nonsuch Park (otherwise known as Worcester Park) in 1663, nominally in reversion to the queen, then permanently resident in France. He later spent £2,500 on repairs to the property. The terms of the lease included the park be converted to pasture and the trees preserved in case the king wished to use it as a deer park in the future.

During the Great Plague of 1665 the Exchequer was relocated to Nonsuch Palace. The following year, on 4 September 1666, the Great Fire of London had already been raging for two days when the Privy Council issued an order to Sir Robert to hire 'loiters' to carry the

---

112   Alice Dryden, *Memorials of Old Wiltshire*, 1906, pp. 174-5
113   Eva Scott, *The King In Exile: The Wanderings Of Charles II From June 1646 To July 1654*, 1905, p. 474
114   John Ferris, 'Long, Sir Robert, first baronet (c.1602–1673)', *Oxford Dictionary of National Biography*, Oxford University Press, 2004; online edn, Jan 2008

records of the Exchequer up the Thames to the safety of Nonsuch. He was not impressed when the Exchequer staff later used many of the trees in the park for timber and fuel, contrary to his lease, leaving the estate in a dilapidated condition.

Much matured from the incompetent young secretary of 1626, he now showed himself 'exceptional among seventeenth century Exchequer officials in having a conscientious devotion to the personal performance of his duties',[115] and he was finally restored to the Privy Council in July 1672. Sir Robert had served Charles as secretary since the days of his boyhood, and was regarded by his master with a kind of affection born of long habit, which probably explains the king's tolerance when Hyde, in particular, was against him.

In late April 1673 he was in the last stages of a long and persistent illness, when the Earl Cholmeley wrote to Lady Harley:[116] 'there is much robbing of houses in town, and at Sir Robert Long's in Westminster a servant was killed'. An account of the crime[117] was privately published shortly afterwards. While Sir Robert was out at church, William Ivy, a young man in a depressed state of mind after a failed love affair, was admitted to the house by Pew the butler, an acquaintance of Ivy's. They drank wine together and toured the house, Ivy admiring Sir Robert's pictures and gun collection. While in Sir Robert's bedchamber Ivy suddenly shot Pew in the back, and before he was finished off with blows to the head Pew had time to cry out: 'Mr Ivy, how could you have so much cruelty to serve me thus?' Ivy then proceeded to ransack Sir Robert's money chest, taking 'seven hundred pound baggs'. Burying some, he took the rest and changed the money for gold, intending to flee England but he was arrested and later hanged.

Two weeks after this incident, in early May 1673, Sir Charles Harbord wrote that 'Sir R. Long though alive is getting weaker.' Sir Robert lingered another two months, and on 13 July he expired. He

115   H. Roseveare, *The Treasury, 1660–1870: The foundations of control*, 1973, p. 30

116   Sir Robert Harley was described in 1633 as cousin of Sir Robert Long – *Calendar of State Papers* vol. CCXXXVIII

117   *The Penitent Murderer*, Anon 1673

had never married, and was buried in Westminster Abbey according to the Anglican rite, 'over against the most Eastwardly Cloister door',[118] but no memorial survives. He had secured a special remainder to his baronetcy for his nephew James Long (later Sir James, 2nd baronet), and his estates were entailed on James's son, James junior.

Connections to the Family of Sir Edward Hyde, Earl of Clarendon

In the nineteenth century Scottish author and publisher Robert Chambers said the fact of two queens-regnant of England being granddaughters of Edward Hyde, 1st Earl of Clarendon, made the genealogy of the Hydes of some interest to poking antiquaries. Some twenty-first-century poking in the maternal lines has revealed the Longs of Monkton Farleigh can claim a direct line of descent from Clarendon's aunt Joan Hyde, and Hyde's mother was from the family of Langford, prosperous clothiers of Trowbridge, also allied to the Longs by marriage.

Hyde's father Henry also owned a house at Trowbridge and had married Mary, daughter of clothier Edward Langford, in April 1597. Langford, who died in 1594, makes mention in his will of his cousin Henry Long of Trowbridge, later of Whaddon, whose nephew William Long, inn-keeper of Trowbridge, married Anne, another of Edward Langford's daughters. Langford's widow Mary (*née* St Barbe) left money to William and his children, as well as her grandson, the young Edward Hyde, and named as one of the overseers of her will Henry Long's grandson, Gifford Long of Rood Ashton.

One of the four confidential counsellors during the Protectorate, Sir Edward Hyde's influence over King Charles was eventually undermined by accusations he had misappropriated state revenue for his own use, which he vigorously denied. By the king's command he resigned the great seal in August 1667. The House of Commons instituted proceedings against him, but their proposal was rejected by the House of Lords; Hyde was only accused of treason in general, and

---

118   Joseph Lemuel Chester, *The Marriage, Baptismal, and Burial Registers of the Collegiate Church Or Abbey of St. Peter, Westminster*, 1876, p. 181

not any one specific misdeed. A storm of disagreement arose between the two Houses and Hyde was advised by friends to remove himself from the kingdom. In November 1667 he sailed for Calais.

A Bill for banishing and disenabling Hyde was passed in December, by which his failure to surrender within two months would result in banishment for life, unable to ever again hold high office. He would also be subject to the penalties of high treason if he returned. His public life now at an end, Hyde was reluctantly permitted by the French king to reside permanently in France. He had been there only four months when he was saved by Oliver Long from assassination. After spending the rest of his days working on his *History of the Rebellion and Civil Wars in England*, a classic account of the English Civil War, he died peacefully at Rouen in December 1674, enfeebled by repeated attacks of gout. His body was returned to England and buried at Westminster Abbey, though no monument or memorial was erected.

Sir Walter Long the Younger (c.1593–1637)

Walter, elder brother of Sir Robert Long, received an annuity of £30 from his father's will while in his minority, increasing to £50 while he lived with his mother. When he came of age he came into possession of Draycot. He was admitted to Lincoln's Inn in 1614, the same year he went to Beckington, a hundred miles away in Somerset, to marry Ann, daughter of future lord treasurer, Sir James Ley (created 1st Earl of Marlborough in 1626). Walter purchased more property, including most of the land at Draycot and Langley from his half-brother John, and part of his marriage settlement to Anne Ley included Draycot House and another two parcels of land in Draycot, Sutton Benger and Kington Langley.[119]

Sir James Ley had moved his family to Beckington before 1613, where he purchased Beckington Castle from William, brother of Henry Long of Whaddon. He also built a new residence at nearby Heywood, about 20 miles from Draycot, having acquired extensive

119   T. Couzens, *op. cit.* p.41

lands in Westbury between 1590 and 1621,[120] and consequently he spent a great deal of time at the home of his daughter and son-in-law. So much so, he had a gateway built at Draycot, according to Aubrey, embossed with his own coat of arms. A quarrel later arose between Ann and her father, possibly because of his choice of a new young wife. In 1621 Ley, by then aged in his seventies, was appointed lord chief justice, and the same year he married seventeen-year-old Jane Boteler, following the death in 1618 of his second wife. The quarrel was never resolved, the old earl in his will 'begging pardon of Lady Ann on bended knee of his heart for his conduct towards her'.

The tendrils of the Ley and Long families later became more intertwined: of the earl's seven other daughters, Elizabeth (his eldest) married Maurice Carent of Toomer, whose son Maurice junior married Eleanor, daughter of Gifford Long of Rood Ashton. Ley's fourth daughter Dionysia married John Harington of Kelston, and their granddaughter Dionysia Harington married firstly Henry Long, son of Robert Long of Stanton Prior, and secondly Henry's cousin, Calthorpe Parker Long of Whaddon. When the earl's youngest daughter Phoebe died in 1653 her husband Richard Bigg married Mary Wade, granddaughter of Henry Long junior of Whaddon and his wife Rebecca.

Sir Walter Long was appointed a JP in 1623 but his name is rarely mentioned in the quarter sessions minutes, and his contribution to Parliament was equally negligible, despite being elected to the seat of Westbury in 1621, 1625 and 1626. In May 1625 he was knighted. By this time James, his only son with Ann, was about ten years old. After Ann's death in 1627 Sir Walter married Elizabeth, daughter of George Master of The Abbey, Cirencester, and widow of Edward Oldisworth.

Sir Walter's death in July 1637 was sudden, just one year into his second marriage with a new baby son, and he had made no will. His eldest son James was just two months short of his majority. According to one of Sir William Waller's men, writing to Cromwell of the triumphant wartime capture of James eight years later, his father

'Sir Walter Long who lately deceased . . . being in drinke, fell from his horse near Chichister and broke his necke.' Sir Walter's youngest son from the second marriage, Walter junior of Marlborough (d. 1673), never knew his father and appears to have had a close relationship with his mother's family. He later appointed his nephew, Robert Oldisworth of Bradley, his sole heir.

Sir James Long (1616–1692), 2nd Baronet

Seen as providing an education for a cultured elite, universities offered status, entry to government office, or admission to the clergy, however Aubrey may have been mistaken when he said Sir Walter Long's son James was educated at Westminster and later Magdalen College, Oxford; his name doesn't appear in their records. He was probably educated at home and travelled in France before being admitted to Lincoln's Inn in 1634. Not quite of age at his marriage to Anne, daughter of Sir William Dodington, he was settled with jointure lands, and at his father's death in 1637 he inherited the bulk of the Wiltshire estates, including Draycot, although he did not immediately gain control.

It is assumed Anne died shortly after their marriage, possibly in childbirth, and there were no surviving children. James was frustrated that the revenues and management of his late father's estates were still out of his hands, under wardship, 'which put him into much travell and paines, for which he almost spurred the horse to death that had broke his father's neck; for he had vowed before he came off his back to get his Wardship'.[121]

A second marriage took place in the early 1640s to Dorothy, daughter of Sir Edward Leche (or Leach) of Shipley, Derbyshire, a master of Chancery and member of the House of Commons. It was a loving and happy marriage, as evidenced by many affectionate letters to his wife held in the archives of the Wiltshire & Swindon Record Office. Well educated herself, Lady Dorothy (whom her husband addressed in his letters as 'My Only Dear') ensured all their six children had the best tutors. Historian John Aubrey became a close friend of both Sir James and Lady Dorothy, 'a most elegant beautie and witt'.

121   James Waylen, *Chronicles of the Devizes*, 1839, p.149

Sir James Long 2nd Bt, © *National Portrait Gallery, London*

The satirist Robert Gould, a significant voice in Restoration poetry, was especially attached to her, his 'Portia', and wrote many poems in tribute. Dorothy was, if both Aubrey and Gould can be believed, as excellent a woman as her husband was a man.[122]

In contrast, the account of a lone critic in *The Complete Letter Writer* (1789) promotes Dorothy as an example of the disagreeable

---

122   Eugene Hulse Sloane, *Robert Gould: Seventeenth Century Satirist,*1940, p. 32

Old Draycot House by Aubrey, Wiltshire and Archaeological and Natural History Society. Courtesy Mandy Ball

consequences of 'false breeding'. 'Mariana' tells of a visit from James and Dorothy, who was so effusive with compliments the hostess attempted respite by offering her snuff. Dorothy insisted on donning her glove, as she 'could not be so rude as to touch it with her naked fingers'. A minor debacle ensued over unwanted sugar added to her cup of tea – for which Dorothy blamed her husband – and on leaving she gave so many curtsies her hostess's 'knees ached for an hour after by returning them'.

James entered the royal army and served in Sir Thomas Glemham's regiment at the beginning of the Civil War, later rising to the rank of colonel of horse in Sir Francis Dodington's brigade. Two years later, in 1644, he was appointed High Sheriff of Wiltshire in the king's interest. Early in 1645 the conflict between the Cavaliers and Roundheads of North Wiltshire brought Oliver Cromwell into the fray, sent by Parliament to join Sir William Waller. While both generals were travelling across the south they received word the Prince of Wales was moving towards Bristol under escort of Colonel James Long, the sheriff. They were too late to intercept the cavalcade, and the prince passed safely through Marlborough and Devizes to the west, while Waller, hoping to cut off James on his return, marched northwards.

The proposed ambush did not occur and, unaware, James made it back safely to Devizes. Waller and Cromwell marched on to Potterne and Lavington, attacking the latter with an overwhelming force a few days later. Aided by soldiers garrisoned at Chalfield, James's troops were ambushed by Cromwell on the road between Devizes and Bath and 'virtually annihilated', the high thick-set hedges preventing their escape. Waller wrote: 'Of four hundred horse, there escaped not thirty; three hundred soldiers were taken prisoners, with three hundred and forty horses, and a good store of arms; and this, in the worst of ways, and the basest weather that I ever saw.'[123] Perhaps still seething with animosity towards Sir Robert Long, Sir Edward Hyde later wrote scathingly in his *History of the Rebellion,* that James's capture was the result of his 'great defect of courage and conduct'.

When news of her husband's capture reached Lady Dorothy, afraid Draycot might soon suffer the fate of Rowden, a nearby mansion belonging to Sir Edward Hungerford that had been dismantled and set on fire, she was convinced James should lay down his arms and submit to Parliament. She offered to compound for his personal estates. Her alarm was well founded: an order had already been issued for the sequestration of rents of Draycot manor, and £400 worth of goods was plundered from the house.

The Wiltshire Committee's report to Parliament relating to the compounded goods was signed by John Goddard, commissary-general, in November 1645. Lady Dorothy was offered a deal: namely, Parliament would return her house and goods and guarantee protection in exchange for an immediate fine of £100, followed by similar payments on an annual basis. She accepted, much to the fury of her imprisoned husband. A few months later the agreement was broken by musketeers on behalf of the garrison at Malmesbury.[124]

James was exchanged after a few weeks of captivity for Colonel Nathaniel Stephens, sheriff of Gloucestershire who had been taken at

123   John Jeremiah Daniell, *Lays of the English Cavaliers,* 1866, p.105
124   John Wroughton, *An Unhappy Civil War: The Experiences of Ordinary People in Gloucestershire,* 1999, p. 261

Rowden. Returning to Devizes, James borrowed a troop of horse and fifty foot soldiers who, with swords drawn and trumpets sounding, stormed the Parliamentary garrison at Chippenham, chasing them off for ten miles and securing the town. Despite this success the king's cause was now becoming desperate and the war fast drawing to a close. However, there was one small victory to come.

In January 1646 a formidable party of a thousand horse headed by Colonel Long and Sir John Causfield surged from Oxford into Wiltshire, travelling from north to south down the country, gathering money, prisoners and horses along the way. At Salisbury their plunders were considerable and they released forty Cavaliers from prison. Having some success at Warminster, they failed at Devizes; the Castle remained impenetrable. At Marlborough they captured the commissary-general John Goddard and others, together with three troops of horse, infantry and a large store of ammunition, sustaining few casualties in the process.[125]

But the war was lost and the Cavaliers of Wiltshire had sacrificed everything for their king. With Parliament proceeding harshly against them there were many confiscations of property, and seventy-five Wiltshire gentlemen were returned as malignants or delinquents. Those who were able to compound for their estates paid a high price; Draycot was restored to James in 1649 on payment of a £700 fine. Not long after this, according to Aubrey, 'Oliver [Cromwell] Protector, hawking at Howneslowe heath, discoursing with him, fell in love with his company, and commanded him to weare his sword, and to meet him a hawkeing, which made the strict Cavaliers look on him with an evill eye.'

Many years later at Bath, James met Sir Edward Southcote, son of his old comrade-in-arms Sir John Southcote. Daily bathing had become a newly fashionable ritual, during which James regaled Southcote each morning with his war-time adventures – no doubt with embellishments. Southcote repeats one story thus:

---

125 *The Monthly Packet of Evening Readings* 'The Cavaliers of North Wilts', 1866, p. 183

When they were in garrison at Oxford their diversion was in going a-birding together (as they called it), which was, each of them had a long fowling-piece, and these charged with a single bullet, they could hit any little mark as well as with a stone bow, so their way was to walk at a proper distance within the works, over which the Roundheads would frequently be peeping, just to look over them, by which they exposed their foreheads, which they scarce ever missed, and could knock down twenty or thirty of them in their morning's walk.

This was published in *The Troubles of Our Catholic Forefathers, Related by Themselves* (1872), with a subtle comment added by the author John Morris in a footnote: 'It is to be feared that Sir James Long is here drawing the long bow.' Doubtless the Roundheads would have agreed.

The following lines are taken from a book of poetic verse commemorative of the sufferings of the English Cavaliers written in 1866 by J. J Daniell, the Perpetual Curate of Langley Fitzurse, Wiltshire, on the 'Discomfiture of Sir James Long', giving expression to his admiration of the Cavalier's courage and the cause in which they suffered:

> When Will Waller reared his standard
> 'Gainst our King, the great, the good,
> And the men of Wiltshire nobly
> To their faith and honour stood;
> With the first the lord of Draycot
> To the field his yeomen drew,—
> Men of Langley, Sutton, Seagry,
> Lusty troopers, bold, and true;
> Where the danger, toil or glory,
> In the foray, or the fray,
> Foremost rode the Draycot troopers,
> Long of Draycot led the way;
> And the name of Long of Draycot,
> In a thousand straits and fears,

Stirred the hearts, as with a trumpet,
Of the Wiltshire Cavaliers.[126]

After the Restoration, James joined the Royal Society on the proposal of Lord Brouncker. In 1661 the word 'science' had yet to be invented, however records of the society list items related to his activities and experiments, including 'to try whether Pebble-stones, inclosed in glasses with water, will grow'; an account of the 'spawning of Frogs and Toads, of Newts and Lizzards, the raining of Frogs'; of the 'Serpent with wings like to those of a Batt'; and to try the feeding of 'Carps in the Air'. He was also something of an antiquary, and in a letter he wrote to Aubrey, preserved in the Bodleian Library dated 1688, there is an interesting description of a number of Roman coins found at Heddington, Wiltshire.

Aubrey, also a member of the Society, says his friend was 'for insects exceedingly curious and searching long since in naturall things'. He also took an interest in 'unnaturall' things. Prosecutions for witchcraft began with the accession of King James I, and in England a great many alleged witches were executed before 1680. It became an obsession, particularly among the most educated. The king himself exposed a few frauds, and despite his efforts and that of his council, the episcopate and the Star Chamber to quash the growing frenzy, the executions continued unabated.

On one occasion James anticipated a threat to his tenantry after an alleged witch had been acquitted at Salisbury and was allowed to go free. As a favour to him and to save his estate, the judge ordered she be kept in gaol at a cost of 2s 6d per week. But on reflection he asked the judge at the next assizes to allow her back to the town, which would cost a shilling a week less.[127] It was a matter of economy. In his *Brief Lives* Aubrey recounts another event during the 1670s when James was a magistrate:

. . . there was a Cabal of Witches detected at Malmesbury, they were

126   John Jeremiah Daniell, *op. cit.* p. 99
127   Roger North, *The Life of the Right Honourable Francis North, Baron of Guilford*, 1808, p.253

examined by Sir James Long and committed by him to Salisbury Gaole. I think there were seven or eight old women hanged. There were odd things sworne against them, as the strange manner of the dyeing of H. Denny's horse, and of flying in the aire on a staffe. These examinations Sir James hath fairly written in a book which he promised to give to the Royall Societie.

The *Gaol Books* give the actual date of the executions as 1672. Aubrey's recollection was slightly exaggerated: there were three women committed at Salisbury and only two hanged, not seven or eight.[128]

Besides the problem of local witches, a fictitious conspiracy of a so-called Popish Plot resulted in the rounding up by the Wiltshire magistrates of recusants in 1680, prompting the Privy Council to congratulate four of the justices for their zeal. In April a fifth magistrate, Sir James Long, ordered a special search be made throughout the Hundred of Malmesbury. This yielded thirty-seven names of suspected popish and other recusants, most of whom were innocent citizens minding their own business. In 1682 a group of Quakers had been accused along with recusants and prosecuted as dangerous subjects, liable to the forfeiture of two-thirds of their estates. They sought and obtained protection of the local magistracy, who collectively informed the king that Israel Noyes of Calne, Serge-maker, Arthur Estmead of the same place, Woollen-Draper, John Harris of Goatacre, Clothier, all prosecuted at the Exchequer as Popish Recusants, were of peaceable and quiet behaviour, no threat to the government and neither reputed papists nor popish recusants. This certification was signed by Sir James Long and four other Wiltshire magistrates.

Family

Sir James was nearly sixty when he succeeded to the baronetcy of his unmarried uncle Sir Robert Long in 1673. His only son James predeceased him and it was his three grandsons who were successively the third, fourth and fifth baronets. The eldest of these, Robert,

---

128   Cathy Gere, *William Harvey's Weak Experiment: The Archaeology of an Anecdote*, 2001

enjoyed the title for four days before dying from smallpox; his brother Sir Giles died six years later of the same disease. The next heir was the youngest brother James junior, who became fifth baronet.

Of Sir James and Lady Dorothy's five daughters, the eldest, Anna Margaretta married Sir Richard Mason of Sutton, Surrey, second clerk comptroller of His Majesty's Household and knight of the green cloth. A sometime MP for Bishop's Castle and Yarmouth, Isle of Wight, Mason acted as secretary to Lord Percy, general of the Royalist Artillery until 1644. During the Interregnum he was denied a licence to come to London to compound 'for being in the King's quarters as servant to Lord Percy, though he never bore arms and has been living one and a half years quietly in France'. Percy, like Sir Robert Long, was one of the trusted inner circle of Queen Henrietta Maria 's royalist exiles, and Mason, as a servant of Percy, was viewed with suspicion by Sir Edward Hyde, who described him as a 'foolish, busy fellow'.

Mason returned to London in April 1659 after Percy's death. At the Restoration he was rewarded with various appointments at court and his rapid social ascent probably owed more to his marriage to Sir Robert Long's niece than the benefits of office. He acted as Sir Robert's deputy auditor of the receipt, and was appointed agent for taxes in 1673. Between 1668 and 1670 Mason had loaned the king several sums of money amounting to £1,533, which was later repaid. He was present at the death of Charles II in February 1685, and immediately afterwards his wife Anna wrote a long letter to her mother Lady Dorothy Long at Draycot, relating the events her husband had witnessed in the king's last days. This letter only came to light among other papers found at Draycot House in about 1850, which Charles Dickens published that year in his weekly journal, *Household Words*.

Anna wrote: 'Methinks I owe my dearest a particular of his late Majesty's sickness and death, with the intervening accidents which escape one's memory, if they are not written in the instant.' There followed descriptive details of the doctor's treatment and its effects. He 'applied a warming pan of coals to his head and blisters to his back, arms and thighs. In the meantime seeing him much foam at the mouth they wished a vomit . . .' There were convulsions, bloodletting and purges, 'which worked mightily well', but 'he was so ghastly a sight (his eye-balls were turned that none of the blacks were seen, and his mouth drawn up to one eye)' and after two days 'he then died as peacable as a lamb'.

> They left the corpse in bed covered with a sheet till next day that he was opened. I think it was till Sunday – and in that time anyone might see him. They say he looked then as in health, his blisters having made him raw, and the covering made him stink without, but his organs were all good and sound, and might have lasted many years, though one little part of one side of his lungs was tainted and perished.

Anna's father Sir James was spared a drawn-out and painful death; seven years later, on the morning of 21 January 1692, he was found unexpectedly dead in bed having attended the House the previous day. He was buried at Draycot on 3 February. Leaving a lengthy will, he referred to his 'many years of white hairs' and desired 'to be buried without any worldly pomp (as a common man)'. His widow was left a life interest in Draycot and four other manors, and ultimately his grandson Sir James Long, 5th baronet, inherited the bulk of his estates.

The 'Notorious' Countess of Macclesfield

Even before she contracted smallpox in May 1686, Sir James and Lady Dorothy 's granddaughter Anna Mason was no great beauty. Described as 'a middle-sized woman, pretty full in the cheeks, disfigured with the smallpox and pretty large pit holes, with thick lips and of a brownish hair',[129] to which other witnesses added the undesirable traits of 'dark complexion' and 'little eyes'. Her portrait of 1687 is rather more flattering.[130] Anna was a headstrong fifteen-year-old when she, with a fortune said to be variously between £12,000 and £25,000, married Charles Gerard, Viscount Brandon, in June 1683 in London.

An unfortunate choice of husband, he had killed a footboy

---

129   Samuel Johnson, Harold Spencer Scott, *Lives of the English Poets, 1905,* *p. 429*
130   Printed by John Smith, published by Edward Cooper, after Willem Wissing

seven years earlier in St James's Park in a drunken rage,[131] reinforcing his reputation as an unprincipled and opportunistic character prone to random violence. However he is better known for his central role in what was perhaps the most sensational divorce of the age. Married barely a month, their union was doomed from the outset. Gerard was arrested and imprisoned in the Tower, accused of treason.

By the time he was released in November 1683 Anna realised her mistake. With a litany of grievances on both sides they parted company about six months later when he dispatched her to his father's house after a furious row, vowing never to live with her again. She endured two weeks with her bad-tempered father-in-law before he too turned her out of Gerard House in Soho, and she went back to her parents at Sutton.

Still at home was her younger sister Dorothy – or 'Doll' as she was known – somewhat prettier than Anna, with the added attraction of a dowry reportedly of £16,000. Dorothy inherited £5,000 at her father's death in 1685 and three years later married Sir William Brownlow, 4th Baronet of Humby. Society scandals were a favourite target of satirists, and after her sister's separation and before her own marriage, in what was probably a case of guilt by association, Dorothy, Anna and their mother came under lampoon attack in a merciless clandestine verse satire entitled 'Julian's Farewell to the Family of the Coquettes' in 1687.

The anonymous versifier alleged their mother Lady Mason, *née* Long, was yet another who had been 'fluxed in France', while Dorothy is accused of concealing a pregnancy by Sir Henry Hubbard (this possibly refers to Henry Hobart) and references are made to Anna's recent smallpox disfigurement and alleged wanton behaviour. Word of her granddaughters' growing reputations had reached the keen ears of Lady Dorothy Long at Draycot, prompting the younger Dorothy to write: 'You think I am such a gadder but I am not mightily abroad.' Being the target of scandalmongers was inevitable, even after her marriage, when Dorothy complained to her grandmother that the

---

131   Edward Maunde Thompson, *Correspondence of the Family of Hatton* (1838) vol. 1, p. 135

lampoons were 'without number': 'I bear a share with my poor spouse in 2 or 3 tho' they are so favourable as to lay no particular crime to my charge & I am sure I have given the poets no occasion of scandal to my knowledge.'

After her separation from Gerard Anna lived with her sister Dorothy and her husband for about fifteen years, during which time, according to the gossips, she had many lovers. Preoccupied with his political career and private pursuits, her estranged husband had little interest in the woman he so despised, even when she became Countess of Macclesfield by virtue of his succession in 1694. It was only after she had two children clandestinely by Richard Savage, 4th Earl Rivers, a reputed womaniser estranged from his own wife, that he realised his reputation was at stake. The first child, a girl named Anne, was born in 1695 in Queen Street, Soho, but died not long after Anna had returned from Bath to take the waters. The second child, born at Fox Court, Holborn, in January 1697, was christened two days later as Richard, son of John and Mary Smith. As soon as they were born both babies were placed at nurse and cared for elsewhere in London, their expenses paid jointly by their parents, Anna and Lord Rivers. In 1718 the poet Richard Savage came forward claiming to be their son.

His friend Samuel Johnson published his *Life of Savage* in 1727, and regardless of their improbability repeated Savage's claims of his parentage and unrelenting hostility by his supposed mother, the Countess of Macclesfield. Savage said he had been cared for by his godmother, a Mrs Lloyd, and his alleged grandmother Lady Mason, who had put him in a school near St Albans. He said his mother had prevented his receiving an inheritance from Lord Rivers by claiming he was dead, and had tried to have him abducted to the West Indies. Anna claimed her real child was indeed dead and Savage an opportunistic imposter.

Author James Boswell 's doubts about discrepancies in the story were confirmed by 'information and remarks' he received from Francis Cockayne Cust, a grandson of Anna's sister Dorothy, and together with his own inquiries Boswell sought to render it doubtful at the very least, publishing the findings in his *Life of Samuel Johnson* in 1791. It was not until 1858 that a thorough investigation[132] was made by W. Moy Thomas, who found the original manuscript depositions in Doctors Commons and the House of Lords from divorce proceedings instituted by Macclesfield in the summer of 1697, which he began only after discovering his estranged wife had borne the two illegitimate children. In an unprecedented action the case was debated by the Lords between January and March 1698, with airing of much salacious detail. It is from the original documents we learn the following:

A few days after their separation in 1684 Macclesfield wrote to Anna, denying any wrongdoing on his part and laying the blame squarely at her feet: 'Your youth and folly did long plead your excuse, but when I saw ill nature in you, and ill will (not to say malice) in your mother join against me, I then had reason to despair of your amendment.' He complains that their marriage had been a bitter disappointment to him, his wife being neither 'a faithful nor cheerful companion'. He denied having preyed on her, as she so often accused him, and felt her family considered themselves the worse for the alliance, 'your mother showing her contempt by writing one of the unmannerly letters to me, and sending back the pittyful jewels, as if they were the worse for wearing'.

During one of their many arguments Anna had told him she had agreed to their marriage only to make herself 'more easy' than she was at home; given her very young age this was probably true, and suggests the sort of domestic conflict typical between wilful teenagers and their parents. She replaced them not with an indulgent lover but a violent and temperamental husband.

His letter goes on to outline all his complaints, including her attempts to provoke him into striking her, threatening to leave him for her parent's lodgings at Whitehall, inconvenient though they were, and her point-blank statement that she had no desire to have his children 'but always pretended yourself with child when I went out of town from you. Your design in it I cannot imagine.' After signing

132 Published in *Notes and Queries* 2nd series, vol. vi, 149, 6 November 1858 p. 361

off 'I am yours, C. Brandon', he added: 'This show to Sir Richard [Mason] and my lady, for I will never live with you for as long as I live.' Witness depositions record the letter being delivered at 7am by the earl's servant, and on reading it Anna 'was mightily concerned and fell a-crying'. Judging by events that followed a year later, Anna still had hopes of their continuing marriage.

In 1685 a sentence of death was passed against Macclesfield, together with others, including Anna's distant cousin William, Lord Russell, son of the 5th Earl of Bedford, for their part in the Rye House Plot. Russell was executed, but in August 1687 Macclesfield was unexpectedly pardoned. The family had been busily working behind the scenes, and in January 1686 Anna's grandfather Sir James Long wrote to his daughter Jane, then staying with her sister Lady Mason in Leicester Fields, London: 'You appear to have good assurance with His Majesty's clemency in pardoning my Lord Brandon.' There were great exertions made personally by Anna on his behalf to secure the pardon, 'both with money and jewels', but the hoped-for reconciliation was not forthcoming. In 1689 she made an unsuccessful attempt to reclaim some of the jointure lands from her marriage settlement.

In the meantime her grandmother Lady Dorothy Long was kept informed of the society gossip in London. Anna's sister Dorothy relayed news of the death of Nell Gwynne, and 'Ld. Elland is marry'd to day to ye uglyest pugg in England'.[133] She only briefly mentions her 'dear sister's unhappy business'. 'He plays ten thousand Devills, gives no reason against her, but will do all ye mischief he can. Nobody knows wt Vipers we have to deal with.'

> I will not say anything of Cos W. L. [William Leche]. Nobody but you had ever ye art to make one laugh so much in talking of him. But I desire to know if ye rain yt had almost drown'd him has wash'd of his greasy hair, for coming two or 3 days after dinner I was ready to spew. I would have, my dearest Gran:Mother . . .[134]

133   William Saville's marriage to Elizabeth Grimston
134   The estate papers & records of Viscount Long, WSA ref 947:2101/3

The Brownlows would have known of Anna's affair with Lord Rivers, and her sister at least would have been aware of her two pregnancies. Evidence was related by servants and midwives of Anna's attempts to conceal the births and her identity, wearing a mask during the birth of the second child. Nothing in the depositions corroborates the later claim of Richard Savage. A divorce on the grounds of adultery was granted to Macclesfield in March 1698, the first such case decreed without judgement from the ecclesiastical court. An annuity was settled on Anna, who despite assertions by Samuel Johnson had never publicly admitted adultery, probably to prevent the loss of her title and fortune. Macclesfield was indemnified against her debts and free to remarry.

Anna, who now signed her letters with her maiden name, became a lady-in-waiting to Princess Anne, and two years later, in January 1700, her sister Dorothy died. Just nine months before, Anna had written to their grandmother that Dorothy had been safely delivered of a son, having 'had an extraordinary good time'. Sir William Brownlow, Anna's brother-in-law, wasted no time after his wife's death, less than a year later marrying Henrietta Brett. He died eight weeks later, intestate and deeply in debt.

Dorothy's death coincided with Anna's remarriage to Henrietta's brother Colonel Henry Brett, and their daughter Anna Margaretta was born ten months later in October 1700. In 1727, the last year of George I's reign, Anna Margaretta was, according to Horace Walpole, inducted into the king's harem by being given a ground-floor apartment in the palace of St James. Much to the annoyance of his older German mistresses – 'the long and emaciated Duchess of Kendall and terrifyingly corpulent Countess of Darlington' – she became the fresh favourite of the king of England. The king died suddenly and his supposed promise of making her a countess never fulfilled.

Marriage was widely rumoured between the Earl of Macclesfield and Letitia Harbord, daughter of the prominent Whig MP William Harbord, but Macclesfield died in November 1701, a little over three years after his spectacular divorce. Having no legitimate children, he left most of his estate to his friend Charles, 4th Baron Mohun. James Douglas, 4th Duke of Hamilton, also made a claim to the estate and challenged Mohun through the courts. Macclesfield was dead, but still his influence lingered. After more than a decade of legal dispute the pair fought a duel in Hyde Park, ending in the deaths of both men.

Savage persisted with his claims that Anna was his mother, successfully blackmailing the family and publishing *The Bastard* in 1728. Anna's nephew, John Brownlow, 1st Viscount Tyrconnel, bought his silence by taking him into his house and allowing him a pension of £200 per annum. Savage not only inveigled his way into the family but also the public consciousness; ten years after King George's death two separate marriage announcements appeared in the *Gentleman's Magazine*, between Anna's daughter Anna Brett and Sir William Leman.

The first, on 17 September, makes no mention of Savage, but the second, on 8 October, is more specific: 'Miss Brett, half-sister to Mr Savage, son to the late Earl Rivers'. The second insertion, so Walpole says, was made by Savage to countenance his own pretensions. Mrs Anna Brett, formerly Anna Mason and sometime Countess of Macclesfield survived her husband Henry by nearly thirty years and her daughter by ten. She died in October 1753 at her home in Old Bond Street, London, aged in her eighties.

James Long Esquire (c.1645–1689)

Sir James and Lady Dorothy had high hopes for their only son James, affectionately known as Jemmy, but despite their best efforts his later drunkenness and gambling proved him to be a bitter disappointment. He was born some time during the mid-1640s, and letters between his mother and her friend Sir Justinian Isham indicate James suffered a serious illness in 1651. In 1653 Dorothy entrusted his religious education to Sir Justinian and her uncle, the Rev. Dr Richard Chaworth, in case she should die in childbirth. But there were early signs that gave rise to his mother's concerns about her son's 'capacity and industry'.

She would gladly accept responsibility 'if he make not an accomplisht Man' but in his 'disaffection & incapacity to Musick' she blamed his father. She was impatient to send him abroad, and he might easily have learnt French with his sisters Anna Margaretta and Dorothy, but his tutor was against it: 'He lost that opportunity. Though not irrecoverably I hope.'[135] James's relationship with his siblings was not always harmonious, his father later writing of the 'wrangles and malice'.

Some time before 1673 he married Susanna, daughter of leading Civil War politician Colonel Sir Giles Strangways, whose enormous wealth – estimated at £3.1 billion today[136] – put him high on the list of richest Britons in the seventeenth century. The Strangways lived at Melbury, Dorset, not far from Athelhampton House, the only residence once owned by the Longs of Draycot that still survives.

Athelhampton was home to the heir until he succeeded to the Long estates, and James and Susanna lived there after their marriage. All six children were baptised at Melbury. The marriage soured early, and it is likely the younger children were brought up at their maternal grandparents' home, with several of their letters addressed from there. In 1674 James's father unsuccessfully contested the Yorkshire seat of Aldborough, and correspondence during the campaign from Sir Henry Goodricke (MP for Boroughbridge) to Sir James's opponent Sir John Reresby leaves no doubt as to the situation on the home front:

> Wee both have the satisfaction to be asured that Sir James Long and his son have both forfeited their interest with Coll. Strangeways; the father by high unkindnesse and folly, the son by hard usage of his wife, who has betaken herselfe wholly to her father's (Strangeways) house, and by the foolish loss of £15,000 in one year at play, and to avoid his creditors, in so much that hee dare not stirr out of his house in the country. [137]

James and Susanna must have reconciled their differences, temporarily at least; their youngest son James junior was born in about 1682. However, their marriage seems to have lurched from one crisis to another. Two years later a curious series of events occurred: one

---

135   Couzens, *pers. com.*
136   Philip Beresford, William D. Rubinstein *The Richest of the Rich*, 2007
137   Roy Carroll, *The By-Election at Aldborough, 1673* (Reresby Corr. 8/18), Huntington Library Quarterly, 28 February 1965, p. 157

Athelhampton House, Dorset

of James's creditors, Mary Keightley, in an attempt to recover a debt, instituted a chancery suit that resulted in the court sanctioning the sequestration of James's estates. In the course of these proceedings it came to light that in 1683 James had gone to some lengths to avoid paying his debts.

When three men from London arrived at Athelhampton, armed with a commission from the court, their request for information from the villagers concerning his whereabouts met with an eager response. They were warned he always kept a vigilant eye out for any creditors who might approach the house, and kept two cases of pistols and several swords near the door ready for use. Just the previous evening, they said, he had been heard firing his pistols towards the entrance gate. It was well known too that bullets were being made in the house. When James received word the men were in town he sent four of his servants who threatened them with violence if they proceeded towards the house.

Somewhat daunted by this antagonism, the leader of the three, Thomas Burgh, lawyer of Gray's Inn, decided to see what could be accomplished by peaceful means. The minister of the parish was later sent to the house and returned with the good news: Mr Long was not at home. Preparations for an offensive movement began. The commission was read to the neighbours and a party of men headed by Burgh and the parish constable set off, arriving at the house about noon.

There they encountered a locked gate, and James's wife Susanna appeared at an upper-storey window. After Burgh explained the object of their mission and demanded entry, she shouted down to them that her husband was abroad and they would enter at their peril. On being told her refusal to grant admittance would be reported to the court, great laughter came from within the house.

Burgh and his men then decided to tackle the sequestration of the farm. The tenant, Robert Grosse, assaulted their ears with 'morose language' when they waved their commission under his nose. He said they were mistaken if they thought they could 'fright the country with wax and parchment'. The farmer told them he paid his rent to Sir Richard Mason, James's brother-in-law. This was in fact true; Mason had leased Athelhampton farm on a long term from James. But Burgh didn't believe it and threatened Grosse that he would 'lay him by the heels' if he didn't tell the truth. Grosse left them to it, and for four days Burgh and his men went about the farm locking gates and putting up bars, with no interference.

Their victory was short-lived. The constable, backed up by twenty local men, went to the lodgings occupied by Burgh and his companions, and arrested all three on a charge of rioting. The lord chief justice, the formidable 'Hanging Judge' Jeffreys no less, had issued a warrant against them, probably at the instigation of James or his father. After a short spell in the local gaol they regained their liberty at the next assizes, and hastily returned to London.

The story that bullets were being made in the house was contradicted on oath, and it may be that the rest of the talk regarding James's activities was just mischief-making on the part of the villagers. The whole episode would have strengthened James's determination to be unco-operative and obstructive, but it had a deeply devastating effect on his wife Susanna. Her brother later asserted that when Burgh confronted her from the gate demanding entry she was 'soe affrighted' by his deportment that she languished and died a short time later.[138] She was buried at Puddletown, about a mile from Athelhampton and her estate administered by her husband in 1686–7.

Mary Long, née Keightley (1652– ?)

Intriguingly, shortly after Susanna's death James married the instigator of the suit, Mary Keightley, a spinster in her mid-thirties. The manor of Burleston in Dorset was settled on her for life, with her stepsons Giles and James junior as lessors. This marriage may have followed a clandestine affair, or it may have been merely a convenient financial arrangement, given recent events. Whatever the case, James must have seen potential in a union with a woman who had influential connections of her own.

Mary's brother was the Right Honourable Thomas Keightley, subsequently uncle by marriage to two queens, and son-in-law of Sir Robert Long's old foe Sir Edward Hyde, Earl of Clarendon. This royal connection came about when Keightley's sister-in-law Ann Hyde married the heir presumptive to the throne, the Duke of York (later James II), whose two daughters each successively ruled England as Queen Mary II of England and Queen Anne of Great Britain.

Mary Keightley seems to have had quite an effect on James, initially at least. His sister Anna wrote approvingly to their mother Lady Dorothy that 'by her patience Mrs Keightley has brought my brother [out] of his drinking, in a great measure, and to love home'.[139]

They had one daughter during their brief marriage, just a small child when James died in 1689. He was also buried at Puddletown. Administration of his estate was granted to his principal creditor Thomas Sherman on 22 October, with Mary his relict renouncing. Yet another creditor, Gabriel Armiger, was granted administration in July 1692.

Mary was staunchly Roman Catholic, and it may be that James had already secretly converted to Catholicism before their marriage. Certainly there was suspicion his great-uncle Sir Robert Long did so

---

138   *Somerset and Dorset Notes and Queries*, vol. IV, 1915, pp. 102-104
139   WSA ref 947:2101 and 2102

while with the exiled court in Europe, and a codicil to Sir Robert's will might be similarly construed: he asked that Sir Richard Mason expend £600 'for the good and benefitt of my Soule . . . as I have Privately directed and ordered him'.[140]

Growing up in an intellectual Catholic household at Hertingfordbury, Mary Keightley and her siblings were cousins of diarist William Evelyn, who was dismayed at the family's conversion to Catholicism. In 1650, two years before Mary's birth, her uncle Thomas had converted to Rome despite Evelyn's attempts to dissuade him, and her father William soon followed suit. Evelyn wrote of Thomas's conversion: 'He hath ben made a Popish proselyte some months & now from a young gallant, a zealous bigot.'[141] Nevertheless, the Keightley children were baptised in the Church of England at Great Amwell, Hertfordshire.

After Mary's brother Thomas inherited his father William's estate he sold it and emigrated to Ireland. His career in Irish government commenced with the appointment of his brother-in-law Henry Hyde, 2nd Earl of Clarendon, as lord lieutenant of Ireland, and Thomas went on to become revenue commissioner and privy councillor.

William Keightley's widow Amy (*née* Williams) married historian John Belson, a prominent and controversial Catholic, although his son Thomas returned to Protestantism, probably to further his career. During the crisis leading to the overthrow of the Catholic James II in 1688, Henry Hyde enlisted Thomas Keightley's assistance to dissuade their royal brother-in-law from leaving England and effectively abdicating. Keightley, as a Protestant, claimed to have no credit with the king and suggested more success might be achieved by his Catholic stepfather Belson.

On his arrival at court Keightley saw King James who pretended to agree to meet Belson the next morning, but he slipped away in the night to France. In what was later termed the Glorious Revolution, King James's nephew William of Orange, together with William's wife Mary (James's daughter and Henry Hyde's first cousin), ascended the

140   PRO, PROB 11/341/236
141   John Evelyn, E.S. De Beer, *The Diary of John Evelyn*, 2001, p. 634

throne as William III and Mary II.

Thomas Keightley's marriage to Lady Frances Hyde, the 1st Earl of Clarendon's daughter, ended in separation. The Hyde family laid no blame on Thomas; indeed Frances spoke kindly of him in a long letter she wrote to their young daughter Catherine in 1681 not long afterwards: 'yr dear Father, a patron of ye best & evenest temper I ever knew'.[142] Early in their separation Frances's brother Henry accommodated her in his house, referring to her as 'this unfortunate woman'. Her behaviour was erratic, and he implied she had a drinking problem. Her unsettled state of mind may have been due in part to a long series of tragedies in her life. The fifteen sons she had with Thomas had all died in infancy leaving only Catherine, later Mrs Lucius O'Brien.

Frances's niece Queen Anne suffered similar misfortunes; perhaps there was an inherited gene in the Hyde family. On thirteen occasions Anne miscarried or gave birth to stillborn children, and four died before reaching the age of two years. Her only son to survive infancy, William, Duke of Gloucester, died at the age of eleven in 1700, precipitating a succession crisis. Her sister Queen Mary's three pregnancies also ended in miscarriage or stillbirth.

Lady Frances Keightley was, like her sister the Duchess of York and sister-in-law Mary Long, a devout Roman Catholic. The secretary of state, James Vernon, in writing to diplomat George Stepney in March 1701/2, advised that the Austrian ambassador Count Wratislaw, concerning himself in solicitations for Roman Catholics, had sent him a petition from 'the widow Long' and her unmarried elder sister Frances, to be given to the king. Vernon makes the point that they were both sisters of Mr Keightley, living in Dorset (probably still at Athelhampton), and 'furiously bigoted.' 'On that account their neighbours have no good will towards them'.[143] Those neighbours must have felt quite pleased when Mary was ordered under a statute to pay the large sum of £20 each month for failing to attend church.

There were also others who were upset by Mary's fanatical zeal.

142   Inchiquin MS 45,720.1
143   James Vernon, [George Payne Rainsford James, *Letters Illustrative of the Reign of William III from 1696 to 1708*, 1841, vol. 3, p. 188

A prosecution was brought by her nephew's widow, whom Vernon doesn't name; both the widow and her husband had been Catholic, but she had since changed her religion and wished to raise her children as Protestants. Mary, who had been appointed guardian to her nephew's children, opposed this. Vernon solicited the mediation of an MP, one of the neighbours known to both parties. The unfortunate children at the centre of the furore were living with their aunts Mary Long and her sister Frances, Vernon writing that had the mother not been deprived of her children the old ladies might live unmolested – but they kept a busy priest in their house who 'calls in foreign aid'. 'It is much fitter that we should send him away, and perhaps that will be the end of it.'

The tug-of-war between Catholics and Protestants within the family caused considerable tension. At about the same time James and Mary Long's only child, also named Mary, was the subject of a letter written by her cousin Catherine Keightley to 'my dear Aunt' Lady Clarendon, wife of Catherine's uncle Henry, the 2nd earl. Mary, then aged about fourteen, was apparently in need of religious guidance and a father figure, and Catherine recommends 'my Cosen Long to my Father's care [to] embrace the protestant Religion wth as much cincerity as I have don[e]'.[144]

Young Mary was more influenced by her mother in her religion, later marrying Colonel Walter Butler of Munfin, a member of a staunchly Catholic Anglo-Norman aristocratic family. The Butler clan had been feudal overlords in Ireland since the twelfth century and included the House of Ormond with whom Thomas Keightley had frequent dealings.

Walter's father, Walter Butler senior (MP for Wexford in the Patriot Parliament at Dublin of 1689), had married as his second wife Eleanor White, widow of his stepbrother, the 2nd Viscount Galmoy. Finding themselves on the wrong side of the political fence, he, his brother Edward and his son Walter were all attainted for treason in 1691. Ten years later Walter senior was forced to sell all his property, and a petition was raised by Walter junior relating to his own forfeited estates and those of Viscount Galmoy.

144   Inchiquin MS 45,720.2

Eventually clearing his name, in February 1703 an Act was passed that all outlawries and attainders of treason against him be repealed. Another petition on behalf of his son by Walter Butler senior in 1704 to the new secretary of state, Charles Hedges, was presented by 'the German Emperor's envoy in London', the aforementioned Count Wratislaw. This may be the link between the Keightleys and the Butler family of Munfin. By the time he married young Mary Long Walter would have hoped all these troubles were well behind him, but a lack of money would prove to be an ongoing problem for the family. This also had an impact on her mother, Mary Long senior.

By 1715 Mrs Long had left England for Ireland to live with her daughter and son-in-law at Munfin, still receiving an income from a life interest in the Longs' estate at Burleston, Dorset. [145] News of their financial difficulties spread. After the death in 1717 of Walter Butler senior, Mrs Margaret Ford[146] wrote to her niece Catherine O'Brien (*née* Keightley) requesting assistance for Mary Long's daughter:

> . . . my Cosen Buttler of Munphin who is a most deserving worthy young woman but not soe well favour'd by fortune as she deserves and has a numerous familie of children. I know not what condition they are in since the father's death but they were in ill circumstances during his life and I don't hear they are much better now.[147]

To compound the family's misery, in 1721–2 young Mary's husband Walter Butler spent a year in Wexford gaol, the old charge of treason having caught up with him once again. On his release he wrote to Catherine O'Brien,[148] shortly before the commencement of her son Sir Edward O'Brien's Grand Tour.[149] To this letter Mary added a postscript of her own, apologising for having written only once in four years to Catherine's mother Lady Frances, since the

---

145   Valued at £339 2s 1d a year. *Roman Catholics, Nonjurors, and Others, who refus'd to take the oaths to his late Majesty King George*, 1746, p. 20
146   Sister of Lucia Hamilton, Sir Donough O'Brien's first wife
147   Inchiquin MS 45.346.4
148   Inchiquin MS *op. cit.*
149   2nd Baronet, son of Mrs Mary Long's niece Catherine, *née* Keightley

death in 1718 of her 'Deare Brother', Thomas Keightley, Frances's estranged husband.

Arrangements were under way for the Butlers' son to accompany his cousin Edward on tour, and Walter intended 'taking all measures imaginable' to find the money, making recommendations for people of interest in Europe for them to visit. Foreign travel was considered a rounding-off of the education process, but expensive, and the opportunity to share Edward's tutors and servants was too good to be missed.

That one letter of Mary's in four years caused Lady Frances some distress. 'I am in great concern for your poor Aunt Long and her numerous family. I could not read her letter without a real grief; I wish I was in a capacity to be any help to her I am sure.'[150] Mary also wrote to Catherine that her 'trubbles and misfortunes of late' and the fate of her 'numeris family' had been weighing on her mind. Frances had offered to 'take up' Mary's fifteen-year-old granddaughter, for which Mary was grateful, having already 'done my best to give her all the learning this little hole is capable of'.

For the impoverished Butler family the relative comfort of Munfin House was a distant memory, and 'this little hole' was probably somewhere considerably inferior in the wilds of Scarawalsh, Wexford. Their troubles only multiplied when Walter Butler died in 1725 giving them little choice but to rely on the charity of the family whom Mary Long was so loathe to burden just two or three years before.

A lack of money was a recurring complaint too in the letters of Lady Frances Keightley to her daughter Catherine, and also for Catherine herself, whose husband Lucius was in considerable debt to his friend Oliver Long, amongst others.

The numerous family so often referred to in these letters consisted of Mary and Walter Butler's six children, including Walter junior, Pierce and three girls,[151] one of whom (Mother Margaret of St Francis Assisi), became a nun in Paris, who in 1767 together with her cousin, Mother Nano Nagle, established the Ursuline convent at

150   Inchiquin MS 45,348.5
151   *Equity Exchequer Bill Books 1674-1850, Court of Exchequer Ireland*, 1717-1718, vol. 20, p. 98

Cork. Nothing further is known of Mary Long *née* Keightley. Portraits of eleven members of the Keightley family, including Mary's parents and her brothers Thomas and Francis, were at Dromoland Castle in 1946, former home of Lucius and Catherine O'Brien.

The Toast of the Kit-Cat Club

The life of James Long and Susanna Strangways' daughter Ann was a tragically short one. She spent her teens living with her mother's family at Melbury, Dorset, later moving to London. She wrote dutifully to her grandmother Lady Dorothy Long at Draycot, passing on poems and the latest gossip, occasionally sending her snippets cut from the newspapers for 'ye scandall Drawer'.[152]

Renowned for her beauty and intelligence, she became a celebrated figure in fashionable London society from about 1703, when in her early twenties. Apologetically bereft of gossip, 'loves, emulation, jealousyes etc' to send her grandmother, she wrote that 'a large dullness' had seized the town for some while, which had kept her from 'being as impertinent as usuall'. The town was at 'a very low ebb of discourse', visiting ladies reduced to 'the old thread bare theam of weather, politicians'. 'We have been soe far from our usual way of inventing mallicious storys, that if people have played the fooll noe notice has been taken of itt. So that I make itt a question whether tis London that I am in, butt I believe I will recover.'

She took a keen interest in England's victories in the War of Spanish Succession, noting after the battle of Blenheim in 1704: 'Soe much rejoyces us here, for we recon we have quite ruined the French & the Duke of Bavarie' and her London neighbour, naval commander Sir George Rooke, 'regained his creditt taking Gibraltar from the Spaniards'. Commenting on Abigail, wife of her cousin Henry Heron of Surfleet, Lincolnshire,[153] she says 'she is grown fatt, butt I heare itt does not proceed from being contented, for they say he makes a sad husband'. Ann had earlier told her grandmother Henry had been fined £300 for ravishing 'some woman'.

---

152   WSA ref 947:2109
153   Son of her aunt Dorothy Long and Sir Henry Heron

While she had an easy rapport with Lady Dorothy, the relationship with her siblings was less congenial. In 1707 she complained that her brother James and sister Dorothy were behaving very strangely towards her for no reason she could think of. She had not seen James for a month, and when 'I meet her [Dorothy] att my Aunts, she will scarce speak.'

Ann first met author and poet Jonathan Swift in 1707 at the London home of their mutual friends the Vanhomrighs. Encouraging a flirtatious epistolary relationship Swift wrote 'A decree for concluding the treaty between Dr Swift and Mrs Long', in December 1707 or January 1708. It was published in 1718 by Edmund Curll in a volume of miscellanies, *Letters, Poems and Tales: Amorous, Satyrical, and Gallant*. Swift developed a great admiration for her, although it lacked the intensity of his slow, tortuous and passionate affair with the Vanhomrigh's daughter Esther.

A celebrated toast of the Kit-Cat Club, Ann is mentioned in a poem 'Describing the Most Celebrated Beauties at St. James's, the Park, and the Mall' entitled *The British Court* (Joseph Browne 1707). Her closest associate was fellow-toast Catherine Barton (d. 1739), niece of Sir Isaac Newton, and it is believed the two women shared a house in London. The club, which continued until about 1720, had about forty-eight members who were prominent politicians, artists and writers, wealthy landowners and the nobility, all Whig party members. Other members of the club included the Duke of Marlborough, Sir Robert Walpole and the writers Joseph Addison, Richard Steele and William Congreve. Their main purpose was to ensure the continuance of the Protestant monarchy.

The cost of living fashionably in London was high. Whatever little money Ann had at her disposal was clearly insufficient, with debts incurred in expectation of the inheritance from Lady Dorothy Long.[154] But 'that odious grandmother', as Swift described her, didn't die until 1710. To avoid her creditors Ann was forced to pack up

154   Swift says this was £2,000, the amount bequeathed by her grandfather Sir James Long

her household and flee London for King's Lynn, Norfolk. In Swift's *Journal to Stella*, a series of letters he wrote to his friend Esther Johnson (nicknamed Stella), he paints a rather sad picture of the last months of Anne's life, and Charles Dickens in the 1850s published her story in his *Household Words*.

'Bailiffs were in her house,' Swift wrote to Stella, 'and she retired to private lodgings; thence to the country, nobody knows where: her friends leave letters at some inn, and they are carried to her: and she writes answers without dating them from any place. I swear it grieves me to the soul.' A little later he wrote: 'I had a letter today from poor Mrs Long, giving me an account of her life; obscure in a remote country town, and how easy she is under it. Poor Creature!' A second letter, not preserved, quite turned his stomach against her: 'no less than two nasty jests in it, with dashes to suppose them. She is corrupted in that country town, with vile conversation.' Her last letter, endorsed by Swift from 'poor Mrs Long' five weeks before she died, was found among his papers. Living under the pseudonym 'Mrs Smyth' near St Nicholas's church at King's Lynn, Ann wrote:

> I pretend to no more than being of George Smyth's family of Nitley, but do not talk much for fear of betraying myself. At first they thought I came hither to make my fortune by catching up some of their young fellows; but having avoided that sort of company, I am still a riddle they know not what to make of . . . I am grown a good housewife; I can pot and pickle, Sir, and can handle a needle very prettily.[155]

She mentions her 'poor cousin is taken for an hermaphrodite', a reference to certain masculine qualities of Esther Vanhomrigh (Swift's 'Vanessa'). The relationship to the Vanhomrighs was probably through Ann's stepmother Mary Keightley, whose brother Thomas was appointed to the Irish revenue service with Esther's father. Swift was also acquainted with Commissioner Thomas Keightley ; he mentions his intention to speak to him on behalf of a friend, although he had 'no personal credit with any of the commissioners'.

---

155   Charles Dickens, *Selections from Household Words: A Weekly Journal*, p. 552

After two years in exile and having almost paid her debts with careful management of her income, which included a £100 annuity and £60 rental from 'Newburg-house' in London,[156] Ann hoped to be able to leave King's Lynn by Christmas 1711. When Swift arrived in London at the Vanhomrighs' house for Christmas dinner, he was shocked to learn that Ann, not much more than thirty, had died suddenly three days earlier. He wrote to Stella:

> Poor Mrs Long died at Lynn in Norfolk, on Saturday last at four in the morning. She was sick but four hours. We suppose it was the asthma, which she was subject to as well as the dropsy. I never was more afflicted at any death . . . She had all sorts of amiable qualities, and no ill ones, but the indiscretion of too much neglecting her own affairs.[157]

He was convinced 'melancholy helped her on to her grave', blaming her 'brute of a brother' Sir James Long, who by all accounts was callously indifferent to her misfortunes, refusing to advance any of her grandmother's inheritance. Despite their minor quarrels, the death of Ann was a great loss felt by Swift. He ordered a paragraph to her memory be inserted in the *Post-Boy* on 27 December, and with malice tinged with grief told Stella it was to spite her brother Sir James, who 'would fain have her death a secret' to save the expense of a funeral or going into mourning.

Further evidence of the affectionate interest Swift took in Ann's unhappy fate is a letter he wrote to the Rev. Mr Pyle, minister of King's Lynn. He sang her praises unreservedly: her 'every valuable quality of both body and mind . . . valued by everyone here above most of her sex, and by the most distinguished persons'. He requested she be buried in the church at King's Lynn.

---

156   Johnathan Swift, *Journal to Stella*, 2.446
157   Dickens, *op. cit.*

Sir James Long (c.1682–1729), 5th Baronet

Ann's only surviving brother was heir to their grandfather Sir James Long, 2nd baronet, after the death of his elder brother Giles from smallpox in 1698. Seventeen-year-old James was the last of three brothers and continuation of the line now rested squarely with him. Once he reached his majority he received the profits of the family estates, and on the death of his grandmother Lady Dorothy Long in 1710 he inherited Draycot together with Athelhampton, other land in Wiltshire and Dorset, and an estate near Ripon in Yorkshire as part of the entailed estates of Sir Robert Long. He used part of his inheritance to purchase more land in Dorset, adjacent to Athelhampton in the manors of Southover and Burleston.

The buzz of society in April 1702 was the coronation of the new Queen Anne, who declared war on France a week later. Twenty-year-old James on the other hand, had more important things on his mind. In June he married his fifth cousin once removed, the Hon. Henrietta Greville, great-granddaughter of Francis Russell, 4th Earl of Bedford. Her dowry would have been generous, provided by her father Fulke Greville, 5th Lord Brooke of Warwick Castle.

Sir James entered Parliament as MP for Chippenham in 1705, re-elected in 1707 and again, unopposed, in 1708. He also actively supported the Tory interest at Devizes, and in a letter to an unknown recipient he advocates the use of bribery to secure a majority vote for the Tory candidate, Mr Child, 'who can with such a majority elect a Mayor and as many Burgesses, living in or out of the borough, as they please; and by that means secure the election of members to serve in Parliament forever'. These votes, he thought, could be purchased for about £500:

> . . . and if the matter succeed you shall ever afterwards be elected without any expense. Now as to the bribing of the five votes, you know what will be the issue of that if discovered, and Child thinks they'll make a discovery; and as to the £500, that will not be bribery within the power of the House of Commons, it being only to elect a Mayor which must be done Friday in the next Whitsun week.[158]

158   MSS Duke of Portland, preserved at Welbeck Abbey, vol. 4

Sir James sat again for Chippenham in 1710. In March 1712 he was granted leave for a month from Parliament 'upon extraordinary occasions', but lost the election in 1713, ironically claiming his majority had been undermined by bribery on behalf of the successful Whig candidates. He was elected for Wootton Bassett in 1714, two years before Parliament introduced the Septennial Act 1716, increasing the maximum period between general elections from three years to seven. This allowed him longer enjoyment of office and postponed the need to invest more money to secure the seat at the next election.

He died at his London residence in Jermyn Street, aged forty-seven in March 1729. He'd had a fit of apoplexy 'soon after he was risen from bed', leaving his widow and four children bereft. His corpse was returned to Draycot for burial. A few weeks later Lady Henrietta began preparations for leaving London and advertised for sale the coach they kept at Jermyn Street with its lining of 'green caffoy and with a whole fore-glass'. A while later she vacated the house there too, occasionally residing at Bath where she eventually died, some thirty-six years after her husband. Of their children, Susanna and her brother Robert were the only two to marry. The future of the family name and estates lay therefore with Robert, Sir James's heir.

Robert's sister, twenty-three-year-old Susanna became the subject of gossip after eloping in 1732 with a family servant, Thomas Roston, reported by the *Gentlemen's Magazine* to be a footman. Her mother, a difficult woman at the best of times, was understandably not at all pleased. Susanna's cousin by marriage, Viscount Perceval, wrote in his diary in August 1732:

My Lady Long's daughter has also just married her mother's gardener. The gardener, when it was over, sent a message to my Lady to acquaint her with it, and to desire she would order a lawyer to settle his wife's fortune, which is £7,000, in such manner as she pleased for the advantage of his wife and the children she might have by him; but my Lady's answer was, that she hoped he would spend it fast, that she might have the pleasure to see her daughter a beggar.[159]

159   Dairy of Viscount Perceval, 3 vols, HMSO for Historical Manuscripts

Considerably in disgrace and probably keen to avoid further maternal wrath, Susanna and her new husband escaped to his native Stafford, where their daughter Sarah Susanna was born. Whether Lady Henrietta forgave her daughter is not certain; Susanna is not mentioned in her mother's will written in 1765, although she may have predeceased her. Rachel, her sister, apparently did forgive her, leaving a substantial legacy in 1781 of £2,000 to Susanna's daughter Sarah Susannah,[160] wife of John Awdry of Notton.

At least one of Susanna's descendants found their way back to Draycot; her great-grandson the Rev. Charles Roston Edridge Awdry (son of the Rev. Jeremiah Awdry) became rector of Draycot from 1852 to 1875. It was during this period that Draycot was controversially bequeathed away from the Long family. The Rev. Francis Kilvert mentions in his diary in 1872 that the Rev. Awdry had made sure the inheritor, Lord Cowley, was in no doubt of his heritage when he bluntly informed him: 'My ancestors owned this estate when yours were peasants!'[161]

Sir Robert Long (1705–67), 6th Baronet

Sir James's son Robert was admitted to Balliol College, Oxford at the age of twelve in January 1717, succeeding his father as 6th baronet in 1729. In 1734 he sat as MP for Wootton Bassett and for Wiltshire in 1741. During this period the costs involved in electioneering had risen so much that only the wealthiest gentry were capable of securing a seat, leading to resentment among the lesser country squires who lacked the power and patronage of their wealthier counterparts. The result ultimately, was a division among the landed classes.

While campaigning costs may have risen, Wiltshire's once flourishing woollen industry had declined. Some of Sir Robert's cousins whose ancestors had made their fortunes in cloth now preferred politics to cloth-making, with the exception of one or two of

Commission,1920–3

160   Her first husband the Rev. Mr Derbyshire was named to inherit the Draycot estate in case of failure of the Tylney-Long entail

161   William Plomer, *Kilvert's Diary, 1870–1879*, p. 202

the less-well-off who still employed weavers at Melksham. They were among the Wiltshire clothiers who in 1742 expressed gratitude for his support of their cause in Parliament, which resulted in the removal of the prohibition of Spanish wool.

His marriage to Emma Child in 1735 would lead to a sudden ballooning of the already substantial fortune of the Longs of Draycot. Emma's father Sir Richard Child, 3rd Baronet,[162] later Viscount Castlemaine (1718), and 1st Earl Tylney (1732), was the son of Sir Josiah Child, governor of the East India Company. Earl Tylney had amassed a great fortune and was said to be possessed of 'almost revolting wealth'.

Cassandra, Duchess of Chandos, Emma's great-aunt, wrote shortly after the marriage that there was more joy in the family than she had ever seen, and the newlyweds were to live at Wanstead House with Emma's twenty-three-year-old brother John, (later 2nd Earl Tylney). 'Sir Robert Long's goodness has charmed them all.' He so delighted his new father-in-law that 'he is equally dear to him as his own children . . . and his merit far exceeds all that has been said of him'.[163]

Many letters written to his wife still survive; he addresses her affectionately as 'my dearest life', 'my dearest little one' and 'my dearest angel'. These letters give an insight into the tender and loving relationships he enjoyed with his family, with evidence of his kindly good nature that extended to all the members of his household. One of his main concerns was 'to promote the welfare, the comfort and prosperity of my children', four of whom survived to adulthood. Reporting to his wife on his shopping expedition in London to buy dress material for Emma and her lady companion, he said he hadn't forgotten Miss Wayte, 'but she must not set up her chops for anything fine. I have only bought a plain Irish stuff for her.'

Sir Robert comes across as a thoroughly nice fellow who loved and appreciated his wife. After a night out to see a play, a domestic tragedy called *The Orphan*, or *The Unhappy Marriage* (Thomas Otway, 1680), he felt so moved by the lines lamenting the scarcity of good

162   And his wife Dorothy Glynn
163   Rosemary O'Day, *Cassandra Brydges, Duchess of Chandos, 1670–1735: life and letters*, 2007 p. 320

women, he afterwards wrote to Emma 'that I was ready to have jumped up in an ecstacy and said "but there is one such person, and she is fallen to my Lot."'

Like his siblings, he had an uneasy relationship with his mother. His sister Dorothy, writing in 1732 while he was on the Grand Tour in Rome, said their mother was in uncharacteristically good humour with her and sister Rachel, and they were relieved that 'Mama has not ask'd us to live with her & (to my great comfort) I am told she does not design it, as expecting we shall ask her.' Lady Henrietta's rare amiability was worthy of another remark five years later, Sir Robert telling his wife he had dined with her at Draycot, making the point that she was 'in great humour' and much pleased with a pineapple Emma had sent, grown in a hothouse at Wanstead. His mother had so many airs, 'I mean complaisant airs', he said, that their dinner guest Lord Forester 'took her for a mad woman. But prodigiously civil, both to him, and to me.'

Taking a hands-on approach to everything in regard to his own household, Sir Robert was a very dedicated parent when his children were ill, 'distemper' and smallpox being the scourge of the age. He wrote that his eldest son 'Jemmy' was almost recovered from the disease, but still extremely itchy. In 1749 young James was at Wanstead with his maternal grandmother, Lady Dorothy Child. He was doing 'vastly good work at school and is mighty well, but Extremely ragged, and I do not think he can wear [his clothes] a week longer'. James was now twelve years old and had just advanced to the second form. His teacher was so pleased with his diligent work he rewarded him with a silver tuppence, but his grandmother despaired of his wilfulness at home, refusing to change his clothes until ordered by his father.

In 1758, after almost two and a half decades of happy marriage, Sir Robert's beloved Emma died, aged fifty-one, from 'gout in the head'. This was a devastating blow, but he carried on, attending to his affairs in London and Draycot, maintaining regular correspondence with his children and taking an interest in the latest society gossip.

He was hopeful of a match for his only son with a Miss Estcourt, a young lady recommended by Lord Tylney. Twenty-three-year-old James, with his regiment near Winchester, knew nothing of this, and Sir Robert wisely suggested it 'might be contrived for him to see her and fancy her himself'. He wrote in 1760 to the Tylneys' agent at Wanstead to arrange an accidental meeting between the two, recommending he invite James to spend a fortnight under any pretext whatsoever. 'Hunting in the forest might be named, or not seeing him a good while or anything else you think of.' But nothing came of these well-laid plans, sadly for Sir Robert, who did not live long enough to see any of his children married.

He kept his spirits up, taking an interest in the latest court cases, balls and quadrille parties. A letter to his daughter Dorothy (Dolly) in 1763 describes the aftermath of one eventful evening which ended with some of the gentlemen becoming very inebriated:

> ... the Sheriffe being in high spirits at [the ball] being so well attended, he made us drink much more liquor than I approved of ... The Sheriff could not get back to his lodgings, and Lord Webb Seymour had the misfortune to befoul his [clothes] and came out the most dismal figure with the most dreadful smell that can be contemplated, for he had been in the common sewer.

Sir Robert died at his London residence in February 1767, and a few days later his remains were carried 'in great Funeral Pomp' to the family vault at Draycot.

Sir James Tylney Long (1737–94), 7th Baronet

Sir Robert's only son was educated at Oxford and joined the Wiltshire Militia in 1759. He rose to the rank of captain, and major in 1769, two years after inheriting his father's title and estates. While James was probably still enjoying himself in Europe on his Grand Tour, Charles, his younger brother by eight years, married Hannah Phipps in 1771, and it was another four years before James, at the age of thirty-eight, married Lady Harriot Bouverie in London in July 1775. Her father, Jacob, Viscount Folkestone of Longford Castle, according to the garrulous gossip Horace Walpole, was a considerable Jacobite who had bought his title for £12,000 from the Duchess of Kendall, George III's 'long and emaciated' mistress.

James seemed to enjoy a friendly relationship with his in-laws both before and after the marriage, but his friendship with Harriot's brother, the Earl of Radnor, was tested on at least two occasions. The earl wrote to James in January 1777 to express his annoyance over one of the latter's servants taking away without notice some slate the earl had ordered dug to make repairs to the almshouses at Corsham. James's much-anticipated marriage lasted a little over two years: a few months after returning from a visit to the Continent, Harriot died at Draycot in November 1777, possibly in childbirth, and they had no surviving children.

He took the name Tylney-Long on inheriting the estates of his unmarried maternal uncle John, 2nd Earl Tylney in September 1784. Seventy years earlier John's father, the 1st Earl Tylney, had commissioned Scottish architect Colen Campbell to design a grand mansion in the Palladian style at Wanstead, Essex, to replace the older one on the estate. This building rivalled such palaces as Blenheim and Houghton, and when built it covered an area of 260ft by 70ft. The main front had a portico with six Corinthian columns, and with the grounds further enhanced with the advice of George London, one of the most famous gardeners of his day, it would also have rivalled Versailles. In addition to this vast estate there were others in Hertfordshire and Hampshire,

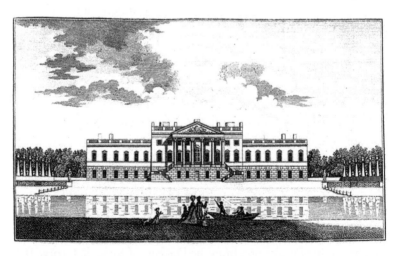

Wanstead House, The Complete English Traveller, Nathaniel Spencer, 1772

all of which passed to James.

It was perhaps in expectation of the inheritance that James completed the rebuilding of Draycot House. The combined income from all these properties made him one of the wealthiest commoners in England, but he did not take up residence at Wanstead. The house had fallen into decay over a period of twenty years and remained empty. Instead he stayed true to his Wiltshire roots at Draycot, for the time being at least.

He represented Marlborough and later Devizes in Parliament, when he made an address to George III on behalf of his constituents congratulating him on avoiding assassination by Margaret Nicholson, who tried to stab the king outside St James's Palace in 1786. James likely rounded off a hard day in the House by unwinding in one the private gentlemen's clubs at St James's, such as the Cocoa-Tree, Boodles or the Pantheon. If he was in the mood for an evening of music and theatre he might go to Drury Lane where he had a private box, before making his way back to his townhouse in Bond Street. At Draycot evenings were spent in conversation, music and cards, with packs purchased by the dozen. Dinner guests included his friend Lord Shelburne of Bowood House.

Sir Francis Burdett once said of Shelburne, renowned for his own 'good dinners', he 'talks volubly and graciously and wreathes his Whiskered Smiles from side to side.'[164] Another on Shelburne's guest-list, philosopher and political radical Jeremy Bentham, a man quick to dismiss ideas he disagreed with as 'nonsense upon stilts', was not backward about describing in uncomplimentary terms some of his fellow dinner guests at Bowood. Mr Tongue was an 'insipid and insignificant man' and the daughter of Lord Coventry was 'as ugly as a horse'.

During the 1780s Bentham spent several weeks at Bowood. Lord Bristol was there too, 'a most excellent companion – pleasant, intelligent, well-bred – liberal-minded to the last degree. He has been everywhere and knows everything.' By comparison, Sir James Long

164   *The Journal of the Rev. William Bagshaw Stevens,* ed. Georgina Galbraith, 1965, p. 332

was 'a little stiff-rumped fellow, who knew nothing except persons and so forth.'[165] This was perhaps a generalisation based on dinner-table conversation. James was apparently a modest and unassuming man with a charitable disposition who made donations to many public and private institutions. As a large landowner, he lived up to his obligations to the local community, regularly providing poor families on his estates with food, clothing and winter fuel.

The pressing necessity to have an heir to his empire could not be ignored however, and after eight years in marital limbo and by now aged forty-eight, James chose for his second wife, Catherine, the twenty-nine-year-old daughter of Other Lewis Windsor, 4th Earl of Plymouth. The nuptials were performed in July 1785, and a few weeks later he announced his intention to use Wanstead as a summer residence. The same year he bought Seagry House, afterwards purchasing Aldersbrook House intending to demolish it and farm the land. This brought his total landholdings across six counties to 22,539 acres.[166]

It may have been around this time that he borrowed £12,000 from his rather less wealthy, but still immensely rich cousin, Walter Long of Bath.[167] By 1787 he was well into the programme of restoration works at Wanstead, reviving it 'with all the splendour of the times', and it was thought it might 'eclipse all other houses in the kingdom'. The press reported that he accommodated his friends with tickets of admission to see the house at their own convenience, and continued the tradition of opening it to the general public every Saturday.

A further example of his goodwill was demonstrated in 1790 when the house was opened for a 'very superb' public breakfast, in which the yeomen and cottagers of Wanstead were entertained by the king's chaplain, Dr Samuel Glasse,[168] 'and the poor and fatherless were not forgotten'. But despite all the trappings of wealth, at a personal level James's dislike for parade and ostentation led him to take things

165   Lord Fitzmaurice, *Life of William, Earl of Shelburne*, McMillan & Co. 1912, p. 322
166   Couzens, *op. cit.*
167   This loan is mentioned in a codicil to Walter Long's will 1807
168   Presented to the rectory at Wanstead by Sir JTL 1786

to the other extreme, and when dining *en famille* the attendance of servants was kept to a minimum, as he preferred a dumb waiter placed at his elbow.

Sir James and Lady Catherine spent what must have been an anxious four years before she finally fell pregnant. In July 1789 the press described the 'singular circumstance' of the young Countess of Plymouth and her four sisters – Lady Catherine Tylney Long, Lady Sarah de Crespigny, Lady Elizabeth Townsend and Lady Anne Broughton [169] – all expecting 'to be in the straw at the same time'. Three months later while travelling either to or from Bath, it became apparent the heir to the House of Long was about to make his, or possibly her, appearance.

The soon-to-be parents hadn't expected the happy event quite so imminently and quickly took up emergency lodgings *en route* in Hungerford at the Bear Inn. Their daughter Catherine was born there on 2 October, and they stayed on at the inn for at least six weeks. As time passed the proprietress Mrs Whale became concerned her business was suffering as a result. Word had got around that due to the presence of Sir James Tylney Long and Lady, no one else could be accommodated, forcing her to inform the nobility and gentry travelling the Bath Road that this was not actually the case.

James was aged fifty-two by now and still hopeful of a male heir. He was not alone. Horace Walpole remarked at the time: 'Lord Tylney hoped for an heir, but his niece, Mrs Long, has only produced a daughter.' James's last remaining brother Charles had died six years earlier leaving an only daughter (Emma, later unhappily married to the heir to Castlecombe, William Scrope), and the future of the estates depended on James and Catherine ideally producing a son.

Their next two children were also girls, Dorothy and Emma, before the jewel in the crown, James junior, was born at Draycot House in October 1794. For some time before, James had been in poor health, necessitating a lengthy absence from Parliament. His infant son was baptised at Draycot on 4 November and James died twenty-four days later, at least secure in the knowledge of a male heir. Shortly afterwards

169   Died without issue 1793

the sheriff of Wiltshire, his cousin Richard Godolphin Long of Rood Ashton, announced a meeting at Devizes to elect a successor for his constituency.

James left a lengthy will, with two equally lengthy codicils, intent on leaving no doubt about the distribution of his vast and burdensome fortune. Besides the valuable estates, legacies of many thousands of pounds were distributed among his widow, children and last remaining sister, Dorothy. With the exception of servants, the smallest amount, 100 guineas, went to 'my friend William Long of Baynton '.

There would be no more grand entertaining at Draycot in the foreseeable future, and the *Morning Advertiser* announced the sale of the contents of his cellar, the bulk of which comprised 'about one hundred and twenty dozen of curious East India Madeira, forty dozen of Old Hock, forty dozen of Sherry, twenty dozen of Lachrymae Christi, thirteen dozen of Claret, thirty-six dozen of Mountain, eighty-eight bottles of Champagne of the year 1788, fifty bottles of Champagne of Noyo', and sundry other varieties of port, brandy, cider, wine and rum. There was also a public sale of his livestock and farm implements.

The tiny one-month-old heir, now Sir James Tylney Long, 8th baronet, was completely oblivious to the great upheaval and grief his father's death had caused. A constant worry to his mother, he grew to be a much pampered but delicate and sickly child. The family doctor thought him rather too pampered, and on his advice the precious boy was packed off to boarding school. All seemed well for a while, but it soon became apparent the boy's constitution had not been strengthened by the school routine, and he died at the age of ten. It was a terrible blow to his mother and sisters, and the fate of the family estates was irrevocably doomed.

The Tragic Heiress

By most accounts Sir James's eldest daughter Catherine was endowed with youthful beauty, but according to one of her contemporaries she was not as pretty as her sister Dorothy, 'though a pleasing looking fairy creature'. She was just fifteen when her young brother died in 1805, passing to her the combined fortunes of not only

Notice of the death of the last Baronet, Sir James Tylney Long, 1805

the Longs of Draycot[170] but also those of the Child family and the Tylney family of Rotherwick, Hampshire. The media exaggerated her wealth of course, reporting that her estates in Essex, Hampshire and Wiltshire were worth between £40,000 and £60,000 per year rental income – more than £2 million per year at current values – with an additional £300,000 'in the funds'.

During Catherine's minority Wanstead House was occupied from time to time by Prince de Conde, Louis XVIII and other members of the exiled Bourbon family. When she came of age on 2 October 1810 there was great rejoicing at Draycot which continued throughout the week, the events recorded by the Rev. Francis Kilvert in his diary. An ox was roasted whole in the park with a troop of

170   The inspiration for some of Jane Austen's characters could well have been drawn from the Longs of Draycot. Her novel *Pride and Prejudice* (1813) included a character by the name of Mrs Long. With regard to the naming of the character of Tilney in Northanger Abbey, Austen's biographer Professor Park Honan PhD says of her home town of Steventon, Hampshire: 'Elms and beeches along the turnpike clung to banked hillside as "hangers"; there would be a line of northerly hangers not far from Basingstoke and Tylney Hall, of Sir James Tylney Long Bart.'

yeomanry cavalry riding around it to prevent anyone getting close, which might explain why when it was cut down one half was burnt and the other half raw. The festivities drew crowds of thousands from far and near, and while the cavalry were distracted by their own dinner inside the house the kitchen chimney caught fire. When they went to investigate, the hungry crowd rushed in and swooped on all the unattended food.[171]

Catherine was often described as the great heiress, an allusion of course to the size of her enormous fortune. But great also was the magnitude of error in her choice of husband. She was under constant public scrutiny and would hardly have known which way to turn, besieged as she was by every would-be suitor with their eyes unwaveringly on the prize. The press kept the public informed of each minute development, her unwanted celebrity status ensuring she was persecuted by fortune-hunters. Crowds pursued her wherever she went. Lady Charlotte Bury, a former lady-in-waiting to Princess Caroline, described these hopefuls as 'packs of truffle hunters'.[172]

An example of the attention Catherine drew in public is described in a letter written in 1810 by Lady Harriett Leveson-Gower (afterwards Countess Granville), to her sister Lady Georgina Morpeth:

> My drive [in Hyde Park] was pleasant because Lady Harrowby is always so, and it was droll to see Miss Long's admirers riding about her carriage as the guards do about the King's. Lady Catherine [her mother] bolstered up in one corner, and all the minor constellations backwards, each of whom is to have a hundred thousand.[173]

Besides the 'minor constellations', Catherine's two younger sisters Dorothy and Emma, Catherine's mother also came under scrutiny. In the same letter Lady Harriett recalls an incident described to her by playwright Richard Brinsley Sheridan, a fastidious man who disliked the spectacle of women gorging themselves, and who

---

171   Plomer, *op. cit.* p.229
172   Leslie Winter, *The Lovely Miss Long*, Longman's Magazine Jul 1905, p. 213
173   Harriet Granville, [Edward Frederick Leveson-Gower, *Letters of Harriet Countess Granville 1810-1845*, vol. 1, p. 1

reputedly lived for the first years of his married life at the expense of Walter Long of Bath, former suitor to his wife. One evening at Badminton Sheridan sat by Lady Catherine Long at supper, 'who munched and munched platesful of salad, till he took her for an old sow, and caught himself just going to say to the servants "pray change this lady's trough."'[174]

The young heiress's obvious attractions didn't escape the notice of George III's younger son, William, Duke of Clarence, who for twenty years from 1791 had lived at the royal estate of Bushey Park near Richmond with Irish actress, Dorothea Bland, better known by her stage name, Mrs Jordan. To the great despair of this lady, with whom he had ten illegitimate 'Fitz-children', their long relationship came to an end when the then debt-ridden forty-six-year-old duke began to make overtures towards Catherine.

With the distinct likelihood of his becoming king and needing a legitimate heir, he opened negotiations with Catherine's aunt, Lady Sarah de Crespigny. If successful, his intention was to apply to Parliament for a Bill to amend the Royal Marriage Act, enabling him to marry a commoner. With no tact or sensitivity, he seemed oblivious to the anguish he caused. To Lady Sarah he wrote breezily: 'Mrs Jordan has behaved like an angel and is equally anxious for the match.'[175] Determined to impress Catherine, in November 1811 the duke gave a ball and supper at the Bears Albion Hotel in Ramsgate, 'which in fashion, splendour and elegance, exceeded everything of the kind ever witnessed in that part of the Kingdom' – so said the *Morning Chronicle*, which reported that His Royal Highness danced a considerable part of the evening with Miss Tylney-Long.

With the duke cutting a conspicuous figure alongside a much younger rival – a certain well-connected and determined young man – the cartoonists were kept busy. A gossipy anecdote of Clarence's advances was related by novelist Monk Lewis in a letter to Lady Charlotte Campbell.[176] The duke was said to have commissioned

174   *Ibid*
175   Linda Kelly, *The Kemble Era: John Philip Kemble, Sarah Siddons, and the London Stage*, 1980, p. 187
176   Winter, *op. cit.* p. 215

a certain Mrs F. to offer Miss Tylney Long his hand and his heart, but his ambassadress bungled it badly by leaving Catherine with the impression she would merely take Mrs Jordan's place, churning out babies left and right.

Having no ambition in that direction, Catherine supposedly fell into a fit of weeping and called the woman a few unpleasant names, before unceremoniously dismissing her. The story was perpetuated in the *Scourge,* a vicious satirical journal, aptly named. After her refusal the duke went to her house at Ramsgate and proposed a further four times, but Catherine wasn't even slightly interested.

The Disconsolate Sailor (W. Long Wellesley, D. of Clarence & Catherine Tylney Long) © Trustees of the British Museum

He returned to London and wrote to ask one last time, adding that 'the Queen sends her best wishes and regards'. Upon this last and final failure the duke then made his addresses in the direction of Miss Elphinstone, daughter of Lord Keith, again receiving a stern refusal. Several more attempts with different ladies also failed, keeping the rampant gossips busy until he eventually secured the hand of the virtuous Adelaide.

Had Catherine been persuaded, she would have become Queen Catherine when the duke ascended the throne in 1830 as William IV – and even possibly a happy queen at that. But it was Adelaide who got the job; there was a very different fate in store for the reputed richest commoner in England.

The leading contender in the competition happened to be the young nephew of the Duke of Wellington. One of many observers, Sir George Jackson recorded in his diary for 9 March 1811 that 'Whether Pole will be the successful competitor remains to be seen. She flouts him now, but he has a real *longing* for her large dowry; he has, at least, to undergo many an uneasy quarter of an hour, when she bestows smiles elsewhere.'[177] The Honourable William Pole Wellesley was indeed the triumphant victor, but honourable he wasn't, as Catherine and her family would discover.

Many years later Wellesley said of Catherine's capitulation in a letter to the Lord Chancellor, Earl Eldon : 'it was agreed upon between that lady and myself, without the advice, intervention, or even knowledge of the relations on either side'. The Rev. Kilvert wrote that Catherine was weak and obstinate, the servants were bribed and the courtship carried out clandestinely. Wellesley would drive his tilbury to the Langley Brewery, leave it there, and hide himself behind the fence at Langley Rectory:

> When he had watched Lady Catherine drive across the Common into Chippenham with her four or six long-tailed black horses, leaving Miss Long the heiress locked up at home, he would run down to the Brewery, get into his Tilbury, and gallop over to Draycot, where he saw Miss Long by the connivance of the servants.[178]

Young Catherine was hopelessly infatuated and refused to heed the warnings of her family and friends, who rightly insisted that

177   The Bath Archives, *A Further Selection from the Diaries and Letters of Sir George Jackson*, 1873, vol. 1, p. 244
178   Kilvert *op. cit.* p. 394

Draycot House c. 1900. Courtesy Tim Couzens

Wellesley was a self-interested opportunist whose prime intention was to get his hands on her money. In that regard he was probably no better or worse than any of the other disappointed hopefuls she left in her wake, but he would indeed prove to be exactly the sort of man every sensible mother warns her daughters against.

But it was too late. Later, during an election campaign, Wellesley would boast how he 'got up the old lady's legs and married her daughter',[179] a statement that would no doubt have mortified Catherine's 'pious and exemplary parent' Lady Catherine Tylney Long, had it reached her delicate ears.

The entire country was abuzz with gossip about the impending marriage. Wedding jewels, fit for a queen, were supplied by the royal goldsmith, jewellers Rundell & Bridge of London. An associate of the firm wrote to a friend from Bath in December 1811: 'Her diamonds, which they are preparing, are much more splendid and magnificent than ever were furnished to a subject.'[180] No expense was spared: 'her gown cost seven hundred guineas, the bonnet one hundred and fifty guineas, and the veil two hundred guineas. The lady's jewels consist principally of a brilliant necklace and ear-rings;

179   Kilvert *op. cit.* p. 246
180   *Littell's Living Age*, 1863, vol. 79, p. 487

the former cost twenty-five thousand guineas'.[181]

In January 1812, three months before their marriage, William received royal permission to assume the added surnames of Tylney and Long, thus becoming the unwieldy William Pole Tylney Long Wellesley, a name which would soon become synonymous with reckless and indulgent extravagance, traits already well known to his friends. Lord Byron wrote in December 1811: 'Pole is to marry Miss Long, and will be a very miserable dog for all that.'[182]

The only son of Lord and Lady Maryborough, William Wellesley had been a dissolute character since his youth, much to his parents' despair. In their desperation they farmed him out to his uncles, the Marquess Wellesley and Duke of Wellington, his father's brothers, who did their best to give him what guidance they could, but it seemed to go in one ear and out the other. Wellington was completely baffled by the behaviour of 'Wicked William', as he was known to his family: 'He appears pretty well in health but his is the most extraordinary person altogether I have ever seen. There is a mixture of steadiness & extreme levity, of sense & folly in his composition such as I have never met with in any other instance.'[183] This was William's character in a nutshell: he could be quite charming and eloquent one minute and completely irrational the next.

Money + Marriage ÷ Wicked William = Misery

The careful planning and preparations for that fateful day in March 1812 completed, the groom arrived at St James's in Piccadilly without a ring. The ceremony had to be suspended while a local jeweller was rounded up to provide one. Once they were married Catherine's assets transferred to her husband by law, but in this case only for the term of his life. William made himself unpopular from the beginning, by attempting to close the road through Wanstead Park to public use. He padlocked the gate and ordered a trench to be dug across the road, but the locals took the matter to court and won.

181   Lewis Saul Benjamin, *The Beaux of the Regency*, 1908, p. 138
182   *Lord Byron, Letters and Journals*, vol. 2, 1811–1814, p. 146
183   Wellington to his brother Henry, 1st Baron Cowley, 25 August 1838, Stratfield Saye, *Wellington Papers*

In October 1813 Catherine and William's first son William junior was born, followed two years later by James. While Catherine was pregnant with their third child, William was in the midst of his election campaign for the seat of Wiltshire, on the nomination of the sheriff, John Long of Monkton Farleigh, brother of retiring member Richard Godolphin Long. In anticipation of William's election success he announced the expected addition to the family would be called Victory. A month later, in May 1818, the baby girl was named Victoria.

William was subjected to a scurrilous campaign in the local press by his opposing candidate John Benett, who labelled his private life extravagant and dissipated; he was a stranger and adventurer unsuited to public life. Benett argued that as son of a cabinet minister and heir to an Irish peerage, William was unfit to represent Wiltshire. William strenuously denied it all, insisting he was an Englishman born and bred and intended to reside in the county: 'I am governed not so much by any political motives, as by the ambition of restoring to the house of Draycot an honour which has been so frequently conferred upon various branches of that ancient family.'[184]

He splashed money around like water, borrowing the huge sum of £32,000 at 16 per cent interest to cover his expenses, according to his running mate Paul Methuen.[185] The freeholders were given a sumptuous dinner by William at Marlborough, which went on till dawn with singers from London, Bath and Salisbury. After the famous fête he had hosted at Wanstead in 1815 to celebrate the triumphal return of his uncle after the battle of Waterloo, everyone knew his relationship to the national hero, but not yet so well-known was the contrast in their characters. His canvassing talents were not inconsiderable and he secured the majority vote. Afterwards Admiralty High Court Judge Sir William Scott wrote from London to the Duchess of Somerset: 'Wellesley Long *has* succeeded, and I admit *partly* by his purse – but not entirely – the name and family of Long did a great deal for him; they have been, and continue to be, much connected to the county . . .'[186]

184   *Kaleidoscopiana Wiltoniensia*, 1818, p. 3
185   R.G Thorne, *The House of Commons 1790-1820*, 1986 vol. 1, p. 412
186   Guendolen Ramsden, *Correspondence of two brothers: Edward Adolphus,*

The novelesque history of Wicked William 's profligacy both
before and after his wife's premature death is well documented in court
records, newspaper archives and personal correspondence – too many
instances to detail here. Certainly the press of the day kept the general
public enthralled (Lord Chancellor Eldon actually said 'nauseated')
with the salacious details that emerged. Catherine initially had seemed
happily married, or so she had her family believe, perhaps reluctant to
admit she had been naïve in her choice of husband.

By 1821 William's debts had grown considerably and pressure
from his creditors finally forced his hand. On legal advice he conveyed
his life interest in Wanstead House to trustees for the benefit of his
creditors, which led to the sale of the extravagant contents, and also
the contents of another of Catherine's properties, Tylney Hall in
Rotherwick.

The London press assured the public they were not exaggerating
when they said the carpets and hangings from Wanstead alone had cost
£60,000. Actually they were; William's bank account shows this was
in fact the cost of the whole refurbishment of Wanstead. The carpets
were made from silk and embroidered with the arms of Tylney and
Wellesley. The walls and windows were hung with the richest Genoa
velvet with three borders of real gold lace, costing 3½ guineas a yard.
All this finery took thirty-two days to sell in over 5,000 lots, raising
a grand total of £41,380 – a few million pounds in today's money.
In the midst of this William took his family to Europe, leaving the
unpleasant task of dealing with his creditors to others – although he
later insisted he had more honourable reasons for doing so.

He gained some breathing space for a while at least, but the
newshounds were still on his tail, following him to France. While he
may have imagined he was travelling incognito, they found him 'a quiet
inmate of Dessaing's Hotel at Calais, occupying the apartment usually
occupied by the common run of travellers'. Gone were the numerous
and costly equipages, and also his 'retinue of proportionate extent and
splendour'.[187] The Americans were kept abreast of developments too,

---

eleventh Duke of Somerset, and his brother, Lord Webb Seymour, 1800 to 1819,
1906, p. 235
187 *Manchester Iris,* 22 June 1822

but in a somewhat haphazard fashion: the Washington *Daily National Intelligencer* was at pains to correct an earlier report in August 1822, which inexplicably described Catherine's father Sir James as 'one of the leeches that draw the blood out of the English people',[188] and that William's supposed half-million pound debt was the result of gaming and other extravagances by him and his wife.

The newspaper informed its readers nine days later that William's present embarrassment was not as everyone thought, the result of a fatal passion for gambling, but the enormous cost of the fine furniture purchased for Wanstead and the vast income required for the maintenance of the estate. This was probably true, and William vehemently denied losing any more than £50 at play in any one sitting.

But Wicked William and the truth were rarely on speaking terms and he denied a lot of things, often in the face of incontrovertible evidence. In his letter of 1827 to Lord Eldon he claimed the manager in control of expenditure for three years at Wanstead had robbed him of £50,000, had subsequently 'become mad, and died in a private mad-house'.[189]

The Long Wellesley family was not destined for the workhouse just yet, however. Although it was only about a sixth of her usual income, Catherine still had an independent income of £7,000 a year guaranteed by a trust jointure, nonetheless a very tidy sum, and there was the income from a further £6,000 legacy from her godfather, old Walter Long of Bath.[190]

They travelled on to Geneva from where Catherine continued regular correspondence with her sisters, who reported that their mother Lady Catherine was in failing health. She died at Draycot in January 1823. Catherine wrote from Naples to her sister Dora of 'her heartfelt pain at hearing the sad, sad news, that their excellent mother was no more'. William displayed uncharacteristically good behaviour, Catherine writing that she had received 'the greatest kindness and affection from Mr L.W. No human creature could have

---

188   *Niles' Weekly Register*, vol. 22, p. 402
189   William Long Wellesley, Hume Tracts, *Two letters to the Right Hon. Earl Eldon Lord Chancellor*, 1827
190   Will, Prob 11/1456

been more kind, or shown greater feeling upon the sad occasion, than he has done.'[191]

Back in England, the expectations of William's restless creditors were still unsatisfied. With his disapproving mother-in-law now permanently out of the picture, and after finding no willing buyers, William took the drastic step of ordering the complete demolition of Tylney Hall and Wanstead House so the building materials could be sold. Reputedly built at a cost of £360,000, the elegant pile dismantled from Wanstead House realised only £10,000. Catherine's father may well have turned in his grave.

Reluctantly taking control of William's affairs in England, his father Lord Maryborough advised that in order to avoid arrest he should not return for another three years, by which time he hoped to satisfy the remaining creditors and restore his finances. This self-imposed exile was necessary as William now had no immunity from prosecution for debt, since losing his seat in Parliament in 1820.

On the home front, Catherine had been aware for at least two years that William was an unfaithful husband, having paid an annuity of £600 to keep away one Mrs Maria Kinnaird (not her real name) who claimed she had been seduced from school by him in 1821.[192] Catherine also implied in a letter to her sisters that she thought William had given her venereal disease. Indeed, he was later accused during a court case of having 'a disease'.[193] The last straw came while she was in Naples with William and the children.

He had begun an affair with Mrs Helena Bligh, wife of Captain Thomas Bligh, a Guards officer, which was soon conducted right under Catherine's nose. In despair she left her husband and went to Paris. William was hot on her heels to attempt reconciliation – with Helena Bligh still in tow – but Catherine knew the hopelessness of the situation she now found herself in. Evidence would later be given that Lord Maryborough had come to Paris at her request to try and

191   Barry, *op. cit.* p. 36
192   Couzens, *op. cit.* Hartley Library Southampton, Wellington Letters, p. 94
193   James Russell, *Reports of Cases Argued and Determined in the High Court of Chancery during the time of Lord Chancellor Eldon, 1826, 1827*, vol. II, 1829. *Wellesley V. Beaufort*, p. 249

'effect a dissolution of the scandalous connexion' between his son and Mrs Bligh. When the furious William discovered the visit was at the instigation of Catherine he bellowed at her so loudly, he was 'audible all over the Place Vendôme'.[194]

In a depressed state of mind and failing health, Catherine returned to England with her children, and on obtaining legal advice she commenced divorce proceedings. Ever mindful of the debts still hanging over his head in England, William dared not return. Instead he wrote pleading letters to Catherine, and informed his father that his wife had left him. Maryborough wrote a scolding reply, rejecting his son's accusation that 'your good and sensible wife' had acted too hastily, and laid the blame almost entirely on 'that horrible monster' Helena Bligh. 'If you do not separate yourself from this profligate witch you must share her fate.'[195] But William as usual paid no heed to good advice, however colourfully worded, and a year later, in August 1825, Helena gave birth to a natural son, William Wellesley-Bligh.

Leaving Draycot in early September, the desperately miserable Catherine moved in with her sisters Dora and Emma at the Paragon, Richmond, not far from London. On 12 September 1825, within five days of her arrival, she died, just a few weeks short of her thirty-sixth birthday. In what was subsequently termed a 'moral murder', both sides of the family, and probably everyone else, blamed Wicked William for her death. He would later write to Lord Eldon that he was 'totally ignorant of her having made a will'. This is contradicted by Emma Long. Catherine had been under the care of the royal physician, Sir Henry Holford, and Emma wrote to her uncle, Henry Windsor :

> On the evening of that day she was seized with spasms which occasioned her so much alarm that she called my sister Dora into another room and told her that as spasms in the stomach often proved fatal, she considered it her duty to revoke without delay a will she had signed some years before and which had been made under Mr Long Wellesley 's direction and probably, she added, to the disadvantage of

194   Wellesley v. Duke of Beaufort, *Glasgow Herald*, 10 March 1826
195   Couzens, *op. cit.* p. 100. From Wanstead Papers, Redbridge Library, Wellesley Pole's correspondence, transcribed by Georgina Green

her children. She then wrote a short revocation of that will and signed it in the presence of two witnesses.[196]

Among the chief mourners at her funeral was the Duke of Wellington, despite being warned by Lady Maryborough not to go for fear he would be pelted by an angry stone-throwing mob targeting anyone with the name Wellesley. The day before, William had sent a courier message that he would not be attending, advising that his children should be given into the custody of the courier in order that they be conveyed to France to live with him. Since Catherine's arrival in England she had received threatening letters from William demanding the return of his children, which so concerned her she employed a police officer to guard them against possible abduction. She had made a death-bed plea to her sisters to have them made wards of Chancery to keep them from William's destructive grasp, but it soon became apparent he would stop at nothing to try and extort custody.

And so it began.

Two months after her death Catherine's Uncle Henry Windsor (later Earl of Plymouth), together with her two sisters Emma and Dora, were appointed temporary guardians pending a court settlement to make the Duke of Wellington the children's permanent guardian. William was furious and once again demanded custody, but the public's attention was momentarily diverted when Helena Bligh's cuckolded husband began proceedings against William for having 'assaulted and debauched his wife' in a suit of criminal conversation, a quaint euphemism for adultery. The resulting media frenzy probably compromised his cause during the long drawn-out guardianship case, but eventually in February 1827 a judgement was made against him. It was the first time a father had ever been deprived of all his children for reasons other than alcoholism or madness (although he was close to both).

William immediately appealed the decision, and during his campaign to discredit those he held responsible he became quite

---

196   Couzens, *pers. com.* From Wanstead Papers, Redbridge Library, Wellesley Pole's correspondence, transcribed by Georgina Green

irrational. His unconscionable utterings knew no bounds, threatening 'most scandallous expositions of family secrets' unless his parental rights were restored. In pamphlet rants against the morality of those who deemed him an unfit father, he dragged through the mud the names of not only the Duke of Wellington but also his parents and sisters-in-law Emma and Dorothy Tylney Long. He hoped if he could 'prove that all members of the Wellesley and Long families were as vicious and immoral as he was himself, the Court of Chancery would have no choice but to grant his appeal for custody of the children'.[197] Furthermore:

> He laid an affidavit against the Misses Long [with] a string of invented horrors: that the Misses Long had picked a playfellow for their nephews who was having intercourse with his aunt; that their niece's governess and her sister were prostitutes, both living with the Misses Longs' uncle; that the younger Miss Long had committed incest with this same uncle, that all the rest of the Long family were drunken blasphemers, and that finally the children's two aunts had 'a libidinous relationship' with one another.[198]

William was a man possessed, it seemed, and during a conversation at dinner with James Grant, a colonel in the 18th Hussars, William said he would shoot the Duke of Wellington if he defeated his appeal. A panicked Grant was convinced he would carry out his threat and told a friend to expect 'a most awful catastrophe'. Fortunately for the duke, William must have had second thoughts about 'expiating the crime on the scaffold', as he told an incredulous Grant, and the crisis was averted.[199]

The House of Lords finally dismissed his appeal for custody. He lost the 'crim con' case too, despite his protests that his relationship with Mrs Bligh was always of the 'most unobtrusive kind', carefully omitting the damning fact she had given birth to his child.[200] Captain

197   Elizabeth Longford, *Wellington Pillar of State*, 1972
198   George Caunt, *The Wellesleys in Essex*, Couzens, *op. cit.* p. 97
199   Longford, *op. cit.* p. 252
200   James Russell, *op. cit.* p. 237

Bligh was awarded £6,000 damages, although extracting this amount from the Hon. William Long Wellesley would have been near impossible at best.

William seemed to be under the delusion he was a continual victim of injustice. In July 1827, five months after his original defeat in Chancery, he turned his attentions to the Draycot estate, which had not been part of the marriage settlement with Catherine. Appealing to public sympathy (which, in light of recent events, the newspaper that published his letter thought laughable), he complained Draycot was 'fast going to ruin', ridiculing its mismanagement by Mr Awdry,[201] 'a needy relative of the Misses Long'. William claimed he had nurtured it at great expense, 'which has been peculiarly injurious to my interests', conveniently forgetting that under his management

'A Bright Thought' W. Long Wellesley, © *Trustees of the British Museum*

201   Henry Awdry of Chippenham, appointed by Court of Chancery

the once magnificent Wanstead House had completely vanished from the face of the earth.

Helena Bligh's husband died at a rather convenient point in proceedings, allowing William to marry Helena in 1828. But in 1835 he denied most emphatically in a Brussels court that she was his 'legitimate wife' in an attempt to avoid paying the £1,000 per annum agreed to on their separation,[202] possibly hoping no one there had noticed their marriage announcement in the English newspapers seven years earlier.

By 1828 the Duke of Wellington was finding his duties as Prime Minister allowed little time to devote to fulfilling his role as guardian of the three children, opting primarily for dual guardianship with his wife Kitty. After refusals from several others, Sir William Courtenay agreed to take on the role, aware of the risk of exposing himself to Long Wellesley's unpredictable temperament and penchant for libel and calumny.

William continued to be a disruptive influence and was twice imprisoned in the Fleet, once briefly for debt in 1830 and again in 1831 after he kidnapped his daughter from the custody of her aunts.[203] He was by then MP for Essex and claimed parliamentary privilege, but this was disallowed by the committee after a few words in the ear of the speaker by the Lord Chancellor. William was released after young Victoria was returned to her aunts a short time later.

He succeeded his father as 4th Earl of Mornington in 1845, and throughout the remainder of his life he continued battling against perceived injustices, including with his second wife Helena and his children over money and property. Unlike the unfortunate Catherine, Helena lived long enough to be Countess of Mornington, but by then it was in name only. Seeking relief from parish authorities she claimed she was destitute.

Wicked William's reputation was now forever cemented in the minds of the public, but towards the end of his life this hardened old litigant faded into obscurity, sustained mostly by the charity of his

202   *Morning Post*, May 25, 1835, Issue 20113
203   Barry, *op. cit.* p. 67

cousin, the 2nd Duke of Wellington, who paid him an allowance of £10 a week. He received little or no benefit from an entitlement to a life interest in certain Irish estates left by his father, which were massively encumbered by his own mortgages. In his will, dated February 1854, he complains of having 'the gravest cause of dissatisfaction with the members of my family for ingratitude in leaving me to starve after having enjoyed immense benefit from my prosperity'.

He died all but destitute in London in July 1857 at the age of sixty-nine 'from a natural disease' according to an inquest held a week later at the Coachmaker's Arms. He was buried at Kensal Green Cemetery – not at Draycot, which no one would have expected, and, as the *Morning Chronicle* said, 'redeemed by no single virtue, adorned by no single grace.

V

The Last Offspring of Long of Draycot

The Heir Apparent

After the death of Kitty, Duchess of Wellington, Catherine and William's eldest son, the ponderously named eighteen-year-old William Richard Arthur Pole Tylney Long Wellesley, became rather a handful for the remaining guardians. He had been born at Wanstead House in October 1813, and at the age of ten was still unable to read, but he did expand his vocabulary under the influence of his father.

Five years earlier during the appeal of 1826 a long series of affidavits had been read to the Chancery court to show the unfitness of Wicked William as a parent, the details considered 'too gross' for publication. He had taught his children to swear. And his advice to William junior when hunting was to 'play hell and Tommy – to catch all the cats he can lay hold of – to hunt every animal on the estate, from the elephant in the forest to the fleas in the blanket'.[204]

The *Satirist*, a scurrilous rag founded in 1807 supposedly to expose impostors, considered the Long Wellesleys too irresistible not to poke barbs at, and Wicked William became known to its readers as 'Vampire Wellesley'. His son William junior was 'Young Wellesley' or 'Young Vampire'. In 1834, on William junior's coming of age, the *Satirist* reported that he came into possession of £180,000, which he had advanced to his father to enable him to discharge his numerous debts. It had been rumoured his father had already spent £30,000 of his son's fortune in eight months, and the fear was that on gaining his majority he would 'rob him of the rest'.[205]

A year earlier Wicked William had fled to France with his sons after a separation from second wife Helena. William junior had become desperately ill from what Lord Byron euphemistically termed

204 *Wellesley v. Duke of Beaufort, The Times,* 10 March 1826
205 Longford *op. cit.*

'a general subscription to the ladies',[206] prompting the Duke of Wellington to dispatch Sir William Courtenay to Brussels on a rescue mission, but this ultimately failed.

Two years later word got round of William junior's large gambling losses, the *Satirist* claiming he had been fleeced of £14,000. When his father was informed he replied 'with a burst of savage joy as if delighted that he had a son who was likely to emulate him in his multitudinous vices'. An easy target, in 1837 William junior again became the victim of play-table conspiracy after several acquaintances got him drunk. This time he refused to pay up and a pen and paper war ensued. This was finally settled by a duel at Paris between himself and the claimant, Captain Cauty.[207]

William Long Wellesley, 5th Earl of Mornington, Lady Victoria Long Wellesley, a Memoir, O. Barry

Styled Viscount Wellesley in 1845 when his father became 4th Earl of Mornington, by the time he succeeded his father as 5th earl William junior was forty-three. His father's debts had probably been the catalyst in 1848 for selling the manor of Athelhampton in Dorset, originally purchased by the auditor Sir Robert Long in 1665. The house by this time was in a poor state of repair, and had it not been held in trust for him as heir it would no doubt have already gone the same way as the other properties his father had squandered.

The last of Sir Robert Long's former properties in Yorkshire also went under the hammer. After Wicked William's death in 1857 the outstanding debts were partially settled, thanks to an insurance policy of £207,000, allowing the return to his son possession of some of the mortgaged estate of Wanstead. William junior's finances continued to improve, and while dividing his time between Paris and Draycot he began revitalising the Draycot estate.

He grew closer to his sister Victoria in his final years, and she doted on him after the premature death of their brother James. Nevertheless, he seems to have been persuaded in his final illness at Paris to change his will at the eleventh hour. Whereas in an earlier will Victoria had been sole beneficiary of what remained of the Long and Tylney properties, Lord Mornington, as William junior was now known, left these to his cousin Lord Cowley – a Wellesley. As Dorothy Tylney Long would later complain in disbelief to the Longs of Rood Ashton, the properties had passed 'into the hands of comparative strangers'.[208] Possibly Lord Mornington was reminded that Victoria would come into a small fortune on the death of their aunts, and he only bequeathed her an annuity of £1,000, a mere quarter of the annuity he bequeathed to his mistress Lucille Bruchet, also an inmate of the Hotel du Rhin, where he died.

In the midst of the profound shock and indignation his actions caused, his body was returned from Paris to Draycot for burial in the family vault. His funeral was boycotted by the Rood Ashton Longs, so appalled were they by his actions, and possibly frustrated that the last opportunity to reunite an estate of historic importance to the Long family was lost. Having no sons, his titles were merged in the Dukedom of Wellington.

208   Couzens *op. cit.* p. 116

The Lion-Hearted Dandy

The youngest son, James Fitzroy Henry Pole Tylney Long Wellesley, was also a challenge to his guardians. Elizabeth Longford says in her biography of Wellington that fourteen-year-old James was completely possessed by his father's demon; this was probably the reason he was gazetted at an early age to the 12th Lancers. 'The Facer', as he was known in certain circles, an allusion to his plucky character, was the embodiment of fashion with his fastidious dress, symmetry and style – an effeminate dandy whose affectations and appearance often made him a target.

One ardent follower of prize-fighting, Bromley Davenport MP, gives a brief description in his book *Sport* (1895) of one such altercation in 1846, 'a long remembered deed of a dandy', when James was aged thirty-one. He recalled that James was 'pale, slim, delicate and even cadaverous in appearance, with the voice of a woman; the gentlest, shyest and most unassuming of manners, and an almost irritating lisp'.

James and his companions had arrived for an evening of entertainment at one of the many 'not over-respectable night-haunts' at Haymarket, when he became the butt of coarse jokes delivered by the notorious 'Birmingham Bone-Crusher', a bruising hulk of a man who resented James's white tie and ultra-aristocratic appearance. After a while James's consummate good humour finally gave way. He walked up to the bully, and much to the astonishment of everyone present, in his sweet womanly tones said: 'Look here thir, if you behave like thith, I'm afraid I shall have to beat you.' 'Beat *me!*' roared the Crusher, amid a roomful of derisive laughter. 'Yeth,' lisped James, 'becauth you've inthulted me.'

Bystanders attempted to intervene, unaware the puny James was not exactly what he seemed, but the 'inthult' was too great to let pass. An improvised ring was formed, rules were declared and the muscle-bound Crusher quickly stripped to the waist. Like most others present, he was confident of a swift victory. But James had learned a thing or two since fracturing his thigh six years earlier during a wrestling match at an infamous saloon, when he was thrown heavily to the floor and incapacitated for several months afterwards.

Now, in his calm and deliberate manner, he peeled off his finely embroidered shirt to reveal a colourful tattoo, a large convoluted serpent encircling his body, its fangs appearing to bite into his heart. The Crusher was visibly taken aback by this, flailing a series of swashing blows artfully evaded by his lithe opponent, who twisted and jumped about until his adversary exhausted himself. Finally, with one of his long wiry arms, James dealt the decisive blow.

Together with his constant companion Lord Waterford, James was conspicuous for his wild recklessness among a certain set of young men-about-town who were both the terror and amusement of London. They made their headquarters at Limmers Hotel where James's bill was reputedly seldom less than six or seven thousand pounds at any given time. A large proportion of this was said to be money he had casually borrowed in small increments to fund his evenings out on the town. He would often be heard lisping to Sam, the old waiter at Limmers, 'Tham, give me ten pounds,' and on his return, 'Tham, pay my cab.'

Occasionally he would return in the early hours with the floor of the cab strewn with door-knockers, drunkenly wrenched off, and once with a gigantic wooden carved Scots Highlander in full kit, torn from the outside of a tobacconist's shop. It was incumbent on the faithful Sam to stow James's collection of purloined curios in Limmers' cellar, which soon became so full that recourse had to be made to his friend Captain Billy Duff's 'museum' at his house in Bruton Street, adding to an already diverse collection of souvenirs, similarly acquired.

Since James and his brother William had spent much of their childhood under the guardianship of their great-uncle, the Duke of Wellington, they saw little of their sister Victoria, living with their maternal aunts Dorothy and Emma. Towards the end of his short life James wrote to Victoria from Carlow in Ireland where he was stationed with his regiment, anticipating a reconciliation with her and their aunts on the same terms 'that I was when I was a child'.[209] Inevitably as time passed and his debts continued to mount, the courageous 'Facer' evaded responsibility by removing to Geneva.

209   Barry, *op. cit.* p. 89

In a later court case brought by Victoria against her father it was stated that in January 1847 James was in a very infirm state of health, both bodily and mentally, from which he never rallied up to the time of his death, though he had 'never been found lunatic by inquisition'. From Geneva he moved to Nice, and was later confined at Turin. A large part of an annuity administered by his brother had paid for his hospital care, and he died unmarried in October 1851, aged thirty-six. He had lived a life without regard to the consequences, probably just as his father had ordered, and he left no will. As administrator of his estate, his father was the one from whom James's creditors now sought restitution, an action all too familiar to Wicked William, and several court cases followed.

The Heir Presumptive

Their only sister, Lady Victoria Catherine Mary Pole Tylney Long Wellesley, grew up with mixed feelings for her father, who included her with her brothers in the swearing lessons, taking special delight in hearing his little girl repeat words no small child should. It was the only part of her education, the Chancery court heard in 1826, that he ever took any interest in. For the first part of her life she led a mostly reclusive existence with her aunts, away from the scrutiny of the public in whose memory the scandals lingered.

After the custody battle Victoria was allowed to see her father once a year at Apsley House, the Duke of Wellington's London residence, but only under the supervision of the duke's wife Kitty. The inheritance in 1857 of £13,542 on her father's death (protected by a trust fund) allowed her to set up her own household in Sussex at Eastbourne, and later at Bolney Lodge, near Cuckfield. According to her goddaughter and biographer Olivia Barry, it was later while living at Madehurst Lodge on the Goodwood estate, leased from the Duke of Richmond, that she developed a close friendship with the family of her cousin Captain John Stuart Lindsay Long, grandson of Walter Long of Preshaw. Captain Long lived four miles away at Walberton, Arundel, in a house he inherited from his father John, called The Firs (now Firgrove).

Victoria felt a deep sense of loss and betrayal over Draycot, and soon after her brother William's death in 1863 she wrote to Walter

Lady Victoria Long Wellesley c.1879, Lady Victoria Long Wellesley, a Memoir,
O. Barry

Long at Rood Ashton: 'the pointed insult intended to myself is very evident'. Legal advice confirmed her suspicion that her brother's last minute change of will was 'not uninfluenced'. But she did not hold him responsible, rather 'a concoction of the terrible set with which he was most unfortunately surrounded. My wish would have been that after our own immediate heirs, all Long property should have returned to your family as the elder branch.' [210]

Her aunts had lived with her at Bolney Lodge for two years until just after the death at Paris of Lord Mornington, and during the difficult time that followed they provided what moral support they could. Victoria held up remarkably well under the circumstances, her aunt Dorothy writing to Walter's son Richard Penruddocke Long : 'our niece bears most cheerfully the loss of property to which she seemed so fairly entitled . . . but she feels the disrespect to her poor mother's family'. Commiserating with him over 'poor lost Draycot and the Long property generally', she lists a number of missing portraits, referring to an incident several years before when a quantity of significant family possessions had been passed out of the library window to George Robins, the original auctioneer during the sale of Wanstead. He had sought to recover a £3,000 debt incurred by 'Mr Long Wellesley, the great spoliator'. [211]

Dorothy's death at Madehurst Lodge in November 1872 was followed seven years later by Emma's in July 1879, aged eighty-seven. At probate their effects were valued at under £140,000 and £180,000 respectively. With the exception of several charitable bequests, most of this money, together with the last remnants of the Tylney Long estate preserved by various trusts, passed to Victoria. She was now just over sixty years old and at last very wealthy in her own right.

Her biographer Olivia Barry paints a glowing picture of Victoria as an example of piety and generosity, the remainder of whose blameless life was spent doing good works and supporting charities, which she certainly did. A lasting memorial to her beneficence is the Italianate-style All Souls' church at Eastbourne, which she had built between 1881 and 1882 with nearly £30,000 of her own money.

210   Couzens *op. cit.* p. 131
211   WSA ref 947:2122

The cosseted life with her aunts had been far preferable to the unthinkable alternative under the 'care' of her unstable father, but if she felt bitterness about all that had happened she kept it to herself, saying only that 'the greatest sorrow of her life' was losing Draycot. The estate was sold in 1920 after the death of Lord Cowley and the house was commandeered by the army at the outbreak of the Second World War. It was demolished between 1952 and 1954 after being earmarked for destruction since 1949, having long lain empty.[212] After the death of her remaining aunt Emma in 1879, Victoria leased from the Duke of Richmond another of his Goodwood estate properties, West Stoke House, together with over five acres of gardens.

Victoria died at West Stoke at the end of March 1897 after a paralytic seizure. Her remains were conveyed to London before being taken to Draycot church for a funeral service. The Right Hon. Walter Hume Long MP (of Rood Ashton) sent his apologies, unable to attend owing to a cabinet council meeting. After a second funeral service at Eastbourne the coffin was returned to Draycot where she was finally laid to rest.

Her personal estate was valued at just over £332,000, and she appointed Captain J.S.L. Long one of her executors. Her cousins received large bequests of money and jewellery, and a long list of charitable organisations benefited under her will. The Bolney Lodge estate was settled on Captain Long, her residuary legatee. Walter Hume Long was left most of the books from the library at Draycot, the reversion of the sum of £12,500 and the option to purchase her London house in Portland Place.

And so, with the last of the family safely tucked up, the Long family crypt at Draycot was finally sealed.

212   Couzens, *pers. com.*

VI
The Descent of South Wraxall Continued

Here we leave the now extinct Longs of Draycot and return to the seventeenth century to pursue the line of South Wraxall, the estate once again restored to the previously disinherited John, son of Sir Walter Long the elder and stepson of the scheming Catherine Thynne. This manor was destined to follow a tortuous route between different branches of the Long family due to failure of issue. John had married Anne, daughter of Sir William Eyre of Chalfield, and the properties passed sideways via their grandson, Hope Long of South Wraxall, to another grandson, Walter Long.[213]

Walter would have to manage his newly-acquired estates with care. Towards the latter half of the seventeenth century and into the beginning of the eighteenth, estate revenues had progressively slowed from their previous buoyant post-Civil War levels. Agricultural prices too were trending downwards, affecting the tenants' ability to keep up their rents. Perhaps Walter spent more time making improvements to his farms hopeful of maintaining good paying tenants rather than turning his eye with any enthusiasm towards Westminster.

But turn it he did, and after his election as MP for Calne in 1701 Walter appears somewhat half-hearted in his commitment to political life. Although he pledged his loyalty by signing the 'Association' drawn up by the Commons in response to a papist conspiracy to assassinate the king, he was otherwise inactive in the House. Dying unmarried in 1731, he left his estates to the sons of his cousin Katherine[214] who had married her cousin John Long of Monkton.[215] These sons were the Rev. John Long of South Wraxall

---

213   Son of Walter Long and Barbara Brayfield. Based in Bristol, he resided occasionally at Gloucester and South Wraxall
214   Sister of Hope Long
215   Son of John Long senior and grandson of Edward Long, both of Monkton

(d. 1749) and his brother Thomas Long of Melksham.

Thomas Long of Melksham (1678–1759)

Thomas, Katherine's second son, had moved from South Wraxall to carry on his cloth-making at Melksham, five miles down the road. He rented a house near the old Melksham Bridge from its previous occupier and owner Thomas Smith, who had built himself a new house just out of town at Shaw Farm. At the time of his marriage to Mary Abbot of Chippenham in 1709, Thomas Long was, according to their marriage settlement, 'really and bonafide worth in personal estate' £1,200, half of this being in ready money and stock in trade.

One of his pattern books still survives, covering the entire time he was in trade from 1699 to 1728. It details the cloth, quality and length, name of the clothworker and the buyer, price per yard and total price realised. At the back are various lists of cloths, accounts of wool bought and notes of household expenses, with a few samples of dyed cloth and wool still attached to the pages. Thomas's business was modest compared to some Wiltshire clothiers; he averaged 39 cloths a year, some years as many as 70 and in a lean year only 22. Much of the spinning was done at Yatesbury, where he also had a house. Weaving alone took two to three weeks, which could only commence once all the wool had been scribbled and the warp had been spun, taking the total production time for one cloth to two or three months. Thomas sent the finished cloth to Blackwell Hall in London where middlemen, or 'factors' controlled the sale of cloth to customers.

But just getting his cloth out of Melksham was a hazardous business. The roads had been flooded by the Avon so often each winter that they were rendered impassable by horses and carriages, 'to the great danger of travellers, and the disappointment and prejudice of the woollen manufactures and other traders'. It had become so bad, that in 1752 an Act of Parliament was initiated and supported by Sir Robert Long of Draycot to raise money by way of toll gates to repair the roads.

Thomas Long's landlord Thomas Smith kept a diary detailing his own day-to-day business and social encounters around Melksham. His tenant Thomas Long, whom he frequently refers to as 'Mr Long of the Bridge', was also part of his social circle. Their wives appear to have had a close friendship, along with 'Mrs Horton of Broughton', who took day trips with them to Bath. In March 1716, while on one of his frequent visits to Thomas Long, Smith was surprised to find the company still seated at the dinner table as late as four o'clock in the afternoon, celebrating the baptism of the Longs' third daughter, Ellen.

Alongside his usual business Smith mentions evenings spent in the tavern, visits to neighbouring houses to drink 'a dish of tea', dinners, card games afterwards and conversations about politics and local affairs. Sometimes their hosts were more than liberal with their hospitality, and on one occasion Smith 'was so overcome with Liquor and in so bad a State that I knew not what I did and too bad to be mention'd; only I make my sincere Acknowledgement to my Creator and Preserver, and stedfastly promise never to commit the like beastly Wickedness.' The next morning he awoke with an enormous hangover, 'not in scarce a sensible condition', hardly able to eat or drink anything all day. Smith died just over a year later, although probably not from the effects of a habitual overindulgence in alcohol.

Besides 'Mr Long of the Bridge', Smith also mentions 'Mr Long of the Farm'. The latter was a cousin, also named Thomas Long (c.1657–1730), a justice of the peace who owned Rowden Farm five miles from Melksham.

Thomas Long of Melksham 's unmarried elder brother, the Rev. John Long, was sometime rector of Meyseyhampton, Gloucestershire and a fellow of Corpus Christi College, Oxford, hence the moniker 'the Oxonian' in Smith's diary. At John's death in 1748 Thomas inherited South Wraxall and the former estates of their cousin Walter Long in entail, which included the manors of Whaddon and Tytherton Kellaways, property in Box, Atworth and Chalfield.

Thomas died in January 1759, two months short of his eighty-first birthday. He appointed as executrixes the elder two of his four daughters, Mary and Anne Long, then living at Whaddon House, who with the help of their stewards, managed all these properties in more than twenty-eight locations in Gloucestershire, Somerset and Wiltshire, let on a bi-annual rental. The heir to this great fortune was Thomas's only son Walter.

A Man of Parsimonious Habits

According to his obituary, Thomas's heir 'entered into the fashionable world, and partook of its various pleasures, but never so far as to injure his own constitution'. A posthumous whitewash perhaps; Walter did indeed sample some of the dubious diversions offered to a young man residing in early eighteenth-century London, while at the same time pursuing his legal studies at the Inns of Court.

His father had apprenticed him to Thomas Moore of New Inn, for which he paid £225 in 1730. He wrote to his son encouraging him in his studies, but bemoaned reports of his wanton behaviour and extravagance, pressing him to cultivate the good favour of his uncle, the Rev. John Long,[216] then life-tenant of the entailed estates. While acquiring a smattering of legal knowledge which would ultimately prove of little practical value, Walter enjoyed the variety and comparative bustle of London, sending letters home to his four spinster sisters with entertaining snippets of news.[217]

Probably to increase his chances on the matrimonial front, Walter chose to live at Bath in Gay Street rather than under the watchful eyes of his four spinster sisters, now living at the old manor house at South Wraxall. The *Antiquary* (Vol. 21, 1889) says of these ladies' night time routine at the Manor: '[the] four old ladies, sisters, chose this room [next to the Raleigh Room] to sleep in, as it commanded on each side a small staircase leading to the upper rooms, so that the old ladies could despatch their men and maid-servants to bed in good time and in discreet order, and then, locking each door across the stairs, sleep themselves the sleep of the just, with, however, an eye upon each staircase'.

Walter was nine months short of his fortieth birthday when in February 1752 Mr T. Robinson, one of his London friends, wrote him a letter warning of the perils of marriage, having heard a rumour emanating from Bath that Walter was seriously involved with a young lady there: 'in short, that the Matrimonial Trap is baited and set for you and that you are soon to be caught in the noose'.

216   WSA, ref 947:1874
217   *Ibid,* ref 947:1875

Robinson thought this an 'improbable article of intelligence' in light of their previous conversations on the subject, and his observation 'that most of the dispositions [of women] I have met with stand in a near relationship to the Barometer and under at least as many variable influences. By this piece of knowledge I have come not to be surprised at anything they do, or by applying the modern word Humbugg to most things they say, am now seldom deceiv'd.' He also hoped the lady in question had not insisted Walter give up his pipe-smoking habit.[218]

At the age of forty-seven, and his wild days long behind him, the inheritance in 1759 of Whaddon, South Wraxall and the other estates made Walter an extremely wealthy man. Despite his reputation as a miserly squire, he had on numerous occasions been generous and extremely liberal.[219] He was sheriff of Wiltshire in 1763 and the following year stood as parliamentary candidate for Bath, losing by one vote. This vote was afterwards the subject of contention in the House of Commons, but the result was upheld and his opponent John Smith duly elected.

Despite his wealth, Walter's lifestyle was not ostentatious, and in that sparkling town of the conspicuously well-dressed he must have looked incongruous in his unfashionable garb and three-cornered hat, long out of vogue. Perhaps he had taken the advice of his London friend Robinson to heart on the subject of marriage, avoiding the 'baited matrimonial trap' of 1752. But then in 1771 at the age of sixty, Walter finally found the real Miss Right. Or so he thought. The object of his desire was Miss Elizabeth Linley, the beautiful sixteen-year-old daughter of Thomas Linley, an impoverished composer of Bath. Elizabeth was a celebrated singer, guileless and romantic, surrounded by admiring fops, but her mercenary father eventually persuaded her to accept a marriage proposal from the vastly wealthy Walter, which Linley had engineered, all the while with his own eyes on the prize.

No doubt Walter could hardly believe his luck, and it was a shock to the world of pleasure-seekers at Bath to learn that Elizabeth, who had turned a cold shoulder to so many others, had promised her

218   WSA ref 947:1877
219   For example, he made a 'voluntary contribution for the service of the State' of £2,000 in 1798, *St James's Chronicle*, issue 6274

hand to such an elderly and unattractive suitor, a man old enough
to be her grandfather. They were the talk of society, and tongues
wagged ceaselessly in scorn and derision at the odd match, but Walter
optimistically loaded his bride-to-be with costly presents, showering
jewels on her and buying her a trousseau fit for a queen.

Playwright Samuel Foote, the great social agitator, seized the
opportunity to make it the subject of his next play. Fearing ridicule,
Walter attempted to persuade Foote to stop production, threatening
violence when he refused. He then commenced legal action[220] and
made an unsuccessful appeal to the lord chamberlain. But all his efforts
were in vain; *The Maid of Bath* opened at the Haymarket Theatre,
London, in June 1771.

It was a great success: Foote added his own embellishments to
the story which mostly had a ring of truth. The character of Walter
Long, played by Foote himself, was named Solomon Flint, described
as miserable and battered, a fat, fusty, shabby, shuffling, money loving,
water drinking,[221] mirth-marring, amorous old hunks, who owned
half the farms in the country, being sixty at least and a filthy old goat.
He had a rumbling old family coach and an old haunted house in the
country. Walter's sisters also received a lampooning: they were 'sour
as fusty malicious old maids, as ever were sour'd by solitude and the
neglect of the world'.

In September, on the eve of the wedding, it was suddenly
announced that the nuptials which Bath had been excitedly anticipating,
would not take place. The cruel London wits made great fun of this
new development. Elizabeth's father was furious, threatening Walter
with a lawsuit. The story goes that Elizabeth confided to Walter that
she could never be happy as his wife, and he reluctantly agreed to
honour her wishes, ultimately appeasing her father by settling £3,000
on her, allowing her to keep the valuable jewels and other presents.
The furore and adverse publicity the whole affair generated ensured
Walter's reputation was further tarnished. Not only was he – in the
eyes of the public at least – a miserly old codger, but a bounder and cad

---

220   *Lloyds Evening Post*, 5 July 1771
221   Water drinking was avoided except by those in extreme poverty

to boot. Either way, he was going to be the subject of cruel criticism, whether he married Elizabeth or not.

Elizabeth's thoughts meanwhile lay elsewhere, and the breaking of the engagement eventually led to her elopement with the man she really loved, the young handsome playwright and poet Richard Brinsley Sheridan. When the opportunity arose he took her off to London before clandestinely crossing the English Channel to Dunkirk, where they were married. Their only income for the first few years was said to be the interest on the money Walter had settled on her, much to the gratitude of the notoriously lazy Sheridan. But Elizabeth's life was cut short by tuberculosis, and she died at Bristol in 1792, aged just thirty-eight.

Thwarted in his marriage plans and publicly humiliated, Walter was still left with the dilemma of who would inherit his fortune. He was no longer a young man, but even so, like his father who also lived to a great age, he faced another thirty-five years of bachelorhood to ponder the point. He didn't sit around twiddling his thumbs however. Four years later in 1775, Walter's housekeeper Sally Roberts gave birth to his daughter, Augusta. In 1778 another daughter was born, named Sally after her mother. But as children born out of wedlock they could never inherit their father's vast wealth.

The goal of landed families such as the Longs had always been to ensure the continuation of name, seat, estate and title under the laws of primogeniture, occasionally supplemented by other devices. A demographic crisis occurred in the late seventeenth and early eighteenth centuries, during which the proportion of males who left no sons to survive them promoted the probability of extinction in the male line, thus precipitating the practice of name changing. The Long family frequently found themselves having to resort to a collateral branch, a prospect which Walter would ultimately embrace in search of an heir.

A nineteenth-century correspondent of the antiquarian magazine *Notes & Queries* claimed Walter attempted to make Mr John

Palmer, MP of Bath, his heir. Palmer's mother was allegedly Jane Long, born 1715, supposedly from the Baynton family of Longs. The *Oxford Dictionary of National Biography (Vol 43)* states vaguely that Jane was one of the Longs of Wraxall Manor. C. R. Clear in *John Palmer Mail Coach Pioneer* (1955) says Palmer's mother was *née* Figgins of Devizes, married to Palmer senior at Christmas 1737, so Jane Long may have been the latter's second wife. Whether she was indeed related to old Walter Long has yet to be discovered. According to the story, Palmer was to agree to change his name to Long as a condition of inheritance, which he refused to do.

Over his lifetime Walter had purchased more property and had renewed the leases of many of his tenants at their old rents a few years before his death, despite the value of his estates reputedly rising in value upwards of £100,000. Sums of this magnitude were often a journalistic exaggeration, but it would be fair to say Walter's income was very large; between 1750 and 1815 rents throughout the country nearly trebled.[222] In short, he had more money than he knew what to do with. Apparently still sharp as a tack and able to quote the Odes of Horace from memory, Walter died at Bath in January 1807 aged ninety-five, survived by his eighty-nine-year-old sister Katherine, who still lived at South Wraxall manor. She died in 1814 at the age of ninety-six, apparently the last legitimate descendant of the Longs of South Wraxall. This point would later be contested by one Mr Walter Chitty.

Despite Walter's final request to be buried 'without pomp and ostentation', his remains were carried from Bath in a great funeral procession to Whaddon: 'first, seven men on horseback, then men with plumes of feathers, his own mourning chaise and four, the hearse and six, Lord Hood 's coach and six, and post-chaise and six, six chaises and pair, and the concourse of people that follow'd were not to be numbered'.[223] He was buried in the elaborately carved marble mausoleum he'd had built for himself, decorated with amphorae and Roman torches.

222   Mingay, *op. cit.* p. 94
223   Philip Lybbe Powys, *Passages from the Diaries of Mrs Philip Lybbe Powys of Hardwick House, Oxon. AD 1756–1808*, p. 364

To his sister Katherine he bequeathed the manor at South Wraxall for her life, together with the interest on bank stocks said to be worth £200,000, and the proceeds from rents on the various estates. After her death this fortune passed in trust, at Walter's direction, to Richard Godolphin Long of Rood Ashton, his brother John and their cousin Daniel Jones,[224] both of Monkton Farleigh. He bequeathed several other large sums to many different individuals.

Of the £12,000 his cousin Sir James Tylney Long of Draycot had borrowed from him, the principal and interest Walter bequeathed to his sister Katherine, and after her decease £6,000 in trust for his god-daughter, sixteen-year-old Catherine Tylney Long, Sir James's eldest daughter. The remaining £6,000 was put in trust for her sisters Dorothy and Emma equally. Some errors in the detail of Walter's will appeared in the press shortly after his death, one newspaper claiming that Catherine Tylney Long, already wealthy beyond imagination, inherited his estates. Another contradicted this by saying she only inherited the reversion, but neither was correct.

By the time Walter died both his illegitimate daughters were married and well settled in life. And he was a grandfather. Ten years earlier Augusta had become the wife of John Biddulph of Ledbury, partner in the London banking firm Cocks Biddulph and Co. Walter provided an estate valued at £2,000 as her marriage settlement. The Biddulphs had ten children, and their grandson Michael, Liberal Unionist and MP, became 1st Baron Biddulph. Walter's younger daughter Sally married Philip Jones of Sugwas Court, High Sheriff of Herefordshire in 1812. Old Walter left his daughters and their mother very well provided for, each receiving cash bequests equivalent to about £400,000 in today's money. He appointed both their husbands, together with the Rev. Charles Coxwell, executors of his estate.

The will of Walter's sister Katherine was proved in January 1814 shortly after she died, her personal effects sworn under £175,000 (approx. £1.2m.) After almost one hundred substantial individual legacies, her two executors Thomas Bruges and the Rev. Charles

---

224   Grandson of Richard Long (d. 1760) of Rood Ashton: thereafter known as Daniel Jones Long

Coxwell received the residue of her estate, which at the time exceeded £100,000. This created animosity between the latter two gentlemen and Katherine's cousins, the Longs of Rood Ashton. The idea of such large amounts of 'Long' property leaving the family was never going to go down well.

The Chitty Claim

Some fifty years later Mr Walter Chitty (b. 1843), headmaster of St John's School at Pewsey, Wiltshire, took a great interest in the estates that had passed from old Walter Long of Bath to the Longs of Rood Ashton. He privately published a book with his grandmother's chronologically unlikely claim that she was a 'kind of' forty-fifth cousin to the Duke of Wellington 'This I afterwards found to be perfectly true, and no one would doubt it after comparing her nose to the Duke of Wellington.' His grandmother also told him she was a descendant in a direct female line of the Longs of Wiltshire,[225] which prompted his own investigations. He became convinced of his descent from Hope Long, believing himself entitled to the estates of Hope Long's great-niece Katherine Long of South Wraxall as her heir-at-law.

Chitty mounted a challenge, putting forward his research and a prospectus for his book, *Historical Account of the Family of Long of Wiltshire* (1889). This provoked a flurry of correspondence from the Longs and their lawyers, refuting his claims.[226] The will of Miss Katherine Long mentions Mrs Catherine Rossiter, whom Chitty names as his great-great-grandmother, who was at South Wraxall at the time of Miss Long's death. Catherine Rossiter was born Catherine Tidcombe Sabin, her grandmother was Catherine Long, daughter of Hope Long and his wife Mary. The Longs of Rood Ashton adamantly stood their ground and Chitty was unsuccessful in his claim. *(See Long of Monkton, Rood Ashton and Melksham)*

Determined nevertheless to claw back something of his heritage, he laid claim to the estates of his ancestor Michael Tidcombe, a lawyer of Devizes, whose properties had been sequestered in the seventeenth

---

225   W. Chitty, *All the Blood of all the Howards, with a Little of Other People's*, 1906
226   WSA ref 947:2189/1

century during the Civil War. He made application to the secretary of state, and also to King Edward VII, who both said in reply the date was too far back for the matter to be considered, and the estates remained the property of the Crown.[227]

Another story of interest to Chitty was that of the peerage claimant Walter Hope Long Howard, son of William Howard and his wife Catherine Tidcombe, and uncle of the previously mentioned Catherine Tidcombe Sabin. William Howard, according to his son, had been acknowledged as a relative by Edward Howard, 9th Duke of Norfolk. Norfolk had supported William Howard financially and paid for Walter Hope Long Howard's education at the English College at St Omer.

In 1793 W.H.L Howard found himself seriously in debt and applied to Charles, 11th Duke of Norfolk for assistance. In late December 1795 Norfolk released Howard from debtors' prison and settled him and his wife on a property at Ewood in Surrey. However, before doing so Norfolk had requested the heralds investigate Howard's relationship to the ducal line. They had been unable to prove a connection, and so Norfolk ordered Howard take the name of Smith.

Howard returned to London to complain, but Norfolk refused to see him and consequently excluded him from the property at Ewood. The correction of the College of Arms pedigree of the ducal family and the resumption of the Ewood property became Howard's obsession. This led him to question the right of Bernard Edward Howard of Glossop, Derbyshire, to be presumptive heir to the dukedom. In 1805 he wrote to Lord Chancellor Eldon, and even attempted to address the House of Lords. Howard gained the nickname 'Heir of Poverty' after his campaign attracted attention from the press.

Thomas Banks, proprietor of the so-called Dormant Peerage Office, took an interest in Howard's cause. He wrote pamphlets inspired by the case – *An Analysis of the Genealogical History of the Family of Howard* (1812) and *Ecce homo: the Mysterious Heir, or, Who is Mr Walter Howard?* (1815). Both implied the rightful holder of the titles was not the present 11th Duke of Norfolk but Walter Hope

227   *Wiltshire Notes and Queries,* vol. 4, pt. 1, 1902

Long Howard. Howard drew up a petition with Banks's assistance, and it was presented to the prince regent in April 1812. Two weeks later Howard waylaid the prince in Pall Mall, for which he apologised in another letter, and on presenting himself at Norfolk House he was taken into custody.

When the debauched 11th duke died the interest of the press and mischief-makers in Howard's cause weakened. His annuity was restored following the accession of Bernard Edward, 12th Duke of Norfolk, and he lived on that until his death in 1830 or 1831.[228] Later independent investigations by various individuals neither conclusively proved nor disproved Howard's claim.

228   Gordon Goodwin, 'Howard, Walter Hope Long (1759–1830/31)', *rev.* Matthew Kilburn, *Oxford Dictionary of National Biography*, Oxford University Press, 2004; online edn, Jan 2011

VII
Long of Whaddon

Although the manor of Whaddon had taken a side-step into the hands of old Walter Long of Bath before it reached the Longs of Rood Ashton in the nineteenth century, it is necessary to turn the clock back a few hundred years to understand where the ownership of this manor began.

Henry Long of Whaddon (c.1510–58)

Henry's grandfather Thomas Long of Semington (d. 1509) was among the legion of West Wiltshire clothiers renowned for their white woollen broadcloth, increasingly in demand in London towards the end of the fifteenth century. Thomas and his wife Johane had eight children, including at least two sons living, both called John – the younger of which is referred to in the will of William, his brother, as 'Litill John'. Henry's father, Henry senior, who was buried at Semington in 1535, had with his wife, also named Johane, at least seven children; Henry Long of Whaddon was the fourth of these.

Known informally as Harry, Henry engaged in agriculture in addition to his clothmaking business, advancing his family by seizing opportunities offered by an expanding economy and a fortuitous marriage. His wife Mary was the daughter of the wealthy clothier Thomas Horton of Iford. Horton had died suddenly in 1549 while in London on business, the same day he hurriedly made his will. This he did in the presence of several London merchants and two notable West Country clothiers: his brother-in-law Robert Barkesdale and son-in-law Henry Winchcombe. He appointed his other son-in-law Henry Long as overseer.

Henry Long and Henry Winchcombe's father John, 'famous clothier of Newbury', were probably similar in age and habits of dress. When granted an audience with Henry VIII Winchcombe went attired in 'a plain russet coat, a pair of white kersie slopps, or breeches, without welt or guard, and stocking of the same piece, sewed to his slopps, which had a great codpiece, whereupon he stuck his pins.'[229] Utilising his codpiece as a pin-cushion might have been unusual, but Winchcombe was obviously a practical man.

Henry Long's in-laws had also prospered as clothiers in Wiltshire: Mary's maternal grandfather Thomas Barkesdale was himself the most successful of the neighbouring Keevil clothiers, who once sold cloth worth nearly 400 marks on long-term credit to merchants bound to him in 500 marks, to be paid either in cash or malmsey wine.[230]

The cloth industry had become the mainstay for this line of the family, with Henry's elder brother Thomas Long of Trowbridge also rising to considerable affluence. Thomas was endeared as a 'friend' by Sir Thomas Long of Draycot[231] which perhaps indicates recognition of their common ancestry, demonstrating a familiarity that otherwise did not exist between the socially diverse clothiers and knights.

Thomas also allied himself to another wealthy clothier family with his marriage to Johanna Yerbury. Well-positioned to take advantage of market trends, the substantial profits he made enabled him to purchase the manors of Calstone, Godswell, Westbury, Maddington, Hilperton, West Ashton and Polston, and land at Whaddon. He received a grant of arms, considered a mark of recognition and respectability. When he died in 1562 Thomas was lord of nine manors; however the cloth industry had already begun to lose some of its momentum by this time. It was still a profitable living for his widow Johanna, who carried on their business for another twenty years until her death in 1582.

As Thomas and his wife were both Catholics he instructed that 'an honest godlie Catholic preacher shall make three godlie sermons for me at my burial'. They had an only child who died young, and

229   Joseph Strutt, *op. cit.* vol. II, p. 143
230   E. Crittal, *The Woollen Industry Before 1550, A History of the County of Wiltshire*, vol. 4, 1959, pp. 115-147
231   Mentioned in the will (pr. 1556) of Sir Henry Longe of Draycot as 'my friend Thomas Long of Trowbridge', to whom he entrusted the custody of a child called 'Franncis' then living in his household

he bequeathed all his property to his brother Henry of Whaddon (who predeceased him), and thereafter to Henry's son Edward, the original purchaser of Rood Ashton. Thomas's legacy became the basis of the widespread estates of the Longs of Rood Ashton right up until the twentieth century. Two of Thomas's brothers left Wiltshire but continued in the wool trade: William at Beckington, Somerset, and Robert, a mercer in London, who also received a grant of arms.

But back to Henry, whose occupation of Whaddon, the main part of the manor purchased with its fulling mill from Sir Andrew Bayntun in 1555,[232] allowed him to carry on his own clothmaking independently of his brother Thomas. Henry's was also a thriving business and he died a very wealthy man in November 1558. When writing his will less than a month beforehand, his wife was 'quick with child'. He specified two alternative provisions, dependent on the infant being either a 'manchild' or a 'maid'. In the event it was a baby girl called Eleanor.

Henry made in excess of sixty substantial bequests including land, houses, money, silver, gold jewellery, cloth, household goods and farm animals to individual family members, godchildren and friends, and not forgetting 'my weavers that now doth weave to me at this present time'. Henry could afford to be a smart dresser: he bequeathed to one fortunate legatee 'my best satin doublet, my gown faced with taffeta, one jacket of chamlett, one coat of cloth adorned with fringe, my best cap and one new night cap of satin'. He left benefactions to the poor and also money to purchase building materials for Whaddon church, and a load of stones to finish the bridge at Semington.

To his eldest son Thomas, besides lands in Westbury, he left the Bear Inn at Reading, Berkshire, previously owned by his wife's grandfather, Thomas Barkesdale. Henry actually had two sons living named Thomas. In his will he referred to them as 'Thomas my oldest son' and 'Thomas my youngest son'; presumably they had nicknames to differentiate one from the other.

At about the time of Henry's death his widow Mary made her own will. She died four years later in 1562, unusually with all

232   H F Chettle, W R Powell, P A Spalding and P M Tillott, 'Parishes: Whaddon', in *A History of the County of Wiltshire:* vol. 7, ed. R B Pugh and Elizabeth Crittall (London, 1953), pp. 171-174

twelve of their children surviving her. Her cautious bequest to her eldest son Thomas was 'on condition that he keep himself in honest testament and good behaviour, and that he [not] trouble my husband's Executors'. Money, household goods, clothing and jewellery were distributed among her family, with the residue of her plate to her third son Edward of Monkton, whom she made sole executor.

Nine years later in May 1571 there was much ado in Parliament after the election of the new member for Westbury. One Thomas Long, called 'Gentleman', the lowest honorific description in the stratum of gentry, considered his ownership of property at Westbury qualification enough for a seat in Parliament. He paid the mayor of that town, Anthony Garland and a man called Watts, £4 for the privilege. Thomas, far from a well-travelled sophisticated man of the world, was deemed not of sufficient capacity to serve. When questioned about how he came to be elected, he readily confessed.

This bribery was unprecedented, causing uproar in the House for two days. It was ordered that Thomas's money be repaid to him. The corporation of Westbury was fined £20 for the queen's use 'for the said lewd and slanderous attempt' [233] and the activities of Garland and Watts were scrutinised even more closely.

The identity of the said 'Thomas Long, gentleman of Westbury' has been adopted on a balance of probabilities as being the elder son of Henry and Mary – the inheritor of property at Westbury, who was only nineteen when his father died. His wardship was granted to his uncle, Thomas Long of Trowbridge, with an annuity of £4. Reading between the lines of his mother's will regarding her hopes for his future behaviour, he may have indeed been a man given to unwise impulse. Called 'clothyer' in his younger brother Thomas's will of 1590, he married his first cousin Joan Yerbury. Making his will six days before his death in June 1593, he was buried at Semington, 'with my ancestors'.

While some elder sons and their heirs carried on the cloth trade, younger sons farmed the land they inherited. Occasionally one or two were placed in an aristocratic household as a kind of finishing school, such as Henry and Mary's great-grandson, Richard Long.[234] He was gentleman waiter to Ludovic Stewart, 2nd Duke of Lennox and 1st Duke of Richmond, a cousin and trusted courtier of James I. The duke's widow, the Duchess Frances (*née* Howard), was a former daughter-in-law to Edward Seymour, the protector. In her will of 1639 she bequeathed to Richard £100 plus another £20 to 'binde out ffranck his Sonne an apprentice if I doe it not in my life time'.[235]

Henry Long Junior of Whaddon (c.1540–1611)

Henry, second son of Henry Long and Mary Horton, succeeded to the Whaddon estates on his father's death in 1558 and built a new mansion there in 1575. By this time he had six children with his wife Mary May, and there were still two more to come. He continued in the trade making high-quality white cloth, outliving his wife by several years. He mentions in his will a number of silver spoons, in particular his apostle spoons, a set of thirteen, which he left to his son Henry and thereafter to his grandson, also called Henry.

The descent of these distinctive spoons can be traced through the Long family, eventually passing into the hands of Thomas Bruges, executor of the will of Miss Katherine Long of South Wraxall. Bruges had his crest – an anchor – engraved on the back of each bowl. Passing from the possession of his heir, great-nephew William Heald Ludlow (later Ludlow-Bruges), they were sold to the wealthy American, William Waldorf Astor, in the late nineteenth or early twentieth century. Dated 1532 by the British Museum and described effusively by *The Times* as 'by far and away the grandest surviving apostle spoons', they entered the Guinness Book of Records after their sale for £120,000 in June 1981 at Christie's, London.

In the unlikely event of his living another 370 years, Henry Long might have been mildly surprised at the value of his old spoons in the twentieth century, but he died in 1611, leaving at least three daughters and three sons surviving him. His heir was his eldest son,

234 Son of Richard Long and Joan Pyke, and grandson of James Long of Monkton
235 *Archaeologia Cantiana xi*, 1877, pp. 232-50, will of Frances, Duchess of Richmond and Lennox

Henry of Southwick. A younger son, William, was the innkeeper at Trowbridge who, with his wife Anne Langford, was implicated in the dispensing of a shower of filth upon one of their guests, Jasper Heily *(see Sir Walter Long, 1st Baronet of Whaddon)*.

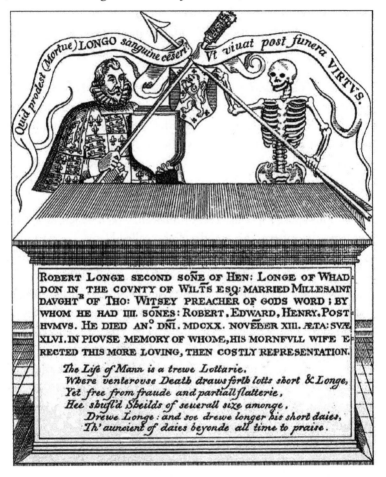

Robert Long of Broughton Gifford memorial, Monumental Brasses of Wiltshire, E. Kite 1860

Henry's second son, Robert Long of Broughton Gifford, was sojourning at his uncle Edward Long's house in Monkton when he died there in November 1620, aged forty-six. The unusual memorial to him at Broughton Gifford commissioned by his widow Millicent

Witsey, was 'more loving than costly'. It depicts death as a skeleton crossing his sceptre with a mace held by a herald dressed in royal livery, holding a 'lottery' of shields – the figure of death drawing one shield out emblazoned with the crest of Long.

Robert and Millicent had four sons, the last born after Robert's death, appropriately named Posthumus. Sometime of Corsham, Wiltshire, and afterwards of Harbridge, Hampshire, Mr Posthumus Long didn't have an entirely harmonious relationship with his elder brother Robert junior, with whom he had a dispute over money in 1661, taking his case to the court of Equity Pleadings. He was not the only half-orphaned child to be forever labelled posthumus, but with his 'after-death' name he never found a woman willing to become Mrs Posthumus Long. At his death in 1682 he bequeathed his property to his cousin Walter Long, 2nd Baronet of Whaddon, and named another cousin, Edmund Long of Battersea, otherwise of Lyneham, who predeceased him by a year.

Henry Long of Southwick (1564–1612)

The first inheritor of the apostle spoons, Henry, eldest son of Henry Long junior of Whaddon and Mary May, was educated at Gloucester Hall, Oxford, entering in August 1578 aged twelve, and in 1582 he commenced his law studies as a student of Lincoln's Inn. His marriage in about 1588 to his second cousin Rebecca Bailey was probably a contrivance to secure the descent of certain property on her side of the family. Rebecca, daughter and heiress of Christopher Bailey junior of Southwick, was the granddaughter of Maud Horton, sister of Henry's grandmother Mary Long.

Thus began the association of the Long family with this estate, and Henry became known thereafter as 'of Southwick'. Maud Horton had been in possession of Southwick at the death of her first husband Christopher Bailey, and her second husband Walter Bush [236] held Southwick for life in right of his wife, extending the house in 1567. Somehow Henry and Rebecca Long persuaded Bush to let them have the estate which later led to proceedings instituted by his son after they

236   Nephew of Paul Bush, bishop of Bristol

Southwick Court

ejected him from it. The Longs successfully defended their claim and retained Southwick.

Henry aspired to more than land-based prosperity. Driven by dreams of wealth and social prominence, England's maritime supremacy was built on the activities of such men as Sir Walter Raleigh and Sir Francis Drake, making piracy a recognised profession in the sixteenth century. Syndicates of gentlemen, noblemen and even the queen regarded vessels of enemy nations fair game, transforming petty piracy in the English Channel into prolific trans-Atlantic plundering. With a change in the law in 1589 legitimising the pillaging of enemy vessels, prizes had to be divided, usually ten per cent to the Crown. Not one to miss a lucrative opportunity, Attorney-General Sir John Popham equipped his own ship for the purpose in May that year and Henry Long also followed the trend, investing in voyages to the West Indies.[237]

Henry only outlived his father by about a year, dying in May 1612 aged forty-eight, having fathered eight children with his wife. An inventory made soon afterwards related mainly to his

237   Mary Frear Keeler, *The Long Parliament, 1640–1641: A Biographical Study of its Members*, 1954

manor of Whaddon, but also lists his goods at Southwick Court and Littleton Wood Farm, a property owned by the Long family since the Dissolution. Southwick passed with Rebecca's marriage to her second husband Henry Sherfield who held it for his life, afterwards reverting to her eldest surviving son, Sir Walter Long, 1st Baronet, who made a name for himself for all the wrong reasons, outlined in a following chapter.

Sir Walter's sister Martha married Berkshire magistrate, Roger Knight of Greenham, who in 1643 was one of the sequestrators of delinquent estates for that county. In 1647 Martha and Roger's eldest son Roger junior found himself involved in a troublesome affair of the heart, and on his father's advice requested the judgement of Mr William Lilly, astrologer of London. The precarious nature of life in England during the seventeenth century gave rise to the popularity of astrology, and between 1640 and 1650 the consultation of astrologers became ingrained in the daily life of rich and poor alike.

Lilly, known as 'the English Merlin' to his friends and 'that juggling Wizard and Imposter' to his enemies, established his reputation as England's leading astrologer after his prediction of the king's crushing defeat at the battle of Naseby in June 1645. Roger junior, twenty-eight and still without a wife in 1649, sent Lilly an earnest request for a prediction as to the probability of marriage, with a minute description of his birth, personal appearance and temperament for the astrologer's guidance. This letter is preserved at the Bodleian Library. Roger desired an answer be sent by the Bristol post, 'addressed Mr Roger Knight, junior, Greenhame, neare Newberry, to be left with the postmaster at Speenhamland, to be conveighed unto me. I have sent here inclosed a 11s. peece for your present paines.'

Sir,

Haveinge been with you divers times, upon the 24 of December, 1647, and upon the 27 of Sept. 1648, and twise in the latter end of Aprill last, at all which times I made bould to desire your judgement concerninge some thinges I then propounded unto you, wherein you were pleased to give me some satisfaction. You may happily remember me by this character:

I was borne 3 weeks before my time, on the 16 Aug., 1619, neare
Newbury, but what hour I cannot tell. I am very tall of stature, but
stoop a little at the shoulders. I am leane, having a thin flaxen hair
of a longish vissage, and a pale complexion, gray eyed, haveing some
impediment in my upper lippe which hath a small mole on the right
side thereof, also on the right side of my forehead another little mole.
I am of melancholly disposition having been all the time of my life in
an unsettled condition.

He mentions his father had advised a match for him, a brown-
haired heiress born at Worcester, six years his senior. Describing his
potential bride's horoscope and astrological characteristics, he asks
Lilly if he should make any attempt to again bring about the business,
his first attempt having failed, and if so, what time of year would be
best to renew his overtures; and may he rely on the astrologer's promise
that he will be settled by November. Preparing himself for the worst,
Roger requests to be informed 'in case none of the things prophesied
should come to pass', and of the probability of his travelling 'beyond
sea', which apparently was Plan B. What Lilly replied to the credulous
Roger we may only wonder, but there is evidence he did marry –
someone unconcerned by his upper lip impediment with its attendant
mole. He died in 1659, six years after his father.

Robert Long of Stanton Prior (c.1606–97)

A younger son of Henry Long and Rebecca Bailey, Robert Long
of Stanton Prior, like his brother Walter, found a seat in the
Long Parliament as MP for one of the constituencies in Somerset. He
was predeceased by his only son Henry,[238] a master of the Bench at
Lincoln's Inn.

His cousin George Long of Downside had stirred renewed
therapeutic interest in the waters at Bath in 1691, making a spectacular
recovery from various ailments that had crippled him for twenty years,
and four years later the Longs were in the news again when Robert

238   His widow Dionysia Harington married his cousin Calthorpe Parker
Long

also derived a seemingly miraculous but short-lived cure at Bath. As a regular bather he donated a brass ring to the Hot Bath, which he instructed be embedded in the bath wall for the benefit of its patrons.

As might be reasonably expected of a man said to be aged eighty-nine and already well past the usual date of expiry, he was 'much enfeebled by fits of the gout, weak in his limbs and tender in his feet'. After bathing in the Cross-Bath fourteen or fifteen times he 'walked more erect and nimble', had a smooth, fresh, florid countenance and was thought likely to live another seven years. Robert's recovery was brief; he died a few months later – but presumably, thanks to his beneficial bathing routine, feeling a little better.

His will mentions his sister Mary's grandson, Lovelace Bigg, whose own grandson Harris Bigg-Wither (1781–1833) was a wealthy country gentleman who stood to inherit Manydown Park and other landholdings in the parish of Wootton St Lawrence in Hampshire. It was at Manydown Park in 1802 that novelist Jane Austen received, accepted and then the following morning – perhaps after a sleepless night – realised her mistake and rejected Bigg-Wither's proposal of marriage.

Sir Walter Long, 1st Baronet of Whaddon (c.1591–1672)

The second son of Henry Long and Rebecca Bailey, and great-grandson of Henry Long of Whaddon, Sir Walter Long spent the early years of his life at Salisbury in the Puritan household of his mother and stepfather Henry Sherfield, a prominent lawyer who became the town's recorder. The letters of his mother, written to Sherfield over fourteen years until her eyesight failed in 1630, are full of care and concern, and show a strong bond to her second husband, whose business commitments frequently kept him in London.

She had at first resolved not to remarry after her first husband Henry Long's death, writing this to Sherfield in 1614, but he was persistent and she eventually relented. Rebecca hoped their marriage would be 'to God's glory, the true comfort of us both and the comfort of ours'. It was also a second marriage for Sherfield, and he suddenly found himself with fourteen children; only one – a daughter, Matilda – was his own.

Sherfield's first wife Mary Bedford came with six children by her first husband, all still living in 1616 at the time of his marriage to Rebecca, who had eight. Although a loving stepfather, Sherfield found their upbringing and education a costly burden, and the girls still had to be married off and positions found for all the boys. Sherfield occasionally found himself having to extend them a little credit: in 1617 Rebecca's son May Long[239] borrowed £80 from his stepfather, solemnly promising, in writing, to repay it with interest.[240] Sherfield kept meticulous accounts, and this was a typically formal arrangement drawn up in the presence of six witnesses. Obviously he was taking no chances. Rebecca, who keenly felt her husband's inevitable absences in London, wrote that 'every year brings more occasions of business', and thanked him in 1618 for his 'good and godly admonitions and counsels' on her difficulties with her children.

Two of the Long boys proved particularly vexing. One was in the Fleet for debt, and another, who wished to sail with Raleigh, was sent off to the Indies, to divert him from an 'ungodly course of living'.[241] This may have been Henry, who entered Jesus College, Oxford, in November 1607 aged eighteen, and died in 1621. The name of 'Henrie Longe' appears on a list of debts due from various members who sailed in the *Dragon* to the East Indies with Thomas Best in 1613. For Rebecca it was probably by necessity a case of 'love me, love my children', and Sherfield had no choice but to pay the Long children's debts 'to save my wife's life or at least her quiet'. Young Walter was no angel either. In 1618 he found himself in court after having made one of Sherfield's servants pregnant.[242]

Walter had inherited no land at his father's death in 1612, and in 1620, having completed his legal studies at Lincoln's Inn, joined Sir Robert Mansell's fleet at Tilbury as it prepared for an expedition in

239   May Long's paternal grandmother was Mary May, daughter of Robert May of Broughton Gifford
240   Document ref.: SP 14/90 f.92, 7 February 1617, National Archives of the UK
241   J.S. Morrill, P. Slack, G.E. Aylmer, D.R. Woolf, *Public Duty and Private Conscience in 17th-Century England*, 1993, p. 158
242   Subdeans Court presentments, St Edmund, Salisbury, 26 October 1618

the Mediterranean against Algerian corsairs.[243] He wrote to Secretary of State Sir George Calvert after reaching Malaga on 3 November, that they had received great support from the Spaniards. Then his elder brother Henry died suddenly, necessitating his hasty return to England.

He was now heir to the family's extensive but encumbered estates. The main Long property, Whaddon, came to him in December 1621 on his marriage to Mary Coxe in London, who brought with her Rodmarton Manor and a dowry of £500. This manor had been purchased in 1597 by her father Robert, a grocer, in his grave barely a month at the time of his daughter's marriage. In the short term Walter received little benefit from these sudden acquisitions, and his lack of cash meant that by 1623 his debts had increased alarmingly. But money wasn't to be his only concern.

Beginning his political career in 1625, Walter sat as MP for Salisbury, a seat he obtained with the assistance of his stepfather Sherfield. An earnest speaker in Parliament, Walter joined with him in attacks on the Duke of Buckingham, questioning his Protestantism, making the motion to name Buckingham as the cause of the evils enumerated in the Remonstrance. He implied that the duke's activities precipitated the death of James I, prompting the Crown to try to prevent Walter's return to Parliament in 1628. He began to attract a certain degree of notoriety; Sir Francis Nethersole wrote to Elizabeth, Queen of Bohemia (sister of Charles I) in June 1628, calling Walter 'one of the hottest men against the Duke'.

He was pricked as sheriff of Wiltshire, but at the same time secured a seat at Bath in neighbouring Somerset, which he claimed was not unlawful since the constituency lay outside his county. However, the solicitor-general, Sir Robert Heath, disagreed, instituting a Star Chamber suit against him, arguing he had neglected his duties as sheriff of Wiltshire while serving as MP for Bath, living in London, contrary to the sheriff's oath to remain in the county.

---

243   Henry Lancaster, 'Long, Sir Walter, first baronet (c.1591–1672)', Oxford Dictionary of National Biography, Oxford University Press, 2004; online edn. Sept 2010

To prevent censure by Parliament, and to avoid an order to appear before the Star Chamber, Walter quickly retreated to Wiltshire. Benjamin Valentine wrote from London to Sir John Eliot in November 1628: 'Watte Long is sent for by a messenger but he was here in house with me, and is gone again, but he intends not to be found.'[244] The name of Walter Long appears in the court records of Salisbury that year, and it may or may not have been our harassed protagonist, wrangling words with William Burges who lived about a mile from Whaddon at Semington. During the argument Walter Long scoffed: 'Thou art a wittol and canst not pull on a hose [over] thy head for the bigness . . . of thy horns.'[245] He returned to Westminster a few weeks later, but by the time Parliament met in January, Buckingham had been assassinated.

With loyalties to the Crown already under strain from the highly unpopular policies of Charles I, the session of 2 March erupted into tumult when the speaker Sir John Finch refused to read out Sir John Eliot's *Protestations,* condemning the king's conduct and his attempts to take tonnage and poundage without the consent of Parliament. Finch was about to adjourn the House when Walter, together with another member, Denzil Holles, thrust him back into the chair and swore 'he should sit still till it pleased them to rise'. This became one of the most infamous events in the Parliament's history.

In a rage, Charles I declared the ringleaders 'vipers who should have their reward', and on 10 March he dismissed Parliament, beginning the Eleven Years Tyranny, ruling England without Parliament at all. He issued a proclamation for Walter Long's arrest 'for seditious practices and crimes of a high nature', together with his co-conspirators Sir John Eliot, Denzil Holles, Benjamin Valentine, William Coriton, William Strode, John Selden, Sir Miles Hobart and Sir Peter Hayman. Walter, through his own evasive efforts, was one of the last to be finally apprehended, and all were committed on 2 April. The warrant determined their detention was 'by the King's pleasure and commandment'. Appearing before the King's Bench while simultaneously facing ongoing Star Chamber

244   Sir John Eliot, [Alexander Balloch Grosar, *De jure maiestatis* (and the letter-book of Sir John Eliot), 1882, vol. 2, p. 24
245   WSA ref B/DB 10, fol. 6

Speaker Finch being held down by Walter Long and others. Andrew Carrick Gow. Palace of Westminster Collection

proceedings concerning his shrievalty, Walter was fined 2,000 marks for breaking his oath as sheriff.

Beginning on 15 May, the trial before the King's Bench saw an unprecedented amount of legal talent assembled: the attorney-general and four king's sergeants appeared for the crown, and thirteen prominent lawyers of counsel for the nine defendants, among whom were Walter's stepfather Henry Sherfield and Robert Mason, who asserted 'there is no crime in our law called sedition'.

During interrogation by the attorney-general Walter referred to his parliamentary privilege, insisting he had nothing to do with the preparation of Eliot's paper, nor could he remember its contents. In between court appearances he was locked up at the Marshalsea prison where his appeals for clemency fell on deaf ears. His counsel and sympathetic friends also attempted to secure his release.

Walter had initially yielded to the entreaties of his wife and mother to find sureties for his good behaviour, but when he realised his fellow prisoners refused to do likewise he went again before the judges to request he have back his recognisance, alleging 'weak counsel' from his lawyer Erasmus Earle. They informed him it was not in their power to revoke it, 'so he went home melancholy to his mother's house, and the day following received the communion at Mr Shure's church in Lombard Street'.[246] Once again before the judges, Walter was told to renew his recognisance for good behaviour, but having remarked it was a 'ticklish point' and he could not consent to it, he was again returned to prison.

King Charles issued a warrant for Walter and two others to be transferred to the Tower on 23 June, and a suggestion was made by their warder Apsley to Secretary Dorchester (who once referred to Walter as 'the busybody in parliament') that all prisoners be held in safe rather than close custody as stipulated in the original warrants. This forced the prisoners to provide their own food, thus saving the crown £1,200 a year.

Rumours began to circulate that this move to the Tower was part of a scheme to pervert the course of justice. The king quickly retaliated by writing to the lord chief justice on 24 June that it was quite the opposite: rather than obstructing justice, he was respecting it. Having heard of their insolent and 'unmannerly' behaviour towards himself and their lordships, he wanted the court to know how much he had resented it, saying he was not willing to afford the accused any favour till he 'found their temper and discretions to be such as to deserve it'.[247]

A key player throughout, and one of those who also opposed their release was the lord chief justice, who happened to be Sir Nicholas Hyde, uncle of Edward Hyde, later 1st Earl of Clarendon. The processes of the court ground slowly, and the prisoners endured delay after delay. On one occasion their hopes for bail were dashed when the court recessed for three months over the long summer holiday.

Walter and his cohorts remained imprisoned in the Tower where his co-accused, friend and political confidant Sir John Eliot contracted consumption. Eliot, whose friends on the outside were

---

246   For more detail on the trial see *Sir John Eliot: A Biography. 1592–1632*, John Forster, 1872

247   *Calendar of State Papers, Domestic Series, of the Reign of Charles I*, p. 588-9

much concerned for the health of his 'little thin carcass',[248] wrote to the king: 'I humbly beseech your Majesty you will command your judges to set me at liberty, that for recovery of my health I may take some fresh air.' The king was implacable and sent his reply: 'Not humble enough.' Eliot did not survive, dying there in November 1632, aged forty.

A year earlier Jasper Heily, a messenger of the Chamber staying at a Trowbridge inn, had spent the evening bragging about his exploits after the 1629 Parliament in arresting the dangerous outlaw Walter Long. Unbeknown to Heily, the inn was owned by Walter's uncle, William Long, and his wife Anne (*née* Langford, aunt of Sir Edward Hyde, 1st Earl of Clarendon). At first Heily was well received but once his identity became known his hosts refused to give him food or sheets for his bed, and 'abused him with reviling speeches'. They complained their kinsman, Walter Long, had received very hard measure from the king and council. At eleven at night they threw Heily out onto the street, branding him a base knave and broker.

On his way he was doused with 'a chamber-pot full of filthiness' by one of the Longs' servants, 'at which Long and his wife much rejoiced'. Humiliated, and making excuses for the delay, it took Heily almost a year to bring a suit against William Long, who at first denied even mentioning Walter's name, let alone a tirade of abuse. Long said he heard a stranger had cast out a basin of water, some of which, regrettably, happened to accidentally fall on Heily. His defence beginning to unravel, William Long then falsely claimed the eviction was necessary because Heily abused their house by requiring a wench, offering 40s for one.[249]

None of this helped Walter, who languished in the Tower for four years until 1633, missing the baptism in London of his youngest son Thomas in 1630 and the death of his wife the following year. During his incarceration he was still able to conduct his own affairs to some degree, having the liberty of the Tower, and in January 1631

---

248   *De jure maiestatis, op. cit.* Sir Oliver Luke to Sir John Eliot, 28 Dec 1629, p. 81
249   *CSP Charles I, op.cit.* pp. 346-7

he was brought before the Exchequer bar to answer a charge by the attorney-general that he had made fraudulent conveyance of all his estate to his brother Thomas, and William Long, probably his uncle of Trowbridge, in an attempt to avoid the fine imposed by the Star Chamber. Sir Robert Heath also exhibited a Bill against two of Walter's attorneys, Robert Mason and Edward Littleton, for their alleged role in the transaction. This continued campaign of harassment further motivated Walter's defiance; he would neither appear nor answer any such Bill, and they could do what they liked. He was carted off back to the Tower and given the weekend to reconsider.

At Walter's request Secretary Dorchester acted as agent on his behalf, pleading favourable consideration and presenting several petitions for clemency to the king. He was allowed liberty briefly: there exists a fragment of a letter from Walter to Dorchester in April 1631, thanking him for procuring his majesty's leave to attend his wife Mary's deathbed. She had previously visited Walter in the Tower, Eliot writing this to Miles Hobart in July 1630. After she died Walter again appealed to Dorchester to obtain permission to go and provide for his 'motherless, fatherless, and friendless children',[250] all less than nine years old, who were probably under the care of his widowed mother-in-law Mary Coxe, living with the family since at least 1630.

One of his contemporaries, John Lisle, during his trial for treason in 1649, alleges a slightly more rosy view of conditions in the Tower for Walter. Complaining of his own harsh treatment and denial of quality food, Lisle claimed the king had allowed Walter and his fellow MPs £4–5 a week for their diet, and Walter had 'confessed in the Lieutenant's own chamber' that while he was prisoner in the Tower 'he spent the king about £1,500 for his own particular self in Provision.'[251]

Meanwhile, Walter's mother Rebecca had declined in health, suffering heart trouble and eye problems. In 1632 Peter Thatcher, parson of the parish church of St Edmund's, Salisbury, had granted her a licence to eat meat during Lent, on account of her 'sickliness'.

250   *Ibid*
251   *A Collection of the Most Remarkable Trials of Persons for High Treason*, 1735, vol. II, p. 145

Walter's stepfather, who had tried his best for his trouble-prone stepson, must have been under considerable stress by this time, and was himself prosecuted in the Star Chamber in 1633 for breaking a painted glass window in St Edmund's with his pike-staff.

In his defence Sherfield said the depiction of God portrayed as a little old man in a red and blue cloak measuring the sun and moon with a pair of compasses, had troubled his conscience for twenty years. Being unable to enter the church without seeing it, he felt his actions had been entirely appropriate. Chief Justice Sir Robert Heath sympathised with his views, but saw his action as a defiant act against episcopal authority and the Crown. Sherfield's vandalism became his downfall; he was stripped of his office and heavily fined. He died soon afterwards in January 1634, disgraced and ruined, with debts of £6,000. His widow Rebecca may not have felt able to continue at Salisbury; she appears to have been living in Berkshire at Greenham with her daughter Mrs Martha Knight when she executed a quitclaim to Walter in 1636.

Not long after his release from the Tower, Walter married a forty-one-year-old widow, Lady Anne Foxe (*née* Cage) of Shropshire, and he spent most of the 1630s living on her estates at Whitcot. Now a marked man, trouble inevitably followed him like a black cloud. Early in 1636 he was presented as a delinquent for not showing a light horse in Wiltshire the previous summer. He wrote from Whitcot to Earl Pembroke, the lord chamberlain, humbly craving his lordship's pardon and protesting that he had never heard any warning of the muster 'or had the least notice in the world'. He claimed his tenant living in his house in Wiltshire had also heard nothing.

Finally, in May 1638, his brother Colonel Thomas Long paid the 2,000 marks fine imposed on him in 1629,[252] forcing Walter to sell some of his Wiltshire property to cover the debt. For Parliament it was a case of robbing Peter to pay Paul. This money was immediately assigned to John Ashburnham 'in satisfaction of so much due from his majesty to him'. However, in 1645 the Committee of His Majesty's Revenue ordered the receiver general to repay Walter £1,333 6s 8d

252   Warrant of Discharge, Thomas Long to John Ashburnham CSP, vol. 23

restitution,[253] roughly equivalent to the original fine.

Contrary to traditional family allegiances, Walter's political views were shared by his Somerset cousins, in particular, Sir Lislebone Long (son of William Long of Stratton), who like Walter, was also a Presbyterian and outspoken critic of the king. In 1639 their alliance is illustrated by a letter from Walter, writing from London at his house in The Strand to Edward Nicholas, appointing Sir Lislebone as the receiver of £93 16s compensation ordered by the Lords to be paid to him by the constable of Wiltshire, Christopher Merewether. Merewether was branded 'a man so full of malice' by Walter, annoyed at his undue and unequal assessment of ship-money against him, but he at least had the satisfaction of seeing him imprisoned in the Fleet until he complied with the order.

Walter returned to Parliament in December 1641 as member for Ludgershall, Wiltshire. Earlier that month he had written to his fellow Presbyterian, Parliamentarian and 'Good Cozen' Isaac Appleton [254] at Holbrook Hall, Suffolk, that he was about to present Parliament with a petition for compensation for the recent injustices he had suffered. But it would be another five years before Walter actually received any redress.

In 1646 Parliament sympathetically voted Walter £5,000 as an indemnity 'for his damages, losses, imprisonments and sufferings'. That year an outbreak of plague in London caused Appleton to experience an unspecified, but 'sadd disaster'. Parliament was in virtual lockdown and Walter apologised for being unable to visit him on account of the impossibility for any member to absent themselves from the House without leave, even to visit family, 'wch I thinke will hardly bee obteyned' owing to the sickness, 'and for my wife I leave her to her selfe, wch is the course now heald wth everie boddie'.[255] The atmosphere in London had been tense for some months, and in July Appleton's cousin Robert reported that the summer heat and fear of the spreading infection was keeping him close to his chambers at

253   WSA ref 947:1871
254   Son of Sir Isaac and Mary Appleton *née* Cage, Walter's second wife's sister
255   William Sumner Appleton, *Family Letters from the Bodleian Library, with Notes*, 1902, p. 30

Gray's Inn. He knew of 88 deaths that week from 'ye pox' and 56 'of ye plague'.

At the beginning of the Civil War adherents of Parliament had the upper hand in Wiltshire, and Walter's support saw his contribution of £350 towards a loan being raised to equip Cromwell's army, and more particularly, for the speedy advance of Sir William Waller, later responsible for the capture of Sir James Long of Draycot who took an active part in opposing them. This money was repaid to Walter in 1643, about the time of his appointment as chief register of the court of Chancery.

In 1641 collections were made throughout England to raise funds to aid the suppression of a Royalist rebellion in Ireland, in return for an allocation of profits from sequestered lands there. Walter took the lead in the House of Commons with a payment of £1,200, and Waller put up £1,000.[256] Walter's cousin William Long of Stratton also subscribed £50. The amount of just over £249,000 was raised through subscriptions of 1,188 individuals,[257] termed adventurers. The problem in Ireland persisted, and in 1646 Walter was contracted to transport a regiment of 500 men across the Irish Sea that he had readied at Bridgwater, Somerset.

He saw action in 1642 when he charged at the head of a troop of horse in Warwickshire during the battle of Edgehill; he was wounded, his horse shot from under him. Impatient at his slow promotion, he left the army and returned to his seat in the House, later refuting accusations by Parliament of cowardice at Edgehill. He insisted that after being suddenly dismounted he 'did yet, with his single Pistol in his Hand, give Quarter to several of the Enemy'. A sixteen-man Committee for Advance of Money was appointed in November 1642, which included Walter, and he was also involved in the organisation of parliamentary forces in Wiltshire and Shropshire.

In the spring of 1643 the lord general sent him into Essex to take horses for the army and collect tax arrears. He wrote to the committee in April: 'I will do my best to get money for the army, but I

256   John Langton Sanford, *Studies and Illustrations of the Great Rebellion*, 1858, p. 488

257   J.P. Prendergast, *The Cromwellian Settlement of Ireland*, 1870, p. 407

dare not propose a new subscription as the people are so averse; I could do more if you sent me an order to assess the malignants and Papists in Essex as you did in London.'[258] The citizens' aversion to Walter and his tax-collecting activities was coupled with accusations he was abusing his powers. Another group of horse-takers was operating in Essex at the same time, and he blamed them for committing the abuses that he had been accused of: taking horses from well-affected people, and taking bribes to return horses to their owners. He even went as far as arresting them and confiscating the horses they had seized.

On examination by Walter in the presence of local officials, he found this rival group had a warrant from Lord Grey, major-general of the Eastern Association, authorising them to take horses, which meant there were two different armies competing in Essex for the same resources. A tug of war developed between Walter and the other horse-takers. He wrote to Parliament questioning whether the warrant was genuine, but discovered they were authorised by the Earl of Warwick, whose popularity among the people was considerably greater than Walter's. This led to his withdrawal from Essex by Parliament to placate the local gentry, who had continued to complain. The horses he took were never given back to their owners, instead being taken to London to help recruit the Earl of Essex 's army.

After his recall by Parliament Walter continued to oppose the despotic power of the king, who in November 1642 had published a proclamation of 'grace, favour, and pardon' to the inhabitants of Wiltshire, with the exception of only four persons, who were to be proceeded against as traitors and stirrers of sedition. These four were Sir Edward Hungerford, Sir Henry Ludlow, Sir John Evelyn and Walter Long, Esq. His continued opposition had only hardened the king's personal animosity towards Walter, and the feeling was mutual.

Unlike his more popular cousin Sir Lislebone Long, Walter's relationship with his parliamentary peers was fractious. He twice assaulted members of his own party who disputed his views, and by 1647, acting as whip, was reviled as 'the Parliament driver', a charge

---

258   M. A. E. Green, *Calendar of the Proceedings of the Committee for Advance of Money, 1642–1656*, vol. 1, p. 140

he hotly denied. He was accused of purposely placing himself by the door of the House during debates so he could intercept or pursue any member who left before a vote could be taken, in line with his own views, and then 'drive' them back into the House.[259]

He was included among the eleven Presbyterian members the army sought to remove from Parliament that year, who were accused of, among other things, conspiring with other disaffected persons at the lodgings of Lady Carlisle in Whitehall and elsewhere, of 'holding Correspondency with the Queen of England now in France, and her Participants; with an Intent, by such secret and clandestine Treaties amongst themselves, to put Conditions upon the Parliament, and to bring in the King upon their own Terms'. A charge of high treason was drawn up, citing betrayal of the cause of Parliament and endeavouring to break and destroy the army. Continuing to deny the charges, in August Walter obtained leave from the House for six months and prepared to go to France.

He, together with five of his co-accused, paid a certain Mr Green a total of £20 to hire a small ketch to take them across the English Channel. But Green, 'a craftie fellow', had other ideas, and as soon as the boat left with its passengers he informed the harbourmaster at Gravesend that they had stolen his boat with fifteen cases of treasure on board. The harbourmaster immediately authorised a large flotilla of local vessels to make pursuit, and the alleged thieves were brought back to port.

On examination, Green's knavery was exposed when it was found all had passes, signed by the Speaker of the House of Commons. The alleged cases of treasure were not fifteen but only the five belonging to the passengers, each containing one suit of 'wearing apparel and the like necessaries'. They were allowed to continue their journey, although one, Sir Francis Stapleton, became ill while on the boat and died on arrival.

Back in Westminster, Parliament was debating what to do with the tyrant king when the army, furious that they continued to support Charles as ruler, conducted what is arguably the only military *coup d'état* in English history, a march on Parliament on 6 December 1648. The events of that cold and frosty winter's day came to be known as Pride's Purge, named after the commanding officer of the operation, Thomas Pride. Consequently several MPs were imprisoned, and only 83 of the previous 489 members were allowed back in Parliament, including Lislebone Long, after making formal refusal to accept the king's authority. The newly purged House was later nicknamed the Rump Parliament.

By this time King Charles was safely tucked up under close guard at Carisbrooke Castle, and on 30 January 1649, after an Act was passed to try him for treason, he was beheaded on a scaffold in front of the Banqueting House of the Palace of Whitehall. For the first and only time in its history England was now officially a republic.

During his period abroad Walter fell in with Royalists and disaffected Parliamentarians, probably pleased he had missed all the action. Towards the end of 1659 he sensed a change in the political wind and returned to England after nearly a decade in self-imposed exile. The first and second Cromwell protectorates had come and gone, Pride's Purge was reversed on 21 February 1660 and all the barred members reinstated, leading to the restoration of the Stuart monarchy. Charles II was firmly on the throne, although now constitutionally restricted. Legislation which had allowed the king right of wardship was repealed. Church and Crown lands confiscated by the Commonwealth were restored by statute but private landowners who'd also had their property confiscated had to either petition for its return or pursue the matter through the courts.

On that score, Walter came through relatively unscathed, unlike some of his Royalist kinsmen who may have felt more lasting consequences of the Interregnum, their estates reduced and indebted. As one of several erstwhile Parliamentarians who went on to enjoy new honours and greater wealth, he built a large addition to Whaddon House, beginning in 1660. In 1661 he was made a baronet.

His second wife Lady Anne Foxe, sister of Sir John Cage and widow of Sir Richard Foxe, died at Whitcot Hall in 1665. Despite her remarriage to Walter she was still known as Lady Foxe by her neighbours. After her death they often reported seeing her in her carriage drawn by four grey horses being driven around the lawn and through the pond in the meadow. The fear of her ghost drove everybody away from the hall, which became semi-derelict as a result. In January 1666, at the age of seventy-four, Walter married for the third time, pocketing another dowry of £1,150. His new wife was also a Shropshire lady, Elizabeth, daughter of John Cotes of Woodcote.

The effects of age were beginning to catch up with him, and he made the decision to remove from Whaddon House, preferring instead a residence nine miles away at Bath where he could avail himself of the therapeutic waters at his leisure. But just as he looked forward to a quiet retirement, someone had other ideas.

In November 1671 at the age of eighty, he was pricked as sheriff for Wiltshire by Charles II.[260] Regardless of his age, Walter had no desire to live in Wiltshire and be sheriff again. Besides, there were always heavy expenses attached, only a small portion of which may or may not be reimbursed. He wrote to the king requesting a compromise: he would fulfil the duty as long as he could continue to live at Bath. Charles was very accommodating and duly granted his request. However, Walter knew frequent attendance at the assizes in Wiltshire would be required, and the prospect held no appeal whatsoever. His horse-riding days were far behind him and travel by coach held its own trepidations; consequently he preferred being carried everywhere in a sedan chair, a favoured mode of travel around Bath.

Walter wrote again to the king, pleading his advanced age and dependence on cumbersome and inefficient transport, proposing in his stead he make one of his sons or 'some other fit person' deputy to attend the county assizes and perform other public duties. Walter's relationship with Charles II was a considerable improvement on the one he'd had with Charles I, and soon afterwards a letter of royal approval arrived agreeing to his request, 'provided this be no prejudice to the service'.[261]

On 15 November 1672, nine months after receiving this letter, Walter died and was buried at Whaddon. His wealth at death was

260 *London Gazette*, 6 November 1671, issue 624
261 C.S.P Domestic series, Charles II, vol. 7, 1939

substantial, despite his debts amounting to £37,036[262] – in today's money, about £3 million. To his younger son Robert he bequeathed the manor of Rodmarton and property in Ireland that he had bought from Sir William Waller.

During the year following his death, his widow Dame Elizabeth released her jointure in his estate to her two stepsons Walter and Robert Long, in return for an annuity of £250 secured on Weston Farm, near Bath. In April 1683 she was living in London with her spinster sister Jane Cotes at Essex Buildings, St Clement Danes, on the banks of the Thames. Her peace and privacy was shattered one day when a group of armed men, led by Thomas Shirley – described in the court indictment as 'gent' – riotously broke into her house and burst into her bedchamber with swords drawn, putting Elizabeth and her sister in fear of their lives.

At the urging of Thomas, his brother Edward Shirley shouted angrily at the terrified Elizabeth, 'You are a bitch, you are an ugly old witch, you look like a witch, I believe you are one, and that you can ride on a stick up the chimney!' Including her sister in the abuse, he ranted, 'you are a couple of old bawds, here is a guinea for you, help me to a whore, I am sure you can do it!' [263] What Elizabeth and her sister had done to provoke such an angry tirade is unfortunately absent from the court record.

Thomas Shirley had a twenty-one-year lease on the house, and from 1678 he let certain rooms to Elizabeth for £20 a year: 'a dining room, a pair of stairs forwards and the chamber next adjoining on the same floor, with a closet belonging, a garret backwards, a room adjoining the kitchen for beer, and a coal hole, and the use of the kitchen, the jack, the fireplace and river water jointly with Shirley, and the courtyards and privy belonging'.[264] This arrangement continued until the end of the year following the violent invasion, when Shirley assigned his lease to a certain Basill Knight.

Five years later, in 1688, Lady Elizabeth Long died and was

---

262   WSA ref 947:1132; 1676/1, 2
263   Sir John Tremaine, *Pleas of the Crown in Matters Criminal and Civil*, 1793–4, p. 179
264   WSA ref 112/2/1

buried at Harefield, Middlesex. She had appointed her nephew Richard Powys executor and residual legatee of her estate, naming several of her other nephews and nieces. By this time only one of her stepchildren survived her, Walter Long junior, now the 2nd baronet. To him she offered first refusal of a picture of his father, unfortunately now lost, 'sett about with diamonds wch his father told me he bought of Sr Robert Viner [265] and cost seaventyfour pounds'. Walter junior could have the picture for this sum of money if he so desired.

Sir Walter Long 2nd Baronet (c.1627–1710)

Walter Long junior was admitted to Lincoln's Inn in November 1644, and in 1672 succeeded as 2nd baronet, probably having taken over his father's duties as sheriff the previous year. He inherited the family estates, including Whaddon, and also the responsibility for his kinsman George Long, who had lived with his father. Walter senior had left George £20 a year for his life, stipulating he continue to live with his son who must provide his diet. Where George fits into the family is not clear, however his ongoing maintenance is an example of the attitude typically exhibited by the gentry. Charity began at home.

Wealthy men such as Walter supported large households whose numbers were often swelled by friends' children and impoverished relations. This generosity – and indeed their whole lifestyle – depended on the cheap labour of servants. Required for practically every room in the house, a small army was needed to greet visitors, fetch and carry, run errands and attend to all the outdoor work in the garden, park, kennels and stables. After their day was done they went to their hard narrow beds in the cold dark attic. Although a servant's wages might range from just £2 to £10 a year – depending on their job description – adding considerably to household expenditure was the cost of large outgoings of food, drink, heating fuel, and candles. All up, this amounted to several hundred pounds a year.

It was just a drop in the ocean to Walter, and with disposable income to spare he added to his family legacy by acquiring more

265   Banker and goldsmith, he also produced the jewel-studded replica of the Crown of St Edward and the King's Orb, used for Charles II's coronation in 1661

property. In 1693 he made alterations to Southwick Court; this date and his initials are cut into one of the stone walls. Another addition to his portfolio was the Gloucestershire manor of Rodmarton, passed down from his father and inherited after the death of his brother Robert in 1675. The introduction of land tax in 1692 was particularly onerous to the lesser gentry; however Walter was reasonably well insulated from its effects by having more varied estate revenues available to him. With agricultural prices so low and falling or stagnant rents, landowners also buckling under the burden of heavy taxes were compelled to sell up. Walter took advantage of this crisis by purchasing an estate in Sutton Veny in 1706 which included Polebridge Farm.

Still looking to consolidate his existing properties, the next year he acquired a twenty-one-year lease of Monkton Farleigh Manor, and, probably mindful of the fate of his wealth in the hands of his heirs, at the age of eighty-three he purchased further extensive lands in Wiltshire.[266] Letting land to tenants gave security for the landowner,

Southwick Court gatehouse was built in the late 15th century. The 18th century bridge crosses the moat that surrounded the original house

266   In Chippenham, Langley Burrell, Hardenhuish, Pewsey, Biddestone St Peter, Biddestone St Nicholas, Slaughterford, Yatton Keynell, Sherston Magna, Sherston Pinckney and Hullavington, WSA ref 947:956

but rents were low – about three or four per cent return after expenses, compared to mortgages yielding between four and five per cent.[267] But as a place to park his capital, land was the obvious choice; at his age Walter wasn't looking for income so much as a secure asset to pass to his heirs.

No doubt careful to avoid any conflict of interest that had wrought such havoc on his father, Walter was MP for Bath between 1679 and 1681 with Sir George Speke, although it was a close competition. Three polls had been required in 1679 before Walter managed to oust his opponent Sir William Bassett by one vote by proxy. He was defeated by Bassett at the next general election in 1681, and in 1683 after Speke's death he was preparing to team up with John Sherstone, 'a most busy pestilent Presbyterian', to stand against Bassett and Lord Fitz-Hardinge. Sherstone was considered so pernicious to the king's interest that he was expelled from the corporation. Although Walter stood again in 1689, he attracted only three votes.

Appointed to the Commission of the Peace, his subsequent removal from it was a direct result of his support of the Exclusion Bill, which sought to exclude the king's Catholic brother and heir presumptive, James, Duke of York, from the English throne. It was a failure, and James was crowned in 1685 after the death of Charles II. It was a short and troubled reign that began with a rebellion in southern England led by his nephew, the Duke of Monmouth. James eventually fled England and died in exile in France in 1701.

With the throne suddenly vacant, William of Orange was crowned co-monarch with his wife Queen Mary II in 1689. In 1692 William was preparing to renew the war against France, prompting the cash-strapped Parliament to pass an Act for raising a war tax, requiring anyone who owned property to pay 4s in the pound of its yearly value. The Common Council raised further loans by subscription, and Walter enlisted the assistance of his cousin Henry Long of Lincoln's Inn, who on his behalf made a tally secured loan of £500 (about £44,000 today) at seven per cent interest to the Exchequer.[268]

---

267   Mingay, *ibid,* p. 82
268   WSA ref 947:1801

Queen Mary died in 1694 at the age of 32, followed by her husband William in March 1702 from complications after a fall from his horse. He was succeeded by Anne, his late wife's sister. Queen Anne's progress in August 1702 with her invalid consort, George, Prince of Denmark, launched a fad that would make the city of Bath the most celebrated spa in England. She travelled from Windsor to Oxford, staying the night at Christ Church College, after dinner going on to Cirencester where she was entertained by Thomas Master at his house, The Abbey.

Her next stop, the London press reported, was 'Sir Walter Long's near the Bath, where her Majesty will reside till her return'.[269] Just which of Sir Walter's houses this was is not certain, but possibly Whaddon House, about nine miles from Bath and 35 miles from Cirencester. Whaddon House had been built in 1575 by the clothier Henry Long, son of Henry senior of Whaddon, replacing the original mansion. Enlarged by Sir Walter's father forty years before the queen's visit, it was destroyed by fire in 1835.

In stark contrast to his trouble-prone father, Sir Walter lived a relatively quiet life – apart from the odd minor skirmish in Parliament as member for Bath. As he neared his end he made a detailed inventory of his valuables kept in chests and drawers in his London house in James Street, Covent Garden. Aged almost ninety, he died there on 21 May 1710, the estimated value of his estates put at £4,000 per annum[270], or just over £306,000 today.

As he was unmarried the baronetcy became extinct at his death, and he entailed his estates – including Whaddon – on his nephew, Calthorpe Parker, third son of his sister Rebecca, on condition he take the name of Long. In default of issue the male entail thereafter included his sister Rebecca 's grandson Sir Philip Parker, 3rd Baronet, with the same proviso to take the name of Long. Next in line to inherit was Thomas Long of Rowden; then the Rev. John Long of Corpus Christi College, Oxford, and finally John's brother Thomas Long, clothier of Melksham in remainder. This strict family settlement was

269   *Daily Courant,* 27 August 1702, issue 112
270   Basil Duke Henning, *The House of Commons, 1660–1690,* vol. 3

Sketch of Whaddon House, History from Marble, Thomas Dingley 1689

a binding legal contract which could be broken only by a private Act of Parliament.

Of the first four named each inherited the estates in turn; effectively only tenants for life obligated to preserve the settled portion of the estates for payment of dowries, jointure and portions. None had male issue, and it was only the fifth inheritor, Thomas Long of Melksham who finally had a son: old Walter Long of Bath, after whose death in 1807 the estates eventually devolved onto the heirs of the Longs of Rood Ashton in the early nineteenth century, to remain in the family for another hundred years or so.

Parker Long of Whaddon and Arwarton

An April wedding in 1649 at Whaddon celebrated the marriage of Sir Walter's sister Rebecca to Sir Philip Parker, 1st Baronet of Arwarton Hall, Suffolk. Recorded on a monument erected in Arwarton church in 1736 by her grandson Sir Philip Parker Long are details of the Parker family's connection to Anne Boleyn – the ill-fated consort of Henry VIII, who professed to have spent some of the happiest days of her youth at the Parker family seat. Sir Philip's ancestor Sir Philip Calthorpe had married Anne's aunt, Amata Boleyn, sister of Thomas Boleyn, Earl of Wiltshire and Ormond.

Anne developed a great attachment to the home of her Aunt Amata, saying, so the story goes, that her heart would always be in Arwarton. After Anne was beheaded in 1536, according to popular legend her heart was conveyed to Arwarton by one of the Parker family and buried in the wall of Arwarton church. Perhaps this was true. During a complete restoration of the church in 1837 workmen found a heart-shaped leaden casket concealed in the north wall, which when opened in the presence of the rector, the Rev. Ralph Berners, they found nothing inside but a handful of dust. It was reburied under the Cornwallis vault below the organ in the church where it remains to this day.

Notable among Rebecca Long's descendants was her great-great-grandson Spencer Perceval, who in 1812 achieved the unfortunate distinction of being the only British Prime Minister to be assassinated (so far). Her granddaughter Catherine Parker had inherited £500 from Sir Walter Long in 1710, and four weeks later she became the wife of John, 1st Viscount Perceval (later 1st Earl of Egmont, created Baron Perceval in 1715).

Catherine had recently given birth to their first child in March 1711, when their friend Jonathan Swift noted in his journal that he had dined at their house with her husband, 'and saw his lady sitting in the bed, in the form of a lying-in woman'. This child was named John junior, who later succeeded his father as 2nd earl. John senior's royal connections would later prove useful in procuring a position for his son as lord of the bedchamber to the Prince of Wales.

As a nineteen-year-old in 1730, John junior made a good impression on his first meeting with Queen Caroline, consort of George II, Lord Perceval telling her afterwards he had 'taken care to breed him a loyal subject'. He later served as first lord of the Admiralty, and he became a supporter of Captain James Cook 's voyages to New Zealand. Cook named Mount Egmont in his honour.

Viscount Perceval's diary provides an interesting insight into his own life. He was a member of the Privy Council and sometime recorder of Harwich, Essex. His entries mention informal conversations with the king and queen at Hampton Court. On his birthday in July 1730 he wrote of a reply made to the queen by his son John on the subject of Mr Spencer, younger brother to the Earl of Sunderland:

> It seems this young gentleman is fond of frequently bathing, and has a bath in his house. By mistake a gentleman who came to see him was admitted while he was in the tub, whereupon making a short visit, he took his leave that he might not keep Mr Spencer too long in the water; but Mr Spencer out of a sprightly and frolicsome humour, leaped out of the bath, naked as he was, and waited on him down to the very street door. The Queen at her levée, talking of this action as a very extraordinary one, my Lord Peterborough replied that Mr Spencer was a man of extraordinary breeding to acknowledge the favour of a common visit in his birthday clothes.

It is possibly this extraordinarily clean Mr Spencer after whom the younger John named his unfortunate son, the doomed Prime Minister-to-be. The tone of his diary illustrates Lord Perceval's positive outlook on life and he kept good health. His wife Catherine, on the other hand, suffered constant and distressing headaches which she eased with the help of laudanum. Perceval often refers to her 'Aunt Long of Bath', Dionysia Long, *née* Harington, widow of Rebecca Long's son Calthorpe Parker Long, inheritor of Whaddon. She had bought a house at Bath in 1736.

The intermarriage between the various Long branches created a vast and ever-expanding cousinhood. Dionysia, a descendant of the Earl of Marlborough, James Ley, had double ties to the family. Her first husband Henry Long,[271] whose cousin Sir Lislebone Long signed his admission to Lincoln's Inn in 1657, died about eleven years into their marriage. One of the few who actually took his law studies seriously, Henry took leave to study common law in 1661. He was called to the Bar in June 1664, became a bencher in October 1683 and treasurer in 1691.

---

271   Son of Robert Long of Stanton Prior and brother of Walter Long, 1st baronet

Dionysia's 2nd husband Calthorpe and his nephew Sir Philip Parker (later Parker Long), 3rd Baronet, were appointed co-executors and successive life tenants of the several estates of his uncle Sir Walter Long, 2nd Baronet of Whaddon. With monies realised from his uncle's personal estate, Calthorpe purchased the manor of Iron Acton in Gloucestershire for £2,668, which was eventually sold by the 1st Viscount Long in the early twentieth century. Thirteen years earlier Calthorpe was also co-heir to another uncle, his wife's former father-in-law, Robert Long of Stanton Prior.

There were no children from either of Dionysia's marriages, sparing their offspring any confusion over their degree of consanguinity to the multitude of Long cousins. When she died in 1744 the wealthy Mrs Long left several sums of money for charitable causes, such as £900 South Sea Annuities for the endowment of a school at Marshfield in Gloucestershire, including clothing and education for twenty boys, with six widows to receive £6 a year. A further £500 went to the Society for Promoting Christian Knowledge, and another amount towards the expense of converting the native American Indians of Georgia to Christianity.[272]

Sir Philip Parker Long (1682–1741)

At the age of fourteen, Calthorpe's nephew Philip Parker junior succeeded as 3rd Baronet (Parker of Arwarton) when his father died in 1696. In January 1715 he was elected Whig MP for the Sussex seat of Harwich, and six months later married Martha, daughter of William East of the Middle Temple. After the death of his uncle Calthorpe in 1729, Philip became life tenant of Sir Walter Long's Gloucestershire and Wiltshire estates of Iron Acton, Whaddon, South Wraxall, North Bradley and others, adopting the name of Long in accordance with Sir Walter's wishes. (His full name was Philip Parker á Morley Long.)

He purchased the lease of 25 Leicester Square in London in 1731, commissioning James Gibbs, one of Britain's most influential architects, to rebuild the house, which by the time Philip and

272 *Calendar of State Papers, Colonial Series* 1963

his family moved in on Lady Day 1734 had three lofty storeys, a basement and a garret. Gibbs had not long completed his most important work, the church of St Martin-in-the-Fields in Trafalgar Square. Philip regularly entertained his political cronies, his brother-in-law Viscount Perceval noting on one occasion a dinner with the Parker Longs included such guests as Horace Walpole, and they were also frequent guests of Horace's father, Prime Minister Sir Robert Walpole.

A few years earlier, a curious little story had appeared in the *Taunton Journal*. Out of concern for one of his tenants at North Bradley, Mrs Crabb, an elderly widow who had been bedridden for several years, Philip directed his steward to enquire after her welfare. Upon arrival at the house he was told she was in bed and not willing to be seen. He insisted and obtained entry, but after searching all the bedrooms upstairs found no sign of her. Her elderly sister finally relented and pointed him in the direction of a large coffer at the head of the stairs. Inside was the old woman's withered corpse bent double, wasted of flesh and apparently dead for some considerable time.

At the inquest her relatives claimed she had been dead only four months and they had not the heart to bury her as they loved her too well. It was not her corpse they were so attached to, but the property, a copyhold estate of about £30 per annum, that should have terminated on the old lady's demise.

Philip and his family enjoyed regular sojourns to Bath and occasional trips to the Continent, and in June 1730 he and his wife and two daughters set sail from Dover for a short holiday to the German spa city of Aix-la-Chapelle (Aachen). Viscount Perceval notes that on the return journey, leaving from the Dutch port of Rotterdam, the family was in great danger during a storm that caused Philip's eldest daughter Martha to be violently seasick. In 1732 the Percevals spent a few days with the Parker Long's at Whaddon, and later that year Philip offered assistance to his Aunt Dionysia Long, who had written to Perceval's wife about a charity set up by Mrs Long's father John Harington, which had been embezzled by a certain Mr Bear.

Towards the end of 1740 Philip became gravely ill. He rallied for a week or so in January 1741, and on the 20th, after a pleasant dinner and evening with family and friends, he retired to bed in good, if not better than usual health. At 3am, according to Lord Perceval, he died, 'choked by one of those fits he has had for 12 weeks past at sundry times'. Perceval spent most of that day with Philip's widow Martha and their daughters, until the evening when his will and codicil were opened: 'the will we judged very ill and confusedly drawn'. Philip's daughter Martha was to receive the Wiltshire and Gloucestershire estates, and to Elizabeth he bequeathed Arwarton.

The newspapers reported he had an income of £7,000 a year and died 'vastly rich'. Perceval, by now elevated to the title of Earl of Egmont, thought it 'surprising that he mentioned not the places in the Funds where his money lies, but only bequeathed his personal estate in general terms, and that he kept no book of receipts and disbursements whereby might be known where his ready money lies, which I have to reason to suppose is more than £30,000 but Mr Gösset believes it nearer £50,000'.

The next in line to inherit Whaddon and Sir Walter Long's other estates was sixty-five-year-old Rev. John Long of South Wraxall, formerly of Meyseyhampton, Gloucestershire. Sometime Fellow of Corpus Christi College, Oxford, the Rev. Long owed his paternal ancestry to the Longs of Monkton, and on his mother's side, the Longs of Wraxall. The other estates included the manor and advowson of Tytherton Kellaways, South Wraxall manor, the chapel of St Audoen's, a farm and cottage – all in the tithing of South Wraxall, and several plots of land in Box, Atworth and Chalfield. There were also sundry houses and stables in Bristol.

In 1743, a year before the death of Calthorpe Parker Long's widow Dionysia, the Rev. Long leased from her the manor house at Whaddon with the best garden, coachhouse and large stable, and use of the courtyard, household furniture and contents (reserving specified rooms and outbuildings occupied by her tenant, Henry Collett) for a term of twenty years at an annual rent of £20. In return he was to relinquish all claims to a disputed enclosed plot of land at Outmarsh in Melksham, to be held by Dionysia for the term of her life. His term as life tenant of the rest of Sir Walter Long's estates was brief: he died six years later in 1749, childless and unmarried. The estates then passed to the last in remainder, his 71 year-old brother Thomas, clothier of Melksham, father of Walter Long of Bath.

Sir Philip Parker Long's daughters both married late and perhaps significantly, only after their father's death. Elizabeth, the youngest, died childless in 1757, less than two years after becoming Mrs James Plunkett at the age of thirty-eight. Martha, the eldest, was thirty-five when she married John Thynne Howe, 2nd Baron Chedworth in 1751, bringing her new husband a fortune of more than £40,000. But they were ill-suited and separated five years later.

His attentions were perhaps diverted more towards his thoroughbred racehorses than his new wife, and he was less than generous towards her. In November 1754, before he permanently withdrew himself from their London residence Carlisle House, she wrote in her pin-money account book: 'Received of Lord Chedworth at Compton, the day I went to Bath, £50. This payment is remarkable: It was to satisfy every expense of dress – laundress – table – chair hire – the diversions of the place – (lodging excepted, which my relation paid for), to the 15th of January when I set out for London.'

On the death of her mother in 1758, Martha, Baroness Chedworth, became lady of the manor of Arwarton, although she preferred the more modern comforts of the house at Leicester Square, inherited from her father. Her fine old Suffolk mansion at Arwarton was beginning to decay 'through improvidence or want of love', and some time during the years that followed she wrote what was effectively a death warrant for the old house:

'The mansion house being large and rambling, only fit for a farmhouse now, I give leave they pull down the crazy part of it, and make a compact farm house.' Although she had spent money on it, 'the outbuildings cost me a full £1,000 last year, and two years ago a barn was built, costing £300', she directed the park be laid out in grass again: 'The deer are all gone – and here ends the park and mansion house. Money is best for me.' The estate was put up for sale in August 1769.

The last of the Parker Longs, sixty-one-year-old Martha died at Leicester Square at the end of November 1775, having no children from her loveless marriage to Baron Chedworth, who had died in 1762. The will she wrote twenty-four years earlier on her wedding day was proved a few weeks later.

VIII
Long of Monkton, Rood Ashton and Melksham

The line of Rood Ashton (anciently *Chapel Ashton*) is descended from Thomas Long of Semington, believed to be a descendant of a brother of the first Robert Long of Wraxall, although the name of this brother has so far remained elusive to historians. Walter Long of Preshaw, who compiled the pedigree of the Longs of Semington and Potterne, printed in 1878, thought Thomas was probably the son of Richard, Robert's son, which would fit the dates.

Robert had both Semington and Wraxall, and the theory is that Richard survived his father who provided lands in the manor of Semington. After the Dissolution of the Monasteries a court roll under Sir Thomas Seymour, Lord Sudeley (who married Henry VIII's widow Katherine Parr), recites grants in Semington manor to Thomas Long and his wife Johane. Certainly the early Longs themselves believed in the connection, with names of their kinsmen from different branches mentioned in each other's wills.

Edward Long of Monkton (c.1555–1622)

The third son of clothier Henry Long of Whaddon and Mary Horton, Edward was 'heir by adoption'[273] to his wealthy uncle Thomas Long of Trowbridge, and succeeded to his estates after the death of his father in 1558. He married Ann, daughter of Henry Brouncker of Melksham and continued the family business, together with his brother Henry Long junior of Whaddon.

With lucrative profits to be made on the export of undyed cloth, the enterprising brothers entered the ranks of Merchant Venturers.

273   William Harvey, George William Marshall, *The Visitation of Wiltshire 1565*, 1897, p. 8

During their father's lifetime the cloth industry had been hampered by attempts to restrict the number of looms owned by clothiers who lived outside the towns, with further restrictions later implemented. In 1566 in an attempt to promote local manufacture, an Act was passed prohibiting export of sheep or wool. The offender would forfeit all his goods forever, and after one year's imprisonment, 'in some market town, in the fullness of the market, on the market day have his left hand cut off, and to be nailed up in the openest part of the market. And for the second offence shall be adjudged as a felon.'[274]

Apart from a few prosecutions at Westminster for operating above their quota of looms, for the most part the Wiltshire clothiers had been left to their own devices. That is, until 1575, when Peter Blackborrow, a troublemaking clothier from Frome, indicted a number of West Country broadcloth makers, including Edward and his brother Henry.

The Privy Council immediately stopped the prosecutions, and the following year an Act was passed in Parliament allowing the clothiers to continue their activities unhindered.[275] But there would soon be more difficulties. In 1577 an enquiry was made into the problem of wool supply after the Wiltshire clothiers complained the dearth and scarcity of wool was caused by the 'greedy forestalling' of wool suppliers, constrained by laws with harsh penalties themselves. Among eleven others, Edward's brother 'Harry Longe', signed the original petition of clothiers to the Council.

Despite government-imposed controls Edward prospered. He loaned £33 6s 8d to King James I on privy seals, compared to Sir Walter Long's £20, and double that of his brothers Henry and Thomas.[276] In 1588 he subscribed £25 towards the defence of England against the Spanish Armada and the following year he obtained a grant of arms. As it transpired, the Spanish king Philip II failed in his attempt to invade

---

274   Dorothy M. Hunter, *The West of England Woollen Industry Under Protection and Under Free Trade*, 1910, p. 16
275   George Daniel Ramsay, *The Wiltshire Woollen Industry in the Sixteenth and Seventeenth Centuries*, 2013, p. 59
276   *The Wiltshire Archaeological and Natural History Magazine*, vols 5-6 1859, p. 335

England, partly owing to his own mismanagement, and partly because the defensive efforts of the English and their Dutch allies proved superior.

From at least 1596 Edward lived at Southwick in North Bradley, the manor which would take a zig-zag route of descent and become the subject of at least one family dispute along the way. The next year he expanded his property portfolio, purchasing the manor of Rood Ashton from William Button, its owner since 1548. In 1600 he leased the manor of Monkton at nearby Broughton Gifford from his kinsman Sir Edward Seymour, 1st Earl of Hertford, before purchasing it five years later, including every property within the parishes of Monkton, Broughton Gifford and Melksham, for £2,100.

It was a relatively small sum, but he bought the reversion only, and there was a jointure carved out of the property for Lady Jane, wife of Edward Beauchamp.[277] Edward acted as bailiff of the manors of Bradford and Atworth,[278] property of Sir Francis Walsingham, Queen Elizabeth's notorious 'spymaster'. It was not unusual for the gentry to earn extra income as stewards and bailiffs for their social superiors, and this was probably an appointment influenced through family connections; Sir William Brouncker, Edward's brother-in-law, had married Walsingham's niece. Walsingham's second wife Ursula executed a lease of property to Edward in 1594.[279]

A Chancery suit in May 1599 exposes the opportunistic characters of Edward and his nephew Henry Brouncker. Henry, son of Sir William Brouncker, agreed to sell Edward 60 acres of land at Broughton, but he made no legal conveyance. Edward then offered to sell it to Sir William Eyre of Chalfield[280] whose property it joined, for £100 immediate down payment, with a further £200 to be placed in the hands of Sir Walter Hungerford, the balance of £400 to be paid by the following Christmas.

Although he had received part payment and was close to completing his share of the contract, Edward, 'thinking to make a

277   WANHM ibid
278   WSA ref 947:1350
279   W. H. Rich, J. Beddoe, J. E. Jackson, *Bradford-on-Avon: A History and Description*, 1907, p. 46
280   Father-in-law of the previously disinherited John Long of South Wraxall

greater benefit thereof, refused and denied the bargain' with Eyre, conspiring with Henry Brouncker to say there was no contract for the wood on the property. The scheme came unstuck when Brouncker confessed that the two of them had intended conveyance to be made of the wood in trust for their own use and for Edward's children, and so to defraud Eyre of both the wood and the money he had already paid.

The case came before Lord Chief Justice Sir John Popham, (his granddaughter later married Edward's son Gifford), who suggested a couple of alternatives to resolve the matter. Edward, labelled 'obstinate' by the court, didn't particularly like either of Popham's suggestions but had to choose one, so he elected trial at common law. A verdict was given in favour of Eyre. As a result, Edward was compelled *nolens volens*, to divide the wood, and fined £30 towards the costs of the suit. He next appears on the other side of the bench as magistrate enacting sanitary regulations to prevent the spread of plague when it came to Chippenham and Bradford.

In 1596 his only daughter Susannah married Nathaniel Coxwell, a member of a long-established Gloucestershire family who lived at Ablington Manor. Their patriarch John Coxwell had the dubious distinction of dying after a fall from his horse, reputedly aged 101, in 1618. In a complicated multi-generational entanglement, the Coxwells also intermarried with the Longs of Lyneham.

Their affairs relating to property were no less complicated. Edward and his wife Ann sought the assistance of her brother Sir Henry Brouncker in April 1600 on behalf of son-in-law Nathaniel, requesting he use his influence with Sir Robert Cecil, master of the wards, to help sway a committee decision on an inheritance in relation to part of the revenues from Lushill manor. This money had been withheld from its heir, Nathaniel's nephew, and Cecil's ward. Edward Long and John Coxwell had been lessees of one half of the manor since about 1597 when Nathaniel's sister Mary married Virgil Parker,[281] owner of the manor. Brouncker forwarded the letter 'from

---

281   Virgil Parker's father Walter married Margaret Duckett, widow of Henry Long, son of Edmund junior of Lyneham

my dear and only sister' to Cecil a few days later, and it appears to have had the desired effect.

When writing his will in 1619, two years before he died, 'being sick and weak in body but of sound and perfect memory', Edward bequeathed to each of his manservants and maids dwelling in his house at Monkton, 5s apiece, with one special manservant receiving 40s. His eldest son Gifford inherited his estates, with the exception of Monkton, which went to Edward's younger sons John and Edward junior.

Edward was very specific that after his death Gifford should recruit the assistance of his two good friends and overseers, Sir Henry Viner and Sir John Horton to search his house for the deeds and titles in all the 'chests and boxes, cupboards and other places'. Charging young Edward 'with the fear of God' to carry out his instructions as executor, he didn't trust him entirely; he must not entertain any ideas about opening or unlocking 'any other chests, boxes or cupboards wherein any of [the deeds] aforesaid are'.

By the time Edward died in 1622 the Wiltshire broadcloth industry was in a chronic depression after a market collapse in 1614, caused by the whim of James I, influenced to tamper with the trade by his courtiers and financiers.[282] James withdrew the privileges of the Merchant Venturers and founded the King's Merchant Adventurers, led by William Cockayne, who had convinced him of a scheme to make large profits for the Crown.

With direct contact between clothier and export merchant broken and Cockayne's ineptitude as a businessman, the scheme was a disaster; the Dutch merchants refused to import any English cloth and other European nations soon followed suit. The king dismissed Cockayne in 1617 and the Merchant Adventurers' former privileges were restored. But the damage was done. Hundreds of families went bankrupt in the West Country; they were producing cloth, but the buyers had gone. Inevitably unemployment and riots followed. The clothiers would later face further problems during the Civil War due to a Royalist proclamation prohibiting the sale of cloth to Parliamentarian-controlled London. In a desperate attempt to revive the industry after

282   Roger Lockyer, *Tudor and Stuart Britain: 1485-1714*, p. 388

the war ended, a severe depression prompted Parliament to pass an Act that all persons should be buried in woollen shrouds.

Edward's In-Laws, the Brounckers

Edward's father-in-law Henry Brouncker of Melksham was a man of considerable wealth. MP for Devizes and a member of the Muscovy Company, founded with state assistance in 1555 to develop trade with Russia, he was sheriff of Wiltshire in 1558. Among several overseers of his will dated 1568, he appointed his 'trustie and wellbeloved' friend Sir John Thynne of Longleat, whose daughter Catherine married Sir Walter Long the elder of Wraxall. Thynne (the builder of Longleat House) was steward to Edward Seymour, 1st Duke of Somerset, and he acted as his agent in the dispute over Fasterne between Seymour, Katherine Parr, and Sir Henry Long.

Another familiar name in the circle of friends is Lawrence Hyde (grandfather of Edward, Earl of Clarendon), whom Brouncker names as his trustee, along with sons-in-law Robert Davy and Edward Long. Hyde's name frequently appears with Sir John Thynne as joint grantees of confiscated chantry lands. Hyde names Brouncker's younger son William as one of his overseers in 1584.

Henry's son, Sir Henry Brouncker, sometime president of Munster and father of Viscount Brouncker of Lyons, was also the queen's commissioner, dispatched hither and thither on royal errands. Devoted and loyal, in 1599 his new year's gift to her majesty was 'one pettycote of taffeta sarcenet quylted all over with a border, imbrothered with golde and carnacon silke with poyntes', one of eleven lavishly embroidered 'pettycotes' received by her on that occasion.

At the outbreak of the Gowrie conspiracy in 1600 the queen sent Brouncker to congratulate the Scottish King James upon his escape, but her discovery that James had been in correspondence with her enemy, the Earl of Essex, combined her congratulations with an accusation that he had been accessory to the preparation of her funeral. She was also much occupied with the intrigues of Arabella Stuart, King James's cousin, considered a likely successor to the Scottish throne. Arabella, forbidden by the queen to marry without her consent, spent twenty-seven years of her life under the control of her grandmother, the Countess of Shrewsbury (Bess of Hardwick), which greatly frustrated her. She wrote many rambling and often angry letters, venting her frustrations and baffling their recipients, including Sir Henry Brouncker at Lambeth Marsh.[283]

Early in 1603 the queen sent Brouncker to Hardwick Hall to question Arabella about a rumour of a politically contentious marriage to Edward Seymour, considered treasonous since the Seymours also had a claim to the English throne. Soon after this visit Arabella made an unsuccessful escape attempt from Hardwick, afterwards writing to the queen begging forgiveness, saying 'Sir Henry Brunker hath charged me with many things in your Majesty's name, the most whereof I acknowledge to be true'. She had earlier ranted to Sir Henry: 'all men are liers. Theare is no trust in man whose breath is in his nosthrilles. Farewell good knight.' Arabella was eventually imprisoned in the Tower by James I for marrying William, Earl of Hertford (younger brother of Edward Seymour), without permission, where she starved herself to death in 1615.

John Long of Monkton (c.1581–1654)

Edward and Anne's sons John and Edward junior occupied the manor of Monkton in succession. John, formerly resident of Haugh near Bradford (not to be confused with the other John Long of Haugh whose daughter intermarried with this line), appears to have carried out an extensive building programme in or around 1647, marked by the date on the north gable of Monkton House.

This work involved repairs, alterations and an extension on the eastern side. During the Civil War the household was forced to accommodate soldiers fighting for Cromwell's Parliamentarian army, an imposition particularly objectionable to John, a Royalist supporter, who gave two horses for the king's service, saying afterwards he thought nothing too good to give.

During the battle at Roundway Down in 1643, a Royalist cavalry force under Lord Wilmot won a crushing victory over the

283   Many lengthy letters from the Countess of Shrewsbury, her granddaughter Arabella Stuart and Sir Henry Brouncker are preserved at Hatfield House

Parliamentarians under Sir William Waller, who were besieging Devizes. In an unguarded moment John was overheard to say that 'there were none but rogues and base fellows left in the Parliament at London', and all rogues should be hanged as rebels against the king. The war was lost, but his careless words not forgotten, and John was later labelled a delinquent and his estate sequestered. Ordered to appear before the county commissioners he was charged a fine, which depending on the degree of delinquency was anything from two or three years' value of his estate to as much as eight years. Owing to the weak market during the Interregnum he probably borrowed the money rather than try to sell land.

Monkton House, Broughton Gifford 1938 Wiltshire & Swindon Archives

At the end of hostilities in 1649 one Katherine Symons testified against John, but he was defiant. He feared nothing but being put to his oath, he said, for he had taken the king's protestation already. He petitioned for dismissal from prosecution on the grounds that the case had already dragged on for a year on pretence of new evidence, maintaining nothing fresh had been produced. Proceedings continued for a further two years, and he was eventually discharged on an Act of Pardon in April 1652. He sued out his pardon for £24 6s 8d.[284]

Four months earlier he wrote his will, leaving his second wife Anne[285] half of all his plate and household goods, lands and a cottage in Winsleigh, and also his late brother Edward's diamond ring, for the term of her life. If she foolishly challenged any of her dower 'all bequests to her are to be void and revoked and the same to be given to my loving son Thomas'.

John died in about 1654 and was succeeded by Thomas, whose marriage to Margery Hungerford came with a handsome jointure; even so, with the impact of the late wars on the family's finances and five children to raise and educate, he was in need of money. Margery agreed to the sale of Monkton, on which her jointure had been secured, and in return she would have a cash settlement of £3000 on herself and her children to be raised out of the purchase monies. Sir James Thynne of Longleat apparently bought the manor in 1669 and the family stayed on at the property until Lady Day 1671 at an annual rent of £260. At odds with this sale however, a conveyance was made by Thomas and Margery, dated 21st January 1674, of the manor with all its rights, members, and appurtenances, for £1221.

In the meantime Thomas had his eye on Rowden Farm and in 1670 he purchased a 99 year lease of the property for £2,020 from Sir Edward Hungerford, with a yearly rent of £10. Included was the manor house, barns, stables, orchards, gardens and 340 acres of pasture and meadow. During the Civil War the house had been used as a garrison by Hungerford, a Parliamentary officer. According to popular legend he lost the estate by gambling it, staking the property in a bowling match, calling out when he threw his last chance: 'there goes Rowden.' In reality it was already mortgaged to sometime MP for Chippenham Sir Richard Kent for £3,000.

The battered house was situated at the centre of the old manor of Rowden and was also known as The Ivy. After being surrounded and dismantled during the war by Royalist troops it was restored to some

284   M. A. E. Green, *Calendar of the Proceedings of the Committee for Advance of Money, 1642–1656*
285   Edward's first wife was Katherine Nicholas of Allcannings

of its former glory in the years that followed. The river Avon bordered the western part of the estate, giving the Longs sole rights of fishing, but the river's bounty provided attractive scope for plunder to the habitual poacher. Thomas caught two cardmakers from Chippenham, William Crill and John Webb, who had stolen three of his fish-pots. They were bound to desist in future and required to inform him about any other poachers.

Thomas Long of Rowden (c.1657–1730)

In 1698, a few years after Thomas and Margery's son Thomas junior finished his university education at Oxford, he purchased Rowden outright (hence his title 'Mr Long of the Farm' in the diary of Thomas Smith of Melksham) after a Chancery decree against its former owner Sir Richard Kent. A respected justice of the peace, Thomas was also 'well vers'd in history', the man most able to 'tell many Historical Passages relating to Chippenham and the places adjacent'. He was recommended thus by the sexton of Chippenham, James Harris, to Thomas Hearne, writer and antiquarian.

Aside from peace-keeping and history, his energies were otherwise devoted to farming during what was a difficult period for landowners; the net return on land rental was only about three per cent and agriculture sluggish. Many smaller proprietors came to grief. A document titled 'An Account of Stock at Rowden Farm, Chippenham 1671–73' apparently written by Thomas, illustrates the trade in cattle fattened on the low-lying pastures of the farm.

The cover of this account has the names Katherine Long and 'Hubert' or 'Hulbert' written on it, as though written by one practising penmanship. These were most likely the youthful doodlings of Thomas's teenage sister Katherine, perhaps besotted with Thomas Hulbert of Corsham whom she married in 1679. Before her marriage she lived at the farm with her brother, who did not marry until he was aged about forty. Their sister Elizabeth married Richard Long of Rood Ashton.

In 1722 the good people of Wiltshire were once again stirred with rumblings of plots against the government, and there was suspicion that some of the conspirators were in their midst. Determined to ferret out the troublemakers, the army were ordered to encamp in several places, and as well as London's Hyde Park and Hounslow Heath, they made their presence felt in Wiltshire at Salisbury, Hungerford, and Thomas's neighbourhood of Chippenham, half a mile from Rowden. A concerned citizen of Melksham had overheard a discussion about weapons in Daniel Webb 's house at Monkton Farleigh, enough for 500 men. Webb had taken a twenty-one-year lease of the manor in 1707 from Sir Walter Long, 2nd Baronet of Whaddon, held under the Bishop of Salisbury. Thomas and two other local JPs made a search of the property, apparently without result.

He was seventy-three when he died in 1730, five months after the death of his brother-in-law and cousin Richard Long. His first wife, Anne Goddard, whom he married in 1697, died aged seventy-two in 1724. He took a second wife, a very young Mary, surname unknown, who must have been about fifty years his junior, and was also seventy-two when she died in 1773, forty-three years after her husband and almost fifty years after his first wife. There were no children. He left his estates to his nephew Richard Long junior of Rood Ashton (d. 1760).

Gifford Long of Rood Ashton (1576–1634)

By 1600 clothiers were in serious decline after the introduction of mechanisation, and Gifford, son and heir of Edward Long of Monkton, became a man of social aspirations rather than just another in the long line of clothiers. His rank of 'esquire' was one above the slightly more humble 'gentleman', but he would have to wait for middle-age before he acquired any significant wealth. First, he must be properly educated, a necessary requirement if he was to oversee his estates and take his place on the magistrates bench.

In 1593, aged seventeen, Gifford was admitted to Magdalen Hall, University of Oxford. He was 21 when he married Anne, heir of John Yewe of Bradford on Avon. She brought to the marriage a property known as The Mount, Somerford Manor, which her father had purchased in 1575. They had two daughters, but Anne died soon after the birth of the second child in 1601.

Her elaborate tomb at Bradford has been compared to that of

*Memorial brass to Anne Yewe, wife of Gifford Long, Monumental Brasses of
Wiltshire, E. Kite 1860*

Shakespeare's wife.[286] The memorial brass to her in the church depicts a young woman attired in typical Elizabethan costume, an outer gown open at the front to show the finely embroidered petticoat, and a bodice with its conspicuous peaked stomacher. The ladies of this period wore a farthingale underneath to distend their skirts, the ancestor of the eighteenth-century hoop petticoat. At her neck is a large ruff of the kind popularised by Elizabeth I, held up with a framework of wires called a supportasse or underpropper.

In his book *The Anatomie of Abuses,* published in 1583, poet and pamphleteer Philip Stubbes ridicules 'these cartwheels of the divel's charet of pride', pouring scorn on the evils of stiffening, 'a certaine kinde of liquide matter which they call Starch, wherein the devill hath willed them to wash and dive his ruffes wel, which when they be dry, will then stand stiffe and inflexible about their necks'.

Somerford Manor was to provide a marriage portion and one half-year's rent, worth £65, for their eldest daughter Anne under the terms of her grandfather John Yewe's will, but Gifford sold it almost immediately after his wife's death. Anne married William Bromwich in 1630 but the younger daughter Catherine died in 1610; the churchwarden's accounts record the payment by Gifford of 6s 5d for her burial.

In October 1604 Gifford was in Harlington, Bedfordshire, on family business when he was diverted with several other gentlemen to the house of a man named Brian Gunter, a member of the local gentry in North Moreton, a few miles south of Oxford. Belief in witchcraft was widespread and there were strange things being said about Gunter's twenty-year-old daughter Anne. Word had got around that her garters and bodices unlaced themselves. Bewitched, her father said, and to prove the terrible fact to Gifford and the other observers, Anne was placed in front of them on a chair. She immediately 'fell into a very strange agony of quivering and shaking', with a 'foaming of the mouth' and other 'fearful . . . passions and extremities'.

Gunter insisted Gifford 'should make what trial he would upon his said daughter' in hopes of demonstrating her insensitivity. He

---

286 *Shakespeariana,* Shakespeare Society of New York, p. 119

began by 'violently of wringing her little finger' then progressed to 'violently pulling of the hairs of the temples of her head and moving back and forth and waving of other parts of her body'. Anne, possibly anaesthetised by a dose of sack and sallet oil, showed no response, leaving him convinced she was genuinely insensitive to pain.

Nearly a year later, upon closer investigation by the witch-hunting King James visiting Oxford in August 1605, Anne Gunter confessed she had simulated bewitchment at her father's instigation to further a feud between him and several women she had named as witches. Late in 1606 Gifford was summoned to London by the Star Chamber to give evidence of what he had seen.[287]

It may have been unusual that Gifford would be in Bedfordshire at all, but he was interested in a young widow there, Mrs Amy Wingate – destined to become the second Mrs Gifford Long. No doubt he went dressed to impress, and the large sum of £95 he spent on lace, silk and taffeta for a doublet and hose[288] was possibly for this purpose.

Amy lived with her two sons John and George at Harlington House, ancestral home of her late husband, Robert Wingate, who had died the year before. Her father, Roger Warre, heir to Hestercombe Manor in Somerset, married Eleanor, *née* Popham, which meant that Amy's grandfather was the immensely wealthy and influential lord chief justice, Sir John Popham of Littlecote, who presided at the trials of Guy Fawkes, Sir Walter Raleigh and Mary Queen of Scots, to name but a few.

In 1622 forty-six-year-old Gifford succeeded to his father's estates, including Rood Ashton, but a disagreement with his brother Edward junior over distribution of their father's farm stock and household goods at Ablington and Alton in Figheldean necessitated the appointment of arbitrators. Gifford and his father had already conveyed the manor of Westbury Arundell with its grain and fulling mills to Sir James Ley in 1614, which may have been influenced by the collapse of the cloth trade that year. This manor was among those passed

287   J.A. Sharpe, *The Bewitching of Anne Gunter: A Horrible and True Story of Deception, Witchcraft, Murder and the King of England*, 2000, p. 161
288   British Library, MSS 15567

down from Gifford's great-uncle Thomas Long of Trowbridge.[289]

Gifford was appointed sheriff of Wiltshire in 1624 and he was churchwarden of Steeple Ashton in 1625, the year the market fair was suspended by an Act of the Privy Council to prevent the spread of plague to the village. At a vestry meeting held in Easter week he and George Webb [290] (vicar since 1605, to whom Gifford would later bequeath '40 shillings to buy a ring of gold as a token of my love') agreed that every cottager and householder in the parish of Steeple Ashton would pay a penny each for himself, his wife and each child who took communion, for the provision of their bread and wine for the entire year. If any refused to pay 'hee is to bee pr'sented'.

Fifty years after his uncle Thomas Long shook the foundations of the House of Commons in the infamous £4 bribery scandal, Gifford was elected for the same seat, Westbury, which he represented in Parliament in May 1625. His appointment as justice of the peace afforded him added status and a considerable degree of influence. The qualifications were good moral and religious character and ownership of land worth at least £20 per annum. He received no pay for his work other than 4s a day for attending quarter sessions, which if he performed his duties diligently would leave him out of pocket, not only for expenses, but also personal time to attend his own affairs.

The lists of county JPs were frequently reviewed for a variety of reasons, and while an appointment to the Commission of Peace imputed social prestige, dismissal meant loss of authority and public humiliation. Gifford's cousin Sir Walter Long the elder was one of twelve Wiltshire JPs sacked from the bench not once, but twice, in 1587 and again in 1592-3. Gifford himself was caught up in a great purge in December 1625. Chancery issued new Commissions of the Peace to remove justices, in which 30-40 per cent of JPs throughout twenty counties were abruptly dismissed. However, he was among the first to regain office, returning to the Wiltshire Commission in February 1626.[291]

289   R.B. Pugh and Elizabeth Crittall, *A History of Wiltshire*, 1953
290   Later bishop of Limerick, d. 1641 of 'gaol fever' after being imprisoned in Limerick Castle by Papist rebels
291   Alison Wall, *The Great Purge of 1625: the late Murraine amongst the*

Early in 1632 he was appointed to a three-man committee with Sir James Ley and the sheriff, Edward Hungerford, to ascertain the cost and availability of materials for repairing the decaying thirteenth-century Bradford Bridge.[292] They were to make their report at the next assizes, but the committee still had not reported six months later, owing to 'it being a hard matter to get the said gentlemen together'. In an attempt to expedite matters the committee was enlarged to seven with a quorum of three, and eventually repairs were made, with a contribution by the town ordered by the assizes in 1634.

The liberal use of the word 'cousin' and its variants seems to have covered near and distant relatives equally, and in some instances they may have been nephews, nieces or in-laws, making it sometimes difficult to determine their true relationship. Gifford was executor of the will of Francis Trenchard of Cutteridge in 1622, who left to his 'welbeloved cosin Gifford Longe' for his pains therein 'my blacke amblinge nagg mare I use to ride on'. The Trenchards were allied by marriage with the Longs of South Wraxall and Preshaw more than one hundred years later, and this mention of 'cosin' implies an earlier connection.

So, too, the Langford family, clothiers of Trowbridge: in 1551 Edward Langford names Gifford's grandfather 'my cosyn Harry Long of Trobridge' together with Harry's brother-in-law William Horton, a clothier, also called 'cosyn'. Connections by marriage to wealthy clothier families like the Langfords and Hortons were not uncommon. In 1624 Gifford was overseer of the will of Mary Hyde, *née* Langford, mother of Edward, Earl of Clarendon.

By the time he died in December 1634 aged fifty-eight, Gifford's estates were substantial, including lands in Poulshot, Marston, Worton, Potterne, Chittoe and Cheverell Magna, all held of William Brouncker as part of his manor of Melksham, making the cost of 6s 8d for his tomb at Steeple Ashton seem modest for a man of such wealth. Among many other things, he bequeathed to his 'dear and loving wife'

Gentlemen of the Peace, University of Oxford
292   Ralph Bernard Pugh, [Elizabeth Crittall, [D. A. Crowley, *A History of Wiltshire*, vol. 7, p. 10

Amy 'all my stock without doors at Rood Ashton', also 'all my grain and wood within doors alreadie cutt or without'. His will has many affectionate and sometimes effusive references to his family. He desired that his 'loving brother John Long, Gent', his 'loving kinsman Walter Long of Whaddon, Esquire' and his servant John Tuthill, in token of his love towards them, each have a gold ring to remember him by, with a death's head and the inscription 'Remember Thy End.'

Of Gifford and Amy's five children, four survived: Edward, the eldest; Roger, who studied law; Thomas, apprenticed to his father's 'good friend Mr Isaac Jones of London, merchant', and Eleanor, who married William Carent, grandson of the lord treasurer, Sir James Ley. Amy continued to live at Rood Ashton until her death in 1650. She still had some of her household stuff and goods at Harlington House which she bequeathed to her grandsons George and Francis Wingate; he was later justice Sir Francis Wingate, whose one memorable act was the arrest of John Bunyan for illegal preaching in 1660. Bunyan was imprisoned for twelve years in Bedford jail where he began writing his famous Christian allegory *Pilgrim's Progress*.

Amy wrote her will in 1646, the last year of the first English Civil War, and she had good reason to fear 'these troublesome times'. Just seven miles to the north, near Corsham, between the two Royalist positions of Farleigh Castle and Lacock Abbey, the manor house of the Eyre family of Great Chalfield had been seized and garrisoned by the Parliamentarians. An undisciplined rabble of about 250 soldiers anxious to avoid the horrors of war, they were typical of the garrisons that caused fear among the civilians. They attempted to dominate the surrounding countryside which they used to maintain themselves in money and supplies by whatever means necessary. Early in 1645 this same garrison caused trouble for Gifford's cousin, Sir James Long of Draycot, by blocking the retreat of his Cavaliers, aiding their capture by Cromwell and resulting in Sir James's imprisonment with his men.

Gifford's son and heir Edward began his university education at Magdalen Hall, Oxford, aged sixteen in 1622, coinciding with the death of his grandfather, also Edward, who left him various items of plate, including a dozen silver spoons with strawberry heads. He commenced his law studies in 1625 as a student of Lincoln's Inn, and married Dorothy, daughter of his father's friend Isaac Jones, merchant of Covent Garden, in about 1631. Between 1638 and 1640 we find Edward living at Alton, in Figheldean, presumably residing in the farmhouse there, part of the inheritance from his father.

Henry Long of Rood Ashton (1631–72)

Gifford's grandson Henry, only son of Edward and Dorothy, was baptised in London and also studied law, inheriting Rood Ashton on the death of his father in 1644, when he was still in his minority. The times in which he lived were tumultuous, to say the least. During his formative years the climate of anxiety, mistrust and fear that pervaded the country saw the disintegration of the Church of England, the collapse of the government of Charles I and the accompanying panic that swept through the population leading up to the Civil War in the summer of 1642.

Years later, as the Great Plague ravaged the population of London throughout the spring and summer of 1665, Henry and his wife Dionysia retreated to Rood Ashton. Hot on their heels, Charles II, along with his family and the royal court, also sought sanctuary in Wiltshire, moving to Salisbury where he attended Parliament at Oxford. But by summer the plague had reached there too. Of those who remained in London an estimated 70,000 died.

The journey from London to Rood Ashton was just a little over 100 miles, which today could be accomplished in two hours by car, but in Henry's time, according to one contemporary advertisement, a stage coach plied the Bath Road three days a week, leaving London at five in the morning and 'performing the whole journey in three days (if God permit)' for the sum of £1 5s per passenger, with a maximum of 14lbs of luggage each.[293]

Preparations were under way in October 1670 for the remarriage of Henry's only sister Elizabeth, widow of their cousin Richard Long of Collingbourne, who had been left with six children under the age of ten years. The prospective bridegroom was John Eyre, an

---

293 W. Outram Tristram, *Coaching Days and Coaching Ways*, 1893, p. 4

uncompromising and embittered Wiltshire JP who had succeeded to his father Robert's estates at Chalfield in 1651.

Suppression of Protestant nonconformists had been a particular hobby-horse of Eyre's; he had written in 1662 to Charles II's secretary of state Sir Henry Bennett, bemoaning the fact that despite his issuing warrants for the apprehension of the most dangerous dissenters, sending them to gaol did little good. 'They glory in their sufferings. There will be no safety unless they are kept down with a strong hand, for there are five to one against the present government.'[294]

A year earlier, in January 1661, Sir Robert Long (1st Baronet of Westminster) received a letter at Somerset House from his nephew James Long of Draycot on the same subject, complaining of meetings at Rowden and Bristol, describing the dissenters as troublesome and insolent, determined to defy the law, mostly men and few women. He warned that certain members of the community, 'Gentlemen, Ministers and others of the better sort', were prepared to take up arms to keep the peace.

Evidently Henry Long was one of the better sort; a few months later he disturbed a large Baptist meeting at North Bradley while captaining a body of militia. His men arrested five dissenters who were later taken before two deputies and imprisoned without bail in the disease-ridden county gaol at Fisherton Anger, on the outskirts of Salisbury.

Some were sympathetic to the nonconformists, such as Leonard Atkins of Sutton Benger, a village which 'abounds with fanatics', according to James Long. Atkins was one of James's tenants, formerly a lieutenant in the rebel army. In 1666 he was a constable at Salisbury gaol where James had committed one Hardy, 'a very dangerous fellow' from Yorkshire, but Atkins allowed his escape. James suggested to Joseph Williamson at Whitehall (at that time in the service of the secretary of state, Sir Edward Nicholas), that if Atkins was 'frighted' they might recapture Hardy and 'discover many mysteries if well handled'.

Not averse to a bit of torture to get information, James wrote to Williamson discussing another of the rebels: 'I am confident that if the rack be shewed him hee will declare all the Cheife traytours in our parts.' He had no qualms about threatening Atkins, whose wife was a cousin, Catherine, daughter of Henry Long of Lyneham. Never mind family sensibilities; the object of his interest was to discover the 'nest of vipers' and 're-establish the dignity of the Crown'.[295]

A royal proclamation against conventicles in 1669 had little effect, owing to the reluctance of some magistrates to properly enforce the law. After a lengthy absence in London John Eyre was outraged to discover on his return to Chalfield in 1670 that once again dissenters were openly holding 'tumultuous' meetings in defiance of new legislation.

In August Sharrington Talbot complained that although he was neither a deputy lieutenant nor a justice of the peace, 'the gentry all repair to me upon all occasions of unlawful meetings', having been informed by John Eyre and Henry Long of the wilful determination of a group of Quakers to 'despise all authority'. With his marriage to Elizabeth Long less than a month away, Eyre wrote to the bishop of Salisbury, Seth Ward, telling of the 'great disorders' again being committed in his neighbourhood, of unlawful meetings of Quakers, Anabaptists and Presbyterians.

Many, including Henry Long, considered it highly likely 'these insolent people' would increase in numbers if their activities were not curbed. The bishop heard from Eyre that Henry had been very active in suppressing the meetings, and many convictions had resulted, their goods confiscated. But Eyre complained that 'the things were offered for sale in the markets and fairs, yet not one penny has been bid, but by way of a sneer; as 6d. or 13½d. for a cow, and such like, save what I bought myself, without occasion, but chiefly to encourage others'. Henry Long, he said, had also bought goods at the market to set a good example.

Charles II introduced the Royal Declaration of Indulgence in March 1672, which suspended punishment of dissenters, but its withdrawal in early spring the following year saw renewed judicial fervour against them. By this time both Henry Long and John Eyre were dead, the campaign of persecution against nonconformists left

295   *Ibid*, vol. CXC 2 February 1667

to others. Indeed, throughout the period 1675 to 1678 Wiltshire persecuted more dissenters than any other county, but only fifteen convictions for each of those years were successful.

Aged only forty, Henry was childless at his death in March 1672. Of the many bequests in his will to family and friends he left one of his 'best horse beasts' to his 'dear and loving uncle, Sir Samuel Jones' of Courteenhall, Northamptonshire. Jones, while mostly dividing time between his estates in Northamptonshire and business in London, also had interests in the Longs' neighbourhood, being the owner of the advowson and rectory of Steeple Ashton in 1663.

Jones's sister Susan had married Sir Dru Drury, 2nd Baronet, of Riddlesworth Hall, Norfolk, whose son the Rev. Dru Drury purchased the advowson and rectory from Samuel Martyn in 1676. The Rev. Drury had inherited his father's estates, and before his death in 1698 he remembered in his will three members of the extended Long family, leaving to 'my cousin Richard Long Esq; [1668–1730] my diamond ring and another mourning ring of the value of a guinea' and 'to Capt. [William] Long of Bainton and Capt. [Thomas] Long of Rowden [1657–1730], rings to the value of sixteen shillings apiece with gloves'. Drury left the advowson and rectory of Steeple Ashton to Magdalene College, Cambridge, to found a travelling fellowship for a 'gentleman's son of Norfolk'.

Henry Long bequeathed Rood Ashton to his sister's second son Richard Long junior (1668–1730). His widow Dionysia (née Bassett) remarried the year following his death, to Christopher Pitt of Blandford, Dorset.

Richard Long of Collingbourne (c.1633–69)

We now enter the confusing labyrinth of Longs consecutively named Richard, which include two who married cousins, both called Elizabeth Long, who each in turn begat more sons called Richard. The second son of Thomas Long of Little Cheverell (see Long of Potterne), Richard Long of Collingbourne also studied law at Lincoln's Inn, being admitted in October, 1634, where he probably came into contact with his cousin James Long of Draycot, admitted four months earlier.

Richard succeeded to the estate at Collingbourne by the will of his father in 1654. His death in September 1669 was sudden and unexpected. He was buried at Collingbourne, just one year after the birth of his son Richard junior, future heir to his maternal uncle's estate of Rood Ashton. He left no will, but the inventory of his household goods indicates his main house was large and well-furnished to accommodate a family and household servants, with multiple lots of everything. The kitchen was plentifully stocked with the usual assortment of dishes, pots and pans and other paraphernalia, including 'Nine and twenty-three dozen of pewter plates', indicating sizeable gatherings at some time. The smaller house at Lower Collingbourne Farm also had large numbers of implements, livestock and grain.

The year of Richard's death had already been an eventful one for the family. Just three months earlier a third son Thomas was born, not long after the death of a daughter, Susanna. His eldest son Henry further entangled the branches of the impossibly complex tree by marrying his cousin Anne, daughter of John Long of South Wraxall and his wife Catherine Paynter. According to the baptism register of Great Chalfield, Richard's widow Elizabeth had a further two daughters with her second short-lived husband John Eyre of Chalfield, who lasted barely three years.

Richard Long of Rood Ashton (1668–1730)

Having already inherited Rood Ashton, Ablington Manor and farms at Tollard Royal and Collingbourne Kingston, the next Richard Long married his cousin in about 1689 – another Elizabeth Long.[296] This marriage brought him possession of Walwayne Court, Trowbridge, leased on behalf of his wife, then a minor, in 1687.

With the passing of so much property between family members, inevitably there were disputes from time to time, and with such close intermarriage of the cousinhood they were usually complicated. After the death in 1686 of his elder brother Henry, Richard was next in remainder to inherit an estate at Melksham. He 'entred and enjoyed these lands' but on the birth of his late brother's posthumous son

296   Daughter of Thomas Long of Monkton and his wife Margery Hungerford

(see Henry Long of Melksham, 1686–1730) Richard graciously laid
no further claim to the property, and gave the estate to his brother's
widow[297] as guardian of her son.

A few years later he had a change of heart and commenced an
action of ejectment for the estate. Judgement was given in his favour
but this was later reversed in the House of Lords 'against the opinion
of all the Judges, who were much dissatisfied by the reversal, and
blamed the Judge who tried the cause for suffering a special verdict to
be found'. The case was heard in December 1694.

One month earlier, Richard, or Dick to his friends, had been
elected MP for Chippenham amid allegations of corruption levelled
against him by his defeated opponent Sir Basil Firebrace and his
supporters. He had beaten Firebrace, the sitting member, by sixteen
votes. An enquiry found impropriety not on the part of Richard but
on Firebrace and his cronies, who had bribed voters in an attempt to
retain the seat.[298]

Traditionally the Longs were staunch Tories, but Richard sat as
a Whig. His representation in Parliament was brief, however, though
he was vocal in his support of the Immorality Bill. In keeping with
the Long family's Puritanical values, his remedy for poverty was the
suppression of alehouses. He proposed that to 'hinder the growing
evil' of alcoholism, a clause should be inserted into the impending Bill
to prevent the poor from 'spending their time consuming their weekly
wages in little paltry alehouses, especially on Sundays'. This could be
achieved, he thought, either by instituting more severe penalties for
drunkenness, or by stopping the proliferation of alehouses 'which I am
sure is the most . . . intolerable grievance we have'.[299]

Richard stood down at the next general election, although in
1701 he and his brother Thomas were active in canvassing support for
the Whig candidates. His close association with the two members for
Chippenham, Edward Montagu and Walter White of Grittleton, was
demonstrated in a letter he wrote to White in January 1700, offering

297   Ann, daughter of John Long of South Wraxall
298   *House of Commons Journal*, vol. 11, 5 January 1695
299   David Hayton, *Moral Reform and Country Politics in the Late Seventeenth-
Century House of Commons*, Past & Present, No. 128, Aug., 1990, p. 63

his continued friendship.[300] The determination of the Whigs to keep the seat was supported by many of the local gentry; 'I beg you to be industrious against the election for our county,' wrote Henry Blake to Walter White on behalf of the candidates. 'Ned Bayntun will take care of Melsham and Bromham side, I will of Calne, Compton etc., Tom Long and his brother Dick of Corsham etc., and doe you doe the same in the north part.'[301]

The bye-election of 1705 saw Chippenham fall back into the hands of the Longs, with Richard's Tory cousin Sir James Long, 5th Baronet of Draycot, securing the seat with John Mordant. Nearly thirty years later Richard's son, Richard junior, would keep the flag flying for the Tories, winning the election in 1734.

Richard served as sheriff of Wiltshire in 1702–3, living at Hatt House in nearby Box until at least 1706, while he leased his house and lands at Rood Ashton to a Mr John Pierce of Beanacre for a term of eight years, reserving certain specified rooms for his own use. His wife Elizabeth did not survive long after the birth of their third child, dying in 1691. After nearly three decades a widower, Richard married again in 1720 to Mrs Grace Martyn (*née* Stileman). Writing his will the following year, he directed his widow should live with his only surviving son, Richard junior, 'if it be agreeable to them'. Whether it was agreeable or not to Richard the son, it may have been imprudent for him to refuse the arrangement; his new stepmother was also his mother-in-law, after he married her daughter Anne.

Richard senior had already made a trust settlement in favour of Richard junior in 1711 of the manors of Rood Ashton and West Ashton, five farms and various tenements at Steeple Ashton, Bratton, Westbury, Semington and Great Hinton, consisting of more than 2,000 acres, which according to an indenture dated May 1711 they rented out to a Michael Collins. Dying in January 1730 aged sixty-one, Richard wanted 'to be buried privately and late in an evening with but few persons to attend my funeral, and that the bell shall be

300   David Hayton, Eveline Cruickshanks, Stuart Handle, *The House of Commons 1690–1715*, 2002
301   R.B. Pugh, Elizabeth Crittall, *A History of the County of Wiltshire*, 1957, vol. 5, p. 198

only tolled and not rung out on the day of my interment'. His widow
Grace survived until April 1746.

The Thresher Sisters

A short journey down the line of Richard's sister Dionysia and
her Thresher granddaughters reveals they did very well from
their Long connections. Dionysia had married Edward Thresher of
Bradford, owner of the Chantry House there from 1696, built in 1524
by the clothier Thomas Horton of Iford. Edward was also a successful
clothier, and by 1723 the Thresher family was quoted as one of
twenty-five families whose combined stock-in-trade topped £40,000.
Edward Thresher died in 1725, debatably 'the most famous maker of
fine mix't cloth in the Kingdom',[302] and his only son John returned
from training as a lawyer in London to take over the family business.

John married his cousin Ellen in 1731, daughter of Henry Long,
clothier of South Wraxall. The London press announced that 'John
Thresher Esq., an eminent counsellor, who upon his father's dying
and leaving him near £2,000 per annum, quitted his business and
was last week married to Miss Long, a very agreeable lady of £5,000
fortune,' – adding rather ambiguously – 'to whom he was before nearly
related.'[303] In fact this somewhat mangled attempt at describing their
family connection could be applied to most of the Long family. At
twenty-one, Ellen was half John's age and also descended via both
parents from the Longs of Rood Ashton.

Having no sons at his death, John bequeathed £12,000 to be
equally divided between his daughters, Ellen, Dionysia, Elizabeth
and Mary, all under nine years old. To his widow Ellen he left £1,000
and the income from freehold and copyhold property in and around
Bradford and Winsley. The court of Chancery appointed Sir Robert
Long of Draycot, 6th Baronet, and old Walter Long of Bath, guardians
to Ellen and her four young girls.

Ellen died in April 1753, and her will allows a fleeting glimpse
into her trinket box. To her eldest daughter Ellen junior she gave

302   *Parker's Penny Post*, 28 February 1726, issue 130
303   *Daily Advertiser*, 11 November 1731, issue 242

£1,000 and 'all my roses or starrs of brilliant diamonds for the stays, my diamond solitaire, my brilliant diamond girdle buckle, my mother of pearl snuff box set in Gold, and such two of my diamond rings as shall she choose'. Dionysia got £500, 'my diamond earrings consisting of a TopaNot and three drops to each earring on condition that she shall deliver to her sister Elizabeth the diamond earrings she now hath in her keeping.' In addition Dionysia was to receive her mother's pearl necklace, a rose diamond buckle, a gold watch and chain and her choice of several diamond rings.

To Elizabeth, Ellen left 'diamond rings now in the keeping of her said sister Dionysia, my other gold watch, such one of my gold snuff boxes and such one of my diamond rings after her two eldest sisters have chosen'. As the youngest child Mary received a gold snuff box and the 'residue of my rings'. Ellen also bequeathed the sum of £100 for a monument to be erected at North Bradley in memory of her 'dear mother and father and brother, Henry Long'.

The young ladies, now aged between seventeen and twenty-one, also benefitted from their late father's property, making them quite wealthy orphans, aglitter with gold and jewels. But this was just the appetiser for the main course. Twenty years later their fortunes again increased, when in 1773 Ellen's unmarried elder brother, William Long of Melksham, 'a gentleman of large fortune', bequeathed to his niece Mary Thresher all his property in Melksham including his mansion house and sundry farms, all the contents and other effects. Her sister Elizabeth received Normanton Farm at Great Durnford, and two farms in North Bradley, and Ellen inherited property in Ireland, as well as a share with her sisters of the residue of William's estate.

The eldest daughter Ellen was the first to marry. With a dowry reported variously between £10,000 and £20,000 and a considerable landed estate 'being her least consideration', in May 1755 she became the second wife of 'an eminent Councellor at Law' Sir Bourchier Wrey, 6th Baronet of Tavistock, Devon, former MP for Barnstaple who had a colourful reputation in his youth. Wrey had made his Grand Tour in 1737–40, visiting Paris, Geneva, Rome, Florence and Milan. While living in Rome, Lady Mary Wortley Montagu recorded him sleeping with his landlady with the encouragement of his landlord.

Sir Bourchier and Lady Ellen had six children, and after her husband's death in 1784 she lived at The Circus, Bath, where she died in 1813. Her daughter Florentina Wrey diminished the gene-pool further by marrying her cousin, the heir to Rood Ashton, Richard Godolphin Long.

In August 1756 Ellen's nineteen-year-old sister Elizabeth Thresher married widower[304] Robert Colebrooke, heir to the manor of Chilham, Kent. Reputedly a renegade who inherited and squandered a fortune, Colebrooke was MP for Malden, Essex (1741-61). He was ambassador to Turkey in 1765. His brother Sir George Colebrooke, 2nd Baronet, MP and merchant banker, reputedly lost £190,000 on speculation in hemp in 1771, then failed in an attempt to corner the world market in alum. Much lampooned in the press, Sir George was said to be a rather pompous, self-important man who considered himself the second most influential politician in England.

His brother Robert and Elizabeth Thresher celebrated their nuptials at Potterne, her guardian Sir Robert Long arranging with his wife to meet her there: 'you will Certainly bring Dolly, and pray come as early as you can, for the ceremony must be before 12 o'clock'. Afterwards the couple set off to begin their new life together at Chilham Castle.

It was not a successful marriage, and after six years Robert went abroad to escape his unhappiness, being appointed His Majesty's minister to the Swiss cantons. He was also deeply in debt. Robert placed his entire estate including Chilham in the hands of new trustees with instructions to pay his scheduled debts by instalments and set aside £200 per annum 'in the Nature of Pin Money' to be paid to Elizabeth.

It was now 1762, and he wrote from Switzerland to Sir John Cust,[305] a cousin of Sir Robert Long, asking for assistance and advice on what to do about his failed marriage, complaining he no longer had any conjugal rights and had applied to Parliament for a dissolution. He not only needed the consent of his wife but he also faced opposition

---

304   His first wife was Lady Henrietta Powlett, daughter of Harry, 4th Duke of Bolton

305   Descended from Anna Margaretta Long and Sir Richard Mason

from his brother and children on whom the estate of Chilham was entailed. Colebrooke never gained his wife's consent. Instead, with his finances still under strain Elizabeth was granted £150 for her annual maintenance. She moved to Bath to be near her sisters, taking a seven year lease on a newly built house there.

Colebrooke had no children with either of his wives, but he had at least six children by Mrs Mary Jones, wife of Dr Robert Jones, and he names them all as such in his will. The eldest, Robert Hyde Colebrooke, was born in about 1762, the year Colebrooke sought the dissolution of his marriage to Elizabeth. He died in May 1784 at Soissons, France, at a small abode owned by his brother.

By now Elizabeth was fifty years old, and one year later she married for the second time, to John Crosdill, a celebrated violoncellist at least twenty years her junior, their marriage witnessed by actor Wright Bowden. The unlikely match raised a few eyebrows among the music-loving public, setting the rumour mill in motion. The London newspapers published 'the particulars' of their age difference: 'She is in the full maturity of almost three score years and ten. She carries however, weight for age, having no less than £25,000 in money, and a jointure of £1,500 a year. The gentleman per contra, whose good parts are barely thirty . . .'[306]

Elizabeth might have been surprised to learn that she was seen as an elderly woman of nearly seventy who had snared a man with such young 'good parts'. Apart from all the other indisputable facts, the dates of her mother's baptism and subsequent marriage render this chronologically impossible, although this misinformation continues to be repeated in published works on Crosdill. The original error may account for *Burke's Landed Gentry* also getting her muddled as her mother's sister. William Long of Melksham clearly names her in his will as 'my niece Elizabeth, wife of Robert Colebrook Esq, another of the daughters of my late sister Ellin Thresher'.[307]

In 1782 Crosdill had been appointed chamber musician to Queen Charlotte, and he also gave lessons to the Prince of Wales. After

306   *Morning Herald and Daily Advertiser,* 28 July 1785
307   PROB 11/990

his marriage to Elizabeth he retired from his musical profession, *The Times* in 1790 announcing: 'Crosdill has given up all public practice – and excepting his attendance on the Prince, confines himself entirely to the more pleasing study of matrimonial duets.'

The advantages of having a wealthy wife enabled Crosdill to attain the status of gentleman, and although he remained active in London musical life he appeared publicly for one day only, in 1821, at the coronation of his old pupil George IV. After twenty-two years as Mrs John Crosdill, Elizabeth died in London in 1807 aged seventy-three, bequeathing all her estate equally to her two surviving sisters Dame Ellen Wrey and Mary Thresher, with her husband's name only mentioned briefly in the probate note.

A few decades earlier her sisters Mary and Dionysia must have realised they faced a future without the support of one of Georgian society's most coveted achievements – a wealthy husband – and it was possibly this prospect that prompted them to venture into acquiring more property in fashionable and booming Bath. The sisters resided at 4 Brock Street until 1776, when they moved to 21 The Circus, which they purchased for £1,995.[308]

Dionysia and Mary's wills reveal a little more about their life in Bath. Dionysia wrote hers in November 1805 when she was obviously in failing health, and she died two months later. She bequeathed the majority of her stocks and shares to her three surviving sisters, Mary, Elizabeth and Ellen. These included 8,000 shares in the South Sea company (valued at around £5,000), and 16,000 shares in the 3 per cent Reduced Annuities Office at the Bank of England (valued at around £10,500). Her half share in 21 The Circus was bequeathed to her sister Mary. Dionysia's estate totalled over £30,000 in value, with £3,000 owed as duty. She also owned shares in the New Assembly Rooms, completed in 1771. Among the thirty people named in her will were cousins Mrs Sarah Awdry and John Long of Monkton Farleigh.

Her sister Mary, now sole owner of 21 The Circus, divided her time between Bath and the old mansion at Melksham inherited from her uncle William Long. The diary entry of Charlotte Grove for 4

308   BRO BC153/563/5

March 1811 suggests that 'the old aunt' Mary maintained her social life well into old age: 'We went to a party at Mrs Thresher's, met Mrs & Miss Longs – the old aunt quite lame. The servants ran up and down the rooms with her. She looked like a corpse.' Mary was by then aged seventy-six, and she died five years later in December 1816.

Several codicils were added to her initial will dated 1808, the last just three days before her death. The majority of Mary's freehold properties, estates and lands were left to her sister, Dame Ellen Wrey, which in turn would be inherited by Ellen's children or grandchildren. Many cash legacies amounting to more than £20,000 were distributed, with Richard Long junior of Rood Ashton receiving £50 'as a trifling remembrance'.

Henry Long of Melksham (1686–1727)

The maternal grandfather of the Thresher sisters, and grandson of Richard Long of Collingbourne, Henry Long junior was born a few months after his father Henry's death in March 1686 and baptised at South Wraxall, where his mother Anne[309] was born. Henry, with both maternal and paternal Long ancestry, was brought up at Melksham on the estate left by his father, after the legal tussle that had wrested it from the possession of his uncle Richard.

His marriage to Ellen Trenchard in about 1708 produced seven children, four of whom died young. He was a clothier at Melksham like his first cousin Thomas Long, although the two men probably operated their businesses independently. Nevertheless both must have encountered the same difficulties with their workforce, and it was unfortunate for Henry and Thomas that eighteenth-century weavers held the record for the most number of strikes. Their tactics were collective bargaining by riot, which inevitably led to violence.

Henry was pricked as sheriff in 1726, the same year a clash between clothiers and weavers broke out after a bad harvest coincided with a depression in trade. A Bill was hastily passed through Parliament in an attempt to regain control and prevent possible Jacobite sympathisers taking advantage of the unrest. Later that year increasing

309   Daughter of John Long (of South Wraxall) and Catherine Paynter

discontent led to a great protest march by the workers, beginning with an assembly near Bradford on Avon from where they proceeded through Devizes, Melksham, Calne, Westbury, Shepton Mallet and Bruton.

On encountering two troops of dragoons at Frome, about 1,500 rioters retreated to Melksham where they attacked the house of one clothier, breaking windows and furniture. Henry Long mounted his horse and courageously rode among them, reading the Riot Act and warning of the imminent arrival of more dragoons from Salisbury.[310] As a representative of the law his presence would not have been particularly welcome. As an employer whose wages were so low the weavers found it almost impossible to make a living, even less so.

The mob dispersed, but not before one man was killed in the tumult. The ringleader of the riot was Daniel Webb of Monkton Farleigh, already on record as a troublemaker four years earlier, when his house was searched for arms by Sheriff Thomas Long of Rowden on suspicion he was storing arms for use in a Jacobite rising.[311]

Henry lived only another ten months after successfully quelling the riot, dying in October 1727 aged forty. The next year his eldest son, eighteen-year-old William, entered Sidney Sussex College, Cambridge. Besides properties inherited from his father, William also inherited a moiety of the Mount Trenchard Estate in County Limerick, Ireland, from his maternal uncle, and he purchased more during his life. By the time he died in June 1773 William was unmarried and considerably wealthy. His only surviving sibling, Mrs Ellen Thresher, had already been dead for twenty years, so he divided all his property between her daughters.

Henry's youngest son, Henry junior, was apprenticed in 1731 to London brewer, Joseph Chitty of Mark Lane, a premium of £600 for his training paid by his widowed mother Ellen (*née* Trenchard). By comparison the payment made by the father of Chitty's two other apprentices, Jacob and Joseph Huse, was considerably less at £200 and £150 respectively, in consideration of their kinship with Chitty.

310   *London Journal*, 10 December 1726
311   WAM xli, 444

Henry junior also lived at Mark Lane and perhaps continued with Chitty for a few years. Eventually he was forced by illness to return to his mother at Melksham, where he died aged twenty-six in September 1739, described as 'nephew to the late ingenious John Trenchard Esq'.[312] A few years later his old boss Chitty was declared bankrupt and committed under suspicion of fraudulent intent to the Fleet prison, owing £1,800 in duty to Customs for a consignment of imported raisins.

Richard Long of Rood Ashton (1689–1760)

The third consecutive Richard Long, and the second to inherit Rood Ashton, was baptised at Chippenham, educated at Queens College, Oxford, matriculating in May 1707 aged seventeen, and he went on to study law as a student of the Middle Temple. He married his step-sister Anne, daughter of John Martyn of Hinton and his wife Grace. Anne was sole heir to her father, and the great tithes of Hinton passed with her on her marriage, together with her marriage portion of mortgages on several properties in Wiltshire.

In 1734 Richard stood as a Tory candidate together with Rogers Holland for the seat of Chippenham, having inherited the estate there of his maternal Uncle Thomas Long of Rowden in 1730. After a hot contest he was duly elected, his supporters celebrating the victory in the evening with bonfires and fireworks. While Parliament was in session he rented accommodation in London at Channel Row, Westminster. But his heart wasn't really in it; his only recorded vote, in agreement with Sir Robert Long of Draycot (then MP for Wootton Bassett), was against the Spanish Convention in 1739.

By the time Richard was aged fifty-one he had perhaps tired of the necessary travel to attend Parliament. Extending well into spring, England suffered a particularly severe winter in 1739/40; a violent easterly gale and ice in the Thames damaged shipping in January 1740, and during extremely low temperatures many deaths occurred through exposure. The streets of London were clogged with ice and snow, the Thames was frozen for about eight weeks and London Bridge was damaged by the ice.

312   *London Daily Post and General Advertiser,* 14 September 1739

Richard chose not to seek re-election that year, which he may have felt in hindsight was a wise decision; the events during the campaign put Chippenham well and truly on the map. Characterised by violence stirred up by the candidates, either by hiring or provoking mobs, it exploded into one of the biggest political corruption scandals of the era. The Whigs were determined to secure both seats after losing one to the Tories in the previous election, and two days beforehand a large number of armed men were brought in to terrify and intimidate the voters. Even the sheriff was held prisoner until after the contest, to ensure the desired result.

The Tories won, but the fall-out would lay political waste in ways no one could have predicted. Sir Robert Long wrote at the time: 'I am credibly informed that the Sheriff understanding how dirty and scandalous a thing it is, does not care to have it tried by gentlemen.' The trail of destruction went all the way to the top, and after being defeated by one vote on the Chippenham election petition, Prime Minister Robert Walpole, whose government was already under attack, resigned amid the furore after twenty-one years in office.

An unrelated Richard Long (son of Henry Long of Bayford, Hertfordshire) has often been confused with his contemporary Richard Long of Rood Ashton in relation to Bowood Park, near Calne. This unrelated Richard was a creditor of Sir Orlando Bridgeman, 2nd Baronet, who later became auditor-general to the Prince of Wales. In 1737 Bridgeman was nominated governor of Barbados, but disappeared before sailing. He had earlier built a new house at Bowood Park, near Calne, plunging him deeply into debt, and the Chancery courts started proceedings against him shortly before he disappeared.

In June 1738 a man was found drowned in the Thames near Limehouse, although the body, presumed to be Bridgeman, could not be properly identified because of the length of time in the water. As his principal creditor, the aforementioned Richard Long acquired ownership of Bowood after a Chancery decree in his favour, in 1739.[313]

---

313   'Bowood', in *A History of the County of Wiltshire: vol. 17, Calne*, ed. D A Crowley (London, 2002), pp. 116-123. British History Online

The diary of John Perceval, 1st Earl of Egmont, claims Bridgeman did not go to Barbados, instead he

> made his escape from the world to avoid his creditors, by pretending to make himself away, and accordingly gave it out that he had drowned himself; was ferreted out of his hole by the reward advertised for whoever should discover him, and seized at an inn at Slough, where he had ever since concealed himself.

Bridgeman apparently died in Gloucester gaol in 1746. A painting of Bowood dated 1725 depicts the park originally laid out in a semi-formal style with walled terraces, avenues, wildernesses and ornamental lakes. Its new owner Richard Long was assessed for land tax on the property in 1747 and retained possession for fifteen years until 1754, when he sold it with the still unfinished house to John Petty, Lord Shelburne (created Marquess of Lansdowne in 1784).

Twelve miles to the south of Bowood, the magnificent edifice of St Mary the Virgin dominates Steeple Ashton's skyline, which in the words of Sir Nicholas Pevsner 'fairly bristles with pinnacles; a gay and fantastical sight'. Of perpendicular-style architecture, much of the church had been paid for by the early Long family. In the embattled western tower is a clock and seven bells; three are inscribed with Richard Long of Rood Ashton's name from his time as churchwarden. The vicar, George Webb (so beloved by Gifford Long) delivered a series of six sermons there in 1615, quirkily titled *The Practise of Quietness, or, A direction how to live quietly at all times, in all places, upon all occasions, And how to avoid or put off, all occasions of unquietness.*

But Steeple Ashton could be a very unquiet place at times, meteorologically speaking. Several spectacular lightning strikes are documented and it is notable for its exploding church spire. After one such storm in 1670 the spire was destroyed and two workmen killed while attempting to repair it. One morning in July 1759 another great storm swept through the area, and a large tree on the Rood Ashton estate was struck by lightning. Reportedly 9ft in girth and perfectly sound, it was slivered into 'upwards of ten thousand pieces', covering a distance of twenty yards. During another violent thunderstorm in 1772 a bolt of lightning struck the vicarage house. A ball of fire, 'the size of a sixpenny loaf' crackled and popped like a canon going off inside the house causing the people in or near it to be thrown off their feet. Several people in the village were also thrown to the ground.

A year after his election to Parliament Richard must have had an acute sense of his own mortality when he wrote his will in 1735, 'in reasonable health', twenty-five years before he actually died. With five children, he was at pains to prevent 'any little disputes' between them after his death, making detailed descriptions of items each were to receive. He died in May 1760, his widow surviving until 1768. His heir was their eldest son Richard junior.

Richard Long of Rood Ashton (1728–87)

This fourth Richard Long, like his father, was educated at Oxford, entering Magdalen College in 1746 aged eighteen, graduating Master of Arts in 1754. After six years of carefree bachelorhood he inherited the responsibility of Rood Ashton and the rest of his late father's estates. A wife was next on the list and within four months of his father's death thirty-two-year-old Richard married Meliora Lambe, great-granddaughter of Sir John Lambe of East Coulston and widow of Thomas Polden of Great Cheverell. The London press proclaimed Mistress Polden was 'endowed with every charm and every endearment that can arise from a graceful person, easy address, and an amiable sweetness of temper'. And she was said to be worth £400 a year. Her brother Thomas Lambe had died unmarried in 1741 and as his heir she acquired lands in Coulston. Her first husband Thomas Polden, who well knew 'the prudence & discretion of my said dear wife', had died in 1753 also leaving all his property to her.

With Meliora came not only a good dowry, but also a ready-made family – two young daughters – who were raised at Rood Ashton alongside their five younger half-brothers and sisters. However Richard makes no mention of them in his will written six years before his death, which would explain their general quitclaim to him twelve years earlier, officially giving up any legal interest in his estate. But they were as much family as his own children, and when forty-year-old Ann,[314] the elder of the two, died at Newbury in 1793, she appointed her half-brothers Richard and John two of her four executors.

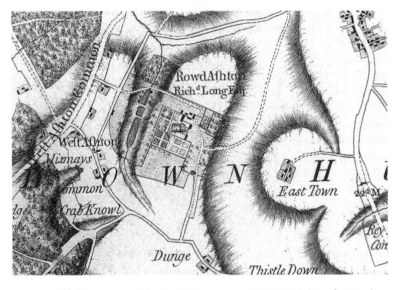

Andrews & Dury map of the Rood Ashton estate, 1773. Wiltshire & Swindon Archives

Their father Richard had no aspirations to enter the world of politics, unlike so many of his relatives, although he did serve as JP on the magistrates' bench. He was content to live a relatively quiet life, passing his leisure hours in the way country squires generally did, supported by the income from his inherited property, including at least four farms and a house in London. He also purchased a plot of land opposite Hyde Park, consecrated as a burial ground and rented to St. Georges Church, Hanover Square.

After his death aged fifty-nine in September 1787, Richard's estates descended to his eldest son Richard Godolphin Long. His widow Meliora went to live with their only surviving daughter at

Devizes,[315] living on an annuity of £200 payable out of Rowden Farm until her death in 1806.

Richard Godolphin Long of Rood Ashton (1771–1835)

Their son Richard was baptised at West Lavington in November 1761, and in March 1786 he married his cousin Florentina Wrey, daughter of Sir Bourchier Wrey, 6th Baronet, of Tavistock House, Devon. Easily distinguishable now as fifth in the consecutive line of Richard Longs, he was the first to be given a middle name, in recognition of his mother's cousin and former guardian, William Godolphin of East Coulston.

His appointment as sheriff of Wiltshire in 1794 coincided with the Duke of York's expedition to Flanders, when a call went out for contributions of various items of clothing for the troops, to which Richard responded by donating fifty flannel waistcoats. As captain of the Melksham troop of Volunteer Yeomanry Cavalry, and with a view to sustaining the war in France, he chaired a formidable meeting in the Town Hall at Devizes in April 1794. It was resolved to augment the militia by a further 400 men and to establish the practice of field artillery. The clergy would receive voluntary donations by 'any persons desirous of showing their zeal for the welfare of their country'.

In 1799 Richard purchased the 38-roomed Steeple Ashton Manor House with the surrounding farm, which remained in the family until the 1970s. Dated 1647, the house has a tall, flat, symmetrical gabled front, and beside it stands a seventeenth-century granary on round pillars. Steeple Ashton church adjoins the gardens, towering over the village in all its glory with its pinnacles, buttresses, battlements and gargoyles.

Inside the church is a special front pew with the Long coat of arms on the side. More than two centuries later, Margaret, the future Viscountess Long wrote that no vicar dared ever go over his time limit when her father-in-law the 3rd Viscount was there; he had perfected a repertoire of deep breathing and ostentatious sighing and wheezing so

---

315   Mrs Dionysia Vince at Belle Vue House, Devizes, later a lunatic asylum from c.1844 and the vicarage 1889-1933

that all concentration on God, both for the vicar and the congregation, was impossible beyond a certain point.

The purchase of the manor house must have put Richard in a celebratory mood; shortly afterwards he regaled the neighbourhood with a 'fine ox roasted whole' on a huge bonfire accompanied by bread and cheese and two hogsheads of strong beer.[316] He was still in good humour by the following year when he made a formal agreement with his brother John (of Monkton Farleigh), John Awdry and Thomas Bruges, entering into a partnership in the Melksham Bank. For Richard, what must have seemed like a sound idea at the time, he would later have cause to regret.

In November 1813 the *Salisbury and Winchester Journal* announced a run on the bank had 'occasioned some bustle among the partners of that respectable firm', caused by the misquoting by two London newspapers of part of an advertisement relating to a bankruptcy. A notice was quickly published by the directors, headed by Richard, declaring their 'perfect confidence' in the stability of the bank.

All was well for another ten years until another bankruptcy reared its ugly head, this time much closer to home. His brother John *and* his bank were declared bankrupt.[317] Described as a 'banker and money scrivener', he had got into financial difficulties, which also proved no small disaster for Richard who had stood as security. In an attempt to mitigate his losses Richard drew up an indenture, whereby John – then aged 55 – was required to repay him the lost money at the rate of £3,000 each year for the rest of his life. This was effectively another ten years; Richard outlived him by two.

On the nomination of his cousin Thomas Grove of Ferne,[318] and seconded by Francis Warneford of Sevenhampton, Richard was elected to Parliament as member for Wiltshire in 1806. He was one of the many elected gentry who were not members of a cohesive country party as such, but instead linked by a concern with common interests, such as opposition to heavier taxation and rising interest rates. With

316   [232] *Bath Chronicle* 534/1799 article 3
317   HOC Parl. Papers1824: 'Country Banks Becoming Bankrupt'
318   Thomas Grove was the son of Philippa Long of Salisbury and John Grove

his tenants forming the majority of the freeholder electorate, he encountered no meaningful resistance during his campaign, although political agitator Henry Hunt did his best. Hunt urged the voters of Wiltshire to disregard the long-established dictatorship of the Deptford and Beckhampton clubs to nominate a member of the Long family. His exhortations fell on the deaf ears of the majority, and Richard was again elected in 1807 and 1812.

By this time the old manor house at Rood Ashton was beginning to become more of a proposition for demolition than renovation, and in 1808 Richard commissioned architect Jeffry Wyatt (later Wyattville) to build a new larger mansion on the site. Nothing is known of the earlier house, although in 1773 it was surrounded by formal gardens with three small lakes to the north-west.

The family fortunes increased considerably when Richard's cousin Miss Katherine Long of South Wraxall died in 1814. At the death of old Walter Long of Bath in 1807, Richard, his brother John and their cousin Daniel Jones were made trustees of the many estates, including Whaddon and Southwick, and the fifteenth-century South Wraxall Manor. Under the terms of the entail the estates were to descend to the male heirs of Richard, and in default of issue to those of his brother John. After Katherine's death they were entitled to rents and profits of the estates until the majority of the next heir, R.G Long's son, Walter. What could have been a lucrative income lasting several years turned into a short-term windfall lasting barely ten months. If only Katherine hadn't lived so long. She died aged nearly 97 in January, 1814 and Walter turned twenty-one in October the same year.

The last sister of old Walter Long of Bath, Miss Long, or Miss Kitty as she was affectionately known to her inner circle, was described on her memorial as having 'maintained a spotless and unsullied reputation throughout a very long life; she lived a very retired life at Wraxall Manor House and did not mix much in gay society.' A 'truly pious and venerated character', declared the *Gentleman's Magazine*, by whose death the poor and unfortunate had suffered an irreparable loss.

Katherine had become blind towards the end of her life, dependent on Thomas Bruges who also acted as her steward. He enjoyed an enduring and friendly relationship with her, and took care planning family events, including her birthday arrangements. His dedication paid off; with his co-executor the Rev. Charles Coxwell, he was left the residue of her estate. This did not sit well with her Long cousins nine miles down the road at Rood Ashton. Feathers were ruffled. Her will included legacies totalling £50,000, and the residue reputedly exceeded £100,000; a considerable fortune.

In a codicil to her will Miss Long left her silver tea kettle 'with the stand lamp' to Bruges, who became extremely unpopular among the late Miss Long's relatives and friends, and there were insinuations her will had been forged or improperly influenced. This may have prompted the comment from one family member some years later, that Bruges 'bagged everything'.

Owing to ill health, Richard announced his intention to retire from public life almost four months before the dissolution of Parliament in 1818, plunging the county instantly into turmoil. With the machinations of the Deptford Club under the spotlight – labelled 'the notorious quorum' – the subsequent election was a controversial one. Richard's brother John nominated as a replacement candidate, the notorious rake William Long Wellesley (later 4th Earl of Mornington), nephew of the Duke of Wellington, and husband of their cousin Catherine Tylney Long, the wealthy heiress of Draycot. His opponent was John Benett of Pythouse.

For several months the Wiltshire press was awash with placards, lampoons, anonymous addresses, scurrilities and personal invectives directed mostly at William Long Wellesley and Benett, but also Richard to a lesser degree, prompting one outraged supporter from Melksham to ask in a lengthy political rant: 'Who is the arch fiend that upholds these beastly idiots, in insulting that most respectable magistrate Mr Richard Long?'[319] A multitude of political ditties circulated at the rallies; for example a verse from "Long Wellesley and Freedom":

PENRUDDOCKE they tried, and GODDARD beside,
The LONGS who a long time did serve, Sirs,

---

319   Sydney Coulton, *Letters to the Gentlemen, Clergy, Freeholders, Manufacturers, Tradesmen, and Inhabitants, of the County of Wilts,* 1818, p. 60

And the great Mister PHIPPS, with his thick cushion lips,
But none could be found with the nerve, Sirs . . .[320]

Henry Hunt kept a critical eye on proceedings. A radical political speaker, he had a well-earned reputation as a vain, domineering and capricious man, jealous of political rivals. In 1819 he had been sent to prison for two years after speaking at an illegal rally in Manchester, causing a riot, during which several people were killed and hundreds injured. This became known as the Peterloo Massacre. *(See John Long Snr of Monkton Farleigh for more on this.)* While in prison Hunt wrote scathingly of Richard's election by default in 1806, which he later published in his biography:

Mr Richard Long, of Rood Ashton, was a fox-hunting country squire, without any other qualification to be a Member of Parliament than that of belonging to an ancient family of the county; in fact, he was proverbially a man of very inferior knowledge, remarkable only for being a stupid country squire, who, although a sportsman, scarcely knew how to address his tenants on his health being drank on a rent-day.[321]

No doubt Richard held an equally low opinion of Hunt. Some 150 years later, Margaret, Viscountess Long would write that Richard's great-great grandson Eric Long, 3rd Viscount and MP for Westbury, had perfected the art of public speaking. He would, whether speaking in the House of Lords or to a local Conservative political meeting with half a dozen farm workers, always address them as though they were an audience of five hundred. 'My Lords, Ladies and Gentlemen' he would say, his eyes disappearing into their top sockets. It was a trick peculiar to the Longs, evolved from years of addressing the Gallery in the Houses of Parliament.

Safe to say, neither Richard nor his supporters were ready for a new landscape in which old political sensibilities and conventions, and

320   John Ebers and C. Fellows, *Kaleidoscopiana Wiltoniensia, Or, a Literary, Political, and Moral View,*1818, p. 403
321   Henry Hunt, *Memoirs, Written by Himself, In His Majesty's Jail at Ilchester,* 1820, vol. 2, p. 216

notions of tradition and elites would be made redundant by reform. Not in nineteenth-century Britain.

1835 was not a happy year for the family. The Longs' old house at Whaddon was destroyed by fire, and the decline in health of both Richard and his wife Florentina prompted her to write to their only surviving son Walter at Chalcot House, informing him of their joint conviction that neither would live much longer. She died in May. Six weeks later at the beginning of July while sitting in his favourite chair at Rood Ashton, Richard also died, aged seventy-three. He kept a well-stocked cellar, bequeathing to his wife fifty dozen of his 'best wines', more than enough to embalm a morgueful of corpses. He was at pains to point out he had already made ample provision for his four daughters during his lifetime, and this, he wrote in his will, was the sole reason he made no further bequests to them.

In 1823 he had made them beneficiaries of his life interest in the annual income arising from £11,000 of a £15,000 principal sum secured to the trustees of his 1786 marriage settlement. In a codicil written in 1832 he changed his mind, leaving them an additional £300 each and a leasehold estate in Steeple Ashton between them. His daughters also received bequests made to their mother by her aunts the Thresher sisters, of property and estates at Bath and Bradford in Wiltshire, as well as valuable Bank of England stock.

Of the Longs' Whaddon property, Whaddon Grove Farm now stands on the site, and all that remains of the original house enlarged by Sir Walter Long at the Restoration, is a seventeenth-century back door in a moulded frame. There are two stone former dairies and a pair of semi-detached stone cottages to the south of Whaddon Farm, which served as the poor house in the 1830s.

Miss Flora Long (1790–1862)

The second of Richard and Florentina's daughters left an indelible impression on those with whom she came into contact. Described by her cousin Harriet Grove as 'a pleasant girl',[322] Flora never married, although there was no shortage of admirers. Card evenings at Rood Ashton were a popular pastime when visitors dropped by, and on one occasion in 1811 Flora impressed her young companions by winning 'the immense pool of 3s 6d' in a game of Commerce.[323]

The Irish writer and reformer Frances Power Cobbe was also impressed by the refined appetites of the young Long sisters when they visited the Cobbe family at Newbridge, Dublin. Much to Frances's amazement and admiration, they never ate anything, except perhaps the wing of a chicken or a spoonful of jelly, and a little wine or water. Some of the children laid a trap for these 'ethereal beings' and caught them 'surreptitiously in the luncheon room – one was eating cheese, another carving a round of beef, and the third . . . had applied a huge silver tankard of beer straight to her delicate lips'.[324]

Flora's maternal aunts Dionysia Harding and Anna Maria Toke of Godington occasionally visited the family of novelist Jane Austen at Chawton, and Jane sometimes referred to Dionysia as 'my Aunt Harding', possibly a connection by marriage, which would explain her reference to Flora as her cousin. After one such visit in 1811 Jane wrote to her sister Cassandra :

> Mrs Harding is a good-looking woman, but not much like Mrs Toke, inasmuch as she is very brown and has scarcely any teeth; she seems to have some of Mrs Toke's civility. Miss H. is an elegant, pleasing, pretty-looking girl, about nineteen, I suppose, or nineteen and a half, or nineteen and a quarter, with flowers in her head and music at her finger ends. She plays very well indeed. I have seldom heard anybody with more pleasure. They were at Godington four or five years ago. My cousin, Flora Long, was there last year.[325]

322   Desmond Hawkins, *The Grove Diaries: The Rise and Fall of an English Family, 1809–1925*, 1995
323   *Ibid.* p. 109
324   Sally Mitchell, *Frances Power Cobbe*, 2004, p. 38
325   Jane Austen, Susan Coolidge, Sarah Chauncey Woolsey, *Letters of Jane Austen*, 1892, p. 175

When she was nearly thirty, Flora began a close friendship with the elderly poet George Crabbe, a man more than twice her age. Crabbe was rector of Trowbridge and not long a widower when he was befriended by the Long family, one of his 'Houses of Call'. Lonely after the death of his wife, he found the atmosphere welcoming when he visited Rood Ashton; 'there is something domestic in a visit there that agrees with my kind of pensive and childish longing for such alliances and associations. I cannot bear to belong to nobody.' He and Flora shared an interest in poetry and mineral collecting, and they had long conversations on their wood-and-grove walks. She rather fancied herself as a poetess and frequently sent verses for his criticism.

Crabbe revelled in 'her good sense, her application, her reasonable piety, her unaffected and simple manners (manners easy and almost rural, for rustic I will not say), and a kind of temperate and cheerful gravity'. The Longs often invited him to visit during their residences at Bath, and in 1819 he enjoyed a much anticipated holiday with them at Exmouth. He wrote of his admiration of their second youngest daughter, Anne Katherine, 'for her extreme attention to her sisters, almost to a kind of self-annihilation'.

Crabbe lamented he was not twenty years younger, but this was, to be sure, no more than an affectionate friendship, and he described as a 'monstrous monstrous absurdity' the inevitable gossip associating him with Flora in any other sense.[326] Crabbe had a number of young female admirers, and although she had never actually met him, Jane Austen harboured fantasies of becoming Mrs Crabbe, so charmed was she by his writing.

In 1823, at the age of thirty-three, Flora became engaged to Henry Cobbe, rector of Templeton and uncle of Frances Power Cobbe. According to his niece, this engagement was a rash and hasty reaction on the part of her uncle, who, owing to his own procrastinations, had recently missed proposing to another. In the few years since George Crabbe had commended Flora's 'reasonable piety', it had somehow along the way transformed into 'such exceedingly rigid piety of the

---

326   S. Paul, *The Romance of an Elderly Poet*, 1913, p. 127

Calvinistic type' that Cobbe was somewhat afraid of his promised bride. His procrastination then began afresh. He stayed away on one excuse after another, until Flora finally wrote to ask whether he had changed his mind about their engagement.

He was not in good health, hoping this would excuse him for a little longer, and before replying he went to Dublin to consult a doctor. After detailing his ailments, he asked what he ought to do about Flora, hoping to get himself off the hook. Instead was told: 'Go and get married by all means!' Now out of excuses, he wrote to Flora to say he was on his way to claim his bride, stopping along the way at his mother's at Bath; but on the morning he was to arrive at Rood Ashton he was found dead in his bed.

The Bristol Riots, 1831

B ristol suffered the worst civil disturbances in its history during the riots of November 1831, which were the culmination of a long struggle for democratic rights. Only 6,000 people in Bristol had the vote out of a population of 104,000. The violence caused great alarm to the Longs at Rood Ashton, who feared not only the potential dangers to themselves 30 miles away but also for the safety of their friends the Oliphants, living at Clifton near the centre of the unrest.

The riots began after the House of Lords rejected the second Reform Bill. Numbering about 500 or 600 young men, the rioters went on a destructive rampage after local magistrate Sir Charles Wetherell, a conspicuous opponent of the Bill, threatened to imprison participants in a disturbance outside the new assize courts. The uprising continued for three days, and a number of people were killed and injured before the mob was eventually dispersed.

Flora's letters to her friend Miss Rachel Oliphant at the height of the riot furnish an interesting side view of events and the effect it had on her family. [327] Each evening they sent to Trowbridge with the coach, seeking fresh intelligence, but the reports were so exaggerated they were unsure what to believe. They found Miss Oliphant's daily

---

327   Ethel Maxtone-Graham, *The Oliphants of Gask: Records of a Jacobite Family*, 1910, pp. 421-426

letters more reliable, although not reassuring. Flora wrote fearfully of the 'fury of the mad populace'. Added to this was a sick baby in the Oliphant family, which prompted motherly advice from Flora : 'surely he should live chiefly on the Donkey's milk'.

In Bristol, the bishop's palace, the mansion of the lord mayor, private homes and property were looted and destroyed, some belonging to friends of the Longs. The demolition of much of Bristol gaol struck even more fear into Flora's heart: 'many bad characters must be wandering about the country, owing to the late dispersion of miscreants from Bristol, and village gossip gathers as it goes, till "four men in Buckram suits" soon becomes forty'. Nor were neighbouring areas spared the violence:

> Melksham is not in a very peaceful state, Longleat is threatened . . . Lord Bath has had threatening letters, having made himself obnoxious by his vote, and is obliged to take measures of precaution in case his noble mansion should be attacked. At Shepton Mallet we hear the Jail has been destroyed and the Prisoners let loose, besides the burning of Ricks in several places in this county.

Flora's father Richard 'was more annoyed than the facts warranted' when news arrived at Rood Ashton that some of the 'idle ill-disposed people of Trowbridge' got the impression Sir Charles Wetherell was concealed in their house, and they meant to come up in great numbers in the evening to search for him. At any other time such an absurd story would have been treated with derision and contempt, but at that moment they knew a search would involve plunder and violence. 'Such a bad spirit always exists amongst the distressed operatives of this neighbourhood, that my Father grew seriously uncomfortable, and was very ill-pleased at any attempt of ours to dispel or ridicule his fears.' The 'Christian views and temperate opinions' of their visitor Major Mackworth, who had 'a situation of command and influence', did not have the effect Flora expected either.

Soon after dark her father, now aged seventy, assembled a defending force at the house, consisting of ten yeomanry from her brother Walter's troop living at Steeple Ashton, and twelve able-bodied workmen – all prepared for the onslaught – in addition to the men of their own household, making about thirty in the garrison. But the night passed uneventfully, and Flora had 'no doubt it was one of the many idle reports which some people take pleasure in magnifying'. But Richard knew how unpredictable a mob could be. A 'perpetual excitation is kept up in my Father's mind', Flora wrote, but she dismissed it as merely imaginary alarm.

After the death of her parents in 1835, Flora lived at Bath with her unmarried sister Anne, their friend Rachel Oliphant and a small household comprising two ladies' maids, a housemaid, cook and butler. She died there aged seventy-two in April 1862, her effects valued at under £18,000. When Miss Oliphant died in 1864 Anne left Bath for London, where she died two years later.

Walter Long of Rood Ashton (1793–1867)

Flora's eldest brother Walter was forty-two when he succeeded to Rood Ashton and the other estates, now considerably swelled by the legacies of old Walter Long of Bath. He was educated at Christ Church College, Oxford, matriculating in October 1811. Eight years later in the presence of his sister Flora and James Graham, 3rd Duke of Montrose, he married eighteen-year-old Mary Anne Colquhoun in Scotland, daughter of the Rt. Hon. Archibald Colquhoun, former lord advocate, lord register of Scotland and member for the county of Dumbarton.

One of Mary Anne's friends afterwards wrote expressing her reservations: 'I hope [the Longs are] a pious family. I do think her rather too young to encounter the cares and responsibilities of a family.'[328] In the early years of their marriage Walter and his wife lived at Hartham House in Corsham, and later at Baynton House in East Coulston, an unexpected inheritance of his cousin John Long junior of Monkton Farleigh. Walter also kept a convenient residence in London, and the family spent a few years at Chalcot House in Wiltshire before inheriting the family estates.

After qualifying as a magistrate in 1825, the next year he found

328   Ethel Maxtone-Graham, *ibid*

himself accused of fathering a child, born in the workhouse at Corsham to a poor serving woman named Ann Davis. In a story considered outrageous and completely implausible, she alleged that a liaison with Walter, whom she'd never previously met, had occurred in a gravel pit. She claimed he had driven from Bath in his gig and accosted her; they went into the stone quarry together where he 'accomplished his purpose'. Later, upon discovering herself expecting a child she went to Walter's house to inform him of his alleged paternity. Telling her

Walter Long of Rood Ashton M.P. 1862. Courtesy Mike Pease

she must be mistaken, he would make a public example of her if she persisted.

The case was heard at the Salisbury assizes, where the jury was told that anyone acquainted with Walter, a most respected magistrate himself, would be in no doubt at all as to the complete falsehood of the accusations. The jury took no time in finding the woman guilty.[329]

Walter sat as a Tory in seven parliaments from 1836 until 1865. For country members who formed the majority of the Commons the debates and resolutions at Westminster were often of secondary interest to matters affecting their constituents at home. This might explain why, in a career spanning almost thirty years Walter made only one speech in the House.[330]

His family was witness to a pace of change in England more rapid in the early decades of the nineteenth century than it had been at any other time in history. Subservient society was passing away, replaced with rising unrest. A year before the disturbances at Bristol, the agricultural riots of 1830 caused much alarm when large mobs of rioters assembled in different towns of Wiltshire and the adjoining counties, led by men 'not of the labouring class'. They burnt ricks, destroyed machinery and plundered houses in all directions.

For some days no force could be mustered in sufficient strength to arrest them, and the storm rolled on towards Warminster, threatening the peace of Heytesbury. There the troop of Yeomanry cavalry, under Walter's command and accompanied by Colonel a'Court, Mr Kavenhill and other magistrates, met the rioters, engaged them, took twenty prisoners and escorted them to Devizes Gaol. Afterwards, Walter's relieved father laid on 'an excellent dinner' at Rood Ashton for 200 labourers as a reward for their good conduct during the disturbance, and ordered a fat bullock to be killed and distributed to the poor of West Ashton.

Their fears were well-founded. Some magistrates unpopular with the mob had found their houses set on fire, putting them and

<hr>

329   *The Age* (London), 16 July 1826, issue 62
330   Walter Hume Long, Viscount of Wraxall, *Memories*, 1921

their families in great danger. In 1839 Walter was obliged to suddenly cut short a meeting in London due to a threatened attack on his house at Rood Ashton by a mob of Chartists, united in their support for a six point charter for parliamentary reform. The centre of Chartism in the West Country was just a few miles away at Bath, and the political message quickly spread to Trowbridge, Westbury, Bradford on Avon, Devizes and Salisbury, where they held torchlight processions and large meetings, attended by as many as 3,000 people.

Although the Bristol riot had resulted in the 1832 Reform Act, allowing a wider vote, there still remained large disenfranchised sections of the population. In a report to the Poor Laws Commission in 1834 Walter insisted no disturbance would have occurred in Wiltshire had an effectual check been put on rioters in the adjoining counties, and the condition and reckless state of the poor been properly addressed. But he was deliberately missing the point. It was the right to vote they wanted, and in the long run the relentless march of democracy could not be denied.

In 1836, his first year as lord of the manor, Walter held the customary rent audit in Steeple Ashton with nearly 100 of his tenantry sitting down to dinner with him. Described in the press as 'kind and affable' and 'a truly excellent landlord', Walter told his tenants he was aware of the difficult times they had to contend with, but he flattered himself that the dawn of better days was appearing and they could be assured he would never take advantage of their prosperity. Indeed, he would do everything in his power to promote it; his chief pride and satisfaction was to see a happy and prosperous tenantry.

Six years later, during a public meeting of farmers at Devizes, a petition was adopted against the proposed importation of livestock and other agricultural produce. In Walter's speech – described as 'curious' by the *Wiltshire Independent* – he said he had travelled a great deal, and in Belgium they could grow barley, mangle-wurzel and turnips to greater perfection, and more cheaply than the English farmers, thereby fattening their cattle cheaply and exporting them to England almost free of duty. On this basis he opposed the tariff that would protect the livelihoods of the English farmers.

Not long after inheriting his father's estates he had begun

Rood Ashton, the panelled hall. Courtesy Tim Couzens

rebuilding work at Rood Ashton, commissioning architect Thomas Hopper to make improvements, and panelling and other material was brought from Whaddon House after being rescued from the fire there the previous year. For a while Whaddon had been tenanted by his cousin Daniel Jones Long who later appointed Walter trustee of his will. He had bequeathed Walter his coin collection with the proviso he not sell or otherwise dispose of it except by will or donation to some public institution.

During the process of making inventory of Daniel's possessions after his death in 1827, Walter panicked when the rare Glenister Petition Crown, struck in 1663, could not be found. An advertisement was inserted in several newspapers offering £20 reward for its recovery and the apprehension of the thief if it was offered for sale. Another advertisement three weeks later sheepishly informed the public they could stop looking: it had been found carelessly put away by Daniel after showing it to a friend.

Little did he know that Walter would sell the collection in nearly 800 lots during a four day auction at Sotheby's in January 1842, many described as 'of the most curious and costly character, and accordingly fetched high, and in some instances rather remarkable prices'. Daniel had paid £210 for the Petition Crown at Sotheby's in 1824; it fetched only £170 (about £7,500) in the sale of 1842. In September 2007 it was sold by Spink's Auction House for a world record price of £207,000.[331]

During rebuilding at Rood Ashton the family's social engagements continued more or less uninterrupted, bringing them into the orbit of many interesting and well-known figures. They were friends with Irish poet and songwriter Thomas Moore, who attended their dinner parties at Rood Ashton, and Moore noted in his diary in 1836 that he had also dined with Walter and his wife at Bowood.

Benjamin Disraeli, who would later twice serve as Prime Minister, dined with the Longs at their residences in both London and Rood Ashton.[332] The two men shared a mutual admiration: in an often repeated quote from Disraeli's *Biography of Lord George Bentinck*, describing Sir Robert Peel's defeat on the Irish Coercion Bill in 1846, he refers to the 'pleasant presence of Walter Long' among the 'men of metal and large-acred squires' whose counsel Peel had solicited in his political speeches in Whitehall Gardens.[333]

The whirl of dinners, banquets, deputations, meetings, royal

---

331   Auction 7023 Lot number: 503
332   Benjamin Disraeli, John Alexander Wilson Gunn, Melvin George Wiebe, *Benjamin Disraeli Letters*, p. 278
333   Wilfred Meynell, *Benjamin Disraeli, An Unconventional Biography*, 1903, p. 321

balls and levees at the palace since entering public life eventually took their toll on Walter's health, and in 1843 illness compelled him to obtain leave of absence for two months from the House of Commons while he recuperated on the Continent. During his frequent attendances at Parliament his wife often remained in Rome or Paris.

Rood Ashton House, lithograph W. Millington c. 1840

In 1847 one scurrilous scandal sheet ridiculed her absence, with Mary Anne's alleged quote that she would rather be an 'Exile of Siberia' than be 'without the pale' of the amusements she had enjoyed the previous season.[334]

While being treated for typhus Mary Anne died at Paris in March 1856, and one year later Walter remarried in London. His new wife was Lady Mary Anne Bickerton Hillyar, daughter of Rear Admiral Sir James Hillyar, and widow of the Rev. Sir Cecil Augustus Bisshopp, 10th Baronet of Parham. Walter's sister Flora had previously written to him expressing reservations about the intended marriage, sentiments which may also have been shared by his now grown children, so soon after their mother's death.

Sixty-five-year-old Walter had one son born in 1858 to the second Mrs Mary Anne Long, then aged forty-one. To ensure appeasement of all the family, the infant was named Walter Hillyar Colquhoun Long,

334   *The Satirist; or, the Censor of the Times* (London), issue 773, 17 January 1847, p. 22

after himself and both his wives. Mary Anne continued to be styled Lady Bisshopp throughout her second marriage.

After retiring from Parliament in 1865 Walter received a private letter from Benjamin Disraeli,[335] then chancellor of the Exchequer, hinting he might expect some recognition of his services to the Conservative party (i.e. a peerage), should the new government survive. But it didn't happen. His failing health eventually induced him to remove to Torquay, Devon, where after a final sudden illness he died aged seventy-four, in January 1867. The funeral was a grand affair, although it rained and thundered throughout the service. His widow survived until 1891.

Walter Long Junior 1 (1823–1847) – The Heir Apparent

Born at Baynton House in 1823, Walter's eldest son from his first marriage, Walter junior was an officer in the Royal Wiltshire Yeomanry Cavalry, founded by his grandfather Richard Godolphin Long. There was a great party at Rood Ashton in September 1844 to celebrate his coming of age, and also the marriage of his sister, Mary, to Brian Edward Duppa, twenty-one years her senior. The journal of one of the guests, author John Hungerford Pollen,[336] contains a minute description, architecturally and artistically, of the house, its furniture, the gardens, park, and grounds.

Not only the manor itself, but every spare room in the village was occupied by guests who were to share the three days of festivities, and an omnibus collected others from outlying places. The wedding was followed by dinner at 6pm in a huge tent on the lawn, and then a ball in the dining room, 'most successful and well attended'. The party continued until at least four in the morning. Each new day of festivities was ushered in by the ringing of bells and firing of guns, with breakfast at eleven, tightrope dancing on the lawn and dinner at 5pm, which on the second day was attended by 150 of Walter's tenants and 70 of his troop, in addition to the other guests, all in the large tent.

Such grand scale entertaining naturally included many cousins

---

335 WSA ref 947: 1849
336 Anne Pollen, *John Hungerford Pollen, 1829–1902*, 1912, pp. 28-29

on the guest list, and Georgiana, a younger daughter of Walter Long of Preshaw, recalled arriving at Rood Ashton with her family at 5pm and sitting down to dinner at six in the large tent, all the ladies wearing bonnets. There were fireworks and 'all sorts of entertainments':

> On Sunday we all walked to church and in the evening played at spelling games. As we went to bed one of the Miss Longs [Flora Henrietta, aged sixteen] and another girl got on the stairs and threw a jug of water down on those going up and then ran away, the water went on my Father's head and we were afraid he would catch cold. Mrs Long was very angry with her daughter who was a school-room girl and afterwards [became] Mrs Penruddock.[337]

Not long afterwards Walter junior became engaged to a daughter of the Rev. J. Sandford, and the marriage was expected to be 'solemnised by the end of the season'.[338] Someone had second thoughts. Eighteen months later Walter again became engaged, this time to Miss Harriet Avarina Brunetta Herbert, only child and heiress of John Owen Herbert of Dolforgan, Montgomeryshire. Walter's cousin John Long of Monkton Farleigh was a party to the prenuptial agreement, and the happy couple were married in London at the fashionable St George's in Hanover Square.

Harriet became pregnant while on their European honeymoon, much to the delight of the family, but in January 1847 back home in Wiltshire at Seagry House[339] she gave birth to a stillborn child. Harriet succumbed to complications and died the next day. Grief-stricken, Walter set off for the Continent, seeking solace with his parents who were holidaying in Rome. Initially the family made attempts to keep news of his daughter-in-law's death from Walter senior,[340] himself recuperating from a serious illness, but eventually they had no choice but to inform him – as gently as possible. He wrote to his sister

337   Recollections of Georgiana Eleanor Smith, *née* Long 1885, private collection
338   *The Times*, 2 May 1844
339   Seagry House originally formed part of the estate of the Longs of Draycot
340   WSA ref 947:2003

afterwards that learning of the misfortune of 'dearest darling Walter' was a 'thunderstroke to me'.

During this unhappy period Walter junior went into a severe emotional and physical decline. His mother wrote to her sister-in-law Anne Catherine Long, on Thursday '…he was seized with the most awful attack of nervous excitement, his heart going like a wheel. I sent again for [the doctor] and he hoped it might be the effect of a first bleeding. I sat up all night and he got calmer, but he said "my wife's death will cause mine"'.

After another similar attack the next day Mary Anne was told by the doctor it was congestion of the brain, spine and marrow. By the Saturday Walter seemed better. Leeches had been applied to the back of his head and mustard poultices to his feet. 'I then saw a clever man here who advised leeches to the nose if excitement extreme.'

Three months after the death of his wife young Walter also expired, aged twenty-four. His bereft mother Mary Anne 'scarcely left his dying bed during his little hour of suffering, I can tell you a thousand little things which none else can do. Now this dream of agony is over….'

Walter Long Junior 2 (1858–92)

Walter senior's youngest son Walter from his second marriage, nicknamed 'Boysie' by his parents, spent his early education at Northam College in Devon, later attending Eton. At the age of eight the sudden death of his father was the first of several misfortunes to blight his luckless life. Embarking on a military career, he soon rose to the rank of lieutenant, afterwards spending some time with the Inniskilling Dragoons, and during the first Boer rebellion he commanded a British garrison of the 94th Regiment of Foot. The garrison was besieged for 84 days at Lydenberg in the Transvaal from early January until the end of March 1881 by a force of 700 armed Boers. Walter, an inexperienced young Lieutenant, suddenly found himself in the most difficult circumstances.

After the departure of his commander Colonel Anstruther, called away on special orders, Walter was put in charge of the regiment. The soldiers of the 94th, numbering less than 100 and some who had seen twenty years' service, profoundly resented being placed in the care of an officer barely twenty-two years old, and especially one who had never been under fire. Walter's wife of two and a half years, Mary Annabella Conway, was also present during the siege and her safety deeply concerned him. The only woman in the fort (named Fort Mary after her), she became a universal favourite among the men, and seems to have exercised a steadying influence over her husband. He had rejected a peace offering from the Boers, and although he improved the defences of the fort there were day-to-day hardships after the water supply ran low towards the end of the first month, with each person limited to a pint a day.

Discipline broke down; the men began to dress improperly, steal chickens and drink to excess. Lieutenant Long closed the canteen and relieved the sergeant in charge on suspicion of improperly selling liquor to the men. Later, when slightly wounded, he was forced to relinquish command for a few days to the regiment's medic, Surgeon Falvey, and he later quarrelled with him after Falvey insulted his wife. Tempers flared and Walter put him under arrest, with Falvey immediately countering that he was placing *him* under arrest for cowardice in the face of the enemy. This was a harsh accusation, given the circumstances, but one Walter would ultimately be called to answer. After the siege ended, a court of inquiry was instituted and numerous trials by court-martial followed. In July 1881 three of the men were sentenced to lengthy periods of imprisonment for insubordination and bad conduct. Walter chose to resign his commission rather than face a decision by a general court-martial. The following year Mary published an account of her experiences during the siege, *Peace and War in the Transvaal, an Account of the Defence of Fort Mary*.

All these events weighed heavily on young Walter's mind for a long time afterwards. Some six years later his problems were compounded when in 1887 both he and his servant Michael Cahill were bitten by a rabid dog. They were sent to the Pasteur Institute in Paris; Pasteur's treatment was still in its experimental stage and Cahill died. Mary afterwards wrote to the *Daily Telegraph*: 'My husband was spared, but his health was shattered.'[341] Their marriage was also affected, and still in a delicate state Walter left Paris for England but there would be no reconciliation with his wife. He went to friends in Dorset while Mary stayed in London. Sometime around Christmas of 1891 Walter, aged thirty-three by this time, arrived in London, taking a room on the fifth floor at the Grosvenor Hotel in Buckingham Palace Road. He ended his life on 18 February 1892, by throwing himself from the window into the street, 135 ft below, fracturing his skull and 'injuring himself in other ways'.

The inquest heard he was a gentleman of independent means who had not conveyed his intention to anyone. Even his friend and the last person to see him alive, John Hallett, a builder, claimed Walter had not mentioned any problems to him. When he visited his hotel room that afternoon his manner had seemed rather strange, with Walter telling him someone was coming to poison him. Anxious about his friend's state of mind, Hallett had asked the hotel porters to keep an eye on him, which they did by taking turns to make sure he remained in his room.

Earlier that morning Walter had repeatedly asked one of the porters for brandy and after initial refusals he was eventually given claret. When it didn't have the desired effect he requested chloroform but was informed it was not within the porters' power to obtain such a thing. By the afternoon Walter was in a highly agitated state; he paced up and down in his room and sometimes outside in the corridor. Unbeknown to his hallway guards, after returning to his room he climbed out onto the window ledge and launched himself into oblivion.[342]

He had written his first will when he came of age in October 1879, and in the year following the rabies infection, from October 1888 to November 1889, apparently in a state of heightened anxiety, he wrote a further six wills which he lodged with his solicitor, William Brewer in London. Walter's friends George Ross and John Hallett

---

341   *The Animal's Defender and Zoophilist, National Anti-Vivisection Society* 1894, p. 312
342   *The Times*, 23 February 1892

Richard Penruddocke Long, by permission of Llyfrgell Genedlaethol Cymru/The National Library of Wales

served a writ on his widow in November 1892 citing a later undated will in which they were named residuary legatees. They demanded probate be granted to them and the administration of a 'pretended' will dated 1889 with his widow as executrix, be revoked. Mary maintained the earlier will was not executed according to the relevant statute of law, and at the time of writing it Walter was not of sound mind.

Richard Penruddocke Long (1825–75)

The next heir to Rood Ashton was destined to be Walter senior's second son, Richard Penruddocke Long. He was born at Baynton

House in 1825 and educated at Trinity College, Cambridge, where he distinguished himself at cricket, becoming a founding member of the amateur cricket club I Zingari in 1845.

He graduated Master of Arts in 1852. In the spirit of the family's centuries-old tradition of unpaid and arduous commitment to public service he qualified as a magistrate in 1854, appointed High Sheriff of Montgomeryshire in 1858 and deputy lieutenant in 1859. He was elected MP for Chippenham the same year, and replacing his father, for North Wiltshire from 1865 to 1868.

Responsibility was thrust on him early, and the death of his elder brother Walter in 1847 was a life-changing event in many ways. In the immediate aftermath Richard told his family he had changed his attitude to religion. But it was only temporary. Not long afterwards his father received a very satisfactory letter from him, 'and it is truly gratifying to observe his altered sentiments on religious subjects, and I think that his poor brother's untimely end will have a salutary effect on him. He's so different to what he was when we left him in October, and when he disgusted Georgina Campbell so much by upholding the infidel Shelley's opinions.'

Two years later at the young age of twenty-three, as co-executor of the will of his cousin John Long junior of Monkton Farleigh, Richard had the burden of the financial management of the widow and children, a task fraught with difficulties lasting many years. In the meantime he fell in love with the beautiful Charlotte Anna Hume, daughter of William Wentworth Fitzwilliam Hume of Humewood, county Wicklow, Ireland. By August 1853 he was engaged to be married and holidaying in France, thinking mostly of Charlotte, but also of the peculiarities of the French. He wrote to his Aunt Anne:

> I am bathing in the sulphurous waters here with advantage. It is curious to see the Frenchmen coming out of the waters looking so strangely clean! What incorrigibly dirty brutes they are! The more I see of them, the more I say this. Pah!

But it was the love of his life he really wanted to talk about:

Oh dear Aunt Nan, you cannot think what a perfect creature she is! Laugh if you like and [tease] me as much as you please. Only promise to believe nothing you may hear and to judge for yourself when you see her, and I will ask no more. Look at the training she has had, I mean the constant obligation to be unselfish for one of the most unlovable of characters. You must promise to be a dear good aunt and love her very warmly, or I won't send you any more bonbons![343]

If that "most unlovable of characters" was Charlotte's father, Richard needn't have worried. 'Papa says his prayers for his child are now fulfilled', Charlotte wrote. She was equally excited about Richard and their new life together at Dolforgan Hall. Charlotte's previous marriage proposals from would-be suitors had left her determined to be not merely a decorative wife whose main function was childbearing and entertaining; she had bigger plans in mind:

Your mother tells me there are plenty of poor people for me to visit, and a school too! to take interest in, why, it seems like a fairy dream that my future life should be permitted to be so completely in accordance with all my tastes and whims, which I have often tried to turn into another course, because I thought it would never be my fate to indulge them; all this is one of the reasons why I so often prevented myself from trying to know and like many who have offered me high rank and wealth. I felt there was so little if any sympathy between us, that tho' after my town duties were over, I should (as is the usual custom) retire to my country home or homes and have much to enjoy – still it would be alone – I mean alone in feeling and tastes. Everything would be enjoyed by the other in so different a way – merely that they bespoke the "possessions of a rich and titled man". The steward's tastes and opinions would have more weight and meet with more real sympathy and be better understood than the unfortunate wife's.[344]

343   WSA Ref: 947/1902
344   WSA *ibid*

Two months later Richard and Charlotte were married in London. There was 'great rejoicing' at Rood Ashton, with church bells ringing and music in the streets. At the Longs Arms a dinner was given to all the principal tenants on the estate, the room decorated with a floral banner: 'Mr and Mrs R.P Long – Long May They Live'. After a brief honeymoon at the estate of his brother-in-law Charles Penruddocke at Compton Chamberlayne, the newlyweds settled at Dolforgan Hall. Richard, a keen arboriculturist, planted many new trees on the estate. But he had been married barely three years when a near tragedy occurred; in 1856 he was accidentally shot by a gamekeeper, losing his right eye.

Seven children were born in their first ten years of marriage, and a further three followed. Walter, the eldest, recalled in his autobiography many years later the carefree days they spent at Dolforgan learning to ride, and milk the cows. Whenever the services of a doctor were required he would come from the neighbouring town and, regardless of the ailment, administer his usual remedy: a linseed poultice, a mustard plaster, bleeding and leeches.

However, when Walter's little brother Henry became ill with diphtheria in 1866 no amount of mustard, linseed, leeches or bleeding helped. Richard was staying with Charlotte's uncle Quintin Dick in Mayfair when she sent him an urgent telegram: 'Don't be alarmed but please return at once if possible. Dr says no visible improvement but no worse. H. won't let me leave him. I am breaking down.' The boy died soon afterwards, the day before his fourth birthday.

As time passed, Richard struggled to make ends meet at Dolforgan, and he soon communicated his discontent to his father at Rood Ashton. There were disagreements over money and property, and what Richard perceived as his father's refusal to help him establish his political career. He felt his income from the estate's rental, and what he believed was an inadequate annual allowance, were insufficient for him to live in a fitting style, carry out repairs and improvements to the Montgomeryshire estates and attend to his parliamentary duties as member for Chippenham. He was concerned about the increasing encumbrances placed on the estates by his father, whom he believed was manipulating sales of portions of the settled estates to his future disadvantage.

After his father's death in January 1867 Richard came into possession of Rood Ashton, South Wraxall Manor, the former Herbert estates of Dolforgan and Machynlleth and many others. The family had been settled into Rood Ashton barely three months when Richard began receiving letters of demand from Walter Chitty, a twenty-four year-old schoolmaster then living in London. He wanted a slice of Richard's magnificent pie.

Chitty was descended from the Longs of Wraxall through a maternal line and had convinced himself he was the rightful heir to old Walter Long's former South Wraxall estates – in particular, the fifteenth-century South Wraxall Manor. In a case such as this old Walter's heir would normally be the next male on the father's side – the first in line being the eldest patrilineal nephew, but since Walter's uncle the Rev. John Long of Meyseyhampton died unmarried, the estates passed to the collateral branch, *i.e.,* Long of Rood Ashton. Chitty, apparently unacquainted with the laws of primogeniture, began a relentless campaign of letter-writing, harassing Richard with increasingly bizarre insults when he refuted his claim. Perhaps accidentally, or even somewhat wishfully, on one occasion Chitty actually signed himself "Walter Long".

Adding a little more ammunition to Chitty 's arsenal of abuse, he targeted Richard's thatch of copper-coloured hair (a consequence his mother's Scottish heritage), although by this time it was beginning to thin. But what he lacked on top he more than compensated for with a fiery red beard and a moustache to match. 'Ginger Moustache,' began the letter of April 1867 – rather than the customary 'Dear Sir'. Chitty accused Richard of being a liar, a thief and a rogue. 'Do you (like your father) reckon on the Wraxall House as yours? If so then you and your father are devils from the lowest Hell.'

Two days later he sent a peculiar list which included a few more of Richard 's supposed traits:

Fool

Devil

Theif [sic]

Liar

B_____r
Beggar
Rogue
Villain
Monkey
Ginger moustache &c &c
Won't you have it
<u>What</u> a lark oh! oh! oh!!!

Chitty believed the supposed wrongful inheritance dated back to Richard's grandfather Richard Godolphin Long. '[RGL] was therefore the sinner and I certainly do not and cannot regard his memory with pleasure. He may be in Heaven but I very much doubt it.'

Not surprisingly, everyone was convinced Chitty was a madman. 'In my life I never saw such an offensive missive as the one you enclose, I should send the police to the address. There can be no doubt of the man being cracked and vicious.' This was the view of the Rev. Charles Awdry, a descendant of the Draycot Longs whom Richard had asked to find the relevant Long pedigree and thus disprove the claim. Chitty continued his campaign for quite some time, threatening all sorts of things including legal action. Oddly, he continued calling Richard rude names in between politely asking he settle the matter in a gentlemanly fashion. But realising he had no chance against Richard's lawyers he eventually gave up and faded into obscurity.

Having shaken off this irritation, Richard and his family spent protracted periods abroad for health and financial reasons, and nearly every winter since they moved to Rood Ashton was spent in the South of France.

His granddaughter wrote many years later that Richard was 'a tall man with a golden beard and a delightful character, from all accounts'. And so he was, but when it came to politics he was not one to mince words. In a lively exchange during the election campaign for North Wiltshire in 1865, he was accused by his opponent Sir George Jenkinson of making a violent personal attack. Richard had apparently forgotten the prepared platitudes with which he had come to the meeting, and 'the spooney young gentleman' began to 'bawl about the plate on his sideboard'. He had claimed the Longs' parliamentary pedigree to support his case; in response, Jenkinson snorted contemptuously, saying *he* was heir to the 2nd Earl of Liverpool. Richard's come-back: 'Well, *I* have as much plate on my sideboard as *he* has!' [345]

Before the dissolution of parliament in 1868 Richard issued an address to his constituents, informing them that the state of his wife's health had compelled him for several winters to live in a warmer climate than could be found in Wiltshire, and he would leave it in their hands to decide if they felt him worthy of re-election now his primary interest was unavoidably elsewhere. Shortly afterwards a deputation of his tenants came to see him.

With tears in their eyes, they thanked him for his consideration and promptly voted for his opponent. The following month a rumour appeared in a weekly Conservative journal, which then circulated in several newspapers across the country. Richard was to be raised to the peerage under the title of Lord Wraxall.[346] But it was only a rumour, quickly scotched by those in the know. Richard – like his father Walter, remained plain Mr. His granddaughter later wrote that both he and his father Walter 'were keen followers of Disraeli and his policies who once told them he regretted he had not had dissolution honours at the time he spoke, or he would have recommended them, in turn, for an earldom.' After some discussion Richard and his father agreed they would have chosen Wraxall for the title.[347]

Richard continued his interest in farming, spending large amounts of money on Rood Ashton draining the land, removing fences and filling up ditches. This expenditure eventually proved unproductive; the drains were too deep. He also grubbed up many acres of woodland in the belief the country would benefit more from the cultivation of corn and other edible crops. The considerable man-hours required to do this made it a costly exercise and it took many years

345   *The Times*, 18 May 1865
346   *Hampshire Telegraph and Sussex Chronicle*, 15 July 1868
347   Anecdote written by a daughter of Richard, 1st Baron Gisborough; Mike Pease, pers.com

before the land was really productive. Without knowing if the returns would ever justify the expense, Richard optimistically continued to spend more money improving the roads and water supply, building new cottages and improving the farmhouses.

Although Chitty was now out of the picture, Richard's problems didn't disappear altogether, and he was still seen as a man who had plenty to spare. Under pressure from his stepmother, who believed she had not been adequately provided for under the terms of her late husband's will, he wrote expressing regret he was unable to help her financially owing to the many demands made by delayed improvements to the estate and Rood Ashton House. Her best course of action, he told her, was to curb her extravagant lifestyle.

In 1865 the debts totalled £51,000 on the Dolforgan estate, and in 1868, under the terms of his father's will, it was put on the market. The greater part of the estate was sold for £76,500 in 1870. James Walton of Cwmllecoediog was the purchaser, and he bought the remainder of Dolforgan between 1871 and 1874.[348] This eased Richard's financial pressures somewhat, but ill-health reared its ugly head once again. In January 1870 the press reported he was in Switzerland 'lying almost hopelessly ill' at Montreux, suffering from bronchitis and pleurisy, and in a critical state. His surgeon in Trowbridge was sent for, and he recovered enough to return home.

Breaking from their usual habit, the following winter was spent in England at the seaside resort of Weston-super-Mare, together with their retinue of seventeen general servants, two governesses, a butler and footman,[349] who all had to be paid. Certainly there was money coming in; the land return of 1873 stated the estimated gross yearly rental on the 13,168 acres at Rood Ashton was £21,878 17s. But there were many expenses, and Richard's attempts to straighten out his finances were countered by Charlotte's propensity for running up debts.

Charlie, as she was known as a child, was born in France. As a seven-year-old she was living with her grandmother at Guisborough in North Yorkshire when her father recalled her home to Wicklow in

348   National Library of Wales, Dolforgan Estate Records
349   1871 census, RG10/2461

Ireland, after the death of her mother.[350] She grew to be a woman of great charm and grace, much loved and admired, and after arrival on the London social scene her portrait featured in an annual publication, *The Book of Beauty*. Her father had never remarried but later had two illegitimate daughters. According to gossip he persuaded Charlotte to present them at court, afterwards rewarding her with a tiara.[351]

She retained her affection for France, and during her marriage she often travelled to Cannes, her favourite watering place, and always in style, with a private carriage on the train, eating off her own silver and eggshell china, surrounded by a suite of couriers, valets de chambre and maids.[352] When travelling from Rood Ashton to London she would drive to the railway station, have her horses confined in a horsebox and her coach lifted onto a rail truck – all while still seated inside. Her coachman and footman spent the whole sooty journey to London mounted on the outside of the coach while Charlotte enjoyed the privacy and comfort of its interior.

Her resemblance to Emperor Napoleon's wife Eugenie was noticed one day when she was travelling in her usual style to the South of France. In 1872 Napoleon III had lost the battle of Sedan and with it his throne, fleeing with his wife to England. The mistaken rumour soon got around that the empress was aboard the train, and a bouquet of flowers was thrown through the open window of Charlotte's compartment with a note in French: 'We implore your Majesty to return to us!' With her beauty and dignified poise she was mistaken for the empress in many places and consequently received very sincere homage, despite her attendant's attempts to inform people she was not the empress but 'Mrs Long, an English lady'; they smiled at the presumed little ruse saying: 'Mais oui, of course, we understand . . .'

Richard and Charlotte spent the last four years of his life continuing to avoid the rigours of the English winters, and he finally succumbed to bronchitis while in France, dying at Cannes in February 1875 at the age of forty-nine. He had spent just eight years at Rood Ashton as Lord of the manor. His younger brother, the Rev. William

350   Margaret Bruce Chaloner of Guisborough, died when Charlotte was seven
351   Mike Pease, *pers. com.*
352   Richard Long, 4th Viscount of Wraxall, *pers. com.*

Henry Long, also met a premature end in Italy less than a year later, aged forty-six.

Charlotte moved to Exeter, firstly to Marley House, and later with her household[353] to a smaller but still substantial house in Louisa Terrace which she named Dolforgan Court, residing there until her death in 1899. She and her daughters joined the local archery club, and in 1891 she officially changed her name to Hume-Long. The same year, at the age of sixty-one, Charlotte adopted a three-week-old baby, dubbed by the local press 'the basket baby', which had been abandoned in a hamper under the seat of a railway carriage at Bristol station. She named him Hilary Dushca Hume-Long, but the child died about six months later from tuberculosis and whooping cough.[354] There was another adopted son, Harry Shirley, to whom she bequeathed £1,000 in her will.

Charlotte's charity work led to her becoming known locally as 'Lady Bountiful'. Like her contemporary, Florence Nightingale, she nursed the sick, and her granddaughter recalled how she selflessly 'gave skin from her arms when needed, so much so, that she was unable to wear a sleeveless dress'. In 1884 she founded the Maud Hospital in Clarence Road which rapidly became too small. She then purchased a further two properties to house both the hospital and the Hope Orphanage. On her death her eldest son Walter added to her legacy, which subsequently created Exmouth Hospital, the foundation stone laid in 1902.

'This is What Comes of Travelling with One's Inferiors!'

A curious story of inflamed passions came before the Oxford Assizes in July 1884,[355] in a case of slander, libel and assault, concerning Richard and Charlotte's youngest daughter Frances. Already married to explorer and author Harry Dewindt for two years, twenty-year-old Frances boarded a train at Paddington with her infant daughter and

353   Fifteen servants including a French chef, a secretary and a nurse (1891 census)
354   *Trewman's Exeter Flying Post*, 27 June 1891, issue 7495
355   Ivor Smullen, *Taken for a Ride: A Distressing Account of the Misfortunes and Misbehaviour of the Early British Railway Traveller*, 1968, pp. 32-37

elder sister Margaret. They had been shopping in London and had a large number of parcels spread all over the seats in their second-class compartment.

When two passengers, Captain John Preston, an officer in the Berkshire Militia, and his wife, arrived to share the compartment with the ladies, as these were the last seats available, Frances announced self-importantly the seats were engaged as they were expecting friends. Preston's wife politely pointed out they were there at the direction of the guard, at which Frances exclaimed loudly to her sister, 'This is what comes of travelling with one's inferiors. We should have gone first class!' She threatened to have the guard dismissed. With the ladies' alleged friends failing to make an appearance Preston and his wife squeezed themselves into the seats between the parcels, with a large hatbox digging into Preston's back. When he tried to move it onto the floor Frances became enraged and demanded to know his name, warning he would receive a visit from her husband.

On arrival at Reading station Frances summoned the guard, telling him loudly she had been grossly insulted – and never more so in her entire life. She demanded he take out her parcels and put her in another carriage. This commotion drew a crowd to the platform, leading to the assumption that Captain Preston was guilty of making ungentlemanly overtures towards her in the train. Three days later Frances and her husband Dewindt, furiously demanding an apology, were ushered into Preston's house by his butler. Feeling he had nothing to apologise for, Preston refused, whereupon Dewindt called him a 'damned scoundrel' and struck him.

A scuffle ensued which ended with Dewindt shouting 'You brute! You've broken my finger!' Preston told the magistrate 'the foulest possible language' was used by Dewindt, who blurted: 'I would not be seen with you at a pig-fight, you white-livered scoundrel,' adding he would do everything in his power to crush Preston and have him blackballed by his club. Dewindt's side of the story was dismissed out of hand by the jury, who awarded Captain Preston £50 damages for assault, and contemptuously threw out Dewindt's bloated counter-claim for £500 damages for his allegedly broken finger.

Perhaps inevitably, the less-than-happy couple would also

find fault with each other eventually; three years after this incident Dewindt attempted to divorce Frances on the grounds of her adultery with Anthony George Lyster. It seems Dewindt was on a losing streak and the jury found her not guilty. She successfully divorced him for adultery the following year. Whether it was his lengthy absences during adventurous exploits to far-off and remote places – giving Frances an opportunity to seek love elsewhere – which contributed to the end of their marriage, one can only guess, but Dewindt married again at least twice. Frances also remarried, in 1892. Her second husband was Dewindt's rival Lyster, a civil engineer whose significant projects included Brunswick Entrance Locks, Vittoria Dock, and Stanley Dock Tobacco Warehouse, the world's largest built from brick.

After Lyster's death in 1920 Frances became a mystic clothed in purple,[356] living in a small and uncomfortable villa at San Dalmazzo di Tanda, near Cuneo in Northern Italy. She died in hospital in 1932 of double pneumonia after a fall, in which she also broke her arm. Her body was taken to Bordighera over the mountains, and her obituary appeared in *The Times:*

> [the] whole population of San Delmazzo waited for hours in the rain to pay the last tribute to one who had made herself the friend of everyone. Not long ago Mrs Lyster was publicly presented with the Fascist Certificate signed by El Duce himself, in a token of their appreciation of her good works.

Frances's sister, Florence Frydeswide, said to have been 'a favourite in society on both sides of the Channel', married Arthur Henderson Fairbairn nine years before his succession as 3rd Baronet Fairbairn of Ardwick. Arthur, grandson of one of Britain's great nineteenth-century engineers, Sir William Fairbairn, had been born a deaf-mute (as had his sister Constance), but not without a sense of humour. One of the mainstays of a large number of philanthropic institutions, in 1908 he acted as toastmaster at a banquet in London laid on in honour of a group of visiting French deaf-mutes. In his

356   Royal mourning

welcome address he quickly twirled off on his fingers the phrase 'Ladies and Gentlemen, pray silence for the toast!'

After her husband's death in 1915 Lady Florence lived for a while in Dublin, and she died in France at Cannes in March, 1941.

Walter Hume Long, 1st Viscount of Wraxall (1854–1924)

The birth of Richard and Charlotte's eldest son Walter was commemorated by planting a 'birthday tree', *Cryptomeria Japonica*, in the grounds of Rood Ashton. He had been a shy, nervous boy suffering from asthma when he first started school at Amesbury in Wiltshire. Not quite twenty-one when his father died, he was suddenly burdened with responsibilities he was not yet prepared for. This, he wrote many years later, was the very worst thing that could happen to anybody, and the loss of his 'wise and good' father so soon fell upon him with undue weight. Virtually overnight he found himself responsible for an estate of more than 15,000 acres[357] and, owing to the indifferent health of his mother, effectively became guardian of his younger siblings.

His mother's excessive spending continued to wreak havoc on the family finances after her husband's death, and the following year she spent £10,000 on what his late father's estate manager H.E. Medlicott described as 'whimsical nonentities'. Medlicott, a cousin[358] and also his father's executor and official guardian of the children, was concerned, convinced that even if Charlotte was allowed £10,000 a year she would spend double that amount. Warning that further headlong extravagance would discredit his name and family, he pleaded with young Walter repeatedly not to advance money to his mother:

> Your lending your mother money is enough to make your father's voice cry out to hold your hand . . . It can only lead to one end, which is your own embarrassment and further sales of Rood Ashton farms

---

357 John Bateman, *The Acre-Ocracy of England – A List of All Owners of Three Thousand Acres and Upwards*, 1876

358 Henry Edmondstone Medlicott, son of Dionysia Meliora Long, and grandson of Richard Godolphin Long

and lands.[359]

Charlotte's father came to the rescue, covering his daughter's debts and providing an allowance. But he made it clear there would be no further indulgences on his part. Walter was in a difficult position, not easily able to refuse his mother; she lived freely off him, adding another £4–5,000 a year to his expenses. Medlicott urged him to 'be firm and hard, and severe even, if necessary . . . to save yourself, your good name and family and property from such disgrace in your time.' Walter's younger brothers were also running up extravagant accounts, and Medlicott was concerned that Walter himself could easily succumb to unwise frivolities.

> So long as you keep clear of racing, I hope you won't come to serious grief . . . The quieter and more economically you can live, depend upon it, the more you will be esteemed and thought well of by those whose opinion is *worth having*, and the less chance you give to malicious or idle gossips to invent lies!

On the first day of August 1878, three years after his father's death, Walter and his fiancée Lady Dorothy (Doreen) Blanche Boyle, daughter of the 9th Earl of Cork, were married at St George's, Hanover Square. This was a lavish society wedding; Lady Doreen was attended by ten bridesmaids, and 'the bridal presents were very numerous'. An understatement typical of *The Times*, given that the published gift list extended over one and a half full-length newspaper columns. Jewellery was at the top of the list, and Walter gave his bride nine separate pieces, mostly diamonds, with some rubies, emeralds and pearls, and from other friends and family she received a great many more.

Lady Doreen's father was a friend of the Prince of Wales (later Edward VII), who usually smoked twenty cigarettes and twelve cigars a day. Walter relates an anecdote in his autobiography regarding the change over the years in attitudes to smoking, a habit he also indulged in with wholehearted enjoyment. One night when he was attending a

359   WSA ref 947:1062

Sketch of Rood Ashton House, drawn for the Illustrated London News to commemorate a visit by Princess Louise in 1889. Private collection

dinner party at the home of his father-in-law Lord Cork, to which the Prince of Wales had also been invited, Lord Cork asked Walter when dinner was over to take HRH and anyone else who wished to smoke to an adjoining room specially prepared for the purpose.

Walter was amazed to learn Lord Cork hated smoking and could not bear the smell of tobacco, and, incredibly, that some houses he had visited didn't even provide a smoking room at all. He wrote in 1921: 'In these days when smoking begins immediately after dinner and is indulged in by both sexes, it is difficult to realise that such rigid rules existed within, comparatively speaking, so short a time ago.'

With Walter's family background a life in politics was probably a foregone conclusion. When Benjamin Disraeli stayed at Rood Ashton when Walter was eight years old he remembered him patting him on the head, saying he hoped one day he would go to Parliament just like his father and grandfather. After leaving Harrow, and while still an undergraduate at Christ Church, Oxford, Walter was offered an opportunity of standing as Conservative candidate for Oxford City. He declined the invitation, later being elected for North Wiltshire in 1880, the seat once held by his father and grandfather, which he retained until 1885 before his election to Devizes. Disraeli lived until 1881, long enough to see his hope fulfilled. Walter also represented Liverpool, South Bristol, South Dublin, the Strand Division and St George's, Westminster.

L-R: Walter Hume Long; his son Richard Eric Onslow Long, (later 3rd Viscount of Wraxall); his brothers Richard, 1st Baron Chaloner; Robert Chaloner Critchley Long and William Hoare Bourchier Long (rear). Courtesy Richard, 3rd Baron Gisborough

In 1882 construction began on the controversial channel tunnel linking England and France, on the drawing board since its first proposal in 1802 by French mining engineer Albert Mathieu. Walter joined an 'emphatic protest' during a political and press campaign to halt tunnelling, citing fears Britain's national defences would be compromised. More than a century would pass before the Treaty of Canterbury in 1986 finally allowed the project to proceed.

By necessity Walter became adept at juggling family and work, but in April 1883 family took precedence when two of his children developed an illness so serious he had to suddenly leave his parliamentary duties and return to Rood Ashton. After the election of 1886 Walter was made parliamentary secretary to the Local Government Board, becoming one of the architects of the Local Government Act (1888), which established elected county councils. He is, however, perhaps best known for his involvement with Irish Unionism, having succeeded the unpopular George Wyndham in 1905 as chief secretary for Ireland.

It would be impossible in just a few paragraphs to do justice to Walter's long political career, about which much has already been written;[360] however, a few notable highlights should be mentioned. His public profile received a boost in 1895 when the Prime Minister, Lord Salisbury, invited him to join the Cabinet as president of the Board of Agriculture, and at the same time he was appointed to the Queen's Privy Council. His Cabinet appointment led to his becoming the most abused member of the government during his campaign to eradicate hydrophobia, through the strict enforcement of a muzzling order for dogs.

Previous failures to stamp out rabies were mainly owing to the spasmodic and intermittent enforcement by local authorities, but Walter was determined it had to be done properly with no exceptions if it was to have any chance of success. The new rules, described by some as absurd and cruel, came into effect in 1896. A few owners of lap-dogs attempted to smuggle their animals out of the country, concealing them in muffs or bags and occasionally chloroforming them to avoid detection by Customs. This practice was soon curbed by prosecutions.

Word spread across the Atlantic, and the *New York Times* informed its readers that Walter was now 'popularly known throughout the United Kingdom as "The Muzzler"'. Walter recalled many years later that his dear old mother supported his policy by parading up and down her driveway at Exmouth in her bath chair with dogs of all sizes and breeds carefully leashed and muzzled. For his single-mindedness over the issue he was subjected to violent verbal abuse and public outrage in the press. The Canine Defence League was formed and campaigned vigorously against the measures, drawing up a petition signed by 80,000 angry dog owners demanding his dismissal. Nevertheless he

360   See *Walter Long, Ireland and the Union 1905–1920,* John Kendle 1992; and *Walter Long and His Times,* Charles Petrie 1936

remained firm in his resolve, and his tenacity eventually paid off.

During an evening session in the Commons in June 1900 his success was celebrated with universal congratulations and cheers from both sides of the House, having finally rid Great Britain and Ireland of the scourge of rabies. But in just a few short weeks he was lying seriously ill, confined to his London residence in Ennismore Gardens, having had little time to savour the victory. He had suffered a severe attack of carbuncle, aggravated by other complications, and after undergoing two operations he and Lady Doreen retreated to Chitterne Lodge, one of his Wiltshire properties, to recuperate. Planned festivities to celebrate the coming of age of his son and heir had to be postponed indefinitely, and Walter must have felt a sense of déjà vu: there were no celebrations for his own coming of age owing to the recent death of his father in 1875. Instead he had been presented with an illuminated address on vellum signed by more than 230 of his tenants.

With a change of Cabinet in November 1900, Walter was appointed president of the Local Government Board, and in July 1903 he sparked a heated debate in the House of Commons when he moved the second reading of the Motor Car Bill. The Bill had been introduced into the Lords by Lord Balfour, proposing among other things, the abolition of the 14mph speed limit, except in particularly dangerous situations. In the second reading it was proposed to raise the speed limit to 25mph in populated areas, but any kind of speed limit elsewhere would be abolished.

In a bid to appease the protesters Walter, a keen motorist himself, reconsidered the point, and a limit of 20mph was adopted as a compromise. In 1905 he earned criticism for his support of the Unemployed Workmen's Act, once again for being too radical. The Act, popularly known as 'Mr Walter Long's Fund', created an unemployment board to provide work and training for the unemployed.

Across the Atlantic, the American press kept the public informed, the *Washington Post* describing Walter as 'an honest, straight-riding country squire, of the Tory persuasion' and a representative of 'the old Wiltshire house of Tylney Long'. In November 1911 he competed unsuccessfully with Austen Chamberlain for leadership of the Conservative party after the resignation of Arthur Balfour, and to avoid a division within the party both candidates capitulated in favour of Andrew Bonar Law, a relatively unknown figure.

When England declared war on Germany in August 1914 Walter returned to office at the Local Government Board, and Asquith's wartime coalition government was formed the following year. In this capacity he dealt with the plight of thousands of Belgian refugees. The previous year he had offered Rood Ashton and another of his properties, Culworth House in Northamptonshire, for use as a hospital and convalescent home for wounded soldiers and sailors.

During this period a public clash over Irish politics erupted between himself and Sir Edward Carson, who had succeeded him as leader of the Ulster Unionist Party in 1910. Like his father, Walter had a peppery temper and didn't back down easily. With the fall of Asquith and the accession of the second wartime coalition government under Lloyd George in December 1916, Walter received a promotion as colonial secretary, and his most important task was the co-ordination and control of oil supplies to the allied forces.

A number of serious illnesses kept Walter from his work at different times over the years, and on doctor's orders a severe breakdown in his health necessitated a trip to the warmer climes of South Africa in 1909 to aid his recovery. The next year, following a concerted campaign against the Liberal's plan of Home Rule in Ireland he again became ill, and had to have his appendix removed.

Having fully recovered, Walter was ready to fight the Votes for Women movement. There is no record of his wife's opinion. He joined the Anti-Woman-Suffrage Appeal, and in company with the likes of Rudyard Kipling, added his name to a letter to *The Times* in 1910, being among those 'unalterably opposed to the grant of woman suffrage in the interests both of women and of the State', describing the prospect of female voters as an 'ill-advised innovation'. Later, as colonial secretary, he had to alter his unalterable opposition when it fell to him to introduce the Franchise Bill, which for the first time allowed the vote to women. His private secretary Sir William Bull, Conservative MP for Hammersmith, later wrote of the difficulties presented by the sheer numbers of women, as if he had only just realised they were not an invisible minority but actually a significant proportion of the population.

After much debate they finally based their scheme on the Local Government Franchise, which gave votes for municipal purposes to widows and spinsters who paid rates. To this were added wives of men who paid rates, but still they felt the numbers were too high and an age limit was applied. Forty was acceptable to the women themselves, they said, and although it was generally agreed by those framing the Bill that thirty-five would be 'less derisory', Walter cut this down to thirty in the final draft.

The first general election to include the female vote was held in December 1918 after the Armistice, when Lloyd George was returned as Prime Minister for the second time. After much speculation in the press the new Ministry was announced in January 1919, and Walter was sworn in as first lord of the Admiralty during a ceremony for which the king had made a special journey from Sandringham. Ironically, some thirty-seven years before, as an eighteen-year-old, Walter had aspired to a naval career and his grandfather W.W.F. Hume had written to the then first lord of the Admiralty, G.J. Goschen, requesting he nominate him to a naval cadetship. This was refused as Walter was over age.

In February 1920 he was appointed lord lieutenant of Wiltshire, replacing the Marquess of Lansdowne. By this time his health was in a state of deterioration after recurring bouts of illness, and in great physical pain he sat through his last Cabinet session, held in the Prime Minister's room at the House of Commons, in October 1920. The wife of Sir Oswyn Murray, secretary of the Admiralty, later wrote that Walter was much loved by his department, and 'although the Admiralty had a little recovered from the horrible results of the War, Lord Long's illness had depressed every one.'[361] Soon afterwards he was diagnosed with arthritis of the spine. Walter and his family never did recover from the horrible results of the war; his eldest son and heir Walter junior (Toby) was killed in action at Hebuterne in France in 1917.

Toby, a decorated general was aide-de-camp to the Duke of Connaught in 1911. Immediately after his death Field-Marshal Sir

---

361   *The Making of a Civil Servant: Sir Oswyn Murray, G.C.B., Secretary of the Admiralty, 1917–1936*, Lady Mildred March Murray 1940

Douglas Haig sent condolences to his father, remarking that he 'was loved and admired by us all for his manly straightforward ways'. Walter also received a telegram from the king:

> The Queen and I are deeply grieved to hear that your son has been killed in action after such a distinguished career and in the prime of youth. I regret that my Army has lost one of its promising young generals. We offer you and Lady Doreen our heartfelt sympathy in your deep sorrow.

The decade from 1910 to 1920 was a life-changing one for the family, and in addition to this devastating loss Walter had to deal with the stresses of what he viewed as the unavoidable sale of his estates under circumstances beyond his control. The second great bereavement came in March 1920, when his eldest daughter Mrs Victoria Gibbs died suddenly of influenza. Victoria, or Via as she was affectionately known, lived at Tyntesfield, the magnificent Gothic mansion in Somerset inherited by her husband George (later Baron Wraxall), who had acted as her father's private secretary when he was secretary of state for the colonies.

In November 1920 several newspapers published the story that Walter had been enjoying a long cruise in the Admiralty yacht *Enchantress* for the benefit of his health at the taxpayer's expense, when, still recovering from a costly war, the nation's focus was on economy. Questions would be asked in Parliament, they promised.[362] Walter was furious and sued for libel: he was actually on public business at the request of naval authorities as first lord, to settle a number of questions at various ports. He was prepared to accept £500 damages, though the jury thought this small amount would hardly be a deterrent. Nevertheless the judge agreed with Walter, and the case was closed.

His health continued to suffer throughout the cold English winter, and early in 1921 his doctor advised he again go abroad to a warmer climate. He reluctantly resigned his office, hoping this would be a temporary absence from Parliament, intending to return as a

362   *The Times*, 6 May 1921

private member. But his ongoing health problems prevented him from doing so, and there ended his career as one of the longest serving MPs, clocking up 40 years and 169 days in the House of Commons.

Following his creation as Viscount Long of Wraxall in May 1921, he decided to occupy his days by writing his memoirs, and in 1923 his autobiography *Memories* was published. His health had improved somewhat, but during July 1924 he was forced by illness to cancel his public engagements. Two months later he seemed to be making a good recovery when he suffered a serious relapse, developing pneumonia. As he lay in a critical condition the family was summoned to Rood Ashton, where a message was received on 26 September: 'The Queen and I are greatly concerned to hear of Lord Long's serious illness, and trust to hear better news. – George, R.I.' But there was no better news, and Walter died that day. In the days that followed, the family received many messages of condolence. The King wrote to his widow:

> The Queen and I are much grieved to hear of your great sorrow and of the loss of one whom we regarded as an old and valued friend. During his long public career he held high office during three successive reigns, while you and he gave your best in our country's cause. – George R.I.

A memorial service was conducted at Salisbury Cathedral and at the same time his funeral was held at Rood Ashton, well attended by a long list of family and distinguished friends, 'representing every phase of public life'. Among the chief mourners was the sole representative of the Longs of Monkton Farleigh, Walter's cousin Miss Alice Long of Bath. By the time they had all squeezed into the little church of St John on the Rood Ashton estate (built by Walter's grandfather) it was standing room only, and Walter's remains were afterwards interred in the family vault in the churchyard, the coffin made from oak hewn on the estate. A substantial memorial to him was later erected in the church.

He left unsettled property with a gross value of £103,990, and the viscountcy was inherited by his thirteen-year-old grandson, Walter Francis David Long, later aide-de-camp to Lord Bledisloe, governor-general of New Zealand. Tragically imitating the fate of his late father, the 2nd Viscount Long was killed by sniper fire at the age of thirty-three in wartime Holland in 1944, reaffirming the family's continued belief in the curse dating back to the death of Sir Walter Long in 1610 and the legend of the white hand. The title passed to the 2nd Viscount's uncle Richard Eric Onslow Long, younger brother of Brigadier General Toby Long.

Eric – as he was known – the 3rd Viscount, was described by his daughter-in-law as 'the archetypal squire of the old school, slowly becoming an anachronism but still with a presence that commanded a desperate standing-to-attention.' A stickler for protocol, during the early days of the marriage of his son, the future 4th Viscount, Lord Long would summon his new daughter-in-law Margaret to his study in Steeple Ashton Manor, where he would sit with an out-of-date copy of Burke's Peerage and test her knowledge of etiquette:

> You are giving a dinner party. You have Her Majesty the Queen of England, the Earl Marshal, a Dame Commander of the Royal Victorian Order, the Chancellor of the Exchequer, the Lord Chief Justice, a Viscount's elder son, a Duke's younger daughter - where do they sit?
>
> You are giving another dinner party with the Bishop of London, the Bishop of Winchester, the Bishop of Durham. Who sits on your right? At the same dinner party you have a Lord Justice of Appeal, a Knight Commander of the Star of India, the Master of the Rolls, the Comptroller of the Household. Who sits on your left?[363]

And then there were instructions quite beyond the future Viscountess's ability to carry out, with any degree of certainty: 'You will give birth to a son first, followed by another son as guard to the King. After that you can give birth to whatever you like.'

Richard Godolphin Walmesley Long Chaloner (1856–1938), 1st Baron Gisborough

363 Margaret, Viscountess Long of Wraxall, *op. cit.*

With the obvious exception of having lost his father so young, fortune seemed to smile on Richard, second son of Richard Penruddocke Long and his wife Charlotte. His maternal great-uncle Admiral Thomas Chaloner had inherited the Guisborough estates in Yorkshire through his mother, a descendant of Robert de Brus, and Richard adopted the surname Chaloner in 1888 after unexpectedly becoming his heir.

He served throughout the Afghan war of 1879–81 and in 1900 commanded the 1st battalion of the Imperial Yeomanry in South Africa, retiring with the rank of lieutenant colonel. His nephew Rob Long told the romantic story that Uncle Dick had married young and impetuously a beautiful but penniless girl,[364] and all they had to live on was his pay as a subaltern in the Carabineers. One day when they were living in garrison with the rest of his regiment he was notified of his aunt's death in Yorkshire, and was requested to attend the funeral. Somehow young Dick Long managed to find the money for the rail tickets, travelling third class, unheard of for an officer in those days. After the funeral they were asked to attend the reading of the will, whereupon he suddenly found himself heir to the great Guisborough estates and an income of about £30,000 a year.

Just a few years before, as a high-spirited young bachelor, Richard had been brought before the magistrate at Exeter charged with toll evasion. He had driven his mother's coach through the toll gates at Haldon without paying, the toll keeper running after him shouting: 'Toll! Toll!' to the great amusement of those on the coach, who laughed at him and called out, 'Come on old man!' The prosecutor asked for the highest penalty provided by law, inasmuch as the offence was committed by a person of 'the higher order' and he should have known better. Penalty: £2. In 1883 he was presented to the Prince of Wales at a levée at St James's Palace, and his niece would later relate a story about Richard one day returning from the races at Ascot and driving his carriage back to London on a clear road, leaving the prince to follow in his dust cloud.

364   Margaret Mary Anne, daughter of the Rev. Weston Brocklesby-Davis, vicar of Ramsbury, Wiltshire

R.G.W.L Chaloner. 1st Baron Gisborough. Courtesy Richard, 3rd Baron Gisborough

Richard, by this time Captain Chaloner, was first elected to Parliament for Westbury in 1895. In the lead up to the election he set about priming the minds of prospective voters by attending various meetings and 'smoking concerts' in West Wiltshire, but a local clergyman, self-proclaimed non-smoking teetotaller, the Rev. W. Attewell of Bradford on Avon, took exception to the supposed 'demoralising tendency' of Richard's campaigning. Attewell preached a bristling and colourfully worded sermon on the subject of 'National Righteousness', proudly declaring he had never attended a smoking concert in his life, and he would sooner rap at the doors of hell. He then proceeded to paint a fanciful picture of what took place there, 'sin in its most degraded form', with thinly veiled references to Richard.

Attewell's sermon, while not actually mentioning Richard by name, was repeated in the *Wiltshire Times*, which did mention him quite pointedly, together with a raft of criticism and the suggestion to mend his ways. He instituted a lawsuit against the proprietors of the newspaper while Attewell reiterated his charge that Richard was, by being present at smoking concerts (to secure their votes), leading the young into debauchery and drinking with prostitutes. The judge awarded Richard £100 damages, and he went on to win the election by 163 votes.

Defeated at the next general election in 1900, he was re-elected to Liverpool Abercromby in 1910. He retained this seat until 18 June 1917; five days later he was created 1st Baron Gisborough of Cleveland, sitting in the House of Lords until his death in January 1938.

The family was still mourning his nephew Toby Long, killed in early 1917 fighting in France, when ten weeks later on 3 April, Richard's eldest son, thirty-three-year-old Richard Godolphin Hume Long Chaloner (nicknamed Huie), was also killed in France, but not as a result of enemy action. While in charge of the 20th Prisoner of War Company he was accidentally shot dead by one of his own sentries in a POW camp; tragically he failed to hear the sentry's challenge during a thunderstorm late at night. Huie's brother, Captain Thomas Chaloner of the Royal Flying Corps, was listed as missing in July 1916 after he failed to return from a bombing raid to Saint Quentin. Piloting a two-seater BE2c biplane, he was shot down behind German lines but managed to land safely, immediately finding himself surrounded by German infantry.

A small group of German Flying Corps officers arrived in a car claiming he was their prize, resulting in 'a lot of scrapping' as Captain Chaloner later wrote, but the Flying Corps officers won the argument and took him to their mess for interrogation. In May 1918, after two years a prisoner of war, Thomas escaped to Holland. Twenty years later he succeeded his father as 2nd Baron Gisborough, and the title lives on in his son Richard, the third Lord Gisborough.

Richard Penruddocke Long's third son, Major Robert Chaloner Critchley Long, was an enthusiastic cricketer and veteran of the Zulu and Great Wars. In 1893 he was awarded the medal of St John of Jerusalem by the future King Edward VII for stopping a runaway coach and four from ploughing into a gathering of civilians. Following in his brother's footsteps, in 1910 he also stood as a candidate for Westbury, but was defeated by the sitting member Sir John Fuller. Robert had three daughters with his wife Maud, and after her death in 1919 he emigrated to Rhodesia, dying there in 1938.

R.P Long's youngest son, William Hoare Bourchier Long – Willie, or Bill as he was later known – was always considered delicate by his mother, and never allowed out without his chest protector and respirator. Not quite seven years old when his father died, he attended a preparatory school for 'delicate boys' run by the Rev. Weston Brocklesby-Davis, his brother Richard's future father-in-law, and later went to Harrow.

Despite repeated bouts of serious illness he became an officer in the Irish Guards, eventually resigning his commission in 1924. After moving to Bordighera, Italy with his wife Vera, he became so frustrated with having to pay the postman the shortfall and a fine to receive under-stamped mail from his friends in England, he inserted a general notice in *The Times* in 1934, admonishing them for their negligence. This would prove to be the least of his worries, however.

When Mussolini declared war on France and England in 1940 there was a pressing need to find a friendlier host, as William was now an Englishman in enemy territory. He escaped with his wife by coal boat from the South of France to Australia via Gibraltar. They arrived at the capital Canberra, and in between friendly games of tennis he organised papier maché classes to produce splints for wounded soldiers. He died there in 1943 aged seventy-five, after a bout of double pneumonia.

His son Rob (Richard Oliver Bruce) Long was an officer in Naval Intelligence during the Second World War. He translated captured German documents for the trials of major war criminals by the International Military Tribunal after the end of the war, and he also translated books from German to English, including *The Sea Wolves*, the story of German U-boats at war by Wolfgang Frank.

The Penruddocke Case

A scandal erupted in 1902 when the wife of Mr Charles Penruddocke junior, a respected justice of the peace, was suddenly thrust into the public eye amid allegations of child cruelty. Owing to their high social standing the case attracted worldwide interest, from London to New York,[365] Canada and even the farthest reaches of the empire, news-starved New Zealand.[366] In 1853 R.P. Long's sister Flora Henrietta had married barrister Charles Penruddocke senior of Compton Chamberlayne, Wiltshire. Charles junior, their only son and heir, was born in Mayfair and inherited his father's estates in 1899, which included Compton Park and Fyfield Manor.[367]

It was Flora's daughter-in-law, Annie, a well-known society lady, who was charged with the ill-treatment of their youngest daughter, six-year-old Letitia Constance, known as Connie. Public feeling ran high in Wiltshire where the family lived, and the trial venue was moved to London's Old Bailey, where she was tried before criminal judge John

---

365   *New York Times*, 30 November 1902
366   *Wanganui Herald*, (New Zealand), 25 November 1902
367   Charles Penruddocke junior sold the manor in 1919. Subsequently owned 1958–66 by Sir Anthony Eden (former PM), and from 1966 to 1977 by the Hon. Charles Morrison, who married Sara Long (daughter of 2nd Viscount Long)

Charles Bigham.

The tortures allegedly inflicted on the child by its well-heeled mother, who for some reason had taken a particular dislike to her youngest daughter, included deprivation of food, clothing and bed-linen, and the use of nettles, birch rods, wasps, with items introduced into the child's gullet and other forms of maltreatment, including belittlement, exclusion and psychological abuse. The case was brought by the Society for the Prevention of Cruelty to Children, already aware of what was alleged to have been happening to little Connie, but it was only when servants of the family agreed to give sworn affidavits that a case was finally brought. Her mother Annie pleaded not guilty. The jury believed otherwise.

On convicting Mrs Penruddocke, Judge Bigham was almost apologetic, giving her a fine of £50 which her husband paid on the spot, and they left the court.[368] Controversy over this decision rumbled on in the newspapers for months afterwards, with petitions and questions raised in Parliament over allegations of favouritism.

Two of the Penruddockes' three sons were killed during the First World War; however Connie grew up and married a young university graduate, later a member of the British consulate. She died in Surrey in 1989.

368   *The Times*, 22 November 1902

IX
Sale of the Estates

To understand the events that led to the sale of the 1st Viscount Long's estates, it is necessary to wind the clock back to the general election of February 1906, when, after a landslide victory, the Liberal government under Prime Minister Henry Campbell-Bannerman introduced the Liberal welfare reforms following a Royal Commission into the country's Poor Laws. This coincided with Walter selling Chitterne Lodge and Chitterne Farm in September 1906, with about 1,650 acres of land. The Longs of Rood Ashton had been lords of Chitterne manor since 1830.

In 1909 Chancellor Lloyd George introduced his famous Finance Bill, which he called the 'People's Budget', imposing increased taxes on luxuries, liquor, tobacco, income and, most significantly, land. This money was earmarked for two main areas of expenditure: social reforms to benefit the poor, old and unemployed, and re-armament to meet the threat from the fleet of dreadnoughts being built by the Germans.

The other intended result was of course the redistribution of land ownership. The nation's wealthy landowners, who had a strong representation in the House of Lords, were in uproar over the proposed new taxes, and Lloyd George vigorously defended his budget in the House of Commons. A pressure group, the Budget Protest League, was formed in June 1909 led by Walter Long, to oppose the new tax rises.

Although the budget passed the Commons, Lloyd George's denunciation of the Conservatives and wealthy classes resulted in its defeat by the Conservative majority in the House of Lords. This changed after the Liberals were re-elected in January 1910, led by Herbert Asquith, and the budget finally passed the Lords. As one of those wealthy landowners, Walter, after much soul-searching, concluded there was only one possible course of action, and on a personal level it was probably one of the most difficult decisions he had ever had to make.

In late September 1910 Walter instructed his Rood Ashton land agent Ward Soames, in conjunction with Knight, Frank and Rutley, to offer the greater part of his Wiltshire estates for sale. This was an historic and unprecedented action for not only the Long family but also the nation, triggering the beginning of an avalanche of selling by others similarly affected. On the eve of his departure to Canada he wrote to his tenants, reassuring them he had no cause for dissatisfaction, nor did he desire to terminate their occupation, instead blaming the financial policy of the government on the need for all large landowners to consider their position. The partnership of landlord and tenant had not been governed by purely mercenary considerations, he told them, expressing deep regret at the termination of their relationship, hopeful they would be able to purchase their own holdings.

In January 1911 several farms were advertised for auction, in the parishes of North Bradley, Hilperton, Melksham, Potterne, Poulshot, Seend, Staverton and Whaddon, with a combined rental income of about £6,900 per annum. As the date of the auction approached, Walter's largest tenants organised themselves into a syndicate, and in February 1911 they negotiated the purchase of 2,500 acres of the first offering of 3,800 acres. The majority of the remaining land went under the hammer at Trowbridge town hall in mid-May, realising £15,000.

The following day more small farms comprising a further 200 acres were sold, raising £9,500, and whatever else remained unsold was disposed of by private treaty. By July many other major landowners had followed suit, with the press full of projected sales and announcements that opportunities would be offered to tenants to buy their farms. The Small Holdings (Tenants Acquisition) Bill was introduced in April 1911 and by the end of that year a little under 278,000 acres were sold for just over £7.1 million,[369] the majority bought by tenants.

The death of his son Toby and daughter Via had caused such depression in Walter that material wealth mattered little to him

369   *The Times*, 30 December 1911

anymore, and over the next few years more of his property was disposed of. Just over 1,000 acres of the South Wraxall estate was sold in thirty-nine lots in 1919, realising £42,000. This sale included five farms, the nine-bedroomed South Wraxall Lodge, allotments, cottages and other land, with a rental income of £1,184 per annum. The historic fifteenth-century South Wraxall Manor was retained.

In November 1919 the Welsh farms in Machynlleth comprising 676 acres were put up for sale, inherited through his uncle Walter's brief marriage with Harriet Herbert. The government's land redistribution plan was working exceptionally well; it has been estimated that from the end of 1918 to the end of 1921 somewhere between six and eight million acres changed hands in England and Wales.

Much of the purchase money was left as mortgage in the old owners' hands at a rate of 5% interest. This was a better deal than the meagre returns on rent, but for the former tenants, now mortgaged owner-occupiers, an agricultural depression between 1921 and 1939 made them realise the enormity of what they had taken on. There was no longer a landlord to soften the blow between farmers and fluctuating market forces. Fixed interest rates were not flexible as rents had been, and the estate office, once helpful with building repairs or costs in changing to new modes of cultivation, was gone.[370]

Since the passing of the Finance Bill, Walter considered the action of the government in regard to death duties 'far and away the most serious effect of their scheme on agricultural land'. This, and subsequent bad financial advice by the wealthy, well-known but disreputable financial speculator Clarence Hatry, wrought havoc on Walter's estate, and in mid-January 1930, a little over five years after his death, *The Times* announced the forthcoming auction of Rood Ashton House and 4,100 acres, to be held on 12 February.

The advertisement described the 'stone-built mansion in the domestic Gothic style', containing six reception rooms surrounding a lofty central hall, forty-six bedrooms but only seven bathrooms, and 'well-appointed offices'. Modern conveniences were electric lighting, central heating and telephone. The timbered park surrounding the

370   Mingay, *op. cit.* p. 173

house comprised about 300 acres with a seven acre ornamental lake, home farm, ornamental gardens and a five acre cricket ground with pavilion, as well as three lodges and a detached stabling and garage block. The estate itself included seventeen farms, 21 smallholdings, 100 cottages, two public houses and a square mile of woodland, all with a combined rental income of about £8,000 a year.

Before auction 2,500 acres were purchased by a syndicate of tenants, and most of the remainder was snapped up on auction day by Mr A.H. Bond of Lowestoft, with a view to reselling. Some of the farms were also sold, and altogether £21,610 was realised; but the mansion received no bids, either with the surrounding property or on its own. It was re-advertised, and by August 1930 finally sold – 333 years after Walter's ancestor Edward Long purchased the estate in 1597. His widow Lady Doreen, who lived at the dower house, Steeple Ashton Manor after her husband's death, died in 1938.

The Demise of Rood Ashton

During the Second World War the house was used as a hospital, and in 1950 it was put on the market again – the asking price a mere £35,000 for the once magnificent mansion, 248 acres with

Rood Ashton House minus its roof and windows. Courtesy Beverley Booty

farmhouse and outbuildings, and two lodges. It was no longer a loved and cherished home, and gradually over a twenty year period it had become run-down; even so, this was an irresistible bargain for someone. The new owner stripped the house. Internal panelling, fireplaces, marble, staircases, and lead roofing were packed into containers and shipped off to the United States.

Now just a roofless shell, the house was vulnerable to the elements and soon became derelict. At the time, Richard, 4th Viscount Long and his first wife Lady Margaret were rebuilding the former dower house, Steeple Ashton Manor, inherited from his father in 1967. It had served its occupants well since its purchase in 1799 by Viscount Long's great-great-great grandfather Richard Godolphin Long, but by the latter half of the twentieth century it was in desperate need of refurbishment. Many years later, Lady Margaret spoke of naked bulbs hanging from the ceiling on long flexes, nettles growing in among the scullery flagstones, stray cats eating out of crested plates, and a ferocious Long family Nanny terrifying everybody. The black iron kitchen range was practically the only form of heating. But Rood Ashton was far worse; a 'dilapidated, deformed and broken kind of grandeur'.

It stood as a gaunt, gutted ruin until May 1975, when the owner, Mr A.J. Green of Trowbridge, decided to demolish it. For their own safety the people of West Ashton were warned to keep away. A large part of the house had already been torn down when the Department of the Environment was alerted, and after an emergency assessment the building was spot-listed on grounds of architectural and historic interest, bringing work suddenly to a halt. But within days Mr Green advised the local council he was proceeding with demolition because the remains of the building were dangerous. Internal walls were standing precariously, and during recent high winds some had fallen. A fire in the ruins caused by partying youths hastened the decision.

Most of the hall was then demolished, leaving just a small wing of the house (the former servants' quarters) rising forlornly from the landscape; today it sits on a 3 acre plot. These remains were purchased by a sympathetic owner who restored the still standing wing, repanelling the previously unadorned servants' rooms with reclaimed timbers from other demolished country houses.

Remains of Rood Ashton House 2010. Courtesy Beverley Booty

South Wraxall Manor

After the death of Miss Katherine Long in 1814 the old manor house at South Wraxall lay empty for some time before being let to tenants. The Rev. Francis Knight DD, formerly vicar of Bradford on Avon, leased the house from 1820 to 1826 and ran it as a school for about forty boys. In his *Recollections of an Octogenarian Civil Servant* (1891), H.W. Chisholm says the 'oak panelled rooms were said to be haunted by two Miss Longs, ancient spinsters who had died there at a very advanced age, however none of the pupils ever saw them, but sometimes sharp and unaccountable noises were heard'. Perhaps the Misses Long were still angry about their portrayal as sour, fusty, malicious old maids in Foote's play *The Maid of Bath*.

During his tenure Knight made a number of 'improvements' to the house, which included plastering over the carved ceilings and painting the oak panelled wainscots, and he and his pupils perpetrated other redecorations and desecrations, their energies also extending to the church. Sixty years later Walter, the future 1st Viscount Long (whose maternal grandfather, W.W.F Hume, was one of the live-in pupils in 1820) endeavoured to rectify these 'mutilations and barbarities' and return the house to its original style.

Walter never actually lived there, though his initials WHL can be seen on several houses in the village. During the remainder of the nineteenth century the house was looked after by caretakers who entertained anyone who wanted to see inside, and it was during this period that 'it degenerated into a show-place where tourists and trippers could have tea parties'.[371]

In 1900 the manor was let on a long lease to Major Eustace Richardson Cox, with the condition that a considerable amount be spent on the estate. In 1912 at least part of the house was exposed to a wider audience when Lady Randolph Churchill organised the 'Shakespeare's England' exhibition at Earl's Court, London, which included a replica of an Elizabethan village designed mainly by architect Edward Lutyens. A scaled-down replica of South Wraxall Manor containing a player piano exhibit was located just inside the Warwick Road entrance.

Richardson Cox leased the manor until 1935, and would have continued longer, considering the amount of money he had spent on the house, but he died unexpectedly while on a cruise. He had kept to the original terms of the lease, undertaking a major restoration programme under A.C. Martin, which included extensive period-matching work, taking two years to complete and costing several thousand pounds. The last time any restoration of this nature had been carried out was in about 1700 when some of the family rooms were refenestrated and repanelled, while in the possession of Hope Long. In February 1936 the house was put up for rent again, and advertised with 50 acres on a short lease at a nominal rent.

Sometime after this, probably between 1937 and 1940, further restoration work was done when the 2nd Viscount Long took over the house, and while he was away in Europe during the war his mother, by then remarried to Baron Glynn, refurnished the manor in anticipation of her son taking up residence there. As he was killed in action the manor was instead used to house refugees from Kent when a large number of inhabitants were evacuated after the fall of France in 1940.

During the 1950s it was occupied by the 2nd Viscount's sister-in-law, Anne, wife of newspaper magnate Lord Rothermere, whom she later divorced to marry novelist Ian Fleming, creator of James Bond.

371   P.H. Ditchfield, *The Manor Houses of England*, 1910

Nearly 400 years after the legendary visits by Sir Walter Raleigh, the old house continued to play host to distinguished visitors. A long-term caretaker later claimed to have seen a photograph of Winston Churchill and Ian Fleming standing in front of the fireplace. If only walls could talk.

The last member of the Long family to live at the manor was Sara, daughter of the 2nd Viscount Long, then wife of Conservative MP Charles Morrison. Her participation in village life is still remembered fondly by the older villagers, but she knew well the economics of maintaining a large medieval house. Eventually this became the catalyst that finally drew to a close the family's 500 year ownership of South Wraxall Manor. Advertised with '847 acres, two excellent farms, a secondary farmhouse, seven cottages, and one let farm' it was sold privately before auction in July 1966.

X

The Junior Branches

Long of Monkton Farleigh

John Long Senior (1768–1833)

The youngest son of Richard Long and his wife Meliora Lambe, John was not baptised in the beautiful church at Steeple Ashton, about a mile and a half from his father's house at Rood Ashton. Instead his parents chose Great Cheverell, eight miles away, the church being in close proximity to a property they were renting at the time.

In 1789 at the age of twenty-one, John was training to be a solicitor at Henley on Thames, Oxford, when he met Mrs Lucy Ann Kinneir, a twenty-seven-year-old widow whose first husband had died three years earlier. They married there the following year, without the blessing of her father, the Rev. John Warneford, Camden Professor of History at Oxford, since he had already been dead seventeen years. The newly-weds returned to Wiltshire, setting up home in Melksham with space for Lucy Ann's widowed mother. [372] They later had five children. Here he conducted his business firstly as a solicitor, and later as a banker from 1792, with his partners John Awdry, Thomas Bruges and his brother Richard Godolphin Long.

---

372 *Née* Lucy Southby, whose mother was Anne Duke of Bulford, descended from Lawrence Hyde, grandfather of Edward Hyde, 1st Earl of Clarendon

Having just turned nineteen when his father died in 1787, John inherited no property, instead receiving cash legacies equally with his only surviving sister Dionysia, of £1,500 and an annuity of £40 per year. He received a further £2,000 in 1797 raised by mortgage on several properties, including Ablington Farm in Figheldean, a property which by then had been in the family for at least 175 years.

A chance find by an antique dealer of a diary wedged inside the casing of a chest of drawers once belonging to John's sister-in-law, Ellen Whinfield[373] gives brief snippets of the day-to-day lives of John and Lucy Ann. In her *New & Fashionable Pocket Book for the Year 1797* Ellen mentions several visits to John and Lucy Ann at Melksham, and they often arrived early enough for breakfast. The Whinfields lived within easy walking distance at Lacock, three miles away, where Ellen's husband was curate. They also regularly dined with the Longs at Rood Ashton, along with John, Lucy Ann and other extended family, and on at least one occasion with Lady Catherine, widow of Sir James Tylney Long of Draycot.

While his elder brother Richard enjoyed the more conspicuous wealth at Rood Ashton, John made the best of whatever windfall came his way with small legacies from dead uncles and cousins. On learning of the benefit he would derive from old Walter Long's settled estates as joint trustee with Richard and their cousin Daniel Jones, acquiring property of his own became a distinct possibility. But he experienced a setback. In February 1822 Lucy Ann died at Cheltenham aged fifty-two, 'after several years of bodily sufferings'. Now a widower with a nine-year-old daughter still to raise, John purchased a five year lease of the manor of Monkton Farleigh.

In S.G. Kendall's *Farming Memoirs of a West Country Yeoman* (1944) he talks about Monkton Farleigh and 'Sir John Long', a member of the 'famous Long of Wraxall family'. He recounts the occasion of a dance party given by a later occupant of the manor house:

There was a suitable room, said to have been built by Sir John Long nearly a century and a half ago now, purposely to please his tenants'

373   Sister of Florentina, née Wrey

daughters, some very pretty girls; here he occasionally joined them in
the dance, not far from Bath, the city where gaiety and society dwelt
in those days.

Monkton Farleigh Manor

To all intents and purposes John was now a bona fide landed
gentleman in his own right; he qualified as a magistrate and served a
term as High Sheriff in 1819, with George Moule, fellow solicitor and
banker of Melksham, as under-sheriff.

With property the backbone of the family fortunes for centuries,
his intention was to provide the same foundation for his own son and
heir, John junior. He had his eye on seventeenth-century Tilshead
Lodge, a sporting estate used by members of the racing elite, just come
onto the market. Once occupied by William, Duke of Cumberland and
the earls of Godolphin and Portmore, among others, it was advertised
as 'a very important and commanding freehold estate', comprising
over 1,050 acres with an elegant mansion, newly erected farmhouses,
'buildings of every description', sundry cottages and a school, known
as Tilshead Academy. The property had been owned by old Walter
Long of Bath in 1760, and now John purchased it for himself.

Before its eventual demolition in the twentieth century, the house had become large and rambling with additions by successive owners, but in 1833 the ground floor comprised 'three good bedrooms, dressing-room, a vestibule, handsome hall, study or boudoir, water-closets, capital dining-room, 33 feet by 20; ante-room, or hall, leading to a breakfast-parlour, 18 feet by 17; drawing-room, 23 feet by 20. At the back of the house, nearly connected with the dining-room, is a building which might at a trifling expense, be converted into a billiard-room.'

Coinciding with John's term as sheriff, dissatisfaction with England's long-entrenched Parliamentary system was beginning to accelerate, with agitator Henry Hunt advocating parliamentary reform and repeal of the Corn Laws. In August 1819, some two hundred miles to the north, the Manchester Patriotic Union organised a demonstration at St Peter's Field to draw attention to their grievances, engaging Hunt to address the crowd. The magistrates had initially allowed the assembly that day, but the mood of the crowd changed after Hunt was arrested on the hustings. Fearing a riot, the magistrates ordered the dispersal of the crowd of some 60,000–80,000 people, which the cavalry undertook with sabres drawn. In the confusion

Tilshead Lodge, 1949. English Heritage, Swindon

fifteen people were killed and an estimated 400–700 were injured. The massacre was given the name Peterloo, an ironic comparison to the Battle of Waterloo four years earlier.

News of the massacre reached Wiltshire just as William Long Wellesley was pitching himself to be elected to replace John's brother Richard. As sheriff, John was drawn into the aftermath by Lord Arundel of Wardour representing an influential group of about 360 freeholders. Weighty additions to the list were the Duke of Somerset, Lord Andover, John Cam Hobhouse, Sir Francis Burdett and Fulwar Craven, who invited John to call a county meeting to arraign the conduct of the Manchester magistrates and the government which had protected them.

John's public announcement proposing the meeting was met with opposition by Lords Pembroke and Montgomery, Beaufort, Bath, Ailesbury, Radnor, Malmesbury, Nelson and Bronte, and nearly one thousand respectable citizens of Wiltshire, who all signed a letter of protest citing a tendency to unduly influence public opinion on matters already under legal investigation. By the time the government enquiry got underway Long Wellesley had been elected MP for Wiltshire and he stood in Parliament in defence of John after Henry Brougham MP questioned his conduct.

The Whig, John Cam Hobhouse, defeated in a contest earlier in the year for a seat at Westminster, carried out his own investigation into the Peterloo Massacre, which included a visit to John. He wrote in his diary on Monday 1 November 1819:

> Came down ready to go, but only sent my groom off to Methuen's, telling him I should come the next day, and sending him also to John Long, High Sheriff, at Monkton Farleigh, who has answered Craven, saying that he declines calling the meeting because he has received a counter-requisition, very 'respectable', and more numerously signed. Craven came here today. Hallett and Craven dined here, determined I should ask the High Sheriff what he would do if he received another requisition, more numerously signed than the counter-requisition. Hallett is a strange, unpopular man.[374]

374   B.L. Add. Mss. 56540

The next day Hobhouse went to Calne, where he saw the counter-requisition for himself, signed by 971 names. After breakfasting with Paul Methuen and his wife at Corsham, he remonstrated with him over his conduct in relation to the recent Wiltshire election, Methuen telling him tearfully that '[Long] Wellesley was a disgrace to the country, but he would still support him against Bennet, who was a liar, and a coward':

> I took leave of him, and rode over well-known ground not seen these five years, to Monkton Farleigh, now the property of John Long, once attorney at Melksham, now High Sheriff. I got there about half-past [ ], and found the man out shooting. I sat down impatiently and waited, reading Crabbe's Tales of the Hall (dull and tiresome), until five o'clock, when my Sheriff arrived, accompanied by a little gentleman. I opened my business, and asked him the question. He boggled and hesitated, and said he could not speak without consulting a friend. At last I got from him that he declined giving an answer. He asked me to dine, but I went away. It was past dark, and I had a headache. [375]

Dissatisfied with John's evasiveness, the question of who had organised the counter-requisition remained in Hobhouse's mind. Two weeks later he got the answer, adding a facetious nudge to Long Wellesley's notoriety: 'Tom Clutterbuck told me at Ricardo's that he was at the bottom of the counter-requisition, together with that honest man Lord Wellesley, the other member.' In early December an enquiry began in the House of Commons with the intention of introducing the Seditious Meetings Prevention Bill, effectively a crackdown on reform and an attempt to avert further incidents like Peterloo.

Six weeks after his visit to John the spotlight fell on Hobhouse. He was committed to Newgate Prison for publishing a pamphlet, *A Trifling Mistake and Reform of Parliament,* which the House of Commons held to be a breach of privilege. He was released at the dissolution of Parliament a few weeks later.

375   *B.L. ibid*

With John beholden to his brother Richard to the tune of £3,000 a year for the rest of his life after his bankruptcy of 1823, there were also ongoing maintenance expenses on his estates, and the following year while repairs were being carried out on the roof of Monkton Farleigh Manor, a workman fell to his death from the battlement. Nevertheless, confident of his financial situation, in 1827 he renewed the lease on the manor for a further twenty-one years, held under the Bishop of Salisbury. He improved the estate and planted the woodland known as Kingsdown Plantation. While he lived at Tilshead Lodge his cousin Daniel Jones Long was his tenant for a while at the manor, where he kennelled his pack of harriers and greyhounds. Dog coursing was well-suited to Wiltshire with its large areas of open space and John and Daniel coursed their dogs competitively against each other.

Tilshead had been a desirable acquisition but it must also have proved a financial strain; before he made his will in March 1830 he sold the estate to George Watson-Taylor of Erlestoke, a serial acquirer of property whose large fortune was eventually depleted by 'an insatiable thirst for something he did not possess.' Parts of the estate including the manor house were sold to the War Department in the early twentieth century and used as an army base during and after the Second World War. The house fell into decay and was eventually demolished.

Despite his earlier financial problems John appears to have recovered a reasonably comfortable position by the time he died in 1833, secure in the knowledge his children would be well provided for – in particular, his son and heir John junior, to whom he left the manor of Monkton Farleigh and other properties at Melksham, Box, Bradford and South Wraxall, including the public house called the Longs Arms.

But the wave of prosperity his family had ridden for centuries was about to hit the rocks.

John Long Junior (1793–1849)

A laconic epitaph written by Richard Penruddocke Long sums up in a nutshell the fate of his cousin John Long junior, 'a soldier with a good estate in Wiltshire which in an evil hour he sold, and being swindled was worried to death'.

In the spring of 1849 a dark cloud hung ominously over the rented three-storeyed terrace house overlooking the wide Georgian boulevard of Pulteney Street, Bath. Fifty-six-year-old John was dying and he knew his wife and children faced an uncertain future. Locked in a desperate battle to recover several disastrous investments, heavy legal fees were draining his capital while a cash-flow problem and an overdrawn bank account conspired to keep him stuck firmly in the mire. As each month passed with no resolution, his situation worsened. Mentally and physically exhausted, he finally ended his struggle, succumbing to the inflammatory disease which ravaged his lungs. But for his devastated widow and their young family, that fateful April day was just the beginning of a long and tortuous journey of anxiety and financial hardship, entangled in purse strings over which they had no control.

How had it come to this? When John was born at Monkton Farleigh in 1793 his proud parents naturally had every hope their eldest son would have a prosperous life. A former officer in the Royal Horse Guards (Blue), in 1836 he was appointed magistrate alongside nearly 300 other Wiltshire gentlemen, however his involvement was negligible. Similarly, he had no political ambitions. Instead he aspired to the comfortable life of a modestly landed gentleman, deriving his income from farm rents, urban property and other small investments. Four months after his marriage in May 1821 to 19 year-old Mary, daughter of barrister Edward Daniel of Bristol, John received an unexpected windfall: he inherited the manor of Baynton in East Coulston.

His benefactress and cousin by marriage, the late Mrs Long of Baynton was also aunt to John's wife, no doubt a decisive factor in his favour. *(See Long of Baynton for more on this.)* John leased Baynton House for the first few years to his cousin Walter, next in line to inherit Rood Ashton. For his own family he rented a furnished house at Freshford, paying £130 for a year in 1823, and thereafter he appears variously resident at Cheltenham and his father's house, Tilshead Lodge.

Baynton House, East Coulston. Wiltshire & Swindon Archives

In August 1830 while living at Bath in a rented villa John and Mary welcomed their sixth child, a daughter who lived only ten weeks. A few days earlier another child, three-year-old Daniel had also died, necessitating a double burial. A further rapid cycle of births and premature deaths followed over the next few years, effectively punctuating their married life.

But the mortality of his children wasn't all John had to worry about. The changing conditions meant rents were falling. The new industrial age engendered poverty and desperation with more workers deprived of their livelihood every year by the introduction of new machinery. In a questionnaire circulated in the lead-up to the Poor Law Amendment Act of 1834 he outlined part of his own stake in the rural economy: 'All the parish [of Monkton Farleigh] belongs to me, except a few acres of Glebe, and 40 acres belonging to other persons. There are no large farms.' For his poor tenants it was a hand-to-mouth existence. During the summer in Monkton Farleigh women supplemented the income of their household with farm work, earning 8*d* a day plus beer, and the children earned anything from 3*d* to 6*d*.

His cousin Walter, whose family were better insulated from the economic changes, had been a strong advocate of emigration of the poor to America and Canada. But John believed many emigrants who had been removed at considerable expense had returned 'and become more burthensome than they were before their immigration.' He saw a bleak future, not only for the poor, but also his family. With more small farmers forced off the land and rents diminishing he worried his property would become a millstone around his neck.

Less than three months after his father's death he advertised the sale of 'the extensive and truly valuable manors of Monkton Farleigh and Cumberwell', including about 1,600 acres, several farmhouses, cottages and quarries, a further estate at South Wraxall with 'capital mansion house' and the freehold public house, the Longs Arms. With the reckless purchaser of Tilshead Lodge, Mr Watson-Taylor, deep in debt and no other buyer interest John withdrew them from the market.

When Walter vacated Baynton House after inheriting Rood Ashton in 1835, John, Mary and their growing family moved in. But John didn't want the responsibility and maintenance of two large properties with minimal income. He decided to divest himself of the contents of Monkton Farleigh Manor first before putting it on the market again.

His late father's 'excellent and substantial' household furniture and other effects were put up for auction. There was an enormous amount to be disposed of; some had probably come from Tilshead Lodge when it was sold in 1830. In the bedrooms alone at Monkton Farleigh there were no fewer than 43 beds, including '17 four-post and tent bedsteads with hangings, 26 prime feather beds, mattresses, bedding and the usual chamber requisites'. There were three chariots gathering dust in the coach-house which also had to go.

Considering his father had lived there alone – except for occasional guests and necessary servants, he had an inordinate amount of possessions for just one man. Such an accumulation was not particularly unusual for the Long family at that time, however.

Death again visited the household when John and Mary's eldest son John junior died aged eighteen in 1840, but it would be another three years before the arrival of the 'evil hour' to which his cousin Richard had referred. In 1843 John once again put into action a plan to liquidate his assets. This time he did sell Monkton Farleigh with the manorial rights, all the other properties *and* Baynton House, surrounded by 24 acres of parkland.

Cashed up and promised a good financial return, John trusted the advice of his wife's brother, solicitor Morton Daniel, who persuaded him to put his money into a variety of investments in London. Between 1844 and 1846 he invested £12,500 in the advowson of St Giles's church, Camberwell by way of mortgage, which included several building leases of glebe adjoining, and he laid out a large sum for the bankrupt stock of 26,000 rare and valuable books from well-known London publisher and bookseller, James Bohn. He now had diversification, and although he had retained some of his old Wiltshire estates at Bradford, exchanging most of his safe-as-houses inheritances for several smaller ventures was risky.

Defaults on the Camberwell investments were the first ominous sign. Ownership of the Bohn books was disputed and they were seized by the sheriff. John's income was drying up and his capital in danger; as far as the rest of the family was concerned the blame lay squarely at the feet of his sometime financial adviser, Morton Daniel.

So began a series of long and complicated law suits which threatened to suck dry John 's remaining resources. As the legal bills mounted, his younger brother, the Rev. Walter Long tried to persuade him to sell some shares, but he refused. Nor would he borrow money to pay off some of the bills. Stressed and anxious, for the last fifteen days of his life he languished on his deathbed. With no return of his money in sight he elicited a solemn promise from his cousin Richard to continue the fight. His family depended on it.

The story of their struggle is contained a collection of more than 300 letters spanning a period of fifteen years, almost the time it took for John's executors, Richard and Walter, to extricate the family from the legal quagmire. By the end of the whole sorry saga what lay at the bottom of that deep, dark hole was a mountain of John's money, several bankrupts, a bigamist, a couple of broken marriages, Walter's sanity, a few dead bodies and a lot of broken dreams.

The first letter begins in June 1849, seven weeks after John's funeral at St. Peters Church, Monkton Farleigh, where five of his eleven children were already buried. His eldest surviving son, 26 year-old Walter – a Lieutenant with the Ceylon Rifle Regiment – was stationed in Hong Kong and still unaware of his father's death. But with five other children ranging in age from six to twenty years looking to their mother for support it became immediately apparent to Walter and Richard that his widow Mary would have to drastically cut costs.

Walter took upon himself the onerous task of persuading her to give up her townhouse at Bath, but Mary was determined not to move just yet. 'With strict economy' she calculated all her expenses for the ensuing year. Rent and taxes on the house at 56 Pulteney Street: £70; schools and clothing for her two boys: £130; two servants' wages £20: housekeeping, about £100; clothes for herself and the three girls: £30. In total: £350. After allowing for other expenses such as coal and doctor's bills, Mary thought she could almost scrape by for the time being on £400 a year, plus the £2,000 cash legacy due to her from her late husband's will. So all her brother-in-law would need to find was £400. How hard could it be?

Walter firmly disapproved of her desire to stay put and he also disagreed with her budget. He surmised that her 'aim appears to be seeking independence, which at present is quite out of the question.' Taking into account other upcoming expenses which included ongoing legal fees and other debts against the estate, he set to work to determine what would be, by necessity, a very meagre annual allowance.

Three weeks later and anticipating the worst, he enlisted the support of his sister Kate who also lived at Bath, and they both arrived at Mary's house to personally break the news. Bracing himself for the storm, Walter delivered his blunt message: the executors were unable to pay even part of her legacy, and certainly not £400 for her next year's income. All she had to live on was the interest on money left to her children by John's late cousin Daniel Jones Long, plus the interest on a small sum in the Funds; altogether £200 a year.

Mary's 'sadly excited feelings' so upset Walter he was reluctant to entertain personal visits again any time in the near future, and he 'left the house with feelings of very much pain.' But it was Mary who felt most acutely the 'accumulation of distress', now having severe financial restrictions to compound her grief. She sent a despairing letter to Richard, referring to the misery Walter had caused 'when he told me to what a pittance I am reduced. All I had, my John received, and he promised when he sold Baynton dear Lord that he would make a settlement before me & my children. My boys need to be educated & clothed, and how are my girls and myself to live?'

John had already downsized his household considerably since moving to Pulteney Street. Gone were the four servants, the French governess, and the large inventory of furniture that once graced the twelve bedrooms, three large reception rooms and all the other grand spaces at Baynton House. Furnished lodgings at Bath, Weymouth and elsewhere "for the season" were, for the time being, out of the question. Mary would now have to dispense with her two remaining servants altogether and she was worried she would also lose what little remained of her furniture.

Mary was still lumbered with a large quantity of Long family portraits, including one each of Sir Robert Long, 1st Bt., Sir Walter Long, 1st Bt. of Whaddon and old Walter Long of Bath, inherited from Daniel Jones Long in 1827. They were taking up much room, according to Walter, and he hoped Richard would offer to take them to Rood Ashton. Adding to her woes was young Stanhope, aged fourteen, rebelliously rejecting any parental control. It is 'quite indispensable', Walter urged, the boy be immediately sent to school. Worry over a wayward and defiant teenage son was the last thing Mary needed. But she did worry, constantly, about the unaffordable opportunities that might be forever lost to her children.

In his letters the Rev. Walter Long reveals himself as an unassuming man, unambitious and prone to anxiety. The archetypical mild-mannered country clergyman, every week for the previous thirty years he had devoted his time to preparing and delivering sermons to his fifteen-strong congregation in the tiny church of St Giles, Kellaways, a small hamlet near Chippenham. Certainly he was well-meaning. But the stresses put on him as his brother's co-executor caused a deep-seated antipathy towards Mary and her three brothers to rise to the surface.

He was bitter about John's disastrous investments, knowing Mary's brother Morton Daniel had recommended and even facilitated them. It was expected Mary and her brothers would close ranks to try and protect Morton from legal action, and Walter and Richard did entertain ideas of suing him, since they held him solely responsible for the financial mess. This effectively made all of Mary's brothers the enemy, and also by association, Mary herself.

It didn't help her position with Walter when she told him of her misgivings about Charles Gunning, his wife's brother. John's solicitor from the outset, Gunning was still actively engaged in trying to recover the lost investments. For his part, Walter had the utmost faith in his brother-in-law's honesty and integrity; indeed, Gunning was also extremely well thought of by his late client who had intended making him a handsome present when the law suits were advantageously concluded. But Mary had lately heard worrying things about Gunning from his aunt. While acting as her agent he had been caught misappropriating some of her rents. 'C.G was in a <u>dreadful</u> state respecting what had been discovered' and 'my poor husband told me language Mr C.G had made use of respecting his Aunt – too gross for me to write.' Mary urged to have him replaced but Walter blindly refused to hear a bad word against him.

Armed with a degree in Common Law from Cambridge, Walter considered he could handle the complicated law affairs but he felt intimidated and outnumbered by Mary's family; all three brothers were solicitors and they were advising Mary behind the scenes. He strongly resented their interference, calling it Mary's 'game', which 'is very disgraceful to her and I must say disgusting to me.' He reminded Richard repeatedly to be guarded in the information he gave her, since she was a conduit to her brothers. Consequently she received only the barest information despite repeated requests for updates, which only fuelled her dislike of him.

Two weeks had passed since Walter's disastrous visit to Bath, and with no word from Mary the ominous silence unsettled him. She was struggling. Two of her children suffered ongoing illnesses and she was finding it difficult to nurse them on her own. She was 'almost overpowered having <u>everything</u> to do for them, not having a servant, but the Lord I trust will give me strength. Yesterday I was so ill I could scarcely move about.' Flora, the youngest, also needed an operation on her leg which would require accommodation in London as well as the cost of the procedure. Mary appealed to Walter's good nature. He complained to Richard: 'She must be surely wilfully blind not to be aware that means will not be at our command until after conclusion of the [Camberwell] Suit.' Charles Gunning weighed in: find the extra money, if only to keep her quiet.

Walter speculated that in a years' time the Camberwell advowson would be sold 'and then we shall be in a better condition'. It had already been at least two years since this particular lawsuit began, so it wasn't an entirely unreasonable assumption; however his optimism would fade as the years went by. John had bought the advowson from the Rev. Mr Storie, an untrustworthy character and rector of St Giles's church. Storie was later declared insolvent with debts to the tune of over £51,000. But unbeknown to John, Storie had also sold the advowson to several other individuals as mortgages, and all claimed ownership.

Camberwell was a significant part of John's investments and the executors were diverting a large portion of his estate's income trying to recover it. Both Richard and Walter were convinced that spending a small fortune to recover a larger one would see the family's finances restored, but as time went on, the expenditure grew while the value of the unrecovered investments diminished. Mary was forced to live extremely frugally in the meantime, to the detriment of her children's health and education. Camberwell's sale was their only hope of deliverance.

Anticipating a suit against him by the Longs after they refused to grant him indemnity, Morton Daniel prepared to flee the country with his family. He had already begun to liquidate his assets and had dissolved his partnership with his son-in-law at Melksham shortly before John died.

Unbeknown to the Longs he sold all his inherited property, including Marley Hall at Ledbury in Herefordshire, and also a house and land in Limpsfield, Surrey, bequeathed to him by Charles Stanhope, grandson of Philip Dormer Stanhope, 4th Earl of Chesterfield. Charles had been a life-long friend of the Daniel family, having studied law with Mary's father. Morton left England in early August but Walter only got wind of his departure in September. 'He has left with his family some weeks since for Australia, and secretly, having plainly told his maidservant, who was connected with Melksham people, that if she made known to anyone there his intention of going, he would instantly destroy himself.'

The *Candahar* arrived safely in Port Adelaide early in December after a voyage of 115 days, but there had been sickness on board and 46 year-old Morton came down with measles. Just as the family was preparing to disembark he developed complications and died without ever having set foot on Australian soil. With all the clandestine preparations and sacrifices he had made for their new life wasted, his devastated widow Penelope now had an agonising decision to make. To stay and make the best of a bad situation or leave Australia behind with her dead husband buried in the churchyard at Adelaide.

Either way, she and her family would struggle. Her eldest daughter Eliza was still in Wiltshire with her husband Alexander Smith who was carrying on the solicitors' practice in Melksham. For the sake of her four other children – the youngest just nine years old – Penelope decided to make the long and tedious voyage back to England. But with no funds for such an unexpected journey immediately to hand, they had to wait for the money to be arranged by Smith.

If Mary thought she was badly off, she needed only look to her poor sister-in-law. Within three years of returning to England, Penelope – then living with her daughter and Smith – had fallen out with her son-in-law who cast her and the children onto the street, forcing her to apply for charity. Morton had left no will, and Smith, administering the estate and behaving evasively when questioned by Walter, was suspected of defrauding the widow. Richard and Walter briefly considered bringing a suit against Morton's estate, and at the same time deprive Smith of his ill-gotten gains, but they quickly realised the futility of it.

All the while Mary was sending desperate requests to Walter and Richard for information about the progress of the affairs and, most importantly, an increase in her allowance. Each time the answer was the same. With 'the intricate embarrassment of the invested property,' – meaning Camberwell – there was just not enough money for an increase as long as they had legal expenses to pay, nor could they say when the affairs might be concluded. She had to accept that her allowance must remain at £200 for the next three or four years. Instead, Richard had the idea to send the troublesome second son Stanhope off to Australia to relieve his mother of the burden of his upkeep. Mary was apprehensive, since he was still only sixteen and not in the best of health. Walter was very keen, Richard thought the sooner the better and Charles Gunning advised against it altogether.

It took Richard two years to finally persuade both Mary and Stanhope that he 'might soon do well – without employing himself in any way that a gentleman need be ashamed of.' And there was still the future of his younger brother Edward to consider. He wanted to be a soldier like Walter, his eldest brother, and when he was old enough Richard's father Walter Long of Rood Ashton agreed to finance his army training at Sandhurst, at a cost of £70 per year.

Stanhope, it was agreed, would be accompanied to Australia by another young gentleman, Alward Wyndham, then visiting family in England but planning to return home to New South Wales. Alward's father George had settled in Australia twenty-five years earlier and established a farm and winery at Dalwood in the Hunter Valley – still the home of the Wyndham Estate Winery today. Under the watchful eye of George, Stanhope would learn about farming until he was able to purchase his own property.

In 1853 planning for Stanhope's "going out" began in earnest. At the same time, Alward Wyndham took rather a shine to Stanhope's twenty-four-year-old sister Emma. And she was not entirely opposed to his attentions either. In March a surprise marriage proposal had her also considering a new life in Australia, but there were financial considerations, information about which only Walter and Richard could provide. Her mother wrote to Walter explaining vaguely that 'a circumstance has occurred' and it was necessary for her to be fully acquainted with the state of their affairs.

Neither Mary nor Walter relished the thought of face-to-face meetings, but given the circumstances she thought it the best option.

Could he please come to her lodgings at Clevedon? Emma also wanted the advice of her uncle; 'it is a serious thing going such a distance from all those I love.' For the moment Walter declined the invitation, 'being kept indoors by a cold & cough', and as for Mary's request for information – yet again – he made it clear with a tersely-worded reply that his patience was wearing thin having to repeat the same bad news every time.

While Walter 'did not much over-relish' the meeting, he finally saw Emma and her mother at Clevedon almost two weeks later. After discussing Alward Wyndham's prospects, he was quite impressed with the young man's character despite his lack of independent means. He seemed to have a steadying influence on Stanhope too. But a seed of doubt was growing in Emma's mind. She felt the tyranny of distance would affect her happiness and the prospect of possibly never seeing her mother or siblings again was too daunting. Reluctantly she called off the engagement. Stanhope, eighteen by this time, upset his sister with an ill-timed and tactless remark, necessitating Richard, himself newly-engaged, to calm the waters, Mary telling him, 'Stanhope is very thoughtless and naturally unstable, and you know he is just at an age when it is difficult to resist temptation.'

With preparations for his voyage well underway, Stanhope went to London to organise his berth, staying with his uncle Henry Daniel. Naturally prejudiced and convinced of a conspiracy, Uncle Walter worried Henry had influenced their nephew, wanting a more expensive cabin than they could afford. Rather than have Stanhope travel in cattle class, and to prevent him from meeting 'with individuals probably not in all respects desirable', Walter, in an uncharacteristic move, gave Stanhope the money in advance to pay for a small first class cabin.

Stanhope had been told about the sufferings of those who had crossed the tropics crammed into a small cabin. And so, with money burning a hole in his pocket he purchased a roomy one-man version instead of the less expensive claustrophobic two-person cubbyhole his uncle had recommended. Walter was extremely displeased. Stanhope argued it wasn't his fault, and after many indignant denials and explanations he managed to redeem himself, with Walter finally agreeing it was the fault of the shipping clerk. But ultimately he laid the blame on Mary. Her sending Stanhope up to London caused the whole 'sad annoyance and expense – <u>very painful</u> to <u>me</u> – I candidly confess – disturbing my mind, morning noon & night.'

With all the other problems he had to deal with, 58 year-old Walter was becoming an emotional wreck and he may well have wished for a less stressful life. Still not reconciled to what he considered an enormous sum for the extravagant bare cabin, he now had the expense of furnishing it. Stanhope would also need new clothes, a horse on arrival at Sydney, and pocket money. Alward Wyndham produced a list of items 'he thought quite needful and proper' including carpet bags; a pistol; rifle; a quantity of shot and eighteen pounds of gunpowder, as well as a saddle and spurs. The bills were mounting. 'Mr J. Gunning is fitting up the cabin – that is, getting a berth fastened by a carpenter, wash stand etc, which he says will cost about £4.13s, and there will be a bolster, pillow, blacking – brushes etc – with a metal tub basin etc – which I expect £6 more will cover.'

While Walter counted the days before he could finally farewell Stanhope, he felt under pressure to get everything done in time. He apologised to Richard for all the trouble his nephew had caused, saying he could endure 'willingly & cheerfully any amount of exertion, bodily or mentally' in attending the legal difficulties of his brother's estate, 'but Stanhope's conduct & behaviour went very deep into my feelings and shook me very much.' There were many frustrating delays. The proposed date of sailing came and went. The ship was still at the dock by the first day of March 1854, and everyone – especially Walter – was getting very twitchy.

And then, after a lot of preparation, expense, and a great deal of aggravation endured by his uncle, two weeks later Stanhope left for Australia. And a year after that Emma got her man. Not the personable Alward Wyndham, but a young Civil Engineer, Alexander Bassett – duly endorsed by Walter. 'The marriage went off very nicely, but <u>between ourselves</u>, rather overdone, vexing me somewhat, yet I had no voice in it.' With Emma nicely married off and Stanhope safely on the other side of the world, Walter could relax, just a little. But evidently Australia wasn't distant enough and much to his dismay, a year later Stanhope returned to England.

Another matter threatened to come back to bite him; he began to think perhaps Mary had been right about Charles Gunning, who demanded more than £500 towards payment of his bill. When Gunning suggested there was plenty of money in the kitty, Walter's reply 'was rather peppery, perhaps, not <u>uncalled</u> for', but he didn't realise that Gunning was up to his ears in debt himself. On examination of his accounts it would later be discovered that an 'alarming sum' was paid to Charles Gunning throughout the family's ordeal.

At the beginning of November Mary's youngest son Edward, now a fully-fledged officer in the 77th regiment of foot, was preparing to fight in the Crimea. Walter somehow had to find money for his uniform and he panicked on learning Edward had already been to London and ordered it without his knowledge. Letters bounced back and forth, full of accusations. Edward was sure he'd done the right thing. 'Uncle Walter's fears are all imaginary – I have only ordered what is necessary.'

Richard's father had compiled a list of things he considered Edward would need and agreed to advance £54 to help cover the cost. When Walter saw the list he was astonished at the extent of it. Included were 36 pairs of socks and 18 towels. 'Is he going to set up housekeeping?' He disputed many of the articles, and for the next few weeks he and Mary wrangled over the details, Walter describing her ideas as 'wretched folly' and extravagant. Edward at last set sail for the Crimea, fully kitted up, prepared for the fight of his life.

But Walter was still as 'harassed & over anxious' as ever. The Bohn suit kept him awake at night and he was wary of Morton Daniel's son-in-law Smith, working in the interests of the Daniel family against the Longs. Walter was half expecting Smith to present some unsettled account from Morton's time as John's solicitor, '& if so, we must meet it by a claim on Daniel's property to repay damage done by him to my late brother's property.'

Then Charles Gunning presented another outrageous bill. Richard was nominated by Walter to write firmly to him, disputing the amount. Intending to make him an offer, Richard emphasised the desperate situation of the family and the urgent need to recover Camberwell, 'this most vile unfortunate investment'. Even before

John's death the law affairs were a tricky tit-for-tat game of suits and counter-suits, and despite all the expense and aggravation, by year's end the money situation was at least as bad as it had been at the start.

It was now six years since her husband's death and Mary continued to manage her enforced poverty with great difficulty. The letters she received from Edward in the Crimea only added to her worries. In January 1855 he was camped at the heights above Constantinople. Conditions were so bad, he told his 'dear Mama', men were dying from exposure and one had committed suicide. In April Mary was alarmed to hear of his harrowing exploits after taking a Russian rifle pit against a 1500-strong enemy side during the Siege of Sebastopol.

Ten days into the battle the 77th and 90th regiments attacked the rifle pits, but vastly outnumbered they suffered heavy losses, including Edward's Commanding Officer, Colonel Thomas Egerton, who at 6' 8" was too tall for the depth of the trench. He was shot in the head as soon as he stood up. 'The Russians got into confusion and killed several of themselves, amongst whom was a Col. (so one of the prisoners said) – we could hear them fighting after we had retired from the 1st Pit. 29 Russians are now lying dead outside our works – & three of our men, besides the killed & wounded they carried away. We lost altogether 41 killed, wounded & missing.' Edward and his comrades were later awarded medals for their bravery.

Towards mid-1856 Charles Gunning ingratiated himself into Walter's good books briefly with news of an imminent payment to John's estate, but then ruined it by applying it against the outstanding amount the Longs owed him. Walter was livid. They would sue if the money was not immediately paid to their credit. His disenchantment with his once-trusted brother-in-law complete, it would be 'the family against C.G'.

For Walter, 1856 was memorable for all the worst reasons. He had begun treatment in London with a certain Doctor Fell for a 'threatened attack of cancer'. He'd had a decayed tooth which caused a large lump to grow on the inside of his cheek and he now had to cut his food into very small pieces before he could comfortably eat it. He was in constant pain 'more or less severe from the applications to the inside of my cheek and not allowed to speak for fear of displacing the dressing – so that I am useless.'

He had taken lodgings in Pimlico while he underwent treatment and hoped not to be out of action for too long. Despite the imminent removal of more of the tumour, Walter couldn't help worrying about the Camberwell affair which, all going well, appeared close to resolution. What they hoped to sell was the valuable advowson and Right of Presentation, the Vicarage of Camberwell, and the recently erected vicarage house (demolished 1967) standing in its own grounds opposite the church. Included in the sale were ground rents on twenty plots of land with a house on each, and there were also various interment fees, a £900 Exchequer Bill as well as numerous other assets. As the vicarage house was fairly substantial Walter had considered speaking to the Bishop of Winchester, thinking it might be suitable as an Episcopal residence.

The whole package should have been a lucrative income-producing investment for his brother John. If only he hadn't paid such an inflated price, and the incumbent, the Rev. John Storie hadn't deviously pulled the rug out from under him by selling it off to others and becoming bankrupt into the bargain. Nevertheless, it was a prize worth fighting for, although it would not prove easy to sell.

Christmas came and went and by February 1857 Walter's condition had deteriorated. He attended to business as best he could from his sick-bed, but with the financial situation lurching from precarious to critical and back to perilous on a regular basis, he was concerned about Mary 's next allowance payment. He had already overdrawn one bank account in order to pay her previous quarterly payment at Christmas. But with no funds in the other account and the next payment due in a few days, he was eyeing up the last remaining £100 Exchequer Bill – 'shall it be sold out?'

His illness would soon end his involvement as executor of his late brother's affairs. For eight years he had been caught up in a swirling maelstrom of endless law suits, legal fees and letter writing, with sleight-of-hand solicitors, wayward nephews and a distressed widow for good measure. He could no longer keep up. After a visit from Charles Gunning he told Richard it was all too much for him, 'I was knocked up for the rest of the day and had a wretched night. Excitement is very hurtful to me therefore I am obliged to give up business altogether.' Doctor Fell realised he could do nothing more and recommended he go home. In great discomfort Walter returned to Tytherton, resigned to his fate.

Mary on the other hand, hoped for an improvement in her own situation. Her daughter Katherine was again very ill, and she was buckling under the strain of her care. Anticipating a resolution of their affairs she enquired of Richard 'what increase of income you can promise me as I find I <u>must</u> have a servant. Those only who have no servants and constant sickness can imagine the various needful occupations caused by illness.' He could do nothing except tell her once again that an increase in her income would simply not be possible until the affairs were settled. So far it had been the worst eight years of her life and the time well overdue for good news. But there was only sad news of Walter. The disease was making fast progress; his throat was greatly affected and he could scarcely swallow. Under the care of his wife and sister Kate he ended his terrible journey a few weeks later, dying on September 9th 1857.

As sole executor Richard now had the entire workload on his shoulders. He instructed Gunning to advertise the advowson, but the sale would be complicated. A few days later Richard took his family to Ireland for the Christmas holidays. While there he was shocked to learn from Gunning that his law firm had been dissolved and without any consultation or authorisation he had placed the Longs' business in the hands of Messrs. Gadsden & Flower of Bedford Row, London. Walter's sister Kate had also got wind things were not quite right. Worried about what would happen in Richard's absence, she warned him the firm's affairs were in a very shaky condition, 'indeed I have known for some time that C.G's were.' She worried that if Camberwell was sold, 'will the money be safe in such hands? These are not times to leave such affairs in Lawyers hands & <u>I know C.G is not to be trusted</u>.' She warned him not to leave the papers in the hands of Gadsden & Flower either; she was reliably informed 'they are perfect sharks.'

Kate was not surprised at the news of C.G 's affairs; Walter had told her he expected it a year ago. 'The <u>sooner</u> you can sell Camberwell, even at a loss, the better, and settle matters if possible <u>and rid your hands of it</u>'. Richard, who had intended spending Christmas and New Year in Ireland, was so unnerved by Kate's letter he packed up his family and returned to Bath on Christmas Eve. There was another problem. Mary 's quarterly payment of £50 was due, there was only £20 in the bank and he had no idea where Walter sourced the funds for her allowance. Richard had to make up the difference with a temporary loan from his own pocket.

In late January 1858 Charles Gunning left London for Scotland. He often travelled on business so initially this move didn't arouse suspicion within the family. In February while Mary was confined to her bed suffering 'an attack on the liver', she received news that the Camberwell advowson was to be auctioned in London on March 17th with a reserve price of £15,000. With their entire financial future hinging on the sale, the family was worried that Gunning's name was absent from the new Law List; he was gone from London, his office vacated. Stanhope was particularly worried what any prospective buyer would think 'of these queer pranks of C.G.' When Richard sought an explanation from Gunning in Scotland the response was, as usual, evasive and unsatisfactory.

Auction day arrived with great anticipation. It had been a very long time coming and an enormous amount of money had been spent along the way. But the bids didn't come anywhere near the reserve price. Afterwards a bitterly disappointed Richard told Kate 'that we are now utterly nonplussed, grieved, disheartened, bewildered. I know not what they are to do. It is possible that £11,000 may be offered for the advowson – a hint of that sort was from Mr Gadsden, but, £11,000 after all that has been done!! It is too dreadful. I only wish Mr Daniel had been hung as high as Hadnan before he induced poor John to invest his money!'

As bad as this was, Richard's attention was momentarily diverted by another unwelcome development. Gunning was taking advantage of the Scotch Sequestration Act, declaring himself bankrupt, which meant a bond he owed John's estate would never be repaid.

The impact on Mary of the failed auction went to her very marrow. She was suffering anxiety and illness, scarcely able to write. 'My hopes respecting the sale of Camberwell are again <u>vanished</u>.' But she had got her long-held wish regarding Charles Gunning. 'From all I hear I think we ought to be glad our papers and affairs are placed in Mr Gadsden's hands.' Before long the family would be even more thankful to be rid of Gunning. He had departed London with his wife and children in tow, living firstly at Glasgow and afterwards at Dunoon, the loss of his livelihood triggering some sort of mid-life crisis. After two years in Scotland avoiding his creditors, he told Lavinia, his unsuspecting wife of twenty-two years, that he was off to London on business. But a week later he wrote saying he would not be returning; he and a certain Miss Mary Turner were now living as man and wife. Asking forgiveness for his 'cruel and wicked act' he implored Lavinia to remember in her prayers 'her once affectionate husband'.

Disinclined to think kindly of him in her prayers or anywhere else, she eventually decided the only course of action was to divorce him. Before she had the chance, Gunning dropped Mary Turner like a hot potato and bigamously married another woman, Alice Perks, at Liverpool. If ever there was a case for a *decree nisi* this was it. The judge granted Lavinia a divorce without hesitation.

It was now well into 1858 and Richard was beginning to buckle under the stress of sole executorship. Mary and her two daughters were in Cardiff with Emma and Alexander, and Katherine was again 'very poorly'. Richard had sent a timely cheque which she '<u>much needed</u>.' In fact prior to its arrival, things had got so bad Mary was prepared to resort to raiding a few shillings from fifteen year-old Flora's bank account. The 'tremendous law expenses' plus the cost of advertising the Camberwell advowson were also an ongoing source of worry to Mary, as John's remaining investments had been earning no interest for ten years.

For the next three years Mary continued to struggle. Negotiations for the Camberwell advowson continued back and forth in a seemingly endless tide of correspondence and the money situation showed no signs of improving, much to the frustration of Richard and the family. Mary's son Walter had died a year earlier aged 33, Stanhope got married ten months later, Flora had to be withdrawn from school owing to Mary's inability to pay, her sister-in-law Kate died at Bath, Edward was forced to resign from the army suffering ill health, and Mary's brother Philip was run over and severely injured by an omnibus in London, later dying from his injuries. All the while Mary's own health was going downhill, her liver disease worsening. By then she was living permanently in Cheltenham with Edward, Katherine and Flora. Although her furniture was still in storage she was at least grateful to have her servants back, if only a cook and a parlourmaid.

In 1861, after twelve years of anguish, frustration and hardship, the advowson was finally sold. On a scale of significant events the family expected it would be life-changing. But for 58 year-old Mary it was all too late. By March she was on her deathbed, Edward writing to Richard with the bad news. Mary clung to life for another eight weeks, instructing Katherine and Flora to take great care to live within their means after she was gone. Having learned much from their mother's ordeal and with nothing to attract a prospective husband, they knew they too would have to survive on a small amount of interest and dividends. The very last thing they should ever do was spend principal.

On May 22nd Mary was dead.

Richard's clergyman brother Henry assisted at her funeral at Monkton Farleigh, the venue for so many family burials. Stanhope would later comment that death had made a sad inroad into the family in the last few years. His sister Katherine was philosophical: 'After so many months of anxious care we feel what is our loss is her gain, her joys are now unspeakable & full of glory.'

Mary never did receive her full £2,000 legacy from John's will. In fact her children were dismayed to learn that all money which 'Mama has lately been receiving and that we have been living on is to be considered as her legacy.' Her effects were valued at under £800 and she left her jewels between the three girls, her furniture and other household goods went to Katherine and Flora. Stanhope and Edward each received only £390 from what remained of their mother's residual estate, and even then, only after much pleading. The family silver was divided between them all.

As for the Camberwell Advowson being their financial salvation, the sale price of £11,000 was £1,500 less than their father had paid for it fifteen years earlier – hardly the sound investment Morton Daniel had led him to believe. With the first £1,000 paid immediately, the rest was to be paid by mortgage at 4% interest over several years, and out of this all outstanding debts had to be settled. It had been a very eventful, very miserable twelve years.

Francis Stanhope Long (1835–84) 'I Seem Very Unlucky'

It transpired that Alward Wyndham had to delay his departure and was no longer able to travel to Australia with Stanhope in 1854. He had found a ship for him – the *Granite City* – a newly-constructed three-masted wooden barque commanded by Captain Leask. With Alward detained in England for a while longer, Stanhope was eager to set off on his own.

In October his mother was in Wales with Emma when she received his long anticipated first letter from Australia. His ship had come into port at Sydney on June 15th, but it had been a perilous voyage; the stuff of mothers' nightmares. Thirty-nine days after leaving England there was a fire on board and Stanhope told her they were nearly lost. Six days after arriving at port the *Maitland Mercury* ran the story of his brush with death. The *Granite City* was somewhere near the Cape of Good Hope on April 19th when smoke was discovered coming from the hold through the hatchways. A pump was immediately put into action and when it seemed inevitable the ship would be totally destroyed the crew prepared the lifeboats.

Smoke billowed from the vessel for twenty-four hours. The hatches were removed, large quantities of cargo thrown overboard and water poured down into the hold. The flames leapt even higher, and all the passengers had to man the pumps to prevent the inferno reaching the rigging. The ship drifted many miles northward but eventually the fire was brought under control and Captain Leask once again set their course for Sydney.

On arrival Stanhope travelled inland to the Wyndhams' winery at Dalwood in the Hunter Valley, where with the assistance of convict labour they were exporting wine to England and India. His host

George Wyndham had also established a 100,000 acre run at Bukkulla, approximately 300 miles south-west of Dalwood, an arrangement that would prompt Stanhope to recall the niceties of a proper bed after assisting to drove a herd of cattle between the two properties. He much preferred 'sleeping indoors to lying out in the dew'.

His financial needs in Australia seemed endless, as were the letters urgently requesting money. He had almost convinced Uncle Walter he could double or even treble his money by investing in sheep and cattle, fattening them on the Wyndham's run, and although Walter considered it a worthy inducement to keep Stanhope in Australia, there was no money to send him.

Throughout the summer of 1854/55 Stanhope wilted in the scorching Australian heat. 'When the thermometer is 108 in the shade, that is too much to enjoy', he wrote. This understatement accompanied yet another urgent request for at least £1,500 to buy a third share in a farm. With each return post came the same answer. Increasingly frustrated, Stanhope was certain there was money, somewhere; 'surely I am to have some or else where is the money, and what use is there in going on with a law suit with endless expense unless we are to derive some benefit from it?' Even for Stanhope this was a fair and logical question, but one which never seemed to meet with a satisfactory answer. All Richard could say was that it had been his father's dying wish that they pursue it.

Hobbled by lack of funds and resentful at being kept in the dark, Stanhope complained that without financial support he could do nothing and must return to England. 'Not that I wish to do that, but I should do it from necessity'. Once the legal problems were resolved he would one day return to Australia, flush with his inheritance. Despite being 'in such an utter helpless and ignorant state' Stanhope was prepared to give it another four weeks. As time went on homesickness overtook him; he wished he was 'safe and sound back in Old England, and if I could get a farm, nothing should induce me to leave it again.'

He reassured Richard he was willing to work in Australia, 'but it is not so easy for a Gentleman to get on as is thought in England, unless he has money, and if he has not, he must make himself a

common Labouring man, and then he gets with very low society' –
an unpleasant prospect in the rough and ready environs of convict-
populated Australia. He was 'quite sickened' by the 'horrid extent' to
which labouring men spent all their wages and degraded themselves
with alcohol. This was quite a high horse he was on, but he would
later discover it had rather rubbery legs. Nevertheless, he liked the
country life and was still intent on buying a farm in Australia, 'so if
you can kindly get my money ready for me, I shall not be wasting it in
any uncertain speculation.' But with no available funds to send him,
Stanhope's ambitions seemed doomed.

To make matters worse, his favourite horse died from stoppage
and another broke its back jumping at a fence. 'I seem very unlucky' was
his woeful conclusion. But then his mother sent some positive news:
the law affairs were nearly resolved! With renewed hope he again asked
Richard for money to buy a farm. This time he wanted £3,000 – and
the sooner the better please. It took about a year and a half for Walter
to finally get through to him: there would be no money available for
him to buy anything. Stanhope resorted to Plan B, putting the hard
word on Richard and his father Walter at Rood Ashton. He outlined
the positives they would all derive from lending him money secured by
his anticipated inheritance. He someday hoped to return 'to thank you
and other kind friends who did me the kindness and made me happy
and respectable, instead of miserable.'

Gambling on such an uncertainty as Stanhope and an
inheritance that may never materialise was contrary to logic. Besides,
they had their own problems to deal with. Not least was the recent
death at Paris of Richard's mother Mary Anne. Stanhope pressed on,
putting forward one or two more schemes, little knowing Walter had
only a £100 Exchequer Bill left. With no money to help him, dogged
by complications with the Camberwell suit and the struggle to make
up Mary's income, the thing Walter feared most – Stanhope's coming
back to haunt him – looked imminent.

Stanhope booked a return voyage in anticipation of getting his
hands on his inheritance all the sooner. But he would be disappointed.
'He will find his ideas in connection with the affairs – moonshine –
& only true what I told his mother, that he, any more than the rest,

could never have much capital from his father's property, and only part, before his mother's death.'

Mary was again in Cardiff staying with Emma – who had just had her first child – when Stanhope's ship arrived at Gravesend in August 1856. Now aged twenty-one he stepped back onto English soil legally an adult. The London air disagreed with him, and after a short stay with his uncle Henry Daniel he obtained the £500 from Chancery left him by Charles Stanhope, part of which Walter wanted to repay some of the costs of his "going out". There would be a confrontation but Walter hoped it would be the last; now Stanhope was of age and his guardianship ended Walter was keen to wash his hands of his difficult nephew. 'I do not mean in any way to make myself responsible in given advice or even an opinion as to which course of life he may pursue'.

By September Stanhope was back in Clevedon with his family, having decided to join the army. But he needed a favour. He'd got word from a friend a cadetship was available in the East India Company. To have any chance of acceptance he needed to attract the interest of the upper hierarchy and he knew Richard and his father had friends in high places. 'If you or Mr Long could use your influence with any of the Directors to obtain a promise if possible, I should be forever obliged.' Richard, happy to indulge Stanhope if it meant gainful employment, immediately sent off a letter to his friend Sir James Weir Hogg, M.P and Chairman of the East India Company, recommending his cousin, 'a young man who has the misfortune to possess expectations. This lad is one of 6 – all wretchedly off for the present.'

It was a few weeks before Richard received a reply, during which time his much-admired wife Charlotte gave birth to their third child. Sir James's letter, when it did finally arrive, was accommodating and loaded with compliments about Charlotte. Everyone was pleased Stanhope was to be given a cadetship, and even Uncle Walter was optimistic. With his failed expedition to Australia still fresh in everyone's minds, Stanhope now had an opportunity to prove all his critics wrong. In December 1856 he began training at the Royal Military Academy, Woolwich, intending to pass all the necessary exams, hopeful of a posting to India.

Just before Christmas he took a break from his studies to see in the New Year with his family, and it was with some reluctance he returned to the barracks in mid-January. He hated it. The Academy was 'the most unpleasant place I ever had the fate to go to. Nothing but Fags and rain, a fine day is quite a rare thing.' Still smarting from an argument with his superior he relinquished his cadetship; no more army life for him. When this unthinkable news reached Richard he was utterly flabbergasted – after all that had been done for him. Having dug an enormous hole for himself Stanhope's explanation was deliberately vague, a mixture of self-justification and over-confidence.

Expressing eternal gratitude for Richard's efforts in securing the cadetship, he cited 'circumstances and reasons' for his resignation. 'I may be blamed, but I hope eventually to be able to prove I did it for the best if my poor endeavours succeed – which I do not myself for a moment doubt.' He was convinced he wouldn't have passed his exams anyway. Whatever those mysterious circumstances and reasons, Richard was not at all impressed. Uncle Walter, whose cancer was well advanced by this stage, was predictably 'disgusted with his folly.'

With more free time than was good for him, in July Stanhope was again with Edward at Colchester, playing the fool. They were arrested with another two young officers after a drunken spree in the early hours one Thursday morning in nearby Ipswich. They had been seen damaging street lamps, a church clock and breaking several windows. After the magistrates established the four young vandals were 'gentlemen', the charges were withdrawn when they agreed to pay for the damage. The prosecutor called it a farce and the mayor was outraged. They 'should not allow gentlemen to come from another town, run amuck at our lamps and then settle the matter by simply paying the expenses.' As a token appeasement, £5 penalty was added to the costs.

With the death of his elder brother Walter in January 1857 Stanhope had moved up a rung in the family hierarchy, inheriting the major portions of two farms at Haugh and Holt, passed down from Miss Katherine Long of South Wraxall in 1814. The rental income was modest, less than £150 a year; hardly enough for the sort of life Stanhope aspired to. He had intimated to Richard his plan to return to Australia, and this would depend entirely on the Camberwell advowson sale. But the lawsuits dragged on expensively with the advowson still as big a thorn in their sides as ever. He despaired for his future. 'I am so completely jammed in a corner I hardly know how to act. I don't wish to be living at home, but I am compelled to do so.'

His expectations in tatters and no sign of a rosy future on the horizon, he joined his family at Weymouth in August for a short holiday. Twenty-year-old Edward, who also laboured under the delusion of post-inheritance prosperity, unexpectedly announced his engagement. He thought his marriage to eighteen-year-old Mary Barthorp 'would not be such a bad thing after all, for she will have ten thousand'. As his guardian, Richard 'had better put a word in for me. She is a regular little steamer.' But once her father learned the true financial position he withheld his consent and the elusive objects of Edward's desires steamed away.

It was an obvious solution, marrying a presentable young lady with the added attraction of the odd few thousand. Even so, it came as a thunderbolt from the blue to Stanhope's unsuspecting family when, just three months later in November he married a local girl from Bath, Miss Julian Elizabeth Brograve. He was 22; she a year older. A 'hasty marriage', his mother said after the wedding. Revealing her misgivings, she told Richard: 'It has caused me many anxious feelings, but I pray it may prove for his happiness.' Stanhope's newly-elevated position as his father's heir may have been enough to convince Julian's unsuspecting father, George Augustus Brograve, only grandson of Sir Berney Brograve, 1st Baronet of Worstead.

Married barely two weeks, Stanhope wrote to Richard complaining about having to pay £10 legacy duty on his already-spent inheritance from Daniel Jones Long, and worse, he was being pressed to explain his finances to Julian's uncle by marriage, Walter Matthews Paul of Highgrove House. Stanhope's financial situation was as much a mystery to him as it was to any outsider; could Richard please furnish the necessary information. Refusing to be drawn in, Richard suggested tersely he read his father's will. He was annoyed with Stanhope over an earlier derailing of the Camberwell sale for which he blamed him.

And there was another sore point: 'Now you are married you probably don't regret refusing India. If I had foreseen your refusal I would never have asked it, for I would now gladly have a cadetship for Charlotte's cousin, but can't ask again.'

About a year later Stanhope's wife Julian gave birth to their first child, Alice. Since their marriage they had been living with her parents at Clevedon, but Stanhope desperately wanted to be independent. Although he did actually own the majority of the two farms at Haugh and Holt, they were both leased to a Mr Bailey. Not that Stanhope considered either of them a suitable residence.

Armed with aspirations of a gentleman farmer he leased a small farm in Devon with a large ten-bedroomed house. At last in control of his life and lord of his own little manor, he adorned the walls of Puddington Lodge with the family portraits, formerly 'taking up much room' at his mother's house at Bath. He employed a labourer and his wife, installing them in a cottage on the property. Mary was very pleased. 'It is a pleasure to visit Stanhope in his own residence. It is very prettily situated. His little girl is a sweet child.'

The next year another child was born, Stanhope junior, followed by the death of Mary a few months later. Stanhope seemed to be enjoying farming and in June 1861 was 'very busy at present tilling'. Although a little older now, he was not necessarily wiser, impulsively expanding his operation and leasing more land on expectation of receiving a half share of his mother's estate. But he had no money to pay for the valuation and other associated costs. 'It will put me to a good deal of inconvenience unless I have [the money] soon', he told Richard.

By the time the last child, Ernest, was born in June 1863, storm clouds had been gathering over Puddington and Stanhope's fleeting contentment with life was evaporating, his marriage disintegrating. With his dream of a home and family lying in ruins, Stanhope unofficially parted company with Julian in late December. Abandoning their three children to his care, she returned to her parents, then living at Weston super Mare, about 30 miles from Bath. They had a large house with plenty of room for the children, but accommodating them wasn't the problem.

Stanhope couldn't possibly manage a six month old baby and two toddlers by himself, nor could he afford to pay anyone to help. It was mid-winter and he abandoned the farm, taking the children to his sisters Katherine and Flora at Cheltenham. The eldest child became seriously ill, and with Stanhope unable to contribute to their upkeep his sisters' finances were under pressure.

Flora was worried that now she was twenty-one she was legally liable for any debts incurred. Pleading with Richard to 'not think your little coz a dreadfully extravagant child', her request for some of her inheritance money hints at her desperation. 'I much want the money & should be very glad if you will let me have £100. Within the last month my brother Stanhope's eldest boy has died of Scarlet Fever in our house. Katherine took the infection while nursing him but I am thankful to say she is now recovering although very weak.' By this time Stanhope and Julian's separation was official. 'Her conduct lately has been such that I am sure it is much more for his happiness to be without her. She has been very extravagant, and her behaviour is most heartless; she even refused to see her dying child although she was in Cheltenham at the time of his death.'

Stanhope stayed under the radar for the next four years. His brother Edward meanwhile had got into debt after a failed business venture in Cheltenham and he fled to London to escape his creditors. But the sheriff caught up with him. He was arrested and briefly imprisoned before being bailed out to the extent of nearly £1,000 – probably by Richard or his father. Stanhope resurfaced in 1868 when his lack of money forced him to sell his only assets, the Haugh and Holt farms. By this time Richard owned a part share, inherited from his father the year before. Stanhope had no trouble convincing him to sell, and they were advertised in eighteen lots.

The 'desirable freehold estates' consisted of farmhouses, gardens, orchards and homesteads, and sundry enclosures of valuable arable, pasture and woodland – altogether 143 acres. The principal farmhouse was said to be Elizabethan, and the views described as 'a perfect panoramic scene, embracing the valley of the Avon, Claverton Manor and Warleigh, and in the distance the confines of the city of Bath are visible.'

With no wife, no house, still strapped for cash and evermore despondent, Stanhope mooched around London, drowning his sorrows. In April 1870 *The Times* reported that a gentleman had been mugged. Richard – lying ill in Montreaux at this point – would have been alarmed but perhaps not surprised to read that the mugger's victim was none other than his 34 year-old cousin Stanhope. That he was an easy target was clearly obvious to at least one young opportunist amongst the minglers in Oxford Street, a young soldier by the name of William Campion who quickly befriended him. Just before 10pm police sergeant Theobold observed them walking arm in arm in Connaught Square, Stanhope so drunk he couldn't walk unaided. Together they staggered off down nearby Seymour Mews in Bryanston Square. His youthful moralising while in Australia against the evils of mixing with low society and the demon drink was by now a long-forgotten memory; Stanhope had become what he once so despised. And his high horse was now completely legless.

Fortunately a resident of the mews was also watching this little spectacle, observing Campion fling his inebriated and by now insensible victim onto a dung-heap. During this extra-close encounter with horse manure Stanhope had the contents of his pockets stolen; four shillings and a bunch of keys. The villain was apprehended not far from the scene by a passing constable, and the next day in court – hopefully after a bath and a change of clothes – Stanhope admitted he probably was quite drunk the previous evening.

With no prospect of getting ahead and his good name tarnished in the eyes of every reader of *The Times,* Stanhope decided he had to leave England, once and for all. But it was in the best interests of his children to leave them behind. Eight year-old Ernest was being educated at a private boarding school at Bath in 1871, and Alice – twelve, was at a ladies seminary in Devizes cultivating the polite arts of music, singing, languages and deportment. Stanhope's destination of choice this time was Canada. After somehow scraping together the fare he sailed to Quebec aboard the *Corinthian* in October 1872. Taking advantage of the Canadian Government's free immigrant transport scheme he arrived by train at his final destination of Barrie, on the shores of Lake Simcoe.

While not the life of gentlemanly pursuits he had once envisioned for himself, Stanhope probably set himself up as a small farmer. His death in January 1884 aged 48 at his home in Elmvale, a rural town north of Barrie, was the result of 'congestion of the lungs'. He and Julian remained estranged and she died at Weston super Mare twenty-one years later in 1905.

For Stanhope's children there had been little time to really get to know their father. As she grew up, his daughter Alice attended her fair share of balls and weddings over the years, acting as bridesmaid on one or two occasions, but never the bride. United in their genteel spinsterhood, she was close to her aunts Katherine and Flora, and spent much of her later life at Bath. Alice evidently maintained a fondness for Richard's third son Robert who died in 1938, bequeathing him a few books and the Meerschaum pipe given her by her Aunt Flora. But Robert never received any of these items; Alice outlived him by three years.

The Long Family c. 1910. L-R: Vivian Edward, Leslie, Flora Elizabeth Alice, Ernest Walter, Stanhope Ernest, Reginald William Walter, Frances Catherine

As for her brother Ernest, his future lay in New Zealand where he established a dynasty of his own. Sometime around 1888 he sailed unaccompanied and unencumbered by old family money or possessions. There was no room for gilt-framed portraits of long-dead ancestors in his new life. Those ghosts he left in the past.

XI
A Diversion to Somerset
Long of Beckington, Stratton and Downside

William Long (*c*.1498–1558), brother of clothier Henry Long of Whaddon, established himself nine miles south-west at Beckington, near Frome. William was also a clothier, a patron of Beckington church and collector of taxes. He maintained ties to Wiltshire with property in Semington, but lived at Beckington Castle, the extremely thick walls of which indicate the edifice may incorporate remnants of a medieval building, and it is likely William rebuilt it. The castle was in possession of the Longs until they sold it to Sir James Ley some time before 1616.

Beckington Castle, 1842

Thomas, one of William's sons, was among the five local gentlemen who provided arms and armour in 1569 when the threat of a French invasion kept the county militia on constant alert. While there was no official conscription of men there were obligations nonetheless, and landowners were required to provide a certain amount of armour and weapons kept and maintained in readiness for muster, the quantity based on the value of their land. The ragtag band of local men who were called to muster about once a month in Beckington in 1569 numbered seventeen 'ablemen', and Thomas's contribution to their armaments was 'one corselet furnished', a heavy portable matchlock gun called a harquebut or hackbut, a crested metal helmet with a curved peak back and front, known as a murrion; a bow, a sheaf of arrows and a skull cap. Another Beckington clothier, Thomas Webb, provided a similar amount.

Thomas Long had four sons with his wife Joanna Burston, and when he died at Beckington in 1608 only one son, Polidore, survived him. Polidore entered Magdalen College, Oxford, in 1592 aged sixteen, and while in London in February 1597 the not-too-streetwise young graduate fell victim to two local conmen, paying ten shillings for what he was told were gold coins. They were in fact copper counters called 'cowpers'.[376] Having learnt a valuable lesson, Polidore left the opportunists of London behind him and returned to Somerset, where he married Maria Pomfret in 1607. They had a daughter and a son, also endowed with the unusual name of Polidore, who did not survive infancy.

Kingsmill Long (c.1588–c.1667)

Kingsmill, son of Thomas's brother William, named after his maternal great-grandfather Sir John Kingsmill of Sidmanton, received his education at St Alban Hall, Oxford, and was a student of Lincoln's Inn in 1608. Despite his education being interrupted by chronic illness, Kingsmill was eventually called to the bar. *The Black Books* of Lincoln's Inn records he had 'long been sick and absent, and so was omitted from the last list for call to the Bar. Nevertheless as

376 *Middlesex County Records* 1886

he is nowe come sicke to the towne, and knowne to deserve well wth the rest, he shall be called with his ancienty, and published at the next moot.'

His one claim to fame is his translation from Latin of John Barclay's *Argenis,* a historical allegory of the religious conflicts in France, originally published in 1621. After a request from James I Ben Jonson translated it into English but his version was lost in a fire which also destroyed many of his other works. Kingsmill's version, which he dedicated to his friend 'the truly noble William Dunch of Avebury', was published in 1625, the year Charles I married the Catholic Henrietta Maria of France. It has been suggested Kingsmill's publication was a gift to celebrate their marriage, based on one point of the story where the daughter of the French king marries a son of Hyanisbe.[377] Kingsmill was truly passionate about the story as his letter to Dunch reveals:

Sir,

When first I viewed the faire and Princely Argenis and her Royall lover Poliarchus, in a curious Latine habit, I was taken (as I think all other men are) both with admiration and delight: there being both variety to please the mind, and Learning to embetter the judgement for, good books I have ever thought like the fattest pastures, which as they are most profitable to the Tenants, so they are ever most pleasing to the eye of each beholder; being as well diapered with the various beauties of delightful flowers, as enriched with a fruitful crop, for the benefit of him that gathers it. And I found myself unable to draw them to the full life with an *English* Pencill, or show them in our native Looking glass; yet, for an essay of my strength, and to the best of my own knowledge, I have adventured (though, I confesse, with more confidence than judgment) to shew them in a dimme perspective.

This rude peece, such as it is, hath long lyen by me, since it was finished; I not thinking it worthy to see the light. I had always a desire and hope to have it undertaken by a more able workman, that our

377 *Catholicism, Controversy, and the English Literary Imagination, 1558–1660,* Alison Shell

nation might not be deprived of the use of so excellent a Story: But finding none in so long time to have done it, and knowing, while it spake not *English*, though it were a rich jewell to the learned Linguist, yet it was close lockt from all those, to whom education had not given more Languages than Nature Tongues: I have adventured to become the Key to this piece of hidden Treasure and have suffered my self to bee over-ruled by some of my worthy friends, whose judgments I have always esteemed, sending it abroad (though coarsely done) for the delight and use of others. I was the more encouraged in this Resolve, that I might shew my gratitude to your selfe, whose many favours though I come far short of ever deserving; yet I have always had the ambition to shew, by my best endevours, that your love and bounty hath not been lost on me. Gratitude is a running Streame, perpetually paying Tribute to his Lord the Ocean, that first filled him. And though I come not in so deepe a Current as my desires would offer; yet in my shallow murmur I have brought you these waters, not that I desire to bee counted able, but thankfull for your accumulated favours.

Vouchsafe therefore, I beseech you, to accept under your Patronage this unpolisht work, whereunto you shall be pleased to give the least approbation, I shall not despaire of the more favourable censure of others. The Originall itself (not to speak any thing of my paines, wherein yet I hope, I have faithfully, though not curiously rendred the History) is, besides the excellence of the Language, not one of the least esteeme that are extant of this kind, both for pleasure and profit to the Reader; which is the true end of every learned Writer. It is so full of wise and politique Discourses, and those so intermixed and seconded with pleasing accidents, so extolling Vertue and depressing Vice, that I have sometimes compared it to a greater Globe, wherein not onely one World, but even the businesse of it is represented; it being (indeed) such a perfect Glasse of State, that I cannot suppose, but every Reader will be drawne by the delight of something in it, to reade the whole. Now my end, in this publication, is not for any vaine hope of praise to my selfe, which, I am not so weake, as not to perceive how little I deserve it; but onely to leave testimony to yourself and the world, how much I am,

Yours in all observance,
Kingesmill Long.

Kingsmill and Dunch were co-owners of the manor of Barwick Basset, an estate confiscated from Thomas Saunders, alias Milles, attainted of high treason. Later in 1636 Kingsmill found himself in a spot of bother when he joined with his friend and others in making several allegedly fraudulent leases relating to Dunch's Wiltshire manor of Avebury, while Dunch continued to receive the rents. At an inquisition taken at Devizes, Kingsmill and his fellow defendants argued that in 1627 Dunch had demised the manor and farm (previously settled on his wife) to them for ninety-nine years at a yearly rent of 12d, in consideration of their paying his debts of about £4,000.

Kingsmill seems to have led a quiet and obscure life thereafter, dying in about 1667 at Newbury, Berkshire, aged almost eighty.

William Long of Stratton (c.1587–1645)

Kingsmill's brother William was keen to increase his fortune, but the timing of at least one of his property acquisitions was unfortunate. He was granted a long lease of Stratton on the Fosse by Charles I when Prince of Wales, only to have it recovered in King James I's reign by Prince Henry's Council. History repeated itself when his son Lislebone purchased the same manor in the Commonwealth sale of Crown lands, and lost it again at the Restoration.

William's business was coal mining, in partnership with gentleman adventurers employing large numbers of men. Coal was in great demand, fuelling many growing industries such as glass, salt-making, brewing and lime-burning, and in domestic fireplaces coal was replacing wood. Occasionally accused of overworking the mines, William, in one incident while following a seam of coal into his neighbour's property, was foiled by the owner's unwillingness to allow mining on his land, despite the offer of generous damages. He merely abandoned the works and resumed after the owner's death. The mining operations were later continued by his grandson George.

William's marriage in 1608 to Mary, daughter of Thomas Lovibond of Whippingham, Isle of Wight, not only produced eleven daughters and two sons, it also reunited two branches of the Long family. Mary's mother was a daughter of Henry Long (d. 1611) of Whaddon, also named Mary. Thomas Lovibond was party to the marriage settlement between her widowed aunt Rebecca Long (*née* Bailey) and the lawyer Henry Sherfield.

During her formative years Mary Lovibond was sent to live with Lady Joan Barrington, a daughter of Sir Henry Cromwell and consequently aunt of Oliver Cromwell, the future protector. Lady Barrington was a remarkable woman whose advice was much sought after, and she kept up a copious correspondence until late in her life. She dedicated much of her efforts to furthering the cause of the Puritans, and also educating young ladies within her household. In 1631 Mary, by then William's wife, wrote to Lady Barrington, expressing her gratitude for giving her 'the best part of my education whereby in my many distresses I have since receaved much comfort, which makes mee bold to present one of my owne daughters to serve your selfe or any of yours whensoever you shall bee pleased to accept.'[378]

Felix Long (c.1598–1667)

A third brother, Felix, was employed as steward by Sir William Calley of Burderop, collecting debts and making payments on his behalf. Letters written by Felix in this capacity during 1638–42 were addressed from Lincoln's Inn Fields in London, but in 1647 he was granted a commission as captain and sent to Dublin. He was appointed a commissioner in Tipperary in about 1655. In direct opposition to his anti-Royalist brothers, Felix publicly pledged his allegiance to the king in 1661, in a 'Loyal Address by the Lords Justices and Officers of the Dublin Headquarters', thanking the king for the restoration of their estates, for giving them others, and for the re-establishment of the Church and civil government. In 1666 he was granted over 1,200 acres of land in the barony of Ballaghkeene, County Wexford,[379] and the following year he was appointed a justice of the peace. He died soon afterwards, and his only child

378   *Barrington Family Letters, 1628–1632*, Arthur Searle 1983
379   *The Wexford Chronicles*, George Griffiths 1877

Lucy, recently married to Edward March of London, predeceased him by a few months.

George Long of Preston Candover (c.1605–55)

Kingsmill's youngest brother George, originally of Beckington, spent a good deal of time in London, where he also studied law. He was, considering the potential consequences, either a brave or foolhardy man. He was certainly a man of principle. Daring to cross swords with church authority in 1636, he was prosecuted for abusing the bishop in the Consistory Court. Eight years later in 1644 he gave damning evidence in the trial against the Archbishop of Canterbury, William Laud, which concluded with Laud's conviction and execution in January 1645. Laud had inaugurated an ecclesiastical reign of terror throughout England, pressing reactionary policies to enforce uniformity of worship. He earned the censure of the inhabitants of Beckington after ordering the communion table in the church be moved to the chancel. Considering it an unacceptable innovation suggesting popery, the churchwardens refused; they were excommunicated for a year and imprisoned in the county gaol.

George had purchased the manor of Preston Candover in Hampshire for £1,110 in 1636, and throughout the Civil War he lived in London. For about two years on and off from 1643 a Royalist garrison occupied the heavily fortified Basing House some nine miles from George's Hampshire estate, defending it against attack by Parliamentary forces. The house was eventually overtaken, ransacked and burnt in October 1645. On his return from London he found his own house also a ruin at Candover, the land laid to waste. A strong adherent of Parliament, he had assisted their cause financially, and by way of compensation Parliament gave him a small farm confiscated from a recusant, Francis Perkins.

George had married Marie Kemp while living in London, where the last of their six children was baptised in 1645. By 1653 Marie was dead and George's second wife, twice widowed Frances Gladman[380]

380 Her first two husbands were the Rev. John Blythman and Farnham Beaumont

appears to have been rather less than honest with him. The daughter of the Rev. Nazariah Gladman, vicar of South Mimms and Ridge, Hertfordshire, Frances had assured George before their marriage that she was in possession of considerable property inherited from her second husband Farnham Beaumont. George, 'out of tender affection and love', settled on her a £100 per year jointure for life. Their union was originally intended to be a double wedding 'consummated both together', the other couple being George's fifteen-year-old daughter Katherine and Frances's son John Blythman junior. The impediment to the double nuptials was not only the youth of the two children, but Frances's absolute insistence that her son not marry Katherine until he was twenty-one.

Only George and Frances married at Ridge in June 1653, and it wasn't too long before he realised he had been duped. Frances had already disposed of her late husband's property to her son and brother, and George later discovered the £400 jointure he had put aside for Katherine on her marriage was missing. This he said was 'imbezzled and surreptitiously taken away by the said Francis out of my box of writing laid up together amongst other writings . . . in my trunke'.[381] Despite this, George still had hopes Katherine would marry his stepson John Blythman, but for whatever reason this did not happen, and Blythman married a certain Elizabeth Norbury in 1659. George had only about two years to rue his poor choice of wife before he died in 1655.

Sir Lislebone Long (c.1613–59)

George's nephew Lislebone, son of William Long and Mary Lovibond, usually signed himself 'Lisle Long', although the register of baptisms at Beckington for 1613 records his name as 'Loveban'. Growing up in a largely female household surrounded by eleven sisters, his attendance at Oxford University immediately transported him into a male domain, where he graduated BA from Magdalen Hall in 1630–1. He was called to the bar at Gray's Inn in 1640. Much respected by his peers, he was later described by

381 Will of George Long, PROB 11/261

Cromwell's ambassador to Queen Christina's court in Sweden, Mr Bulstrode Whitlocke, as 'a very sober, discreet gentleman, and a good lawyer'.[382] He became an elder in Parliament's Presbyterian national church and a member of the committee established to administer the solemn league and covenant in Somerset.[383] Appointed to the committee to settle the form of English church government, he took a moderate stance following his election to the Long Parliament as a recruiter MP for Wells (1645–53).

His reputation didn't hold much sway with Archbishop Laud, however, who in 1643 bluntly rejected his petition on behalf of his younger brother William, then newly beneficed and residing at Magdalen Hall. Lislebone had asked Laud to allow William to continue to live at the university to improve his studies, his parsonage house not being habitable until repaired. Laud declined, saying he would not give William leave for a day, and he must depart the university immediately or leave his living. Lislebone, of the same mind as his uncle George on the subject of Laud's tyranny, felt this a harsh and politically motivated response, arguing that his refusal was based on the name of Magdalen Hall being synonymous with Puritanism because they did not comply with the superstitions and other 'errors' then broached in the university as a whole. Many years later his unfortunate brother William died from the Plague, which hit areas of Somerset in 1661 while he was rector of Priston, part of the Somerset estates of the Longs of Whaddon.

Although he wasn't one of the many MPs excluded from the House after Pride's Purge, acting as teller on a critical vote the next day, Lislebone's strong opposition to the action resulted in his finally absenting himself in protest. He took no part in the trial and execution of Charles I, but by taking his dissent on 22 February 1649 he became a conformist, and resumed his seat in the Rump Parliament, taking a key role. He and a group of conservative like-minded lawyers (including

382   *The Lives of the Speakers of the House of Commons, from the Time of King Edward III to Queen Victoria*, J.A. Manning 1851
383   John Wroughton, 'Long, Lislebone (*bap.* 1613, *d.* 1659)', *Oxford Dictionary of National Biography*, Oxford University Press, 2004; online edn. Jan 2008

Bulstrode Whitlocke, Roger Hill and Edmund Prideaux) who opposed law reform were given the task of organising the Rump's committees, drafting much of the legislation, and he was appointed chairman of the committee charged with defining the powers of the lord protector. He represented Somerset in Parliament, and in December 1656 was knighted by Oliver Cromwell, having that year been made recorder of London, a master of requests, and treasurer of Lincoln's Inn.

The succession of Oliver Cromwell's son Richard in September 1658 as lord protector met with opposition and controversy, resulting in his resignation eight months later. Two months earlier in March 1659, Challoner Chute, the speaker of the third Protectorate Parliament, suddenly became indisposed and died as a result of a nine day continuous session, being 'tired out with the long debates and late sitting'.[384] Highly regarded by his peers, Sir Lislebone was an obvious replacement, and by general consent of the House he was elected speaker. But he lasted just one week, during which Parliament sat for four days continuously, before he too became ill and died on 16 March, leaving an estate that included a number of ecclesiastical and Royalist lands purchased after confiscation by Parliament. He was buried at Stratton on the Fosse, survived by four of his five children and his wife Frances, daughter of John Mynne of Epsom, who later took up residence with their eldest son George at Downside.

George Long of Downside (c.1643–1705)

For centuries Bath has been associated with the treatment of rheumatic and other diseases by virtue of its hot mineral springs, visitors coming from far and wide in the hope of a cure. It is still one of the natural wonders of Britain. Towards the end of the seventeenth century the case of George Long Esquire, of Downside, near Bath, caused an 'immense sensation' throughout the country, prompting the renewed drinking of the waters at Bath, not practised for 150 years.

George was just sixteen when his father died in 1659, but he was able to continue his education, matriculating at Wadham College, Oxford, two years later, and he became a student of Lincoln's Inn the

384   Diary of Thomas Burton, 4.92

same year. After completing his studies he returned to Somerset to continue the mining operations begun by his grandfather at Stratton. There was much controversy over possession of the mines after the Restoration, and in 1678 George was accused of attempting to establish a monopoly by buying up his competitor's lands to close down their works. It was alleged he had advanced the price of coal for his own interest, causing scarcity and oppression of the poor. He was accused of threatening people who had dared collect loads of coal from workings other than his own. Previously, in 1671, George had petitioned for a new grant of lands confiscated from his father Lislebone, and he renewed it again in 1696.[385]

For twenty years he had suffered with 'the gout and stone', and by the age of fifty he was bedridden. His elderly mother Frances, who had lived in his household for some years, died in February 1691, and three weeks later George was taken to Bath. In 1882 John Kent Spender printed the story of George's apparently miraculous recovery in his publication *The Bath Thermal Waters*, from an original account published in George's lifetime by his physician, Dr William Oliver FRS :

> He was brought here in April 1691, with crooked fingers, right knee and hip, and a motionless back. So contracted was he that he could not be extended in bed. He had importunate thirst, no appetite, and a shrivelled skin; the face was meagre and the hair grey. There were several internal troubles also. He was brought to Bath with great difficulty, and immediately drank the water hot in the morning and cold at meals. In a week the thirst was abated; in a month he bathed 'between whiles,' which eased the pains. He returned home at the end of May and came again at the end of August, having gathered some flesh and strength and some small ability to go, though cripplishly. He again stayed here several weeks. By the end of November his grey hairs began to fall off and new ones succeeded; nay, some grey ones returned to their colour. By Candlemass he had few or no grey hairs left, but a good deal of soft brown hair such as he had when 25 or 26,

and it grew so fast that he cut more than an inch every four or five weeks.

Mr Long lived here during the greater part of 1692. His old and ragged toe-nails came off, and new and smooth ones grew. His arms and hands recovered strength, with more motion of their joints; the muscles became plumper, and he daily became more erect while every bathing stretched him half-an-inch. The eye was vigorous, and his face ruddy and youthful (especially when he mixes sherry with his water). So well and young was he that an unbelieving friend inquiring of his health, his wife replied – 'I believe if I were dead he would marry again.' Finally he was returned to Parliament and two months before election he rode from Bath to Oxford in a day, and a few days before that he rode home 12 or 14 miles, went to bed for two or three hours, rose again and dispatched a great deal of business before dinner.

A week before the parliamentary election for Bath in October 1695, George was predicted as the likely winner against Sir Thomas Estcourt, but he lost by a whisker to his opponent. He donated plate to his old college at Oxford, dying in 1705 aged sixty-two, and his wife Mary, daughter of Marmaduke Jennings of Curry Rivel, survived him by thirty-two years. She also outlived five of their seven children. George's descendants continued at Stratton for another two generations; his son William was appointed life steward of the Duchy of Lancaster by letters patent in March 1707, continuing the coal-mining interests at Stratton. His granddaughter Judith Long married Major Norton Knatchbull, son of the 'ambitious, capable Parliamentarian' Sir Edward Knatchbull, 4th Baronet. Judith was the last of the line, dying in 1792.

XII
Long of Potterne

Thomas, uncle of clothier Henry Long of Whaddon, died at Potterne in 1550, possessed of property at Semington, Littleton and elsewhere. His sons continued in the textile trade, and the eldest, Henry, occupied the manor and rectory of Potterne in 1555. At his death in 1557 Potterne passed to his brother William. Two other brothers, John and Thomas, also lived at Potterne, their descendants gradually distributing themselves all along the River Avon – at Keevil, Bulkington, Marston, Worton and Cheverell – utilising the same water for their woollen mills.

John Long, grandson of the first-mentioned Thomas, lived at Marston, and by the time he died in 1597 he had nine children, all of whom survived him. Signing his will only with his 'mark', his illiteracy seems to have been no barrier to accumulating wealth; he held lands in Worton, Bulkington, Potterne, Marston and elsewhere, and had loaned money to Sir William Brouncker. His cash bequests amounted to more than £1,900, roughly equivalent to about £200,000 today. To one of his overseers he left four yards of velvet. His wife Anne Merewether lived for another twenty-nine years, dying in 1626 at Little Cheverell. Their son John junior (called John Long of Tilsitt in his mother's will) was the ancestor of a further four generations of John Longs who successively handed down from father to son a modest estate at Tilshead, initially comprising 83 acres and pasture for 220 sheep. The last of these died unmarried at Tilshead in 1701, leaving his estate to his mother Cicely, later of Chitterne, who had remarried a Mr Strotton.

Thomas Long of Little Cheverell (c.1579–1654)

The second son of John Long and Anne Merewether, Thomas inherited from his father lands at Marston, an estate at Melksham and Hurst Mill in Potterne. Thomas continued as a clothier and purchased more property at Melksham from William Brouncker, including Melksham Farm and six houses, and estates at Collingbourne Kingston and Burbage from the Earl of Hertford. Both these estates he bequeathed to his son Richard, who married his cousin Elizabeth Long, heiress of Rood Ashton. Thomas first leased the demesne farm of Little Cheverell in 1606; this passed to his grandson John (d. 1679 at Devizes), whose widow Eleanor finally left the farm for an annuity in 1719. Amazingly, the Longs had held Little Cheverell for the entire 113 years with no increase in rent.

With civil war disrupting life in Thomas's usually peaceful neighbourhood, the inhabitants were expected to support the king in preserving his kingdom at a time when his own revenues had been seized. In 1643 general levies were made on the Hundred of Potterne and Cannings and the townsfolk were urged to comply promptly and cheerfully and furnish the required sums of money and provisions, unless they preferred the alternative of being proceeded against as disaffected persons. The 'loans', they were promised, would be repaid with interest.

Thomas sent into a royalist garrison twenty-eight oxen, valued at £168, considerably more than the thirty loads of hay from Mr Yerbury of Trowbridge valued at £23, and the eight oxen from Mr Vinor of Staverton worth £48. The head of another prominent Potterne family, John Grubbe, received a letter superscribed with the king's autograph desiring him 'forthwith to lend us the sum of Two hundred pounds, in money or plate, for our necessary support and the maintenance of our army which we are compelled to raise for the defence of our power, the Protestant religion, and the laws of the land'. Another resident, John Harvest, received a similarly worded document with a demand for £100, concluding just short of a threat: 'If you shall refuse to give us this testimony of your affection, you will give us too great cause to suspect your duty and inclination both to our person and to the public peace.'

As a taxable landowner Thomas also received a letter of royal demand, but by backing the losing side he later found himself under the scrutiny of a parliamentary committee. In May 1649 he, together with Francis Allen of Devizes and Thomas Sadler of Elcombe, became answerable to the Committee for the Advancement of Money, which included his cousin on the other side of the political fence, Sir Walter Long of Whaddon, appointed by Parliament. Allen was accused of holding intelligence with the enemy, trading in their quarters and holding £500 belonging to Sir Allen Apsley, a delinquent.

For his part, Thomas was charged with lending money to the king to maintain his army, in particular £100 to Apsley, and furnishing and maintaining a horse and man. Sadler was involved in the collection of money for the king. A few days later the county commissioners were ordered to examine the three men and secure their estates if their delinquency was proved. Whether Thomas had his estates sequestered is not recorded in that particular document,[386] though enough evidence would have been found against him.

Family matters occupied him in 1651 when he filed a Bill in Chancery against Christopher Merewether, once described by Sir Walter Long of Whaddon as a man 'full of malice'. Merewether had dishonestly obtained a £500 legacy from the estate of his late brother John, husband of Thomas's daughter Ann. John died leaving a widow and three children, having appointed Thomas executor of his will. Christopher had duped Thomas into handing over the money intended for John's children, after obtaining custody of the eldest daughter and pretending he was officially her guardian.

In 1652, at the age of seventy-three, Thomas was made sheriff of Wiltshire, and less than two years later he died. He requested his interment in the chancel of the church at Little Cheverell be 'in a decent and comely manner', and his worldly estate he distributed among his children, 'kindred and friends in the world', including £1,200 to his son William, who in the meantime was to be provided with sufficient man's meat, horse meat and lodging at Thomas's mansion house at Cheverell, and be allowed to keep his bed and three pairs of sheets.

John, Thomas's eldest son succeeded to his father's estates at Melksham and Little Cheverell. He was educated at St John's College,

---

386 M. A. E. Green, *Cal. of the Proceedings of the Committee for Advance of Money, 1642–1656* vol. II

Signature and seal of Thomas Long of Little Cheverell, 1654

Oxford, later entering Lincoln's Inn by special admission in 1640. He was afterwards called to the bar. Evidently the life of a London barrister didn't suit him and he returned to Wiltshire where he was appointed sheriff. John Danvers mortgaged his estate of Baynton to him, and in 1673 he purchased it outright, dying unmarried without issue three years later. He left his various estates to his nephews, sons of his three brothers[387] and Baynton descended in the Long family until sold by John Long junior of Monkton Farleigh in 1842.

Thomas's third son, Thomas junior, had a large family with his wife Margery Flower, some of whom branched out to Salisbury. One son, Richard – a grocer – was alderman and mayor of Salisbury, and his third son (also Richard) followed him in the trade. His fifth son William was alderman and mayor of Bath in 1715.

James Long of Wedhampton (1694–1768)

W illiam's youngest son James encountered difficulties with his new wife Mary Turner, which became public knowledge when she ran away from their home at Wedhampton in 1720, after one year of not-so-happy marriage. The circumstances that led to this escape

387   William Long of Little Sutton (d. 1670), Thomas Long of Devizes (d. 1671) and Richard Long of Collingbourne Kingston (d. 1669)

are not recorded, but her brother George Turner took her side and hid her in his house at Penleigh. On discovering this, James retrieved his reluctant wife and took the matter before the next assizes at Salisbury, where he was awarded £150 damages against his brother-in-law.

But this didn't remedy the underlying problem. Soon afterwards Mary was again 'convey'd away' and concealed. James placed a newspaper advertisement in the *Postboy*, warning that anyone receiving or entertaining his wife would be prosecuted. Furthermore, Mary should not be trusted, he would not be liable for any debts she

The Long Monument, Devizes

incurred and he offered a good reward for information that would lead her to 'be secured' by him. The couple seem to have eventually reconciled their differences, although they had no children.

It has been generally thought Long Street in Devizes was named after him. He originated a scheme to build a safer road to bypass Etchilhampton Hill and a monument was built on the hill south-east of Devizes at an estimated cost of £40, raised by subscription from grateful locals. It is inscribed with his name and the crest of Long – a large demi-lion rampant – forming the apex. James died in 1768 just before it was erected. Known as the Long Monument, it was repaired and restored in the nineteenth century by Walter Long of Preshaw and is now Grade II listed.

Of James's two elder unmarried brothers, William junior lived quietly at Bratton and died in October 1751, reported to be 'possessed of a large estate, part of which he hath left to charitable uses'. Often men of wealth set up permanent charities in the form of land held in trust, the rents reserved for relief of the poor. The benevolence of the less wealthy was usually limited to one-off payments; in William's case he left money to the Bath Infirmary and the urgently needy of his parish.

Rev. Thomas Long MA of Finmere (1691–1771)

Thomas, James's next eldest brother, educated at Queen's College, Oxford, began as rector of Little Oakley, Northamptonshire, in 1719. A year later the bishop of Peterborough, White Kennett, a man of formidable reputation, began to make visitations, sending Thomas into a flurry of alarm over the neglected state of his chancel, rectory and outhouses. On taking possession he found things in a ruinous state; 'my Predecessor left his Widow in such melancholy Circumstances, that it was more proper to consider her as an Object of Charity, than as a Person, on whom I could with any pleasure, make demands for delapidations.'

In 1734 Thomas returned to Oxford and was instituted as rector of Finmere. There was no free school but a few children in the parish were taught to read at his expense. He presented to the church twelve acres of land in nearby Tingewick, 'charging it with a yearly payment of fifteen shillings to the Clerk, as a recompense to him for attending on the Fasts and Festivals', and ordering 6*d* to be deducted from the payment for each time the clerk failed to attend on those days 'unless let by sickness'. Continually frustrated by lack of finances and the conduct of his churchwardens, he accused them of not 'making fair and full presentments as their Oath requires', complaining to his bishop that they were 'incorrigible offenders'.

Lancelot "Capability" Brown designed the grounds of the rectory but it would be thirty years before Thomas was able to spend the required amount to refurbish the interior of the church, by which time he was in his seventies. The extent of this work was such that services had to be suspended for the duration 'by reason of being embarrassed by much scaffolding employed in repairing and ornamenting my church and chancel'.

Thomas had once proudly proclaimed to catechise daily all through the year, except at harvest, and the children came to him in the church 'on notice of the bell', but as he began to feel the effects of age these were reduced to a three-yearly course of lectures. He printed his last lecture on the catechism in 1762, *The Holy Scripture, the best Teacher of Good Manners and Civility*, addressed to the 'young persons' of the village 'as a small monument of my care and affection for you'. He had kept meticulous records over the years, and his Rector's Book, which he began in about 1750, was maintained by successive rectors of Finmere until 1956. After nearly forty years of unwavering dedication to his parish, Thomas died in April 1771 in his eightieth year, 'a man of the most exemplary piety and charity'.

Long of Buckingham and Maidsmorton

Thomas's elder sister Mary married the Rev. Francis Turner, son of Dr William Turner, archdeacon of Northumberland, a connection probably influenced by Thomas. Mary and Francis, described posthumously as 'eminent examples of conjugal affection, piety, and charity', lived at Buckingham, where they had an only child also named Mary, the main beneficiary of her uncle James Long of Wedhampton. In 1772 an Act was passed to enable Mary and her husband the Rev. William Hutton to use the name, arms and crest of Long, pursuant to her uncle's wishes.

Rev. James Long Long, formerly Hutton (c.1766–1846)

As a consequence, William and Mary's son, baptised James Long Hutton, became known as James Long Long. Oxford-educated, James was rector of Maidsmorton from 1790, having inherited the advowson at his father's death ten years before, and his wealth further increased with the Wiltshire estates of his great-uncle James Long passing to him after his mother's death in 1784. From his great-uncle Thomas's will he received £200 and 'my model of Sir Isaac Newton'.

A man of great religious fervour, James published a paper in 1805 cumbrously titled *The Christian's Answer to the Antichristian Calumniator*, consisting of a short address to the inhabitants of Maidsmorton. His younger sister Jane defected early in life to the independent church at Buckingham where she met her future husband, the Rev. William Priestley. She later changed her views and returned to the Church of England, outliving her husband by nearly twenty-five years. Dying childless in 1851, Jane bequeathed substantial sums to various societies with mainstream religious affiliations. Unwavering in his own beliefs, James gave a generous donation towards the founding of King's College, London, proposed to counter the secular University College, founded with the backing of Jews, Utilitarians and non-Anglican Christians, which had met with storms of disapproval from the establishment.

In 1827 he lived with his wife Henrietta Thomas and their three daughters at Lillingstone Lovell, a village with a population of about 135, three miles from Maidsmorton. There had been trouble with his servants that year, serious enough to warrant the dismissal in mid-September of three of them; two young women and a male servant, Robert Siddall, aged twenty-two. Siddall applied to join the army the next day but he didn't meet the height requirement and was rejected. This, together with his sudden unemployment and a stain on his character, prompted him to end it all in James's rickyard where he was found the following day by two young lads driving pigs from the cornstacks. He'd slashed himself with a large pocket knife purchased specially and made extra-sharp for the purpose. The inquest held at the tavern in Maidsmorton found he had committed the fatal act when in a state of lunacy.

James's wife Henrietta had been ill for a long time before her death in March 1843, giving him plenty of time to keep an eye out for a suitable replacement. Suitable or not, six months later he set the gossips atwitter and the news ricocheted around the country: at the age of almost eighty it was announced he was to wed a labourer's daughter, twenty-two-year-old Jane Hobbs. James was commended for his 'fine taste in female beauty', and the young lady herself, described as 'beauteous, blooming, lovely and modest', was still employed as maid of all work by a local draper, George King, eight days before the wedding.

Much of the curious population of Buckingham, 'old, young and middle-aged', all 'hasted to the wedding' and the church was 'crowded almost to suffocation'. The reporter of this spectacle seemed to be revelling in journalistic liberties; the population of Buckingham at that time was around four thousand, just a few thousand too many to all squeeze into the church together. After the ceremony the elderly James, with glowing admiration, lifted the veil of his young bride, and in front of the congregation gave her a distinct and audible kiss. No pen could describe the looks of the female auditors, the reporter wrote, and 'a simultaneous burst of applause and a loud clapping of hands followed'.

James's other siblings included an elder brother, Francis Richard Turner Hutton Long, declared a lunatic at the age of forty-one in 1801, and he died unmarried in 1812. His elder sister Elizabeth married Thomas Gilbert, a captain in the Royal Marines, and she became the mother of the Rt. Rev. Ashurst Turner Gilbert, later bishop of Chichester. On failure of male issue, James Long Long at his death in 1846 became the last of this line, and the entailed Wiltshire estates eventually passed to his cousin, Walter Long of Preshaw. James left a long list of bequests to his family, including £200 to his 'beloved wife' of three years, Jane, and as an afterthought he left her parents Abraham and Mary Hobbs, labourers of Croughton, Northamptonshire, ten shillings a week for their lives.

XIII
Long of Preshaw, Hampshire

Walter Long (1690–1769)

A younger son of the grocer Richard Long of Salisbury, Walter suffered a devastating loss during an outbreak of smallpox in 1723 which decimated his family. A total of 1,244 inhabitants of Salisbury contracted the disease and 165 died. His wife of less than six years, Mary Morley, fatally succumbed on 11 April, followed two weeks later by their two infant daughters, leaving an only son, six-month-old Walter junior. A second chance presented itself in 1727 when he married Philippa, daughter of John Blackall of London, which coincided with his purchase of the manor of Muchelney in Somerset. Over the next few years ten more children were born, with eight of them surviving.

Walter was a successful linen-draper at Close Gate, Salisbury, where he owned several premises in High Street. Sometime deputy lieutenant of Wiltshire, he served a term as High Sheriff in 1745. The manor of Preshaw came to him in 1742 on the death of his unmarried brother John, who had purchased it in 1728 for £7,600. Having survived the theft from his house of a 'considerable amount of plate' by his footman two years earlier, he died at Salisbury in January 1769, devising Preshaw to his son John and Muchelney to his eldest son Walter junior. Nearly thirty years a widow, Walter's wife Philippa was in her ninety-ninth year at her death in 1798.

The eldest son and sole survivor from his father's first marriage, Walter Long junior was the previously mentioned heir-at-law to James Long Long of Maidsmorton. Educated at Queen's College, Oxford, at the age of twenty he was apprenticed to John Hitches, attorney of Clifford's Inn, for £150, later becoming a barrister at law and bencher of Lincoln's Inn. For forty-five years he officiated as judge of the Sheriff's Court in London, earning not more than £100 a year salary and without any prospect of promotion.[388]

He was occasionally confused with his cousin and namesake, having to field correspondence intended for old Walter Long of Bath. To add to this confusion the two cousins both died unmarried in 1807, eight weeks apart, aged eighty-four and ninety-five. Walter of Lincoln's Inn was buried in Salisbury Cathedral, where there is a memorial to him by John Flaxman. He devised his estates in Somerset with male entail successively to his half-brothers William and Samuel Long and his young nephew Walter Long of Preshaw, only son of his other half-brother, John Long.

John was the eldest son of his father's second marriage. In 1746 at the age of eighteen he was apprenticed to his uncle John Blackall, merchant of London. Still unmarried at the age of fifty-one he found a wife in Ellen,[389] widow of John Ashfordby of Cheshunt, Hertfordshire, no doubt much to the relief of his seventy-year-old mother Philippa. Walter welcomed his only child into the world in 1788, but joy turned to sorrow a few days later when his wife died from complications at the age of forty-three. The now motherless child was Walter Long of Preshaw, destined to become heir to several estates.

William Long FRS, FSA (1747–1818)

William, the youngest son of Walter and Philippa, built a respectable reputation during a career spanning thirty-three years as a surgeon at St Bartholomew's Hospital, London. In August 1769 at the age of twenty-two he became a member of the Corporation of Surgeons and he was appointed to the Court of Assistants in 1789. He was elected fellow of both the Royal Society (1801) and the Society of Antiquaries (1802). His appointment as second master of the Royal College of Surgeons in 1800 coincided with his post as governor from 1800 to 1807.

Something of a pioneer in his field, William designed various surgical and other devices, with mixed success. His patient John

---

388   Jeremy Bentham, *The Correspondence of Jeremy Bentham* vol. 12: July 1824 to June 1828, p. 272
389   The only surviving daughter and heiress of Robert Hippesley-Trenchard Esq. of Stanton Fitzwarren, Wiltshire, and Mary Gore.

Marsh, one of the most prolific composers of the age, had rented a house at Salisbury in 1779 from William's mother Philippa at 49 High Street, Close Gate, 'a sad old fashion'd house with hardly any outlet', which Marsh thought the best of two offered by her at the time. By 1796 Marsh was becoming quite deaf, and he consulted William at his house in Chancery Lane 'about some tin artificial ears of his invention'. These would prove to be one of William's not quite so brilliant ideas. Giving several instances of successful trials, William persuaded Marsh who immediately 'bespoke a pair', but after trying them once or twice found them to be of little benefit, 'and they rather heated his ears'.[390]

William later lived at 16 Lincoln's Inn Fields opposite the college buildings, and developed close friendships with the architect George Dance and painter George Romney, the sculptor John Flaxman and writers William Hayley, Isaac Reed and William Blake, who, like William, were members of the select eight-member Unincreasable Club formed in 1777. They met at nearby Queens Head, Holborn, and for many years their meetings were presided over by Reed. At the age of about thirty William sat for Romney as his first subject for a portrait,[391] done for his friend Hayley. In his *Life of Romney* (1809) Hayley writes:

> In the year 1776, when I was furnishing the little villa in Sussex to which I had retired, I wished to adorn it with good portraits, as large as life, of a few friends from whose frequent society I precluded myself, in a great measure, by relinquishing my residence in London. The first work that Romney executed for me was a portrait of Mr Long, a gentleman to whom nature had given extraordinary talents for the pencil.

William, as Hayley had observed, was himself an amateur artist and he acquired many of Romney's paintings. One of the

390   John Marsh, Brian Robins, *The John Marsh Journals – The Life and Times of a Gentleman Composer (1752–1828)*, 1998
391   In 1913 this portrait was at Whittington Hall, Kirkby Lonsdale, Westmorland, the residence of the family of Greene, descendants of one of William's executors and related to his wife. It was acquired some time before 1950 by C. John Brooke of Devon, a descendant of the Ley family.

earliest, *Lady Hamilton as Circe*, which remained in Romney's studio until his death, was sold as lot 100 in April 1807 and knocked down to William at 14½ guineas. He attempted to improve it by painting two wolves and a panther into the background, with singularly inappropriate results. His handiwork has since been removed. Romney's delicately painted nude figures *Cupid and Psyche* were 'improved' by William painting in a piece of strategically placed drapery,[392] perhaps to appease his wife. These pictures remained in the possession of the Long family until 1890, when thirteen were sold by Christie's on behalf of his great-nephew, Walter Jervis Long of Preshaw. *Lady Hamilton as Circe* fetched 3,850 guineas, and eventually found its way to the Tate Gallery, London, bequeathed by Lady Wharton in 1945.

Romney's letters make frequent mention of William, whose passion was obvious to everyone he knew. Romney wrote to his brother James in 1793: 'Long is in full business and at the head of his profession.' Despite writing several papers, nothing has been found published in his lifetime, but his untitled notes on two cases of breast cancer are preserved in the donation book of St Bartholomew's Hospital Museum. They were copied out by William Clift, museum conservator in 1818, who refers to them as *Long's paper on The Effects of Cancer*. This paper, 'with preparations of the diseased parts, and drawings made from them', was submitted by William to the Board to be deposited with the papers of the college.

In about 1798 William purchased Marwell Hall just a few miles from Preshaw, and between 1812 and 1816 he made considerable alterations, resulting in the house that stands today. This house was once part of the bishopric of Winchester, wrested away by Henry VIII at the Dissolution and bestowed upon Sir John Seymour (father of the protector), whose daughter Jane was Henry VIII's third wife. There are various stories relating to Henry VIII and Jane Seymour at Marwell Hall, where the king and his new bride are said to have retreated after their wedding breakfast in May 1536.

392 John Romney, *Memoirs of the Life and Works of George Romney*, 1830, p. 143

William was a man of compassion and generosity, and when resident at Marwell he always gave his advice and medicine gratuitously to the poor of the surrounding neighbourhood. He died there in March 1818 aged seventy, having had no children with his wife Alice.[393] She commissioned his friend Flaxman to erect a monument in Salisbury Cathedral 'to perpetuate the memory of a much esteemed husband'. A man of many virtues, 'he added a suavity of manners to a firmness of expression, which was at once perspicuous and convincing', and he was 'warmly and firmly attached to his relations'. That he was highly esteemed by his peers there is no doubt, and his colleagues at the College of Surgeons gave heart-felt tributes to him after his death, noting his refined notions of honour and dignity, which 'promoted a high tone of moral feeling', and by his 'silent benevolence' he 'soothed the pangs of misery'.

William left a 'handsome legacy' to his niece Philippa Grove, daughter of his sister Philippa, who had married John Grove of Ferne. The younger Philippa never married, and was known to her own nieces Charlotte and Harriet Grove as simply 'Aunt Grove'. Harriet, regarded as the first love of the poet Percy Bysshe Shelley, kept long and detailed diaries spanning many years, as did her sister Charlotte. In 1810 Harriet wrote that her brother Charles and Aunt Grove 'had a little squabble on the subject of Mr William Long. A very tender subject (one) always with my Aunt.' Unfortunately Harriet doesn't elaborate, but it is clear from another diary entry written by Charlotte that a special affection existed between Philippa Grove and her uncle William, and she noted her aunt was the only Grove to receive any legacy from him. His sister Eleanor left legacies to Philippa in 1824, Charlotte remarking 'she will come into a great property and is most truly deserving of it'.

William's collection of preserved medical specimens and surgical instruments was presented by his widow to the Royal College of Surgeons Museum in London in June 1818, although some items were destroyed in May 1941 by German bombing raids during the Second World War. The museum also benefitted from a collection of

393   Daughter of Edmund Dawson Esq. of Wharton, Lancaster

494 books from his library selected and presented by his executors.

During the Owslebury riots of 1830 threshing and other farm machinery was destroyed and a mob of rioters besieged Mrs Long and her servants at Marwell Hall, demanding food, money and lower rents. She persuaded them to accept £5 on condition they go away without making any mischief. The mob moved on to Preshaw House, and by threats and imprecations obtained a supply of provisions and destroyed a machine. John Boyes, a local farmer, had taken around a petition demanding higher wages for farm labourers; for his part in the riots he was convicted and transported to Australia. Altogether 245 men were arrested and brought to trial at Winchester. Two of the prisoners were hanged.

After Alice died in September 1840, her husband's nephew Walter Long moved the pictures and remainder of William's library from Marwell to his house at Preshaw, initially placing the Romneys in the 'best bedroom' and on the staircase. Walter's daughter Georgiana later recalled no one in the family was aware of their great value; they had been in a large bedroom at Marwell with their faces to the wall for many years.

Walter Long of Preshaw (1788–1871)

Walter had an unfortunate start in life; his mother Ellen died a few days after his birth and he was orphaned less than a decade later. Firmly focussed on the future, he entered Oriel College, Oxford, in 1805 aged sixteen, graduated BA in 1809 and MA in 1812. He was a student of Lincoln's Inn in 1809, a justice of the peace from 1815, and deputy lieutenant of Hampshire in 1817. Seven years later he was appointed High Sheriff.

His accumulation of wealth began at the unwitting age of nine with his inheritance of Preshaw on his father John's death in 1797; aged thirteen he received a moiety of the estates of his maternal uncle J.W.H. Trenchard in 1801, including the manor of Overcourt, which before ownership by the Trenchards (from 1617) had been owned by Henry Long, grandson of Henry Long of Whaddon. At the age of twenty-nine, now with a wife, seven children and another on the way,

Walter Long of Preshaw. Courtesy Ian MacAlpine Leny

he inherited estates in Somerset and Dorset on the death of his uncle William Long in 1818; these had come from Walter Long of Lincoln's Inn. On the death of his thirty-six-year-old cousin John Blackall in 1829 he inherited further estates in Oxfordshire, including the great manor house Haseley Court, now grade I listed.

Walter's cousins Charlotte and Harriet Grove were frequent visitors to Preshaw, Harriet recording in her diary the long walks they took with the then twenty-year-old Walter, not long before his marriage. He was apparently a talkative young fellow; on an excursion to Farringdon Harriet became quite tired by his 'nonsensical conversation'. His engagement was announced a few months later to Lady Mary Carnegie, eldest daughter of William Carnegie, 7th Earl of Northesk, and his wife Mary Ricketts. They were married in London in February 1810. A year later they celebrated the birth of a daughter, who died soon afterwards. In between another eleven children born during the course of the next fourteen years Lady Mary became an accomplished artist, a talent shared by many of her offspring.

Preshaw House, a large Elizabethan mansion now Grade II listed, was at that time surrounded by approximately 1,670 acres of parkland, woodland and arable fields, and served by a range of barns, stables and cottages. Early in his marriage Walter commissioned John Nash, architect to George IV, to make alterations to the house, the results of which met with the hearty approval of the Grove cousins.

Preshaw House c. 1870. Courtesy Peter Sonksen

Napoleon's abdication in 1814 inspired jubilant celebrations across Great Britain and Ireland, with general "illuminations" lighting up the towns and cities. The Allied Sovereigns whose armies had subdued Napoleon were invited to England by the Prince Regent, prompting Walter and his wife to make a spur of the moment decision to travel to London to witness the arrival of the Emperor of Russia, Czar Alexander. Mary's journal[394] gives a detailed account of their ten day stay in the city, which proved a little more exciting than they had expected. It began sedately enough, with a visit to see Hogarth's paintings at the British Gallery, which far exceeded Mary's expectations. She was much impressed by the balloon and car at the Pantheon, 'which together cost a thousand pounds'.

394   George Smith, *Cornhill Magazine*, vol. 159 pp. 776–792, 1939

Eager to get a good view of the visiting royals and after some difficulty finding a suitable vantage point, Mary found herself minus her husband, shut up in a little room with a window overlooking the street in the company of the Duchess of Sussex, Princess Augusta, Lady Dunmore, and Lady Clanricarde. To the puzzlement of the crowd, the Emperor of Russia and King of Prussia finally arrived incognito in a very shabby carriage. Mary noted the emperor's coachman 'was a curious looking man with a beard who sat on the box . . . I never saw anything like the number of carriages and people, every house in London was almost empty, numbers went without any dinner that their servants might see this famous sight.'

That evening at the opera the Princess of Wales arrived and 'evidently wished to attract notice, but without effect.' Driving into Piccadilly the next morning Mary caught sight of the Emperor on his way to visit the Regent. 'He was dressed in scarlet with very large epaulets. He is very fair and rather bald, his eyes are small but have a very arch expression: he looks remarkably healthy. We afterwards saw the Emperor and the Duchess of Oldenburgh going in state in a glass carriage drawn by cream-coloured horses and preceded by a party of the Queen's Bays. He bowed constantly as he passed. The Duchess is a pretty looking woman, very fair and rather thick lips.'

The next night Walter and Mary again attended the opera, 'in the hopes of seeing some of the great people'. They were not disappointed: 'the performance was several times interrupted from the general idea that the Emperor was coming. He was very much amused at some young ladies in the next box looking at him. He has a trick of always netting his fingers and stroking his whiskers which I do not much admire.'

Mary was disappointed with the art exhibition; it was 'a bad one: most of the rooms were darkened for the illuminations, so that we could not see the miniatures. From there we proceeded to the Panorama of Vittoria, which was so crowded it was almost impossible to see it: and I almost fought a battle with a woman there, who stuck her elbows into my sides till I was quite sore, and upon my remonstrating with her she threatened to call a gentleman to speak to me, upon which I told her she had better hold her tongue.'

On Saturday, after day of sightseeing the visitors set out after dinner for another evening at the opera, which began badly. There was a stampede the moment the doors were opened.

> We went in with the rush. Mr Long soon lost his hat, and my shawl was carried off, but we were fortunately not separated till I was driven up against an iron railing with one of my arms bent back and all the pressure of the people against me. I felt my breath almost gone several times and that unless I made a desperate effort I must have been killed. Mr Long… was so alarmed for me that he kept beseeching the people around me to save me.
>
> As soon as I could extricate my arm, which was with great difficulty, I got over the railing with the assistance of a gentleman behind me, and Mr Long had scrambled over the pay box and received me on the other side. I then got into the turn of the bannisters on the stairs which kept off the crowd, and then climbed, or rather was dragged, over them, then over a poor woman who was thrown down. I had all my clothes torn to pieces and a violent bruise on my arm. Mr Long had his hand cut open.
>
> The screams of the poor woman were dreadful… and I thought hardly anything short of a miracle could have saved my life…I was almost fainting with pain and fright. I got two or three good stares and no wonder, for I looked like I had just come out of Bedlam. There was a dreadful row; the people were clamorous for stage room and broke into some of the boxes, one of which was the Duchess of Richmond's. I expected to have been killed.

Despite Walter's lacerated hand and Mary bruised black and blue with her dress in tatters, they were still able to enjoy the performance.

Back home in Hampshire a few days later they awaited the arrival of the royal party at Portsmouth. They visited the residence of the Commissioner, Sir George Grey, to see the preparations for the Emperor. He 'slept in a very small bed, and the Duchess of Oldenburgh carries her bedding about with her and sleeps upon a sofa. When the servants arrived they disarranged everything, flew into dreadful passions, and began spitting about on the carpets. They put a dirty

Lady Mary Long (née Carnegie) of Preshaw, c.1850. Courtesy Julia Crane

Russian footman into Miss Grey's bed. The King's servants would not do anything, nor the Russians, therefore the Commissioner's servants were obliged to do all the work, and sit up all night.'

Later when the Regent arrived for the festivities he was applauded by the waiting crowd. He held a levee for the naval officers and Mary counted 84 who walked to Government House with the Duke of Clarence. 'Papa dined with the Regent.' The Duke of Wellington was given a hero's welcome and 'Mama was presented to [Czar] Alexander by the Duke of Clarence as the wife of the Admiral, and the niece of Lord St Vincent. The Regent was very ungracious to Lady Ponsonby.' And there was a skirmish at the dockyard after Walter and Lady Mary were refused admittance to the rope-walk, 'the Constable was then going to knock Mr Long down, which frightened me so much that I began to cry.' At the grand ball later that evening the Prince of Prussia asked her to dance, but his father intercepted before it began. The Emperor asked in English how she had hurt her arm. She answered in French that she had been running after him. Was it *un coup,* he asked?

Mary was just a young woman of twenty-five when she wrote of these events. Her father, Lord Northesk, a rear admiral of England and admiral of the red, took a prominent part in quelling the Nore mutiny in 1797, and was later third in command in the *Britannia* at the battle of Trafalgar. His friendship with the Prince Regent may explain why there is no mention in Mary's account of the crowds hissing at the prince during his public appearances, referred to with such emphasis by Lady Charlotte Bury and other diarists.

Walter briefly aspired to a career in Parliament, and in October 1832 put himself forward as a candidate for the Northern Division of Hampshire. According to the *Hampshire Telegraph* he was considered to be of 'Tory principles' and his talents and private character were unimpeachable. Personally canvassing in every direction, his friends believed he had every prospect of success. Their optimism was short-lived and he relinquished his candidacy, much to the incredulity of the press. By this time he was sitting on a very comfortable rent-roll, but unfortunately for Walter his brother-in-law Swyn Carnegie (later admiral) introduced him to a man by the name of Footall who persuaded him to invest heavily in what turned out to be a risky, if not dishonest, venture.

In the 1920s Walter's granddaughter Mary Jane[395] implied that Footall was a swindler. 'Unfortunately after a few years Grandpapa lost by bad speculation in cotton, I believe £100,000, and had to sell some of his land and Haseley included. It was when I was too young to remember.'[396]

Many years after the death of her parents, Walter and Lady Mary's younger daughter Georgiana recorded a few memories of her family life before her marriage to Richard Bowden Smith. 'I think Haseley must have been sold about this time [1845] as we did not go there again. I suppose Mr Muirhead must have bought it with furniture and everything, as I do not remember anything being brought from there.'

395   Daughter of George Long, banker of Portsmouth
396   Letter of Mary Jane Long to her cousin Mary Long *c.*1922, private collection

Haseley's new owner, James Patrick Muirhead, is best remembered as the biographer of his cousin, engineer and scientist James Watt senior, leading member of the Lunar Society and key figure of the Industrial Revolution. Muirhead went to live at Haseley in 1846, where most of his literary works on Watt were written.

Georgiana wrote of the extended periods spent at Haseley and London, where 'the terrible outbreak of the influenza took place in 1836 and 1837; we were all very ill and left London earlier than usual for Preshaw. Numbers of people died and some went mad, the doctors did not know any cure for it.' In the spring of 1838 the family were again in London:

> I think it was about this time that my Mother was much interested in Phrenology and Mr D(?) was all the fashion. People went to him to have their heads felt and he wrote down the character of each person. I saw a bust made of my mother, she was placed on the floor and a man plastered her face all over with plaster of Paris. She could not breathe and I was so frightened for fear she would be suffocated; then the man took a string and divided the plaster into 4 parts and took it off. The bust was afterwards at Preshaw in the passage for many years, and was found broken at the sale of house and effects in 1898.

Walter and Mary's second daughter Elizabeth Mary became the wife of John Etherington Welch Rolls of the Hendre, Monmouthshire, in 1833. The Rolls' first child arrived on the scene with his doting grandmother in attendance, but as Georgiana recalls, Lady Mary arrived home black and blue once again:

> In February 1837 my mother travelled to the Hendre by coach to be with my sister Mrs Rolls at the birth of her son John Allan Rolls. I diligently took care of my father in her absence. On her return the stagecoach she was in was upset near Marlborough, she was inside and the men had much trouble in pulling her out of the window and hurt her arms, but no one was severely hurt. The passengers had to take refuge in a cottage till the coach was again ready, which caused much delay. I remember sitting up with my father, he much frightened

wondering what was become of her. She arrived about 12 o'clock at night having posted I think from Salisbury.

Elizabeth and John Rolls' only son John Allan, created 1st Baron Llangattock in 1892, was the father of England's first recorded aircraft fatality, the Honourable Charles Stewart Rolls (d. 1910), who famously co-founded the motor company Rolls-Royce. Charles' two elder brothers John, the 2nd baron, and Henry – both in their mid-forties – died in 1916 within five months of each other. The barony became extinct. At his death the estate of the 2nd Baron Llangattock, who died as a result of wounds received at the battle of the Somme, was valued at more than £1.1 million, and his sister Eleanor Shelley-Rolls [397] was the main beneficiary.

In October 1837 Walter Long and his family were astonished to receive the news their second youngest daughter, fifteen-year-old Lucy, was engaged to be married to William Barnes, a twenty-year-old university friend of her brother William. The two young students had unknowingly engaged the same tutor to coach them during the holidays, and when Walter heard this he invited Mr Barnes to Preshaw to study, together with their tutor, with quite unintended results. The engagement was allowed, but the young lovers had strict instructions to wait at least three years before tying the knot. A few months short of the prescribed minimum time they were married in Haseley church in July 1840. They had seven children (two of whom would marry their first cousins), but the last one born in 1850 was a stillbirth, followed soon afterwards by the death of twenty-eight-year-old Lucy, much to her family's grief.

The year following Lucy and William's wedding was a worrying one for the Longs; they all thought Walter was dying, and friends and family arrived at Preshaw to say their last goodbyes. The Rolls' travelled from the Hendre, arriving late at night, and the younger son William Long junior and his family made the 75 mile dash from Bath. Dr Budd was summoned from London and after staying half an hour

397   Wife of Sir J.C.E. Shelley, 6th Baronet of Castle Goring, Sussex, a great-nephew of the author Mary Shelley

he presented what was considered a vastly excessive bill for £60. Over the course of a long and miserable winter Walter slowly recovered and by the summer of 1842 he had regained his health. In July Walter and his wife set off for London for the wedding of their youngest son John. It was the first time they had travelled anywhere by train and Lady Mary was so terrified she cried repeatedly, 'Let me out, Let me out!'

John and his wife Georgiana Frances[398] had a tragic beginning to their family life at Marwell Hall. His sister wrote that 'Mrs John Long had a fine little girl, but when it was 6 weeks old the nurse overlaid it, and it was dead in the morning.' They had called the child Georgiana Selina; two years later another daughter was born, and perhaps tempting fate they gave her the same name. This second girl died in Venice aged twelve.

At his death in January 1871 aged eighty-two, Walter devised Preshaw House and all his other estates to his eldest son, Walter Jervis Long, who lived at nearby Belmore House. Lady Mary survived him by four years, dying in March 1875.

Walter Jervis Long (1816–91)

His father had been master of the Hambledon Hounds for many years, a position which Walter Jervis Long filled on and off from 1841 to 1874. As a young boy he took a great interest in the activities surrounding the hunt, and one day when he was about nine years old, mounted on his little pony, he spotted a captain of dragoons among the field sporting a moustache of walrus proportions. As one observer remarked, he was 'by the orderly-book of his regiment, denied the Christian-like operation of shaving', prompting the curious young Walter to ride up to his father exclaiming: 'Papa, who is that gentleman with a wig under his nose?' He later grew his own under nose-wig.

His sister Georgiana recalled that he was 'a very tiny child', and with maternal links to a long line of illustrious seafarers (his godfather John Jervis, 1st Earl of Vincent (1735–1823) was an admiral and former first lord of the Admiralty), his parents were persuaded to send him to sea to promote his growth. In 1829 as a lad of thirteen, he set sail on

Walter Jervis Long. Courtesy Ian Macalpine-Leny

the *Undaunted*, and while anchored in the Azorean archipelago the boys were allowed a few hours' liberty ashore, where they came upon a type of turn-about, a receptacle designed to convey provisions into the nearby Spanish convent. This, of course, would have been irresistible to any adventurous boy, and Walter was hoisted into it and swiftly dispatched. The nuns were astonished to see a boy in their room, 'they petted him and gave him sweetmeats and some beautiful flowers made of birds' feathers; the difficulty was to turn him out again, as he was almost too big, it was easier to get in than out. His companions had run away back to the ship and he was told that they were very nearly going without him.'

Having survived his stint at sea Walter entered Oriel College, Oxford, as a gentleman commoner at the age of seventeen. The death of William IV six days before his twenty-first birthday celebrations presented a dilemma; would all the guests arrive in mourning? There were discussions back and forth, and fortunately for Walter and his parents all the guests agreed to leave off their mourning for that day, as they thought black would look too dismal. The festivities went on for three days, the fun enjoyed by the families of Sir Henry and Lady Tichborne, Sir Henry Rivers and many other friends and relations. There was dancing inside the house and outside on the lawn, and the general merriment was assisted in no small measure by the strong ale brewed at Preshaw twenty-one years before, to celebrate the joyous birth of the heir.

Two years later the neighbourhood was in festive mood once again, when Walter married Emily Jane, daughter of Edward Gregory Morant Gale of Upham. They spent their honeymoon at Haseley, and lived for the first eight years of their married life at Preshaw with the rest of the family, afterwards moving to The Holt, a 950 acre estate at Upham. Over the next fifteen years the couple had ten children, but barely a generation could slip by without at least one of their number espousing a cousin. One of Walter's younger sons, Reginald Gambier Long, carried on the tradition by marrying Agnes Flora, granddaughter of Walter Long of Rood Ashton. Reginald's sister Jessie Annie went one better, marrying her first cousin William Barnes, son of her Aunt Lucy.

Walter was a member of the Hampshire Yeomanry Cavalry for about four decades, before resigning his commission in 1873. He qualified as a JP in 1869, and after inheriting his father's estates in 1871 his landholdings in Hampshire and Somerset totalled 4,801 acres.[399] He was appointed deputy lieutenant of Hampshire in March 1891 but died in November, leaving his widow, six surviving children and numerous grandchildren.

The Tichborne Claimant

During the celebrated nineteenth-century legal case against Arthur Orton, an imposter who claimed to be the missing heir Sir Roger Tichborne, the Longs, long-standing friends and neighbours of the Tichbornes, were eager to give evidence in support of his claim. Sir Roger had been lost at sea in 1854 although his distraught mother always believed he would one day turn up alive. When Orton appeared

399   Bateman, *The Acre-Ocracy of England, op. cit.*

twelve years later she had no hesitation in believing he was her missing son, despite obvious dissimilarities in appearance.

Walter's second son, Jervis Morant Long, had been away in Queensland, Australia, since 1864, gaining experience in stock-keeping and sheep farming, and while he was in a shop in Sydney in August 1866 he overheard a conversation about the imminent arrival of Sir Roger Tichborne. After making enquiries he found Orton at the Metropolitan Hotel where he introduced himself, and the two had a detailed conversation about the Long family, Preshaw, Tichborne and the surrounding neighbourhood.

Orton had obviously done his homework, and must have had his fingers crossed behind his back when he told Jervis he remembered him as a boy on a Shetland pony wearing a scarlet jacket hunting with the Hambledon hounds. Amazed at this, and after meeting with him over several days, Jervis became convinced he was genuine. So taken in was he by the charade, he gave Orton £200 towards the expenses of his voyage back to England to claim the inheritance of the real Sir Roger Tichborne.

Following soon afterwards, Jervis returned to England for the enquiry, telling the court he remembered as a child the supposed death of Sir Roger Tichborne had been the subject of conversation at his father's and grandfather's table, and they too believed he would one day turn up alive. Lady Mary Long also fully identified the claimant as Roger, and the Marquis of Queensberry said he never doubted it. At the conclusion of the enquiry Jervis Long returned to farming in Queensland, but didn't live to hear the verdict. He was drowned in 20ft of water on his neighbour's farm in March 1870, while trying to swim to his own house during a devastating flood. He was twenty-seven.

Eventually Orton came undone and his criminal trial began in 1873. Finally, after 188 days of evidence he was convicted on two counts of perjury in February 1874 and sentenced to fourteen years' hard labour. The legal costs were enormous, reputedly £200,000. After his release in 1884 he attempted to arouse public interest by alternately confessing and claiming his innocence, but by then he was all but forgotten. He died in poverty in April 1898, and his coffin-plate defiantly bore the name Sir Roger Charles Doughty Tichborne.

The Last Man Standing... Almost

Yet another Walter, the eldest son of Walter Jervis Long and Emily Jane Gale, married Fanny Vansittart in 1866. He inherited his father's estates in 1891. Fanny 's younger sister Constance Mary also became Mrs Long some years later, when she married Lieutenant-Colonel Charles Wigram Long, MP for Evesham, a distant cousin descended from Edward Long of Jamaica. Walter and Fanny had eight daughters but only one surviving son, a situation that would ultimately result in the sale of the estates handed down for so many generations.

In 1883 John Bateman, a landowner himself, published *Great Landowners of Great Britain and Ireland* to try and dispel claims that land ownership was concentrated in the hands of a few. He lists acreages, details of their owners and the amount of income derived from their landholdings, which served only to prove that out of the entire population just 710 individuals owned a quarter of all the land in England and Wales. Bateman's intention had backfired. Walter's 4,798 acres in Hampshire and Somerset, with an annual income of £6,983 was less than a third of his cousin Walter Hume Long over at Rood Ashton, who owned 15,404 acres in four counties, producing £23,213 per annum.

Three years after death duties were introduced in 1894 Walter began the process of diminishing the family's landholdings when he sold Preshaw to Baron de Bush. His sister Agnes noted in her diary the price paid was £35,000. Further property was sold in 1911 and he died in 1919. The only son and last owner on whom the rest of the burden lay was yet another Walter, christened Walter Vansittart Long in 1868. In 1894 with his brother-in-law Captain Robert Eden Richardson as best man, he married Mary Lilian Pleydell-Bouverie-Campbell-Wyndham of Corhampton. These unwieldy appendages were due to several intermarriages in her family dating back to 1846.

After the death of Mary's mother in 1908 and her brother the following year, the manor of Corhampton passed to her. In consequence of this inheritance Walter changed his name by deed poll to Walter Vansittart Campbell-Wyndham-Long. They had no children, and after the death of Walter's father the sale of the remainder of the estates began in earnest. The first to be put up for auction in March 1921 was the Holt estate, former home of his grandfather Walter Jervis Long. The seventeenth-century mansion was in need of a few modern conveniences, such as electric lighting, and included three reception rooms, eleven bedrooms, acetylene gas lighting and central heating. Five months later the Muchelney estate and other property, amounting to nearly all the land in the parish, was sold to the tenants by auction in lots, realising nearly £52,000.

Over the next few years Mary also sold off some of her inherited property in Hampshire and Wiltshire, although at her death in May 1948 she was still possessed of considerable real and heritable estate both in England and Scotland. She devised these properties to a series of heirs, including John Henry Hildyard Robinson, Walter's nephew. The death duties payable absorbed approximately half the value of her gross estate. Walter's unsettled estate when he died in 1944 was valued at £25,910 gross.

William Long of Wrington FSA (1817–86)

William Long, second son of Walter Long and Lady Mary Carnegie, was a graduate of Balliol College, Oxford. He later became a churchwarden, JP for Somerset, a fellow of the Society of Antiquaries and director of Stuckey's Banking Company. He authored two books, *Abury Illustrated* (1858), and *Stonehenge and Its Barrows* (1876), and he was one of the literary editors of the writings of the Rev. Francis Kilvert, whose diary entries are mentioned in relation to the Longs of Draycot.

William settled at Bath after his marriage to Elizabeth Hare Jolliffe where they raised two sons, and a daughter Elizabeth Mary Diana, who married her first cousin, the Rev. George Edward Barnes. In 1850 William was councillor at Bath for the Lansdown Ward, and in 1851–2 served a term as mayor.[400] The good citizens of Bath gained much by his contributions to promoting the institutions of the city, such as a new library and museum, the Mineral Water Hospital and

---

400 An earlier cousin, son of Thomas Long and Margery Flower, also called William Long, had been mayor in 1715

William Long of Wrington. Courtesy Julia Crane

the restoration of the abbey church. The not-so-good citizens received just and courteous treatment when he discharged his duties as chief magistrate.

His diary of 1851–2 gives a deceptively one-sided snapshot of a year in his life. Beginning in November, the first thing he did after being elected mayor was put on the scarlet robes and chain to please his children. Each morning at 10.30am, Monday to Saturday, he left his home at 16 Lansdown Place East with its spectacular southerly views across the city and walked up to the Guildhall to meet his fellow magistrates, where a never-ending supply of petty criminals awaited their turn.

The once exclusive city of Bath now had a seamy side much like any other, and William doled out fines and imprisonment with hard labour to men, women and children alike, for such things as begging, forgery, fortune-telling, assaults on police, pickpocketing, prostitution, vagrancy, theft, the occasional stabbing and, in December 1851, the so-called Priston murder. A close watch was kept on beershops and suspected brothels, and he gave a 10*d* fine to a thirteen-year-old boy who had 'assaulted his mother and torn her hair', or fourteen days' hard labour for breaking one of her windows. In the case of 'a lad playing with halfpence on Sunday in Grove Street', William ordered him to find two sureties of £5 each for his good behaviour for a week.

It was all in a morning's work for thirty-four-year-old William, who spent the remainder of his working day as mayor attending seemingly endless committee meetings interspersed with occasional visits to the lunatic asylum and the gaol, afterwards recommending a prison van with divisions to segregate the prisoners, and segregated cells at the Guildhall when they arrived for trial. William and his family attended church twice every Sunday, and in this his mayoral year, most weekday evenings were filled with dinner parties and musical entertainment. Indeed, quiet evenings at home were the exception rather than the rule, and in the summer months William enjoyed regular games of cricket, despite on one occasion sustaining '2 severe blows on the shin & ankle'.

The other aspect of his life not reflected in his diary for that year has more to do with his literary and antiquarian interests. When William was elected mayor his old Oxford friend James Froude, controversial author and historian, had sent his congratulations through Mrs Long, the 'dear Lady Mayoress' for his courage in undertaking such a 'generally unwelcome office'. 'I am busy imagining your husband in his chain and robes, and yourself doing the agreeable to the ladies of the rosy burgesses. For the first of which entertainments pray let me be invited, as for some time we shall be floating in the neighbourhood of the Great Western'.

Froude occasionally stayed with the Longs, as did another of William's literary friends, notably William Makepeace Thackeray,[401] who in January 1857 arrived at Bath to give his celebrated lectures on *The Four Georges*, on the manners and morals of England during the reigns of the Hanoverian kings. Already rapturously received in America, the audience that crowded into the banqueting hall of the Guildhall was equally enthusiastic. In 1861 William spent some time

401   John Freeman, *Literature and Locality: The literary topography of Britain and Ireland*, 1963, p. 122

in Rome studying the archaeology of the catacombs with another friend, author and publisher John Henry Parker, first keeper of the Ashmolean Museum.

With his eldest son William junior (of Congresbury) recently married, in 1868 William and his family moved to Westhay, Wrington, where he set up his extensive library. This much impressed Parker, who said he could find works there not to be found in the Bodleian Library. The residents of Wrington also benefited from his generous community spirit, William contributing handsomely towards extensive repairs to the church. His health declined after the death of his wife in 1874, and he died at his London residence, Onslow Gardens, in 1886. Highly esteemed by his peers, a glowing obituary appeared in the journal of the Somerset Archaeological and Natural History Society, of which he was president in 1869. Likewise the *Bath Chronicle* described him 'as an English gentleman of the highest type, one who had a cultivated mind and a generous disposition'. He left a personal estate worth over £51,000.

Major William Edward Long (1863–1961)

With eight sisters, William's grandson, the only son of Colonel William Long of Congresbury and his wife Anna Mary Hunter, William Edward Long was the one hope for the continuation of the male line in this branch. Educated at Eton, he later saw service as an officer of the Somerset Light Infantry and 4th Hussars in France and Palestine. His father, who died in 1926, had distinguished himself as commander of the 4th Battalion of the Somerset Militia, and as a freemason, becoming provincial grand master for Somerset. The establishment of a new lodge at Bath was first considered in November 1919 when the name proposed in honour of his father was the William Long Lodge, but the masonic powers-that-be would not sanction a new lodge named after a living person, and it was therefore agreed to name the lodge St Alphege.

William, the son, was a career soldier, wounded during the Boer War in 1901, and he acted as assistant commissioner of police in Cyprus. While with the Remount Service attached to the Desert Mounted Corps in Egypt in August 1918, he received devastating news about his wife.

He had married Violet Beatrix Alice Lambton Way, daughter of Colonel Wilfred FitzAlan Way, in 1901 in London, and they had two young daughters. Together with her sister, Mrs Florence Burleigh Leach, Violet had started the work of the Women's Corps early in the war, rising up the ranks of the WAAC, later known as Queen Mary's Auxiliary Army Corps. Florence was eventually appointed controller-in-chief, with Violet one of the three chief controllers. On 3 August 1918 she was returning from France on the hospital ship *Warilda* to report to her sister on the progress being made by the WAACs detailed for service with the American Army overseas.

Leaving the port of Le Havre, the *Warilda* was escorted by two destroyers. On board were about 660 wounded soldiers, a medical staff of 60, 115 crew and a detachment of eleven women of the WAAC. This was the vessel's 180th trip ferrying war casualties between France and Britain, a relatively short but dangerous journey. The Germans did not grant immunity to any enemy ships, including those carrying wounded; six months earlier the *Warilda* had been struck by a torpedo which had failed to explode.

A few hours into the Channel crossing Violet retired to her bunk at midnight after giving chocolates to her colleague Charlotte Trowell, and enquiring if she was 'comfy'. Just after 1.30am a German U-boat fired a torpedo into the *Warilda*, striking the starboard side and exploding in the engine room, instantly killing seven crew. A further 102 casualties located in a ward just above were also killed.

The movement of the ship had prevented the lifeboats being lowered during the first hour after the attack, but finally a frantic attempt was made when it became obvious the ship was going to sink. After ensuring the safe evacuation of all the WAACs in her charge, Violet was the last woman to leave the stricken vessel. She climbed into one of the lifeboats, but as it was lowered it became lopsided. A davit rope was cut causing the lifeboat to capsize, spilling everyone in it, including Violet and Charlotte Trowell, into the water. Amid the chaos she managed to cling to another lifeboat containing Charlotte, who grabbed her by the hair. Her feet became entangled in a mess of rope, preventing her from being pulled out of the water despite the strenuous efforts of others to get her into the boat. Suddenly she collapsed and sank from sight, one of 123 lives tragically lost that night.

Much loved and respected for her selfless volunteer work, there was a great outpouring of grief for Violet, described as 'a splendid specimen of womanhood' by the vicar of her local church in Chiswick, where her name is listed on the war memorial. For her work with the Women's Legion she was posthumously awarded the OBE in the New Year's Honours List of 1918.

Major William Long never remarried, but after the war spent a good deal of his life at sea. He found with the rate of exchange it was cheaper to travel from the Continent to Japan and back than rent a villa on the Riviera: just 11,000 francs. He informed his companions of this one night during a conversation in the smoking room of a French club, evoking a chorus of astonishment and incredulity. He hit on the idea that he could live in retirement congenially and more cheaply aboard ship than in his family home by becoming a permanent cruise ship passenger, and in 1935, after completion of a voyage to Australia, he decided to spend the rest of his life on an ocean liner. To try out his idea he booked round voyages for a year in the P&O ship *Barrabool*.

This new lifestyle made him something of a minor curiosity in the press, and when he was interviewed by the *Daily Mirror* at the end of his first voyage he was 'thoroughly satisfied with his decision'. Anyone could do it, he said, on £400 a year. After its last voyage from Australia the *Barrabool* was sent to be broken up for scrap and the major was forced to find an alternative. Still hot on his trail, the *Daily Mirror* caught up with the 'tanned and very fit' sixty-three-year-old at the docks, having moved 'just next door' to his new floating home, the *Mongolia*. He intended travelling to and from Australia 'as long as they'll have me.'[402] He died in 1961 at Malaga, Spain, aged eighty-eight.

Eventually the male line of Long of Preshaw petered out, culminating in childless marriages or daughters. With what remained of their wealth greatly affected by death duties, the taxman did quite well out of the estate of Mary Doreen Jane Long, a great granddaughter

402   *Daily Mirror*, 8 August 1936, p. 4

of Walter and Lady Mary Long,[403] who had no children with her husband Commander Alexander Gibson Fleming RN. At her death in December 1962 Mrs Fleming bequeathed her entire estate, valued at £322,043, to her childhood friend Ruby Matthew, then aged sixty-eight.[404]

Long of Arundel, Sussex

Walter and Lady Mary Long's third son John lived at his uncle William 's old home Marwell Hall in the early years of his marriage. By 1861 he had moved his family to The Firs, at Arundel, Sussex, where they enjoyed a close friendship with Lady Victoria Tylney Long Wellesley, the last surviving member of the Longs of Draycot. Seventy-two-year-old John married again after his first wife's death in 1890, to Blanche Kavanagh, a woman thirty years his junior and a survivor of the Siege of Lucknow. He died two years later passing his property to his eldest son, John Stuart Lindsay Long.

His second son Colonel Charles James Long was a career soldier who received what some believed was unjustified criticism after his actions during the 1899 battle of Colenso, which ended in the defeat of the British. Writing *The Great Boer War* a year later, Arthur Conan Doyle had only praise for the man. 'Long has the record of being a most zealous and dashing officer', he wrote. With two field batteries under his command he opened fire on the Boer position at Fort Wylie, but their rifle fire proved too effective against his artillery. 'Poor Long was down, with a bullet through his arm and another through his liver. "Abandon be damned! We don't abandon guns!" was his last cry as they dragged him into the shelter'.

A year earlier in the South African campaign he had commanded the artillery at Omdurman, achieving acclaim for taking his guns to the front and successfully bombarding the Mahdi's dervishes. But then, in what was considered a lack of judgment, he sent the armoured train forward from Chieveley unsupported into Boer-occupied territory, causing the loss and derailment of part of the train by the

---

403   Daughter of George Long, banker of Portsmouth
404   *The Times*, 30 April 1963

Boers, and the capture of a party of Durham Light Infantry and the correspondent Winston Churchill. In 1908, having survived his war injuries and widespread criticism Charles married a young widow and died without issue in 1933.

Charles's brother John junior was a naval officer who retired with the rank of commander in 1879. His marriage to his cousin the following year created yet another complicated, but by now familiar, network of family ties. His new wife was Letitia Blanche Penruddocke, granddaughter of Walter Long of Rood Ashton (d.1867), and sister of Charles junior, the hapless husband in the 'Penruddocke Case'. John and Letitia's two sons were given the middle name of Tylney in honour of Lady Victoria, whose advisor and confidante he became. As an executor and one of the main beneficiaries of her will he inherited her house Bolney Lodge in 1897, along with two family portraits rescued from Draycot House.[405] A decade later he also died, followed soon afterwards by his youngest son.

Nineteen-year-old Robert Penruddocke Tylney Long, an undergraduate of Trinity College in his first year of residence, was found shot in his rooms shortly after one o'clock in the afternoon with a bullet wound to the forehead. Still in his right hand was a revolver with one discharged chamber. A troubled young man with an unfortunate sense of irony, Robert was found with Shakespeare's *Hamlet* lying open by his side. Marked on the page was the first line of the haunting soliloquy 'To be or not to be, that is the question.'

The male line of this branch ended with the death of John's eldest son John Victor Tylney Long in 1951.

---

405   These portraits were given to the National Portrait Gallery in 1968 by John's daughter Dorothy.

XIV
Long of Baynton

John, brother of Richard Long of Collingbourne, purchased the estate of Baynton in 1673 from John Danvers and died without issue three years later at Little Cheverell. He left Baynton to his ten-year-old nephew William, who had little opportunity to benefit from his inheritance; he died aged twenty in 1683 while studying law at Inner Temple. Over the next one hundred years Baynton descended through the male line to another William in 1782, the last surviving son.

The Last William Long of Baynton (1734–1807)

Thirteen years after William's inheritance the manor house was destroyed by fire, believed to have begun in the laundry, 'by putting cloaths to dry too near the fire'. Fortunately the family was awakened by farmer Pepler's servant on his way to Warminster market; otherwise they would all have been burnt in their beds. The next year, in 1796, William purchased an estate at East Coulston from William Evelyn, which included a manor house formerly belonging to the Godolphin family.

With an unexpected extra 100 guineas to spend, left to him by his immensely wealthy cousin Sir James Tylney Long, 7th Bt., William made further alterations and renamed it Baynton House, after the old one. Serving as county justice and captain of the Devizes Yeomanry Cavalry kept him busy for the most part, but with neither brothers nor nephews, he lacked an immediate heir. At Bath in 1792, almost at the eleventh hour, he married the illegitimate daughter of Thomas Estcourt Cresswell of Pinkney Park, thirty-seven-year-old Mary Jenkins.

Cresswell of Pinkney Park, Wiltshire

Mary's father Thomas Estcourt Cresswell, MP for Wootton Bassett, was descended from a line of six consecutive Richard

Cresswells, some of whom gained considerable notoriety for their unsociable behaviour. His father, MP for Bridgenorth, nicknamed 'Black Dick Cresswell', was described as 'a perfect madman, a Judas and devil incarnate' by his son-in-law, who, when obliged to stay with the family for a time at Sidbury, wrote that 'to live with him is to live in Bedlam, for he is made up of noise, nonsense, railing, bawling and impertinence . . .' Having apparently inherited his unstable traits, Black Dick was disinherited by his father, himself a 'roaring Shropshire squire'. His already questionable reputation was sullied further by his arrest in 1716 on thirty-eight separate charges of sodomy 'with a young Genoese boy he had lately dressed up'. From 1726 to 1730 he was known to be in France, travelling with 'one Mrs Smith, called his niece'. In 1730, owing to financial problems, he was forced to mortgage his Pinkney Park estate for £10,000.

Madness seemed to run in the family. Thomas E. Cresswell's grandson Richard Estcourt Cresswell was declared a lunatic while locked up in an asylum in France in 1837. It was said that 'he fancied himself a King, and continually declared that Lord Hungerford, who had conspired against the lives of himself and his family, had shot him in the forehead with a bullet; he had warned his wife that her life would be attempted'. In 1844 Richard's brother, the Rev. Henry Cresswell, was suspended for bankruptcy and violent behaviour, rather unbecoming for a man of the cloth. Proceedings were brought against him by the bishop of Salisbury, charging him with quarrelling and fighting, habitually swearing, frequenting public houses and habitually drinking to excess.

No stranger to controversy himself, Mary's father Thomas Estcourt Cresswell created a scandal by marrying Ann Warneford in 1744, the wealthy heiress of Sir Edmund Warneford of Bibury, Gloucestershire. Another wife came forward, Elizabeth Scrope, who successfully sued on the grounds of bigamy, claiming a prior Fleet marriage. The Cresswell-Warneford marriage was declared null and void and the children were bastardised. However, a third marriage was revealed through a search of the Fleet records that antedated the others;

thus Cresswell's last two marriages were bigamous.[406] In addition to these scandals he had at least four children with Catharine Jenkins of Sherston Magna, between 1749 and 1755. He made substantial bequests to these illegitimate children, Elizabeth, Mary and William Jenkins, on a par with his son Estcourt Cresswell from his marriage to Ann Warneford.

Keeping it in the Family

William and Mary Long, *née* Jenkins had an only child, Emma, who died in 1796 aged eighteen months. Her memorial in Edington church mourns the 'Sweet Innocent, of fondest hope, thus early taken', and her bereaved mother kept a lock of the dead baby's hair in a diamond locket. When William died in 1807 he left an annuity of £50 to his widowed sister Elizabeth Peplar,[407] and the rest of his estate he left to his 'dear wife Mary' who promised her husband to restore Baynton to the Long family. But her death in 1822 set off such a force of divisive resentment among her relatives over the substantial spoils she would've been pleased to have missed it.

In 1773 Mary's sister Elizabeth Jenkins had married Dr Timothy Dewell[408] of Burton Hill House, Malmesbury, descended matrilineally from John Long of Marston (d. 1597). Mary appointed Elizabeth's son Thomas Dewell and her favourite great-niece Jane Dewell executors of her estate. By this time Jane's already eight year engagement to the Rev. Walter Long still had six years to run – and both had expectations. With Walter's brother John junior newly-married to her niece Mary Daniel, such close family entanglements made Mrs Long's decision a controversial one. Anticipating trouble, she began her will by reminding the family she had it in her power to have 'spent all my possessions and what I have left to dispose of I esteem out of kindness.' Jane's father the Rev. Charles Dewell showed 'the most decided antipathy to John, because the property is come to

406   Lawrence Stone, *The Road to Divorce: England, 1530–1987*
407   Elizabeth Long married firstly John Hicks in 1762 at Edington, and secondly Daniel Peplar of Coulston (d. 1801)
408   Dewell's father Timothy senior married as his first wife Elizabeth Knight, granddaughter of Henry Long of Whaddon (d. 1612)

him and not to Walter, as he (Mr C.D.) expected'.

Still shell-shocked, the cousins went into battle, disagreeing over Mary's extensive collection of jewellery which included two diamond necklace and bracelet sets, one she had purchased after writing her will. According to John Long senior, 'independent of these diamonds, Mrs Long left behind her three sets of Pearls – one set of Amethysts – one set of Turquoise – one set of Carnelian and more finery of the same Sort enough to make one sick'. He was very critical of Mary's executors, Thomas and Jane Dewell. Thomas was left Mary's townhouse at Bath, and 'Miss D. Claims to divide the Trinkets herself and Consequently she divides for herself. You would have smiled if you had been present when the furniture etc was under valuation; in fact the executors claimed everything . . . right down to a few broken garden pots.'

Charles Dewell was next in line for the jewels after his daughter Jane's death, which would be soon; she had been ill for years and not expected to survive. John senior knew even her own family believed that afterwards 'the Diamonds given to her will be sold [by her father] and turned into money; such is his fondness for that article.'

Part of the estate consisted of allotments in Steeple Ashton Common, claimed by the Dewells – much to the annoyance of John junior, who commenced legal proceedings to have them returned to him, citing Mary's promise to her late husband to restore the *whole* estate to the Longs. Just before her death efforts were made by the family for clarification, John senior writing that 'Mrs Long was wholly incapable of giving any directions about her property, not only being confined to her bed but her head in a state of great confusion.' He believed Mary had only pretended to entail the estate.[409]

Eighteen months later in 'wretched health', Jane Dewell wrote her will, bequeathing all her money and property, with a few small exceptions, to her father Charles. She directed that all the diamonds from her aunt Mary be sold, apart from the diamond locket containing baby Emma's hair. This was to go to her 'Grand Mamma' Elizabeth Dewell. As had been expected, Charles was to receive the money,

409   WSA ref 947:1694

minus a few cash legacies to be distributed to friends and family. Jane appointed her father sole executor and residuary legatee, but he did not live long enough to carry out this duty nor receive any bequests, his own death occurring a few months after his daughter's, in 1826.

Perhaps relieved to be released from his fourteen year terminal engagement, three years later the Rev. Walter Long married Sarah Anne Gunning of Bath, daughter of the Rev. Peter Gunning, rector of Newton St Loe and sometime chaplain to the Duke of Kent. A few years after Walter's brother John junior lost the proceeds from the sale of Baynton in bad investments, Baynton House was mentioned briefly in relation to the highly publicised 'Road Murder' and the Saville Kent family who leased it in 1852. Their daughter Constance, who confessed to murdering her four-year-old half-brother in 1860, was occasionally sent up to the empty garrets as punishment, defiantly climbing in and out of the windows and sliding down the roof.[410] The Saville Kents left Baynton in 1855 owing to the isolation and expensive upkeep.

John Long's daughter Emma kept alive the fond memories of her childhood there by naming her new home Baynton House, built by her husband Alexander Bassett at Llandaff, near Cardiff after their marriage in 1855. The house was purchased in 1951 by the BBC as a site for their new broadcasting headquarters in Wales, and later demolished. Emma's family's link to her old home in Wiltshire was represented in a collection of Roman coins in the possession of her son Herbert Bassett. Known as the Baynton Hoard, it was dug up in a broken pot in 1830 in the grounds of his grandfather's Wiltshire estate.[411] Many coins were from the reign of Constantinus II (317–37 AD), the majority in mint condition, but by 1907 much of the hoard had already been dispersed. Bassett still had 365 coins from the original hoard, many of which are now kept in the Wiltshire Heritage Museum, Devizes.

410   Mary S. Hartman, *Victorian Murderesses*, 1995, p. 108
411   WAM, vol. IX, p. 27

XV
Long of Longville, Jamaica; Hurts Hall and Hampton Lodge

After the end of the sixteenth century the name of Long became associated with many other towns and villages in Wiltshire, Somerset and Hampshire. One member of the family who ventured further was Samuel Long, grandson of John Long of Netheravon, who accompanied the original Cromwellian expedition that conquered Jamaica in 1655. This led to a new era of wealth creation for this branch of the Longs, making their fortunes from sugar plantations and slavery.

A descendant, Robert Mowbray Howard, son of Henry Howard-Molyneux-Howard and Charlotte Caroline Georgiana Long, published *Records and Letters of the Family of the Longs of Longville, Jamaica, and Hampton Lodge, Surrey* in 1925. This included a narrative by the historian of Jamaica Edward Long, which provides considerable detail about this branch of the family from which some of the information in this chapter is drawn.

John Long of Netheravon (c.1570–1630)

John Long apparently had not learned to write, and as overseer of the will of William Smythe of Figheldean in 1620 he signed his name with his mark. The established thought is that John is descended from the Longs of Semington, about 20 miles from Netheravon, and certainly the notes now held at the Heralds' College in London written by genealogist and antiquary Charles Edward Long while preparing the printed pedigrees indicate that he thought John Long was most likely the son of Thomas Long the Elder of Semington.

This, however, would appear not to be the case, according to the will of Thomas's daughter Jane, widow of Richard Dicke, a

wealthy clothier from Turleigh, Wiltshire.[412] Bearing in mind John of
Netheravon is known to have died in 1630, Jane Dicke made her will
on 21 May 1646 leaving £5 to her brother John Long, and appointed
him overseer together with her son George Dicke. Jane's brother John
was a clothier of Trowbridge in 1599,[413] and John Long of Netheravon
is described in surviving documents as a yeoman, a class whose lack of
wealth, rank and social status divided them from the great landowning
gentry. This is not to say that John was unrelated; sons of gentry
families were often described as yeomen, and Thomas Fuller (1608-
1661) wrote that 'the good yeoman was 'a Gentleman in Ore, whom
the next age may see refined.'

John's estate was administered by his son John junior, and
his residuary account mentions £19 owed to Thomas Long of Little
Cheverell and £24 to Mrs Amy Long of Rood Ashton, widow of
Gifford Long, which certainly implies some close family relationship.

However the question of John's parentage remains. A more
likely candidate is Thomas Long the Elder's younger brother, also called
Thomas, a farmer of Semington whose son John was his father's executor
in 1591, and a first cousin of Gifford Long. John married Catherine,
daughter of Thomas Bushell, owner of the manor of Netheravon.

Samuel Long (1638–83)

J ohn's grandson Samuel, son of Timothy Long, grocer, and his wife
Jane Brunsell, bore the arms granted in 1589 to Gifford Long's
father, Edward of Monkton. He was baptised at the small Wiltshire
village of Wroughton by his maternal grandfather Oliver Brunsell,
the vicar there, and according to his great-grandson, Edward Samuel
was probably named after his uncle, Dr Samuel Brunsell, sometime
rector of Bingham in Norfolk. At the age of sixteen he was attached
as lieutenant to the regiment of Colonel Edward Doyley when he set
out on the expedition that seized Jamaica from Spain, during which he
proved himself to be a young man of exceptional ability.

---

412   The IPM of Richard Dicke mentions the Bear Inn, Reading, formerly in
the ownership of his father-in-law, Thomas Long the Elder of Semington
413   WSA ref 947:1671/2

At the end of the war he received considerable land grants in Jamaica, and he was the first settler of the estate originally called Seven Plantations, later renamed Longville, in the parish of Clarendon. Samuel became one of the largest landowners and sugar planters of his era, and together with the other wealthy residents he committed himself to the process of anglicising the environs of Jamaica as much as the climate would permit. His plantation houses were substantial, but his residence in the capital at Spanish Town was particularly magnificent.

He would come to dominate politics in the island, starting out as secretary of the commissioners, being elected as a member for Port Royal and he was later chosen speaker in four successive assemblies from 1672 to 1675. He was sworn a member of the Council and in 1674 at the age of thirty-six was appointed chief justice. His political views often created controversy, but 'he asked nor desired nothing but his rights and privileges as an Englishman',[414] which included the same privileges in Jamaica as enjoyed by the House of Commons in Britain.

After his involvement in the passage of an unpopular Revenue Act in 1664, Samuel was charged with treason together with his ally and fellow planter William Beeston, but owing to the popularity of his political stance the charges against him were dropped. In 1678 he was suspended from the Council and dismissed as chief justice for his opposition to what he saw as backward law reform, undoing all he had achieved. He was arrested with Beeston and sent as a state prisoner to England in 1680, but gained his acquittal and successfully pressed for a permanent Revenue Act, eventually returning to Jamaica.

Samuel had six children with his wife Elizabeth Streete, four of whom died in the four months between May and September 1677, aged between seven months and ten years. The tragic loss of these children was possibly caused by yellow fever. The West African slave population was at least partially immune to the disease but it was the principal killer of Europeans. His own life was also relatively short; he died in Jamaica in June 1683 aged forty-four, by then owner of seven plantations consisting of 11,183 acres in six parishes, and 288

414   CSP col., 10, no. 1512

slaves. He was buried in the parish of St Katherine's. Not including his landed estates and houses, he also left £12,000, and to his elderly father Timothy in Wiltshire he left an annuity of £50. Among the legacies to his wife he gave livestock and 'ten negroes', and to his daughter 'also two negroe Girls and twenty Cowes such as she shall chuse at her age of twelve years . . .' His only surviving son Charles inherited the rest of his estate. After Samuel's death his widow Elizabeth married the Rev. John Towers, and she died in 1710.

Samuel's younger brother Timothy was a graduate of Queen's College, Oxford, later rector of St Alphege's, London. During the Great Plague of 1665 many of his counterparts left their posts and fled for safety into the country, their pulpits being seized by opportunistic Presbyterian ministers. He was one of the exceptions, who at the risk and cost of his own life continued to hold services and care for the sick and dying in his parish. The parish register records his death from the plague aged twenty-nine in September 1665.

His father Timothy senior died in 1691 with no sons surviving him and he bequeathed most of his estate to the sons of his sister Sarah, who married Anthony Silverthorne.

Colonel Charles Long of Hurts Hall (1679–1723)

Samuel's son Charles, born in Jamaica in 1679, was just four years old at his father's death. His portrait, reproduced in R.M. Howard's book, bears such a resemblance to Sir James Long of Draycot, had there not been sixty years separating them they could be mistaken for brothers. Both are adorned by flamboyant long dark periwigs of the kind made popular by Charles II. At the age of twenty Charles married Amy, daughter of Sir Nicholas Lawes, governor of Jamaica, but she died a year after the birth of their second child in 1701.

Soon after his second marriage in 1703 to Jane, widow of Sir James Modyford, daughter and heir of his father's old ally, Sir William Beeston, he found himself embroiled in a lawsuit with his new mother-in-law. Lady Beeston had taken advantage of her frail and feebleminded husband on his deathbed and guided his hand to sign a will she had drawn up, leaving his whole estate for her own use and to their daughter Jane in remainder, thereby excluding Jane from any

benefit during her mother's lifetime. It transpired that the witnesses to
the will were menial servants who were conveniently in another room
at the moment it was signed.

Charles was determined to try the validity of the will on behalf
of his wife (who had already inherited her first husband's estate), and
in 1706 he instituted an action of ejectment on the Statute of Frauds.
This was tried before a special jury in the Supreme Court of Jamaica.
Charles won the case and took possession of all of Sir William Beeston's
estates in right of his wife, leaving Lady Beeston the option of pursuing
her share in a further suit. The incensed mother-in-law launched a
counter-attack and attempted to have the ruling overturned by writ of
error, but the original verdict was confirmed by the court.

The lady persevered and took her case to the Lords of Council
in England, having in the meantime married Sir Charles Orby, with
whose willing assistance she procured a reversal of all the proceedings
in the courts in Jamaica. Peter Heywood, at that time chief justice of
Jamaica, wrote to Charles Long: 'The order of Her Majesty's Council
confounded all the lawyers at the Bar so that they to this very time
know not what to do, nor in what words to enter up the judgement.'

Heywood disagreed with the English judges who said 'the
laws of England are not in force in Jamaica', and despaired of future
law enforcement in the island. Charles prepared to take the case to
the House of Lords, but Orby's lawyers persuaded him to accept a
compromise and the income from the estates was split 50-50 between
each party. After the death of the former Lady Beeston, Charles and
his wife Jane came into possession of the whole valuable estate.

As a consequence, Charles Long's income was by far the largest
of any Jamaican proprietor of that period, and he removed his family
to England where they lived comfortably off the profits. He purchased
the lease on a house in London at Queens Square, Bloomsbury, and
a country estate in Saxmundham, Suffolk, with the manor house
Hurts Hall. When Charles left Jamaica he had put his estates of Seven
Plantations and Lucky Valley (4 miles apart) under the management
of a certain Mr Hunt.

Little did Charles know that while he was living the privileged
gentleman's life in England his Jamaican estates were fast going to rack

and ruin. Hunt had so neglected them that they were in a terrible state when Peter Heywood and others went to inspect the properties in 1707 after receiving several complaints, and Heywood wrote a lengthy and detailed report to Charles.

He began with the bad news at Seven Plantations, leaving little to the imagination: 'The whole works a Pott of nastiness and in general out of repair.' The mill house was 'half a legg deep in dung', the roof leaked in several places, the boiling house was filthy with molasses everywhere, 'the cureing hous as nasty as the boyling hous, great waste of sugar', and the steward room was in complete disorder with things 'thrown hogledy pogledy together'. Although Heywood was unable to look over the entire plantation in one day, what he did see were 45 acres newly planted with corn 'soe horrably overran with weeds' that it would need to be cleared and completely replanted. This corn should have provided food the following year for the 'poor slaves, the mules and the stock'.

Overjoyed to see the visitors, the slaves were hopeful at last of deliverance from Hunt's neglect, complaining they had not had a grain of salt since Charles left, and their fowls and hogs had been taken from them. Heywood did his best by 'giving them such Liberties as we thaught reasonable'. The next day he took his party to Lucky Valley, where the conditions were just as bad: overgrown fields, decaying buildings, a cellar overrun with ants, coppers 'horrably burnt'. 'The negroes are the most ordinary gang that ever I see and ye Doct^r that you imployed, a sad sottish ignorant fellow . . .' whom Heywood immediately dismissed.

On his return to Seven Plantations Heywood confronted Hunt, 'wch he was horrably startled at', remonstrating 'that he had acted in your imployment like a very ill man, that he had in great measure ruined your estates, abused your servants and slaves, and affronted your beloved Sister Mad^m Lowe in a very high degree'. Heywood followed this by immediately terminating his employment too.

Hunt, 'a rogue to you in ye highest degre', was so taken aback 'that he knew not what to say for himself but that he resolved neiver to serve any other Gentleman for as long as he liv'd; he noe more thought of being dismist than I doe of being Governor of Jamaica'. Heywood later found more 'roguerys' committed by Hunt; 'in short, everywhere

he has bin consern'd, you have bin horrably abus'd'. About a year later
he was able to make a favourable report on the new management,
under which many repairs and improvements had been made.

With his affairs in Jamaica under the watchful eye of his friend,
Charles was able to concentrate on business at home. In 1716, while
his slaves toiled under the hot Jamaican sun, a particularly harsh
English winter caused the Thames to completely freeze over for about
two months, allowing the inhabitants to enjoy a frost fair on the ice.
Charles was elected MP for the Suffolk borough of Dunwich that year,
by which time he was thirty-seven years old and had eight children,
later growing to a brood of ten.

Hurts Hall, Saxmundham

A life of relative luxury and ample fortune now seemed assured,
but Charles was about to make another very grave error of judgement.
After his purchase at Saxmundham he made the acquaintance of
William Wood, a speculator who would later be granted a patent for
coining £108,000 worth of farthings and halfpennies to relieve the
distress and inconvenience caused by the shortage of copper money in
Ireland, last issued in 1696. Jonathan Swift cynically called him 'Wood
the Hardware Man', and Edward Long laments the fact his grandfather

was not also acquainted with Swift, who might have 'rescued him in time from the grasp of this ominous Projector'.

In July 1720 Charles, together with his nephews Samuel Lowe and Samuel Long and five other 'particular and select friends', obtained a patent from George I to establish themselves as a company of adventurers to mine silver and gold in Jamaica for thirty-one years, on condition they pay a fifth of the value of all discoveries to the Crown. They divided the patent into 2,000 equal shares which they assigned in trust to William Wood to sell for £75 per share, with the intention of raising £150,000.

The subscription was taken up rapidly, many investors from the top end of town. A large house in London was rented as offices for the new Royal Mines Company with Wood as manager, and Charles acted as treasurer, safely investing the funds in the Bank of England. Miners and tools were dispatched to Jamaica, supervision was arranged, and for a while everything progressed smoothly.

Charles and the South Sea Bubble

It was an unfortunate coincidence that right at that moment the House of Lords passed the South Sea Bill, which allowed the South Sea Company to hold a monopoly of trade with South America in return for a loan of £7 million to finance the war against France. The company, originally founded in 1711, primarily traded slaves, cotton and agricultural goods, and on the passing of the Bill it underwrote the £30 million English national debt on a promise of five per cent interest from the government.

Suddenly everyone in England was gripped by a mad frenzy; speculation on South Sea shares ran wild, the expectations of greedy investors whipped up by artful management. Overtaken by the 'avarice and credulity of the multitude' the share price escalated from £125 in January 1720 to £550 by the end of May, and all sorts of other companies that hoped to cash in on the hysteria, from the fraudulent to the optimistic, were launched, forcing the government to pass an Act of Parliament commonly known as the Bubble Act.

Designed to curb opportunistic new companies, the Act provided a boost to the South Sea Company, whose shares had leapt to £890 by early June. Charles Long was implicitly guided by Wood's desire to jump on the speculation bandwagon as it careered crazily out of control, expecting to increase the capital of the mining fund from five to 600 per cent. But no sooner had he withdrawn most of the subscription fund from the bank and bought the shares, the bubble burst. The stocks crashed and the South Sea Company declared bankruptcy, causing financial ruin for people all over the country, including heavy losses for members of the royal family. Such a catastrophic loss of money and property had been hitherto unimaginable, and suicides became a daily occurrence.

The subscribers to Charles's mining fund had not been consulted before their money was removed from the security of the Bank of England, and despite Wood's 'romantic, visionary and impracticable' ideas Charles knew their losses must be made good out of his own personal fortune. 'Grief, shame and despair all at once rushed to his mind', wrote his grandson Edward. According to many receipts later found among his papers, Charles repaid the shareholders as much as he could out of his own pocket, but the inevitable labyrinth of lawsuits that followed took a toll on his mental and physical health.

Under the accumulated weight of this financial disaster, which had almost annihilated his wealth, he died insolvent on 8 May 1723, just one week short of his forty-fourth birthday. Eight of his ten children outlived him, and to Samuel, his son from his first marriage, he left the wreckage of his estates in strict entail, which included the estate at Saxmundham, the house in London and 14,000 acres of plantations in Jamaica.

His daughter Susanna had an exceptionally long and uneventful life, commemorated with a portrait when she was 102, and she died unmarried in 1820 aged almost 103.

Samuel Long of Tredudwell (1700–57)

It was left to Charles's twenty-three-year-old son Samuel to try and sort out the chaos of his father's affairs, hindered by the inherited estates being heavily encumbered with debts and legacies, and a large annuity to his mother. The first hearing of the Shareholders v. the Patentees and William Wood began in the Court of Exchequer in

December 1727, but there were endless delays, during which time – with the exception of Samuel – all the patentees died.

Finally in December 1745, a full eighteen years later, the court dismissed Samuel from the cause as he was less than twenty-one years of age when his name was inserted in the patent. Nevertheless he was still held responsible as a representative of his father, being instructed to repay the shareholders his portion of £75 per share with interest at four per cent, backdated twenty-five years to November 1720.

There were several appeals by Samuel and the representatives of the other patentees, during which the shareholders contended that 'The Projectors for several months amused the Subscribers with pretences they were actually working the said mines, which soon afterwards came out to be mere Amusement, there being in fact no Gold or Silver mines in Jamaica'. They were therefore guilty of 'Great Frauds'. The Court of Exchequer disregarded the amount of £35,415 which Charles had expended from shareholders' funds to find and work the mines, and ordered this money also be repaid.

The magnitude of the South Sea Bubble debacle had tainted the view of the court, which seems to have agreed with the shareholders' opinion on the veracity of the mining project, giving no credit to Charles Long or William Wood or the other patentees for their genuine belief in the presence of gold and silver. Whether it actually existed or not, it was the object of the Spaniards when they invaded and occupied the island until 1655.

Before the events that so devastated his father Samuel had spent his carefree youth at Eton and later joined the army. He was attendant on Queen Caroline when captain of a troop of Horse Guards; she called him her 'Handsome Captain'. Just after the death of his father, and while he was still in the army at Northampton, he met his future wife, Mary, daughter of Bartholomew Tate of Delapre, Northamptonshire. After their marriage he left the army and they went to Jamaica, where in 1725 he passed a conveyance to cut off the entail of his inherited estates there. Over the next few years Samuel and Mary divided their time between England and Jamaica, adding to their brood along the way. He kept racehorses for a time in Dorset, but according to his son Edward he was 'wretchedly cheated by his grooms'.

Edward says rather vaguely that when he was born at Rosilian in Cornwall in 1734 his father had been absent in London, 'employed in soliciting some post of profit' for Sir Robert Walpole, the then Prime Minister. Samuel and his father Charles had become very attached to the family of Walpole after Sir Robert, in his capacity as Chancellor of the Exchequer, had provided some protection to the embattled father and son during the Exchequer suits. In recognition of this attachment Walpole bestowed upon Samuel the office of keeper of the king's house at Newmarket and a position in the Customs Office, which came with a combined salary of £400 a year.

He moved his family into the Newmarket mansion and under the watchful eye of their Welsh governess, whose previous charge had been the young Lord Paget, the children occupied their own separate apartments so their noise would not disturb the numerous and often high-ranking visitors to the house. The living expenses in London soon proved too great for Samuel's salary, and returning to Cornwall he purchased a property about 20 miles from Plymouth called Tredudwell, overlooking the sea. He enlarged and improved the old farmhouse ready for the arrival of his wife in 1741, while the children were sent away to school.

Edward believed his father had expected to end his days in peaceful retirement at Tredudwell, but the income from his estates in Jamaica had dwindled to almost nothing, once again under gross mismanagement. At the same time other planters were prospering, with the price of raw sugar in England skyrocketing in the fourteen year period from 1733 to 1747. There was also one last Exchequer suit still hanging over his head. With the £400 per annum his only income and none to spare for the education and advancement of his numerous progeny it became an urgent necessity in 1746 to return to Jamaica and attempt to put his affairs in order.

So off he went, with the expectation his wife and elder children would join him later. In Samuel's absence Mary hoped to alleviate their financial problems somewhat by marrying off their two elder daughters Charlotte and Emma, but one of these suitors was so 'perfectly odious' to Charlotte that to 'countenance pretensions of this nature', unauthorised by her father, she intended immediately on her arrival in Jamaica to inform him of her mother's 'very great imprudence' in encouraging men of whom he might entirely disapprove.

Mary would add to her husband's wrath by arriving too late at Portsmouth to board the ship arranged for her by Samuel's half-brother Beeston Long. A West India merchant and partner in Drake and Long, London sugar factors and commission agents, Uncle Beeston was the 'gayest of the whole party' in his younger days, jollying up their entertainments by making fireworks. But now, indulging his sister-in-law's tardiness was a different matter. He lost patience entirely after Mary's refusal to take the next available passage on a merchant ship. She and her daughters would have had to share their cabin with male passengers, separated at night only by a curtain made from old sail cloth, ingeniously rigged up by the captain. Beeston probably informed Samuel of her obstinacy, justifiable though it was from a female point of view.

When she finally arrived in Jamaica Mary was met with a torrent of accusations from her husband and daughter Charlotte on the subject of her 'unpardonable imprudence', which were reinforced by another sister and Mary's maid. The lengthy and stressful process of litigation over the lost shareholder's money and the ongoing problems with his Jamaican estates had soured Samuel's disposition, not surprisingly, and he 'flew into an outrageous passion', would hear none of her attempts at explanation and she was effectively banished as his wife.

Mary moved into a small house before eventually returning to England; she was allowed to take their youngest daughter with her and set her up at school. But Samuel's instructions via his brother Beeston proved his fury to be all-consuming; Mary was forbidden to see her daughter, even at school, although she made a clandestine arrangement with the schoolmistress to peep through a screen on occasions to watch her playing the harpsichord. Mary was given an allowance of £200 a year to live on, but she was never reconciled with Charlotte, the instigator of the rift.

Samuel's anger further fractured the family after he forced his second son Charles to take a seat in the Assembly to vote with him on the question of relocating the seat of government in Jamaica. When the votes were counted Charles's name was found with those in opposition, and Samuel renounced his son forever – stubbornly refusing to speak to him even when Charles became ill. Charles died shortly afterwards aged twenty-five, and Samuel died three months later in January 1757, a bitter man, never returning to Tredudwell.

Edward Long (1734–1813), Historian of Jamaica

Samuel's son Edward is best known as a leading contemporary commentator on the eighteenth-century British Caribbean for his influential work, *History of Jamaica, or, General Survey of the Antient and Modern State of that Island,* published in three volumes in 1774.

Even after the passing of so many years, it must have given Edward some pain to recall the events that had such an impact on his family, but in his narrative he counterbalances the tragedies with a light-hearted and humorous account of his own childhood. His mother told him he was named Edward after his godfather Sir Edward Walpole, a compromise caused by his father's refusal to agree to the name Zouche, in recognition of her family's connection to the name. 'So violent was his penchant for all of the House of Walpole, that I believe if another son had been born after me, he would have named him Horace.'

In 1741, the year his parents moved into Tredudwell, Edward was sent to school at St Edmundsbury in Suffolk, joined by his brothers Robert and Charles who had been at the then unaffordable Eton. Edward was particularly attached to Charles, making the circumstances of his death all the more unbearable:

> I loved him, not only for his amiable qualities of heart and head, for he was intrepid, liberal, sweet tempered and possessed of a genius and understanding which gave promise of the highest future celebrity, but of a manly noble figure of uncommon strength and agility, which he had frequently exerted in protecting me from ill usage at school.

Charles, his 'dearly beloved protector', also stood between Edward and their elder brother Robert, who was 'in his boyish years of a most tyrannical overbearing disposition'.

Edward Long, Historian of Jamaica. Fitzwilliam Museum, Cambridge

Soon after his father had returned to Jamaica, Edward was sent to Liskeard in Cornwall where he attended Bury St Edmunds School. He boarded with a certain Dr Star and his wife, who lived modestly with their two servants and a clutch of rowdy children, and although the house contained 'a vast number of good rooms', such was Doctor Star's limited means that their family time together was spent in the smoke-filled kitchen with walls covered in soot and two of their sons 'pigged together in the same bed' with the manservant.

Young Edward, or Mr Ned as they called him, was treated with the 'utmost civility', though the short-tempered Mrs Star scolded her own children outrageously, and occasionally answered her long-suffering husband with a sharp whack around the ear. Edward enjoyed the quiet solitude of his own spacious and private sleeping quarters during the summer, but 'underwent considerable mortification' when informed the doctor could not afford fuel for his fire in winter. His father had allowed him pocket money of 1*s* a week, but owing to Dr Star's 'parsimonious humour' Edward lacked a suit of clothing that was not 'patched and darned in a thousand places'. When one of the sons came down with smallpox, the other was sent to share the bed with Edward, to whom he transmitted a severe but fortuitous dose of rank itch. Fortuitous because it was the reason Edward left this penurious household, at least temporarily, spending a blissful five weeks at Tredudwell while he recovered.

He spent six years in total with Dr and Mrs Star, and in 1752 on Uncle Beeston's approval he moved to London to the household of Mr Smith, who had recently married his housekeeper, 'a pert and ignorant little Hussey'. His previous sleeping accommodation in Dr Star's house must have seemed relatively luxurious compared with the small inconvenient garret he was assigned at the Smiths; it had no fireplace but a bedful of bugs that never seemed to diminish in number despite, or perhaps because of, a particularly futile basket-weave bug-trap set each night.

After two years Edward entered Gray's Inn. He intended a career travelling the barrister's circuit, but the death of his father and the meagre provision left for him in his will meant he had to abandon his studies and sail to Jamaica. He was later called to the bar *ex gratia*, despite not having completed the full term. After arrival in Jamaica his brother Robert conveyed to him a moiety of the Longville estate, and he also managed the Lucky Valley plantation. It was inevitable he would become involved in administration on the island, and beginning as private secretary to his brother-in-law, Lieutenant-Governor Sir Henry Moore, husband of his eldest sister Catharine Maria, it wasn't too long before he was promoted to the position of chief judge of the Vice-Admiralty Court.

In August 1758 he married Mary Ballard Beckford, second daughter and eventual heir of Thomas Beckford of Jamaica, and widow of John Palmer. The first four of their children were baptised in Jamaica, and Edward was elected a member of the Jamaican Assembly for St Ann parish in 1761, 1765 and 1766. In 1768 he was speaker of the Assembly, an office he held only for one year until the House was dissolved the following September. Plagued by several bouts of illness, he resolved in 1769 to return to 'studious retirement' in England. He never returned to the island, although he retained his judicial office in Jamaica until about 1797.

From 1771, when his twin sons Robert and Charles were born at Chichester, until 1803 Edward relocated his family seven times. During this period, free from the responsibilities of estate management and colonial government, he was able to take a more objective view of Jamaica's affairs, and wrote numerous articles for London newspapers. Between 1772 and 1782 he published several pamphlets, mainly on the sugar trade, but his most seminal work was *The History of Jamaica*, reprinted in 1970.

Apart from a detailed account of the seizure by the English of the island from the Spanish in 1655, for the most part it is an intimate portrait of life in the colony in the eighteenth century, and he was at pains to portray it as a settled and civilised improvement on England. No doubt based on his family's previous experience, he argued absentee plantation owners were inefficient managers, and this he believed could be overcome if estate owners resided in Jamaica rather than returning to Britain.

As a member of the colonial plantocracy Edward attempted to justify the slave trade on both moral and practical grounds, and his account is liberally sprinkled with his own often intemperate opinions. His diatribe against 'goatish embraces' between white men and black or coloured slave mistresses is one example, arguing strenuously that the white and negro were two distinctly different species, and he regarded the latter as inferior and subhuman. Nevertheless his *History* remains one of the most valuable and authoritative works on the colonisation of Jamaica.

Cultivated and intellectual, Edward was also an accomplished musician who encouraged the same qualities in his offspring. His wife Mary died in July 1797 aged sixty-two, and he survived a further sixteen years, to March 1813, dying at Arundel Park, Sussex, the seat of his son-in-law, Henry Howard-Molyneux-Howard. He was buried in the chancel of Slindon church, Sussex, where he is commemorated by a memorial.

Robert Ballard Long (1771–1825)

Robert, the elder of Edward and Mary's twin sons, was educated firstly at Dr Thomson's school, Kensington, and spent nine years at Harrow School until 1789 under Dr Drury, after which he took a course of military instruction at the University of Göttingen, in Hanover. He had an active military career beginning in 1791 as cornet in the 1st King's Dragoon Guards, eventually purchasing a lieutenant-colonelcy in the Hompesch Mounted Riflemen, for which his father paid £2,000. He commanded the regiment in Ireland during the 1798 uprising.

Later in his career, during which he saw service in Spain and with the Duke of Wellington's army in Portugal and various other places, he earned a reputation for incompetence after the British sustained heavy losses during one particular campaign in 1811, the year he became major-general. At Wellington's request in December 1812 the commander-in-chief (Frederick, Duke of York) recalled Robert against his wishes. He returned to England and indignantly declined an offer of a command in Scotland. He was made lieutenant-general in 1821 and settled in Surrey. He died unmarried at Berkeley Square, London, in March 1825, and was interred in the family vault in the church at Seale, Surrey.

During his career he had clashed with his superiors, and his military conduct had attracted much criticism. After his death his nephew Charles Edward Long, the genealogist and antiquary, had attempted to vindicate Robert by publishing two pamphlets in 1832 and 1833, and in a third in 1838 he felt he had succeeded in restoring his uncle's reputation. But Charles was still rankled that Robert's name had been omitted from the list of medal recipients in 1814 after Albuera, the bloodiest battle of the Peninsular War.

Abolition of the Slave Trade

A decade after the formation in 1797 of the Committee for the Abolition of the Slave Trade, led by William Wilberforce, the Slave Trade Act of 1807 was passed following a successful parliamentary campaign. Slaves were still owned, though not sold, and further campaigning eventually brought about the Slavery Abolition Act in 1833. On 1 August 1834 all slaves in the British Empire were emancipated and then indentured to their former owners in an apprenticeship system, which was later abolished in two stages.

The government set aside £20 million to cover compensation of slave owners across the empire, although there was no compensation for former slaves. The House of Commons parliamentary papers show Charles Beckford Long, Robert's twin brother, received £3,092 compensation for 234 slaves in 1835 and 1836, and his son Charles Edward, together with nephews Frederick and Henry received a total of £4,025 between them.

Edward Noel Long (1788–1809), and his brothers Frederick and Henry

Edward Beeston Long had five children with his wife Mary Thomlinson, and the eldest, Edward Noel, was a twenty-one-year-old ensign in the Coldstream Guards who had already served with distinction in the expedition to Copenhagen, when he drowned on his way to join the British forces in Spain in March 1809. Others in his regiment also perished, when in the dark of night, the *Isis*, a fifty-gun man of war, accidentally crashed down on their transport, the *St George*, off the coast of Portugal near Cape St Vincent. Edward had fallen into the sea between the two ships as they collided.

Eight years earlier, in 1801, Edward had entered Harrow and later attended Trinity College, Cambridge, along with Lord Byron with whom he shared an intimate friendship. Edward wrote from Harrow to his father in May 1802 describing two of the new boys at school: Lord Bury, Lord Albermarle's son, was 'the most passionate fellow that ever was; he won't fag', and Lord Byron, 'a lame fellow just come, he seems a good sort of fellow'. When news of Edward's death reached Byron 'he threw himself on the sofa and gave himself up to the most violent grief'.[415] He wrote in his diary:

> We were rival swimmers, fond of riding, reading, and of conviviality.
> Our evenings we passed in music (he was musical, and played on more

---

415   R.M Howard, *Records and Letters of the Family of the Longs of Longville*, 1925, p. 396

than one instrument – flute and violoncello), in which I was audience; and I think that our chief beverage was soda-water. In the day we rode, bathed, and lounged, reading occasionally. I remember our buying, with vast alacrity, Moore's new quarto (in 1806), and reading it together in the evenings . . . His friendship, and a violent though pure passion – which held me at the same period – were the then romance of the most romantic period of my life. [416]

Byron's friendships during his school years had left a great impression on him, recalled in his poem *Childish Recollections*, where he refers to Edward as 'Cleon'. Two years after Edward's death Byron was deeply affected by the deaths of four more of his school friends, all in a four month period in 1811, when his mother also died, prompting the justifiably melancholic observation: 'some curse hangs over me. I never could keep alive even a dog that I liked, or that liked me.' Edward's father had asked Byron to write his son's epitaph. 'I promised – but I had not the heart to complete it. He was such a good, amiable being as rarely remains long in this world; with talent and accomplishments, too, to make him the more regretted.' Byron's poetic epitaph to 'my friend alone' can be seen on Edward's memorial at St Lawrence's church, Seale, Surrey.

Edward's two younger brothers, Henry Lawes Long (destined to become an eminent man of letters) and the youngest of the three, Frederick Beckford Long (whom twelve-year-old Henry playfully called 'Senex Fred') both attended Harrow and Cambridge, and Frederick afterwards studied civil law. He was called to the bar in 1838. His ill-fated appointment as inspector general of prisons in Ireland regularly exposed him to conditions of deprivation and disease, and he contracted smallpox from which he died at Dublin in 1850, aged forty-five. His widow Maria Elizabeth (*née* Daniell) was left with eight young children to care for, and she was granted a state pension of £100 per annum in consideration of her husband having died from illness contracted while in the execution of his duty. Later a further £50 a year was granted in recognition of his services.

416   Byron Diary, 'Life', 1821, p. 31

The second brother Henry was also befriended by Byron, who frequently tipped him with £5 notes, causing Henry's father Edward Beeston Long to write a postscript to his elder son Edward Noel in 1808:

> P.S. I must entreat you to remind Ld B. of my earnest wishes that he w^d not be so liberal in his tips to Harry – it will absolutely ruin him to possess so much money at once . . . A £5 note might do a 5th or 6th form boy but till then a tip sh^d never exceed one guinea. Ld B. is a fine generous fellow, but he must attend to a Parent's feelings.[417]

The marriage of Edward Beeston Long's sister Elizabeth to Henry, the younger brother of Bernard Howard, 12th Duke of Norfolk, hereditary earl marshal, ensured Henry Lawes Long and his brother Frederick were present as gentlemen ushers at the coronation of George IV in July 1821. Exactly one year later Henry married Catherine, daughter of Horatio Walpole, 2nd Earl of Orford. Catherine matched his intellect and became an authoress of some repute. In 1825 Henry inherited Hampton Lodge in Surrey, which his father had purchased in 1799. He stood unsuccessfully as a Liberal candidate for Surrey in 1838.

During his marriage Henry fathered seven daughters and two sons with Catherine, and his estates at his death in 1868 passed to his youngest surviving son Henry Charles Dudley Long, who died two years later in Paris, unmarried. These estates eventually came to the latter's cousin, Robert Mowbray Howard (d. 1928), compiler of the book on the Longs of Jamaica, and custodian of the numerous family letters.

Charles Long (1760–1838), 1st Baron Farnborough

Charles was born in London, the youngest son of Beeston Long (uncle to Edward Long the historian) and his wife Sarah Cropp, and he is known chiefly as a politician and connoisseur of the arts. He received his education at a private school in Greenwich and at

417   R.M. Howard, *op. cit.* p. 400

Emmanuel College, Cambridge, where he matriculated in 1779, but is not known to have taken a degree. At the same time he was entered at Inner Temple, and for two years he explored Rome under the tutelage of James Byres during his Grand Tour, establishing the groundwork for his art collection.

One of Charles's Cambridge friends was William Pitt, who in 1783 at the age of twenty-four became Britain's youngest Prime Minister (although at that time the term 'prime minister' was not used). Charles's own involvement in politics began as early as 1788 after his return from Rome, canvassing for the ministerial candidate in the Westminster election, Lord Hood. A year later he entered Parliament as MP for Rye, with subsequent representations as member for Midhurst and Wendover. Thereafter he held the seat of Haslemere for twenty years until 1826. He was elected FRS in 1792, FSA in 1812, and was later given an honorary LLD by his old university.

Charles Long, Lord Farnborough, by John Jackson. Courtesy William J. Long

In between times he became junior secretary to the Treasury in 1791, acting as parliamentary whip and teller, and during 1796 he was responsible for much of the management of the general election on behalf of the government. After Pitt left office in 1801, as his loyal friend and ally Charles insisted on following suit, afterwards receiving a pension of £1,500 per annum.

Behind the scenes Pitt arranged for Charles to become Treasury adviser to the new Prime Minister Henry Addington,[418] and he became a privy Councillor in 1802. Pitt defected to the opposition after declining Addington's invitation to join his cabinet, becoming very critical of the government. Consequently Charles's house at Bromley Hill became the scene for negotiations between Pitt and Addington over remodelling the administration. With Charles acting as intermediary Pitt's object was to take Addington's place as Prime Minister.

In the meantime England had renewed its hostilities with France, and by May 1804 Addington, who had lost his parliamentary support, decided to resign. Pitt immediately returned to power and made Charles a lord of the Treasury, a post he held until 1806, and at the same time he served as chief secretary to the lord lieutenant of Ireland. Pitt's second term was short however, and he died in 1806. Charles then took office in the new Portland ministry as paymaster-general of the Forces, a post he retained until his retirement from politics in 1826. Charles was unambitious politically, and when Portland's successor Spencer Perceval (a distant cousin descended from the Longs of Whaddon) offered him the chancellorship of the Exchequer and the secretaryship at war in 1809, he refused them both.

Throughout his political life Charles maintained his passion for the arts, and artistic causes benefited under his influence, such as the establishment of the National Gallery and the purchase of the Elgin marbles. His advice was sought from every quarter, and George IV frequently consulted him over the commissioning of paintings, architecture and sculpture, although opinion was divided on his

---

418   Addington had been MP for Devizes with Sir James Tylney Long from 1784 to 1788

personal level of influence. Harriet Arbuthnot, Tory supporter and friend of the Duke of Wellington, thought Charles was 'a complete courtier, [who] always acquiesces in anything the King says and never dares contest a point with him'. On the other hand, the prince's secretary told landscape painter and diarist Joseph Farington that in matters of art, 'The Prince Regent saw through Mr Long's spectacles.'

Also an amateur architect, Charles persuaded Parliament to vote him £300,000 when the king decided to reconstruct Windsor Castle. Sir Jeffry Wyattville implemented the remodelling in 1824 based on the detailed brief Charles had drawn up, which envisaged every important feature of the castle from the formation of the grand corridor to the heightening of the keep, and he made a sketch plan suggesting the sunken garden below the east terrace.[419]

Charles had purchased his country estate at Bromley Hill, Kent in 1801, just a few miles from his friend Pitt's at Holwood. The house had been built in 1760 and he considerably enlarged and modified it in the Italianate style with neo-classical interiors. He improved the extensive grounds which came to be much admired, with long picturesque walks and a distant view of the dome of St Paul's Cathedral. Here he entertained George IV, William IV and Queen Adelaide with the able assistance of his wife Amelia, whom he had married in 1793. A meeting place for artists and royalty, Bromley Hill was also the showcase for Amelia's works as a horticulturist and watercolourist, and she designed the celebrated grounds that subsequently became the main source for her sketches. Her father Sir Abraham Hume, 2nd Baronet,[420] was also a prominent collector and patron of the arts.

Not long after 1806 Charles inherited the manor of Duxford in Cambridgeshire, purchased by his maternal great-uncle Richard Cropp in 1759. In 1820 Charles was made a Knight of the Bath by George IV, and on retirement in 1826 he was created Baron Farnborough. When Charles's wife died in mid-January 1837 he was also suffering ill

419   Howard Colvin, 'Long, Charles, Baron Farnborough (1760–1838)', *Oxford Dictionary of National Biography*, Oxford University Press, 2004; online edn. Sept 2013
420   His second daughter Sophia married John Cust, 1st Earl Brownlow, a descendant of Sir James Long, 2nd Baronet, of Draycot.

health. Taking a sudden turn for the worse, the London press reported he was dangerously ill 'in consequence of a shock occasioned by the death of his lady'. He died childless a year later almost to the day in January 1838, leaving his collection of paintings to the National Gallery, including works by Rubens, Vandyck, Canaletto, Teniers, Mola, Cuyp, and others. He left the Duxford estate to his brother Beeston junior's sixth son, the Rev. William Long of Hurts Hall, and the nominal lordship of the manor was retained by William's descendants until the twentieth century.

Lord Farnborough's Siblings and Cousins

In 1787 Charles's eldest brother Samuel married Lady Jane, daughter of James Maitland, 7th Earl of Lauderdale. Samuel (MP for Ilchester in 1790) lived with his wife and three children near London at Carshalton House (demolished 1822), inherited from his father Beeston in 1785. He died in 1807 and a year later his young widow married Sir William Houston, 1st Bt., who had fathered at least one of Lady Jane Long's children while she was still married to her first husband.

Samuel and Lady Jane's elder son Lieutenant-Colonel Samuel Long junior married, as his fourth wife, his cousin and maid of honour to Queen Victoria, the Hon. Eleanor Julian Stanley. Baron Farnborough's other brother, Beeston Long junior, was a senior partner of Long, Drake & Co., a governor of the Bank of England and also chairman of the London Docks Company. In that capacity he led a group of merchants and speculators in a private venture to construct the docks at Wapping. With the exception of ships from the East and West Indies, the company had a twenty-one-year monopoly to unload all vessels entering the port. Beeston and the other directors oversaw their lucrative trade from the London Dock House in New Bank Buildings.

A portrait of his wife Frances Louisa (*née* Neave) was painted by George Romney not long after their marriage, and Romney painted other members of this family, including Charles's sisters, one of whom married her first cousin, also named Charles Long.[421] Hurts

421   Charles Long junior, son of Charles Long and Mary North

Carshalton House, A Companion from London to Brighthelmstone. James Edwards (1801)

Hall passed to this Charles's younger brother Dudley (1749–1829), a philanthropist who had inherited from their father £25,000 and a joint interest in his Jamaican plantations.

The impoverished poet George Crabbe, many years later rector of Trowbridge and a great friend of the Longs of Rood Ashton, visited Charles and Dudley at Hurts Hall in 1781. Crabbe addressed 'a very extraordinary letter' to Dudley requesting a loan of £5 for travelling expenses which was readily given. Thus Dudley became his patron, and for five years from 1796 to 1801 he allowed Crabbe to live at Glemham Hall, inherited from his maternal aunt Anne Herbert (*née* North). As a condition of this inheritance Dudley assumed the name North, but on succeeding to the estate of Hurts Hall he resumed his former surname, thereby becoming Dudley Long North.

A mourner at Sir Joshua Reynolds's funeral and pallbearer at Edmund Burke's, Dudley counted his friends in both the literary and political spheres, having represented various constituencies in Cornwall, Lincolnshire and Oxfordshire. A speech impediment had prevented him from speaking in Parliament, and his reserved demeanour had given others the wrong impression, including Samuel Johnson, who in 1781 contradicted high praise by diarist and author Mrs Thrale: 'Nay, my dear lady, don't talk so. Mr Long's character is very short. It is nothing. He fills a chair. He is a man of genteel appearance, and that is all.' This is from Boswell's *Life of Johnson;* in a footnote Boswell negates Johnson's glib comment, saying that Dudley Long was 'a gentleman distinguished amongst his acquaintances for acuteness of wit . . . He has gratified me by mentioning that he heard Dr Johnson say, "Sir, if I were to lose Boswell, it would be a limb amputated".'

Dudley married Sophia Anderson Pelham, daughter of the 1st Earl of Yarborough in 1802 and died without issue. Through his mother Mary North he was the last direct descendant of Elihu Yale, benefactor of Yale University.

In 1835 Lord Farnborough's only surviving brother William Long, canon of Windsor, preached the sermon at the funeral of George IV, whose father George III some years earlier had remarked to William while on the terrace at Windsor, 'Mr Long, I hear you are a very good parish priest.' William's death was very sudden; he had just finished showing 'visitors of distinction' through the gardens at Bromley Hill when, a few minutes after their departure, he died.[422]

Archdeacon Charles Maitland Long (1803–75)

Lord Farnborough's nephew and namesake was born at Berkeley Square, London, the younger son of Samuel Long and Lady Jane Maitland, (or so his mother Lady Jane would have everyone believe)[423] and he was educated at Trinity College, Cambridge, graduating BA in 1826 and MA in 1830. He had an almost textbook well-to-do Victorian parson's career. In 1834 his first parish, Woodmansterne, Surrey, was in the gift of Lord Derby, a near neighbour and his brother's father-in-law. Charles's first wife, Harriet Mary Ellice, came with £20,000, but she died in 1835 from complications after giving birth to their first child, a year after their marriage. Before Harriet's death he had moved

---

422   William Long's obituary, *Gentleman's Magazine,* 1835, vol. 159, p. 552
423   A recent DNA test by a direct descendant of Charles Maitland Long has shown significant matches with the name Houston. Sir William Houston was Lady Jane Maitland's 2nd husband.

to Whitchurch, in the gift of his uncle Charles, Lord Farnborough, as executor of the Earl of Bridgewater, the previous incumbent.

In 1846 he became rector of Settrington, Yorkshire which at £1,045 per annum was one of the richest livings in England, with one of the lowest numbers of parishioners. It was in the gift of Lord Brownlow, Lady Farnborough's brother-in-law. Charles was quite a busy man as archdeacon of East Riding (1854–73) and prebendary of York (1855–75), but still he found time for a second wife, marrying Anna Maria, daughter of Sir Robert Wigram of Walthamstow, Essex in 1839. In his spare time he bred racehorses, and children too; he and Anna had ten. Unfortunately two of these died on the same day in September 1855, a boy and a girl aged three and fourteen years respectively, presumably from the same fatal illness.

From the age of eighteen their second son, Lieutenant-Colonel Charles Wigram Long enjoyed a twenty-five-year career in the Royal Artillery, serving at Aden and in Canada before retiring in 1886. He sat as a Conservative for the seat of Evesham from 1895 to 1910. His marriage in 1889 to Constance Mary Vansittart (whose sister Fanny was Mrs Walter Long of Upham, Hampshire) coincided with a timely windfall. Five years before the introduction of death duties he inherited a house in Berkeley Square and the residue of the estate of his late maternal uncle Loftus Tottenham Wigram QC, the effects worth £81,554.

Rear Admiral Samuel Long (1840–93)

Archdeacon Long's eldest son Samuel went to sea at the age of twelve in 1852, fifty years after Lord Nelson had said the practice of sending boys to sea so young should stop. He was promoted to sub-lieutenant in 1859 and lieutenant just over a year later. In 1868 he married Alice Jane, daughter of Vice-Chancellor Sir James Wigram. The same year he was appointed commander, captain in 1876 and rear admiral in 1891.

His involvement in the Crimean War included his presence during the bombardment of Sebastopol in September 1854 for which he received the Crimean Medal with Sebastopol clasp. He served as naval aide de camp to Queen Victoria from 1889 – her golden jubilee year –

Rear Admiral Samuel Long. Courtesy William J. Long

until 1891. He saw service in the Far East and was executive officer in Admiral Hornby's flagship on his non-stop circumnavigation. During his captaincy of HMS *Vernon*, the gunnery school at Portsmouth, he was involved in the development of the torpedo. He was the first to use the term 'battle-cruiser' in a paper entitled *Cruisers and their Function*, presented to the Institute of Naval Architects in 1893.

Samuel's best known act as a naval officer occurred when he was in command of *HMS Agamemnon* in 1885, at a time of high tension between England and Russia. In company with the corvettes *Saphir* and *Swift* he was ordered to shadow the Russian flagship *Vladimir Monomack*. On 6 May he encountered her in Yokohama harbour, and as he steamed up the harbour he noted the Russian guns were manned and trained on him, although his own guns were covered and trained fore and aft.

He told the officer of the watch, Alexander Duff, 'if as much as one gun is fired, put telegraphs to full speed and ram her amidships!' No gun was fired, however, and he anchored and went to call on the Russian admiral, telling him that to train guns on a ship in a neutral port was neither a courteous nor a diplomatic act. He was later complimented by the Admiralty for his restraint. After his promotion to rear-admiral Samuel was due to take command of a cruiser squadron in the Mediterranean, but he never got the chance to fly his flag.

On the evening of 24 April 1893 he went out riding with his twenty-one-year-old son Wilfred, then second lieutenant in the King's Royal Rifles. The rear-admiral was perhaps more accustomed to handling a warship than a horse, and as they were returning to their home in Hampshire at Blendworth Lodge, Horndean, about two miles away, the animal became unmanageable and he was thrown off, his foot caught in the stirrup. Wilfred was riding ahead and when he looked back he saw the horse galloping at a furious speed, dragging his father along the ground. By the time he reached him the horse had fallen and Samuel was unconscious, with the back of his skull badly fractured. He never regained consciousness. In a strange coincidence, the previous occupant of Blendworth Lodge, General Morant, connected to the Longs of Preshaw, was out on horseback with his son the following day, and he also fell from his horse – dead from a fit of apoplexy.

With Samuel's eight children now fatherless, his widow continued to live at Blendworth Lodge with two of their daughters and eighteen staff. An old resident of Horndean, Mrs Lillian Purnell, recalling her school days, wrote of Mrs Alice Long:

> There was a lady on the committee at the school who used to supply us with slippers so if our feet got wet on the way to school we were able to change our boots for slippers. She was a little old lady called Mrs Long, who lived at Blendworth Lodge. She drove a carriage like Queen Victoria used to have. One day, when I was in the village, a farmer came along in his high dog cart. He must have thought she was Queen Victoria because he stopped his cart, took his hat off and made an enormous bow.

Blendworth Lodge was destroyed by fire in 1916 and Alice died in 1928.

The Ghost of Cripple Creek

In 1889, sometime after Samuel and Alice's fourth son George Edward completed his education at St Peter's College, Oxfordshire, he emigrated to America. He bought a farm in Denver, Colorado where he and his English-born wife Ursula Worth raised four children. By 1909 he described himself as an architect. He was also an accomplished artist but later gained a reputation for his fractious temperament and a fondness for alcohol.

He sold the farm sometime after 1910, moving his young family nearly 9,500ft above sea level to Cripple Creek, which in the 1890s had been a lawless Colorado gold rush town that quickly sprouted saloons, hotels and theatres to cater to the newly rich miners. After two separate fires within a week completely devastated the timber buildings in the centre of town during April 1896, it was rebuilt in brick. Among these new buildings was the Collins Hotel, which by the time George bought it was renamed the Imperial Hotel. Over the next thirty-five years or so he built up a thriving business, living with his family in apartments within the hotel.

All the children, with the exception of one, eventually married and moved away. The eldest son, Samuel Godfrey Long, born in 1904, had an interesting and varied career. He was a member of the London

Stock Exchange from 1930 and later a pilot for Imperial Airways. Just before the outbreak of war in 1939 he navigated the first commercial transatlantic flight in a modified Shorts 'C' Class flying-boat *Caribou*, flying 3,000 miles from Southampton to New York.

While serving as squadron leader for the RAF he was shot down in the Bay of Biscay *en route* to Cairo in June 1941. Nine of his fourteen crew were drowned, and Samuel and the other four survived adrift in their lifeboat until they were picked up by the Germans. He was afterwards imprisoned in Stalag Luft III and was present during the famous Great Escape. At the end of the war he became a vicar ministering to various parishes in England and spent a year as a missionary in South Africa in 1951–2. He married at the age of fifty in 1954 and died in 1991.

Alice Jane was George Long's other exceptional child, born in May 1902 possibly with some sort of intellectual disability; she continued to live with her parents until the age of forty. The following may be more folklore than fact. On 7 May 1942, as George picked his way down the rickety stairs to the cellar, he was unaware of Alice close behind him. She had in her hand a heavy iron skillet, but a fry-up was the last thing on her mind. Perhaps fresh from an argument, Alice hit George in the head with such force he collapsed down the stairs and fell in a heap at the bottom, stone dead. And that was the end of George. Or was it?

Alice spent the rest of her life in an institution for her crime, but today (so say the many true believers, including a previous owner) visitors to the Imperial Hotel at Cripple Creek might still encounter the spirit of George Long. Over the years there have been several claims of sightings and unexplained events, and in the 1980s he is said to have appeared, rather appropriately, behind the bar. Now whenever there is a stuck drawer or a slamming door, poor old George gets the blame.

XVI
Sugar Plantations, Australian-Style

Three of George's uncles tried their luck in Australia. William Houston Long, Edward Maitland Long and George Boswall Long RN, hoped to replicate the success of their plantation-owning ancestors, and out of the three it was twenty-two year-old Edward who was the driving force behind their establishment in Queensland. Together with George Nisbett Marten they purchased River Estate at Mackay in 1870, building a house and establishing a plantation called Branscombe.

Marten dropped out of the relationship within a year or two and River Estate was operated by the partnership of Edward, George and William, the enterprise known as Long Brothers and later Long and Co. Like other plantation owners, Edward believed the European workforce would not perform the required field labour apart from ploughing; black labour was a necessity. Although he first considered workers from India, Edward imported much of his labour force from the Polynesian islands. In late November 1872 his brother George left Mackay aboard the schooner *Petrel* on a voyage to recruit natives. A widespread and controversial practice known as blackbirding, it was a profitable exercise for ship and plantation owners alike. There was often coercion, kidnapping and violence involved and the islanders didn't understand the agreements they were entering into.

George didn't make it back to Australia; his ship was lost in a storm. A £500 reward was posted for information regarding the fate of the vessel, and several advertisements ran in the press between October and November 1873. No trace was found, and finally in April 1874 his brother William was granted probate on his will as sole executor and trustee.

Two years later a rust outbreak severely impacted the two remaining brothers' financial position and the Australian Joint Stock

Bank took over River Estate. Queensland was still a self-governing colony and Edward stood unsuccessfully as a political candidate for Mackay in April 1877. Having learned much from the failure of River Estate he purchased a 6,000 acre hilly scrubland estate he called Habana, and in partnership with William Robertson established a plantation in 1881, capable of turning out 70 tons of sugar per week.

The day of the official opening was celebrated with great fanfare and the following evening a ball was held at the School of Arts in Mackay. The mill produced 1,500 tons in the first season and Edward continued to develop his operation with tramways, and he constructed a wharf using his cheap South Sea Islander labour. His request for a school was satisfied in about 1883. When a nationwide depression hit Australia and sugar prices fell by a third he subdivided the estate, so that from early 1884 he only controlled the milling of the cane, leaving responsibility for production to small tenant farmers who leased some of his land. They were not particularly happy about the arrangement.

Moves were afoot to change the plantation system after challenges by the small farmers, and in 1884 Queensland's state premier Sir Samuel Griffith introduced legislation that effectively put an end to South Sea Islander labour. Eventually, after pressure from labour unions, various Acts were passed in 1901 that came to be termed the White Australia Policy, aimed at excluding all non-European immigrants.

In the interim Edward had encouraged migration from Britain and he pioneered the employment of Japanese labourers, the first of whom arrived at Habana in about 1893. By this time there were 85 whites working at Habana mill, and 315 Islanders. In 1895 Edward hosted a visit by the Earl of Yarmouth at his now flourishing plantation, with 1,300 acres under cane and seventeen miles of tramway. By then twenty-six farmers were supplying his mill. At the same time he was also managing the Pleystowe Central Mill Company for which he had purchased land with the assistance of a government grant.

His high public profile as 'one of the most experienced and up to date sugar men in Queensland' was further boosted after his appointment as first chairman of the Mackay Harbour Board (1897–1903), and he was a Pioneer shire councillor in 1880–1 and 1897–

1900. In 1901 he was acting chairman of the Central Sugar Millers' Association of Queensland, the year Queensland lost its colonial status and became a state. It was also the last year cane was crushed at Habana Mill. Financial problems forced its closure, and to add to Edward's problems, complaints by other growers gave rise to an official inquiry into the Pleystowe Mill's affairs in February 1902, while he was away in New Zealand.

Later, as he lay ill in a hospital bed in Brisbane, he was exonerated by the enquiry, but the government foreclosed on the mill in 1903, and although it continued its operations Edward was replaced as manager. His empire was beginning to crumble. Illness plagued him again early in 1905, and he returned to England on the French mail steamer *Australien*, intending to take a year's holiday. He died on board ship in the Thames estuary on 4 August 1905, aged sixty-three, not having set foot again on English soil. He never married.

At what point Edward's brother William returned to England is uncertain, but the family tradition is that he lived for a time with 'a woman to whom he was not married'. Then he surprised everyone in 1907, when at the age of sixty-three he married a lady in London more than thirty years his junior. He died in 1912.

XVII
Conclusion

In the early eighteenth century, possibly up to 75 per cent of the population of England made a living in one way or another from the land. By the mid-nineteenth century this figure had declined to about twenty per cent, by 1900 only ten per cent and by the late twentieth century a mere three per cent,[424] decimating the previously comfortable income of large landowners such as the Longs.

Although many family estates have given way to corporate ownership, the private pursuit of wealth through land has not changed, and by having most of their assets held in trust inheritance tax is avoided and the status quo maintained. Whereas the priority was once to pass the estates to the eldest male heir, assets are now more likely to be divided equally and property sold to accommodate this.

A survey of land ownership in 2010, the most extensive undertaken since Parliament's second Domesday Book in 1872 or John Bateman's revealing report of 1883, has found despite Mr Lloyd George's taxation reform in 1909 more than a third of Britain's land is still in the hands of a small group of 36,000 individuals one century later. They own about 50 per cent of rural land and represent just 0.6 per cent of the population.

The name of Long is now absent from the list of the most wealthy landed gentry, whose centuries-old stranglehold on Parliament has also disappeared. They adjusted gradually to their new circumstances, staving off disaster by diversifying wherever they could. Younger sons were less likely to proliferate in the army, the church or the law, while the legacy of immigration from England to other nations in its once vast empire, such as America, Canada, Australia and New Zealand, has resulted in a broad scattering of their genes. While all but a few

424   Mingay, *op. cit.* p. 78

known family lines are extinct, those that continue to flourish in the twenty-first century do so without the encumbrances of political responsibilities, crumbling manor houses with their armies of servants, and generations of tenants to provide their income.

Appendix
Parliamentary Pedigree

Owing to the disastrous fire that destroyed the old Houses of Parliament in October 1834, some records may have been permanently lost. Therefore the often repeated claim that the Longs produced no fewer than seventy-three members of Parliament cannot be completely substantiated from available sources. The following represents members taken from a list of forty-nine Longs who served Parliament from 1213 until 1702, compiled by Sir William Bull in the early twentieth century, with a further seventeen after this date, which equals sixty-six. Those of uncertain identity have been omitted.

Robert Long (c.1391–1446), Old Sarum 1414, Calne 1417, Wiltshire 1421, 1423–4, 1429–30, 1433, Salisbury 1441–2.

Richard Long (1423–after 1490), Old Sarum 1441–2

John Long (c.1419–78), Cricklade 1442

Henry Long (c.1417–90), Wiltshire, 1448–9, 1452–3, 1472

Sir Thomas Long (c.1461–1509), Westbury 1491

Sir Richard Long (1474–1546), Southwark 1539

Sir Robert Long (c.1517–81), Calne 1544–5

Sir Henry Long (c.1489–c.1556), Wiltshire 1552–3

Henry Long of Shingay, Cambridgeshire 1571

Thomas Long, Westbury 1571 (removed after bribery scandal)

Sir Walter Long (1561–1610), Wiltshire 1592–3

Sir Walter Long (c.1590–1637), Westbury 1620–1, 1625–6

Sir Robert Long, 1st Baronet, Devizes 1626, 1628–9, Midhurst 1640, Tewkesbury 1659, Boroughbridge 1661–73

Gifford Long, Westbury 1625

Sir Walter Long, 1st Baronet, Wiltshire 1625–6, Bath 1627–8, Ludgershall 1640

Sir Lislebone Long, Wells 1645–8, 1654, 1659, Somerset 1656–1658

Robert Long of Stanton Prior (c.1606–97), Somerset 1654

Sir Walter Long, 2nd Baronet, Bath 1679–1681

Sir James Long, 2nd Baronet, Chippenham, Malmesbury 1678–9, 1680–1, 1689–1692

Richard Long (1668–1730), Chippenham 1694–5

Walter Long (c.1647–1731) (of South Wraxall), Calne 1701

Richard Long (c.1690–1760), Chippenham 1734–41

Sir James Long, 5th Baronet, Chippenham 1705–13, Wootton Bassett 1715–22, Wiltshire 1727–9

Sir Philip Parker-a-Morley-Long, 3rd Baronet, Harwich 1715–34

Sir Robert Long, 6th Baronet, Wootton Bassett 1734, Wiltshire 1741

Dudley Long, St Germans 1780, Great Grimsby 1784, Banbury 1808, Richmond, Yorkshire 1812, Newtown, Isle of Wight 1820

Sir James Tylney Long, 7th Baronet, Marlborough 1762–80, Devizes 1780–8, Wiltshire 1788

Charles Long, Baron Farnborough, Rye 1789, Midhurst 1796–1802, Wendover 1802–6, Haslemere 1806–26

Samuel Long of Carshalton, Surrey Ilchester 1790

Richard Godolphin Long, Wiltshire 1806–18

William Long Wellesley, 4th Earl of Mornington, St Ives 1812–18, Wiltshire 1818

Walter Long (1793–1867), North Wiltshire 1835–65

Richard Penruddocke Long, Chippenham 1859–65, North Wiltshire 1865–8

Walter Hume Long, 1st Viscount Long, North Wiltshire 1880–5, Devizes 1885–92, Liverpool West Derby 1893–1900, Bristol South 1900–6, South Dublin 1906–10, Strand 1910–18, St George's 1918–21. Also president of the Board of Agriculture, president of the Local Government Board, chief secretary for Ireland, leader of the Irish Unionist Parliamentary Party, first lord of the Admiralty

Richard Godolphin Walmesley Long Chaloner, 1st Baron Gisborough, Westbury 1895–1900, Abercromby 1910–17

Charles Wigram Long, Evesham 1895–1910

Richard Eric Onslow Long, 3rd Viscount Long, Westbury 1927–31

Richard Gerard Long, 4th Viscount Long, Conservative opposition whip 1974, lord-in-waiting, 1979–97 (removed from Parliament with the majority of hereditary peers in 1999)

Family Trees
(see following pages)

Long of Lyneham and Bradenstoke

Long of Draycot Cerne; descent from Sir Walter Long (d. 1610) and Catherine Thynne

Long of Wraxall; descent from Sir Walter Long (d. 1610) and Mary Pakington

Long of Preshaw

Long of Semington (incorporating Dewell of Malmesbury)

Sir Henry Long m. Elinor Wrottesley

Richard Long
c.1526-1558
m (c.1554) Marian Browne   (d. after1559)

Edmund
(1555-1635)
m (1576) Rachel Coxwell (sister of Nathaniel who m. Susannah dau of Edward Long of Rood Ashton)

LONG of LYNEHAM & BRADENSTOKE

Richard
d. 1639
m 1. (ca 1620) m 2. (ca 1631)
Mary Miles   Susanna Clarke

John
d. 1623

Jane
d. 1643
at Bath

Eleanor
b c.1592
m
Mr Willes

Henry
b c.1593
m
Margaret
Duckett

Walter
(1595-1630)
m (c.1627)
Mary

Mary
b c.1593
m (c.1618)
Thomas
Bishop

Norton
(1606-c.1638)
m (after 1623)
Mr Smith
of Corsham

Edmund
(1621-1664)
m 1. (c.1642)
Barbara Ayliffe (sister of Anne who m. Edward Hyde, E. Of Clarendon)

Richard
(1623-1665)

Mary

Elizabeth

Humphrey
(1633-1679)

Susanna
b c.1635
m.
Rbt Compton

Catherine
(1612-1681)
m Leonard Atkins of Sutton Benger

Edmund
(1642-1681)
m (1676)
Mary Otger

Oliver
(1643-1716)

Martha
(1644-aft 1715)
m (1665)
John Danvers

Barbara
b c.1648

Lucy
b c.1654

William

George
Mariner d. at
sea 1706

Elizabeth
m (c.1680)
Christopher Gulse

Mary

Deborah

Richard
1660-1662

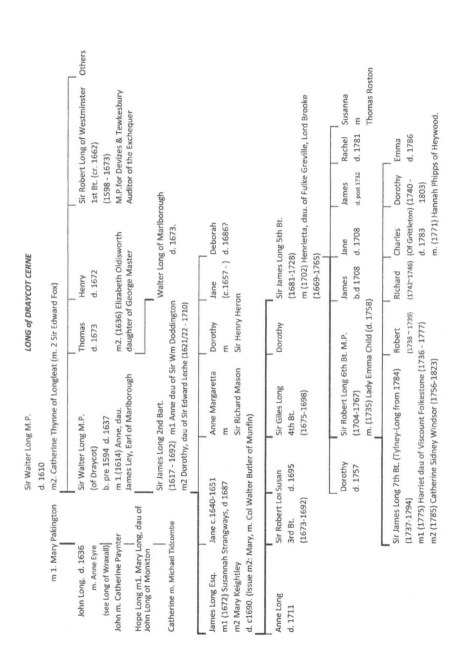

LONG of DRAYCOT CERNE

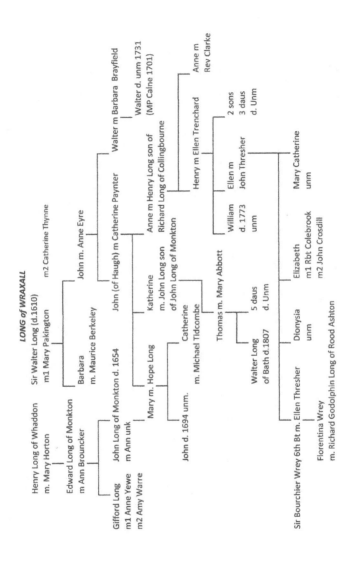

LONG of WRAXALL

Henry Long of Whaddon   Sir Walter Long (d.1610)
m. Mary Horton   m1 Mary Pakington   m2 Catherine Thynne

Edward Long of Monkton
m Ann Brouncker

Barbara   John m. Anne Eyre
m. Maurice Berkeley

Walter m Barbara Brayfield

Walter d. unm 1731
(MP Calne 1701)

Gifford Long   John Long of Monkton d. 1654
m1 Anne Yewe   m Ann unk
m2 Amy Warre

John (of Haugh) m Catherine Paynter

Anne m Henry Long son of
Richard Long of Collingbourne

Henry m Ellen Trenchard   Anne m
                                     Rev Clarke

Mary m. Hope Long

Katherine
m. John Long son
of John Long of Monkton

William   Ellen m   2 sons
d. 1773   John Thresher   3 daus
unm   d. Unm

Catherine
m. Michael Tidcombe

Thomas m. Mary Abbott

John d. 1694 unm.

Walter Long   5 daus
of Bath d.1807   d. Unm

Elizabeth
m1 Rbt Colebrook
m2 John Crosdill

Mary Catherine
unm

Sir Bourchier Wrey 6th Bt m. Ellen Thresher   Dionysia
                                               unm

Florentina Wrey
m. Richard Godolphin Long of Rood Ashton

LONG of PRESHAW, HAMPSHIRE & SOMERSET

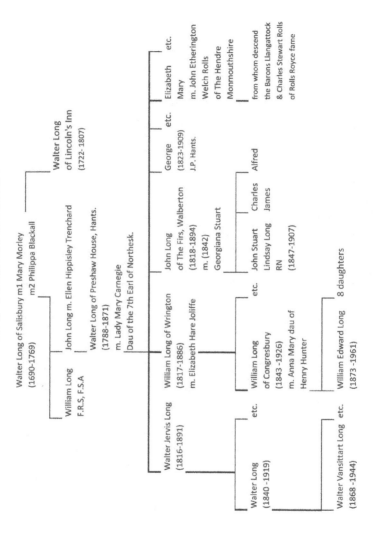

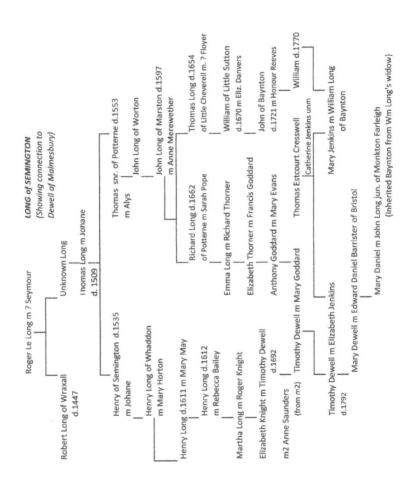

LONG of SEMINGTON
(Showing connection to
Dewell of Malmesbury)

Roger Le Long m ? Seymour

Robert Long of Wraxall
d.1447

Unknown Long

Thomas Long m Johane
d. 1509

Henry of Semington d.1535
m Johane

Henry Long of Whaddon
m Mary Horton

Thomas snr. of Potterne d.1553
m Alys

John Long of Worton

John Long of Marston d.1597
m Anne Merewether

Henry Long d.1611 m Mary May

Henry Long d.1612
m Rebecca Bailey

Richard Long d.1662
of Potterne m Sarah Pope

Thomas Long d.1654
of Little Cheverell m: ? Floyer

Martha Long m Roger Knight

Emma Long m Richard Thorner

William of Little Sutton
d.1670 m Eliz. Danvers

Elizabeth Knight m Timothy Dewell
d.1692

Elizabeth Thorner m Francis Goddard

Anthony Goddard m Mary Evans

John of Baynton
d.1721 m Honour Reeves

m2 Anne Saunders

Timothy Dewell m Mary Goddard
(from m2)

Thomas Estcourt Cresswell

Catherine Jenkins unm

William d.1770

Timothy Dewell m Elizabeth Jenkins
d.1792

Mary Jenkins m William Long
of Baynton

Mary Dewell m Edward Daniel Barrister of Bristol

Mary Daniel m John Long jun. of Monkton Farleigh
(inherited Baynton from Wm Long's widow)

Index